Charles Reade

Readiana

Comments on current events. Bible characters.

Charles Reade

Readiana
Comments on current events. Bible characters.

ISBN/EAN: 9783337093532

Printed in Europe, USA, Canada, Australia, Japan

Cover: Foto ©Lupo / pixelio.de

More available books at **www.hansebooks.com**

CHARLES READE

READIANA

COMMENTS ON CURRENT
EVENTS

BIBLE

CHARACTERS

LIBRARY EDITION

LONDON
CHATTO & WINDUS, PICCADILLY
1896

Printed by BALLANTYNE, HANSON & Co.
At the Ballantyne Press

PREFACE

MANY people think they can discern a novelist's real opinions in his works, and, of course, when he speaks in his own person, they can. But surely the dialogue of fictitious characters must be an unsafe guide to an author's real mind; for it is the writer's business to make his characters deliver their convictions, not his, and as eloquently as possible. My good friend, Mr. Chatto, has thought it worth while to ransack the files for my personal convictions on various subjects and to publish them. In this he has consulted friendship rather than interest. However, honest and lasting convictions are worth something, and this volume contains nothing else.

I find I have gone a little beyond the mark in calling the execution of Murdoch illegal. It is not *primâ facie* illegal to hang a man who kills an officer in the discharge of his duty, but in this country law goes by precedent; Murdoch garroted the gaoler, not with the intention of killing him, but of escaping whilst the gaoler was disabled for a time. The desire for liberty is as natural and overpowering as hunger, and the prisoner acted upon it with no murderous intention whatever. He never left the neighbourhood, sure proof he did not know he had killed the gaoler, and he went into tears when he heard the old man was dead. The people who at that date misgoverned this nation had tempted Murdoch to the act by leaving Hastings Gaol inefficiently guarded. When they hung the youth they had tempted,—hung him to hide their own fault,—the spectators of the execution were fewer than ever assembled to see a hanging before or since, and the only cry that came from this handful of spectators was, "Murder! Murder!!" Just three months after this butchery,

v

an escaped prisoner was brought before a judge : the judge was invited by the crown to inflict condign punishment; he treated the proposal with contempt. "The prisoner," said he, "yielded to the natural and imperious desire of liberty. It was his business to escape, and it was the gaoler's business not to let him."

In two other matters I said too little. Colonel Baker's sentence was beyond all precedent, and the verdict hardly justified. In a court that defies the Divine law, and the laws of civilised Europe, by closing the mouth of the accused, every admission made by the prosecutor ought to have double weight. When a young lady orders a gallant colonel to hold her whilst she projects from a railway carriage, he is her ally in a gymnastic, not an assailant she really fears, or has grave reason to fear. *Quodcunque ostendis mihi sic incredulus odi.* The other example in which I have written below the mark, is the verdict of wilful murder against Louis Staunton, Mrs. Patrick Staunton, and Alice Rhodes : a verdict bloodthirsty yet ridiculous, a verdict obtained by transparent perjury in the witness-box, and prejudice, sophistry, and bad law upon the bench.

But this latter shortcoming I hope to repair, with God's help, before the two victims of perjury, sophistry, false fact, and rotten law are slaughtered in the bloodless but effectual shambles, where the one real criminal has already perished.

CHARLES READE.

October 1882.

CONTENTS

CONTENTS

BIBLE CHARACTERS—

READIANA

READIANA

A BRAVE WOMAN

THE public itches to hear what people of rank and reputation do and say, however trivial. We defer to this taste: and that gives us a right to gratify our own now and then, by presenting what may be called the reverse picture, the remarkable acts, or sufferings, or qualities, of persons unknown to society, because society is a clique; and to fame, because fame is partial.

In this spirit we shall tell our readers a few facts about a person we are not likely to misjudge, for we do not know her even by sight.

31st of August, 1878, a train left Margate for London by the Chatham and Dover line. At Sittingbourne the pointsman turned the points the wrong way, and the train dashed into a shunted train at full speed. The engine, tender, and leading carriages were crushed together and piled over one another. The nearest passengers were chatting merrily one moment, and dead, dying, or mutilated, the next.

Nearest the engine was a third-class carriage, and in its farthest compartment sat a Mrs. Freeland, who in her youth had led an adventurous life in the colonies, but now in middle age had returned to mother England for peace and quiet. She felt a crash and heard a hissing, and for one moment saw the tender bursting through the compartments towards her; then she was hurled down upon her face, with some awful weight upon her, and wedged immovable in a *débris* of fractured iron, splintered wood, shattered glass, and mutilated bodies.

In a few minutes people ran to help, but in that excited state which sometimes aggravates these dire calamities. First they were for dragging her out by force; but she was

3

self-possessed, and said : " Pray, be calm and don't attempt it ; I am fast by the legs, and a great weight on my back."

Then they were for breaking into the carriage from above ; but she called to them, " Please don't do that—the roof is broken, and you don't know what you may bring down upon us."

Thus advised by the person most likely to lose her head one would think, they effected an entrance at the sides. They removed from her back an iron wheel and a dead body, and they sawed round her jammed and lacerated limbs, and at last with difficulty carried out a lady, with her boots torn and filled with blood, her clothes in ribbons, her face pouring blood, her back apparently broken, and her right leg furrowed all down to the very foot with a gaping wound, that laid bare the sinews ; besides numberless contusions and smaller injuries. They laid her on a mat upon the platform, and there she remained, refusing many offers of brandy, and waiting for a surgeon.

None came for a long time ; and benevolent Nature, so-called, sent a heavy rain. At last, in three quarters of an hour, surgeons arrived, and one of them removed her on her mat into a shed, that let in only part of the rain. He found her spine injured, took a double handful of splinters, wood, and glass, out of her head and face, and then examined her leg. He looked aghast at the awful furrow. The sufferer said, quietly, " I should like a stitch or two put into that." The surgeon looked at her in amazement, " Can you bear it ? " She said : " I think so."

He said she had better fortify herself with a little brandy. She objected to that as useless. But he insisted, and the awful furrow was stitched up with silk. This done he told her she had better be moved to the Infirmary at Chatham.

" Army surgeons ? " said she. " No, thank you. I shall go to a London hospital."

Being immovable in this resolution, she had to wait three hours for a train.

At last she was sent up to London, lying upon a mat on the floor of a carriage, hashed, as we have described, and soaked with rain. From the London station she was conveyed on a stretcher to St. George's Hospital. There they discovered many grave injuries, admired her for her courage and wisdom in having had her wounded leg sewn up at once, but told her with regret that to be effectual it must be secured with silver points, and that without delay.

"Very well," said she patiently; "but give me chloroform, for I am worn out."

The surgeon said: "If you *could* endure it without chloroform it would be better." He saw she had the courage of ten men.

"Well," said she, "let me have somebody's hand to hold, and I will try to bear it."

A sympathising young surgeon gave this brave woman his hand: and she bore to have the silk threads removed, and thirty little silver skewers passed and repassed through her quivering flesh, sixty wounds to patch up one. It afterwards transpired that the good surgeon was only reserving chloroform for the amputation he thought must follow, having little hope of saving such a leg.

Whatever charity and science—united in our hospitals, though disunited in those dark hells where God's innocent creatures are cut up alive out of curiosity—could do, was done for her at St. George's Hospital; the wounded leg was saved, and in three weeks the patient was carried home. But the deeper injuries seemed to get worse. She lay six months on her back, and after that was lame and broken and aching from head to foot for nearly a year. As soon as she could crawl about she busied herself in relieving the sick and the poor, according to her means.

Fifteen months after the railway accident, a new and mysterious injury began to show itself; severe internal pains, accompanied with wasting, which was quite a new feature in the case. This brought her to death's door after all.

But, when faint hopes were entertained of her recovery, the malady declared itself, an abscess in the intestines. It broke, and left the sufferer prostrate, but out of danger.

Unfortunately, in about a month another formed, and laid her low again, until it gave way like its predecessor. And that has now been her life for months; constantly growing these agonising things, of which a single one is generally fatal.

In one of her short intervals of peace a friend of hers, Major Mercier, represented to her the merits and the difficulties of a certain hospital for diseases of the skin. Instantly this brave woman sets to work and lives for other afflicted persons. She fights the good fight, talks, writes, persuades, insists, obtains the public support of five duchesses, five marchionesses, thirty-two countesses, and a hundred ladies of rank, and also of many celebrated characters; obtains sub-

5

scriptions, organises a grand bazaar, &c., for this worthy object.

Now, as a general rule, permanent invalids fall into egotism; but here is a lady, not only an invalid, but a sufferer, and indeed knocked down by suffering half her time; yet with undaunted heart, and charitable, unselfish soul, she struggles and works for others, whose maladies are after all much lighter than her own.

Ought so much misfortune and merit to receive no public notice? Ought so rare an union of male fortitude and womanly pity to suffer and relieve without a word of praise? Why to us, who judge by things, not names, this seems some heroic figure strayed out of Antiquity into an age of little men and women, who howl at the scratch of a pen.

Such a character deserves to be sung by some Christian poet; but as poetasters are many and poets are few, Mrs. Rosa Freeland, brave, suffering, and charitable, is chronicled in the prose of " Fact."

A BAD FALL

SIR,—I sometimes get provoked with the British workman
—and say so. He comes into my house to do a day's work,
and goes out again to fetch the tool he knew he should want,
and does not come back till after breakfast. Then I think I
have got him. But no; he sharpens his tools and goes out
for a whet. Even when he is at work he is always going
into the kitchen for hot water, or a hot coal, or the loan of a
pair of tongs, or some other blind. My maids, who, before
he came, were all industry and mock modesty, throw both
these virtues out of window, and are after him on the roof,
when he is not after them in the kitchen. They lose their
heads entirely, and are not worth their salt, far less their
wages, till he is gone, and that is always a terribly long time,
considering how little he has to do. For these reasons, and
because whenever he has been out on my roof, the rain
comes in next heavy shower, I have permitted myself to call
him in print "the curse of families."

Then he strikes, and combines, and speechifies, and calls
the capital, that feeds him, his enemy; and sometimes fights
with the capital of a thousand against the capital of a single
master, and overpowers it, yet calls that a fight of labour
against capital. Then he demands short time, which generally means more time to drink in, and higher wages, which
often means more money to drink with. Thereupon I lose
my temper, rush into print, and call the British workman
the British talk-man, and the British drink-man.

But it must be owned all this is rather narrow and shallow.
"Where there's a multitude there's a mixture," and a private
gentleman in my position does not really know the mass of
the workmen, and their invaluable qualities.

One thing is notorious—that in their bargains with capital
they are very lenient in one respect, they charge very little

for their lives; yet they shorten them in many trades, and lose them right away in some.

Even I, who have been hard on them in some things, have already pointed out that instead of labour and capital the trades ought to speechify on life, labour, and capital; and dwell more upon their risks, as a fit subject of remuneration, than their professed advocates have done.

Is it not a sad thing to reflect, when you see the scaffolding prepared for some great building to be erected either for pious or mundane purposes, that out of those employed in erecting it some are sure to be killed!

All this prolixity is to usher in a simple fact, which interests me more than the petty proceedings of exalted personages, and their "migrations from the blue bed to the brown;" and some of your readers are sure to be of my mind.

The Princess's Theatre, Oxford Street, is being reconstructed. The walls, far more substantial than they build now-a-days, are to stand, but the old interior is demolished, and the roof heightened.

Sullivan, a young carpenter, was at work with his fellows on a stage properly secured. They wanted some ropes that lay on another stage, and sent him for them. Between the stages was a plank, which he naturally thought had been laid to walk on. He stepped on it—it was only a half-inch board. It snapped under his weight like a carrot, and he fell through in a moment.

He caught at a projection, but merely tore his fingers, and descended into space with fearful velocity.

The height was fifty feet—*measured.*

The thing he fell on was a hard board, lying on hard ground. Those who saw him fall, and heard his one cry of horror, had no hope of taking up anything from the ground below but a battered corpse with broken back, fractured skull, and shattered ribs.

Thirty-five feet below the place he fell from, a strong bolt, about an inch in diameter and four feet long, protruded from the wall almost at right angles, but with a slight declension downwards.

The outer end of this protruding iron just caught Sullivan by the seat, ripped up his clothes, and tore his back, and partly broke his fall. Nevertheless, such was its violence that he bounded up from the board he eventually fell upon, and was found all of a heap in a hollow place close by, senseless, and almost pulseless.

8

A BAD FALL

He was taken to the Middlesex Hospital. There he came to his senses and his trouble. His pulse was soon over 100. His temperature 108—a very alarming feature. This, however, has subsided, and they have got his pulse to 98, but he cannot eat; his eyes cannot bear the light. There are one or more severe wounds upon his back parts, and much reason to fear injury to the spinal column. He is in danger; and, if he survives, which I think very possible, it is to be feared he will never be able to walk and work again. These, sir, are the dire realities of life; and very fit to be admitted into your graver columns. Here is a sad fact and a curious fact.

Sullivan was a handsome young fellow, just beginning the world. In a moment there he lies a cripple and a wreck, and that is a sad thing for any feeling heart to think of. The bolt which saved him from immediate death is a curious fact. It is still to be seen dangling from the wall as it did, when it ripped up the workman's clothes, furrowed his back, and broke his fall.

Will it prove his friend or his enemy, that piece of iron? The enemy of his body if it makes him a cripple instead of a corpse; but the friend of his soul if he reads his own story right: wherefore I hope some servant of God will go to his bedside with the true balm of Gilead.—I am, sir, yours faithfully,   CHARLES READE.

July, 1880.

PERSEVERANCE

On a certain day in the year 1819, Mr. Chitty, an attorney in Shaftesbury, was leaving his office for the day, when he was met at the door by a respectable woman and a chubby-faced boy with a bright eye. He knew the woman slightly—a widow that kept a small stationer's shop in the town.

She opened her business at once.

"Oh, Mr. Chitty, I have brought you my Robert; he gives me no peace; his heart is so set on being in a lawyer's office. But there, I have not got the money to apprentice him. Only we thought perhaps you could find some place or other for him, if it was ever so small." Then she broke off and looked appealingly, and the boy's cheeks and eyes were fired with expectation.

Most country towns at that time possessed two solicitors, who might be called types; the old-established man, whose firm for generations had done the pacific and lucrative business —wills, settlements, partnerships, mortgages, &c.—and the sharp practitioner, who was the abler of the two at litigation, and had to shake the plum tree instead of sitting under it and opening his mouth for the windfalls. Mr. Chitty was No. 2.

But these sharp practitioners are often very good-natured; and so, looking at the pleading widow and the beaming boy, he felt disposed to oblige them, and rather sorry he could not. He said his was a small office, and he had no clerk's place vacant; "and, indeed, if I had, he is too young; why, he is a mere child !"

"I am twelve next so-and-so," said the boy, giving the month and the day.

"You don't look it, then," said Mr. Chitty incredulously.

"Indeed, but he is, sir," said the widow; "he never looked his age, and writes a beautiful hand."

"But I tell you I have no vacancy," said Mr. Chitty, turning dogged.

10

" Well, thank you, sir, all the same," said the widow, with the patience of her sex. "Come, Robert, we mustn't detain the gentleman."

So they turned away with disappointment marked on their faces, the boy's especially.

Then Mr. Chitty said in a hesitating way: "To be sure, there *is* a vacancy, but it is not the sort of thing for you."

" What is it, sir, if you please ? " asked the widow.

" Well, we want an office boy."

" An office boy ! What do you say, Robert ? I suppose it is a beginning, sir. What will he have to do ? "

" Why, sweep the office, run errands, carry papers—and that is not what he is after. Look at him—he has got that eye of his fixed on a counsellor's wig, you may depend; and sweeping a country attorney's office is not the stepping-stone to that." He added warily, " at least, there is no precedent reported."

" La ! sir," said the widow, " he only wants to turn an honest penny, and be among law-papers."

" Ay, ay, to write 'em and sell 'em, but not to dust 'em ! "

" For that matter, sir, I believe he'd rather be the dust itself in your office than bide at home with me." Here she turned angry with her offspring for half a moment.

" And so I would," said young master stoutly, endorsing his mother's hyperbole very boldly, though his own mind was not of that kind which originates metaphors, similes, and engines of inaccuracy in general.

" Then I say no more," observed Mr. Chitty; " only mind, it is half-a-crown a week—that is all."

The terms were accepted, and Master Robert entered on his humble duties. He was steady, persevering, and pushing; in less than two years he got promoted to be a copying clerk. From this in due course he became a superior clerk. He studied, pushed and persevered, till at last he became a fair practical lawyer, and Mr. Chitty's head clerk. And so much for Perseverance.

He remained some years in this position, trusted by his employer and respected too; for besides his special gifts as a law clerk, he was strict in morals, and religious without parade.

In those days country attorneys could not fly to the metropolis and back to dinner. They relied much on London attorneys, their agents. Lawyer Chitty's agent was Mr. Bishop, a judge's clerk; but in those days a judge's clerk had an insufficient stipend, and was allowed to eke it out by private practice. Mr. Bishop was agent to several country attorneys. Well, Chitty had a heavy case coming on at the assizes, and asked Bishop to come down for once in a way and help him in person. Bishop did so, and in working the case was delighted with Chitty's managing clerk. Before leaving, he said he sadly wanted a managing clerk he could rely on. Would Mr. Chitty oblige him and part with this young man?

Chitty made rather a wry face, and said that young man was a pearl. "I don't know what I shall do without him; why, he is my *alter ego*."

However, he ended by saying generously that he would not stand in the young man's way. Then they had the clerk in and put the question to him.

"Sir," said he, "it is the ambition of my heart to go to London."

Twenty-four hours after that, our humble hero was installed in Mr. Bishop's office, directing a large business in town and country. He filled that situation for many years, and got to be well known in the legal profession. A brother of mine, who for years was one of a firm of solicitors in Lincoln's Inn Fields, remembers him well at this period; and to have met him sometimes in his own chambers and sometimes in Judge's Chambers; my brother says he could not help noticing him, for he bristled with intelligence, and knew a deal of law, though he looked a boy.

The best of the joke is that this clerk afterwards turned out to be four years older than that solicitor who took him for a boy.

He was now amongst books as well as lawyers, and studied closely the principles of law whilst the practice was sharpening him. He was much in the courts, and every case there cited in argument or judgment he hunted out in the books, and digested it, together with its application in practice by the living judge, who had quoted, received, or evaded it. He was a Baptist, and lodged with a Baptist minister and his two daughters. He fell in love with one of them, proposed to her, and was accepted. The couple were married without pomp, and after the ceremony the good minister took them aside, and said, "I have only £200 in the world; I have saved it a little at a time, for my two daughters. Here is your share, my children." Then he gave his daughter £100, and she handed it to the bridegroom on the spot.

The good minister smiled approval, and they sat down to what fine folk call breakfast, but they called dinner, and it was.

After dinner and the usual ceremonies, the bridegroom rose and surprised them a little. He said, "I am very sorry to leave you, but I have a particular business to attend to; it will take me just one hour."

Of course there was a look or two interchanged, especially by every female there present; but the confidence in him was too great to be disturbed; and this was his first eccentricity.

He left them, went to Gray's Inn, put down his name as a student for the Bar; paid away his wife's dowry in the fees, and returned within the hour.

Next day the married clerk was at the office as usual, and entered on a twofold life. He worked as a clerk till five, dined in the Hall of Gray's Inn as a sucking barrister; and studied hard at night. This was followed by a still stronger example of duplicate existence, and one without a parallel in my reading and experience—he became a writer, and produced a master-piece, which, as regarded the practice of our courts, became at once the manual of attorneys, counsel, and judges.

The author, though his book was entitled "practice," showed some qualities of a jurist, and corrected soberly but firmly unscientific legislature and judicial blunders.

So here was a student of Gray's Inn, supposed to be picking up in that Inn a small smattering of law, yet, to diversify his crude studies, instructing mature counsel and correcting the judges themselves, at whose chambers he attended daily, cap in hand, as an attorney's clerk. There's an intellectual hotch-potch for you! All this did not in his Inn qualify him to be a barrister; but years and dinners did. After some weary years he took the oaths at Westminster, and vacated by that act his place in Bishop's office, and was a pauper—for an afternoon.

But work, that has been long and tediously prepared, can be executed quickly; and adverse circumstances, when Perseverance conquers them, turn round and become allies.

The ex-clerk and young barrister had ploughed and sowed with such pains and labour, that he reaped with comparative ease. Half the managing clerks in London knew him and believed in him. They had the ear of their employers, and brought him pleadings to draw and motions to make. His book, too, brought him clients; and he was soon in full career as a junior counsel and special pleader. Senior counsel too found that they could rely upon his zeal, accuracy, and learning. They began to request that he might be retained with them in difficult cases, and he became first junior counsel at the bar; and so much for Perseverance.

Time rolled its ceaseless course, and a silk gown was at his disposal. Now, a popular junior counsel cannot always afford to take silk, as they call it. Indeed, if he is learned, but not eloquent, he may ruin himself by the change. But the remarkable man, whose career I am epitomising, did not hesitate; he still pushed onward, and so one morning the Lord Chancellor sat for an hour in the Queen's Bench, and Mr. Robert Lush was appointed one of Her Majesty's Counsel learned in the Law, and then and there, by the Chancellor's invitation, stepped out from among the juniors and took his seat within the Bar. So much for Perseverance.

From this point the outline of his career is known to everybody. He was appointed in 1865 one of the Judges of the Queen's Bench, and, after sitting in that Court some years, was promoted to be a Lord Justice of Appeal.

A few days ago he died, lamented and revered by the legal profession, which is very critical, and does not bestow its respect lightly.

I knew him only as Queen's Counsel. I had him against me once, but oftener for me, because my brother thought him even then the best lawyer and the most zealous at the Bar, and always retained him if he could. During the period I knew him personally Mr. Lush had still a plump, unwrinkled face, and a singularly bright eye. His voice was full, mellow, and penetrating; it filled the Court without apparent effort, and accorded well with his style of eloquence, which was what Cicero calls the *temperatum genus loquendi.*

Reasoning carried to perfection is one of the fine arts; an argument by Lush enchained the ear and charmed the understanding. He began at the beginning, and each succeeding topic was articulated and disposed of, and succeeded by its right successor, in language so fit and order so lucid, that he rooted and grew conviction in the mind. *Tantum series nexuraque pollent.*

I never heard him at Nisi Prius, but should think he could do nothing ill, yet would be greater at convincing judges than at persuading juries right or wrong; for at this pastime he would have to escape from the force of his own understanding; whereas I have known counsel blatant and admired, whom Nature and flippant fluency had secured against that difficulty.

He was affable to clients, and I had more than one conversation with him, very interesting to me. But to intrude these would be egotistical, and disturb the just proportions of this short notice. I hope some lawyer, who knew him well as counsel and judge, will give us his distinctive features, if it is only to correct those vague and colourless notices of him that have appeared.

This is due to the legal profession. But, after all, his early career interests a much wider circle. We cannot all be judges; but we can all do great things by the perseverance which, from an office boy, made this man a clerk, a counsel, and a judge. Do but measure the difficulties he overcame in his business with the difficulties of rising in any art, profession, or honourable walk; and down with despondency's whine, and the groans of self-deceiving laziness. You who have youth and health, never you quail

> " At those twin gaolers of the daring heart,
> Low birth and iron fortune."

See what becomes of those two bugbears when the stout champion SINGLE-HEART and the giant PERSEVERANCE take them by the throat.

Why the very year those chilling lines were first given to the public by Bulwer and Macready, Robert Lush paid his wife's dowry away to Gray's Inn in fees, and never whined nor doubted nor looked right nor left, but went straight on— and prevailed.

Genius and talent may have their bounds—but to the power of single-hearted perseverance there is no known limit.

Non omnis mortuus est; the departed judge still teaches from his tomb; his dicta will outlive him in our English Courts; his gesta are for mankind.

Such an instance of single-heartedness, perseverance, and proportionate success in spite of odds is not for one narrow island but the globe; an old man sends it to the young in both hemispheres with this comment: If difficulties lie in the way, never shirk them, but think of Robert Lush, and trample on them. If impossibilities encounter you—up hearts and at 'em.

15

One thing more to those who would copy Robert Lush in all essentials. Though impregnated from infancy with an honourable ambition, he remembered his Creator in the days of his youth ; nor did he forget Him, when the world poured its honours on him, and those insidious temptations of prosperity, which have hurt the soul far oftener than "low birth and iron fortune." He flourished in a sceptical age ; yet he lived, and died, fearing God.

A DRAMATIC MUSICIAN

To the Editor of the "Era."

Sir,—There died the other day in London a musician, who used to compose, or set, good music to orchestral instruments, and play it in the Theatre with spirit and taste, and to watch the stage with one eye and the orchestra with another, and so accompany with vigilant delicacy a mixed scene of action and dialogue; to do which the music must be full when the actor works in silence, but subdued promptly as often as the actor speaks. Thus it enhances the action without drowning a spoken line.

These are varied gifts, none of them common, and music is a popular art. One would think, then, that such a composer and artist would make his fortune now-a-days. Not so. Mr. Edwin Ellis lived sober, laborious, prudent, respected, and died poor. He was provident and insured his life; he had a family and so small an income that he could not keep up the insurance. He has left a wife and nine children utterly destitute, and he could not possibly help it. The kindest-hearted Profession in the world—though burdened with many charitable claims—will do what it can for them; but I do think the whole weight ought not to fall upon actors and musicians. The man was a better servant of the public than people are aware, and therefore I ask leave to say a few words to the public and to the Press over his ill-remunerated art, and his untimely grave.

Surely the prizes of the Theatre are dealt too unevenly, when such a man for his compositions and his performance receives not half the salary of many a third-class performer on the stage, works his heart out, never wastes a shilling, and dies without one.

No individual is to blame; but the system seems indiscriminating and unjust, and arises from a special kind of ignorance, which is very general, but I think and hope is curable.

Dramatic effects are singularly complex, and they cannot really be understood unless they are decomposed. But it is rare to find, out of the Theatre, a mind accustomed to decompose them. The writer is constantly blamed for the actor's misinterpretation, and the actor for the writer's feebleness. Indeed, the general inability to decompose and so discriminate goes so far as this—You hear an author gravely accused by a dozen commentators of writing a new play four hours long. Of those four hours the stage-carpenter occupied one hour and thirty minutes. Yet they ascribe that mechanic's delay to the lines and delivery, when all the time it was the carpenter, who had not rehearsed his part, and therefore kept the author and the actors waiting just as long as he did the audience.

Where the habit of decomposing effects is so entirely absent, it follows, as a matter of course, that the subtle subsidiary art of the able leader is not distinguished, and goes for nothing in the public estimate of a play. I suppose two million people have seen Shaun the Post escape from his prison by mounting the ivied tower, and have panted at the view. Of those two million how many are aware that they saw with the ear as well as the eye, and that much of their emotion was caused by a mighty melody, such as effeminate Italy never produced—and never will till she breeds more men and less monks—being played all the time on the great principle of climax, swelling higher and higher, as the hero of the scene mounted and surmounted? Not six in the two million spectators, I believe. Mr. Ellis has lifted scenes and situations for me and other writers scores of times, and his share of the effect never been publicly noticed. When he had a powerful action or impassioned dialogue to illustrate he did not habitually run to the poor resource of a "hurry" or a nonsense "tremolo," but loved to find an appropriate melody, or a rational sequence of chords, or a motived strain, that raised the scene or enforced the dialogue. As to his other qualities, it was said of Cæsar that he was a general who used not to say to his soldiers "go" but "come," and that is how Mr. Ellis led an orchestra. He showed them how to play with spirit by doing it himself. He was none of your sham leaders with a *bâton*, but a real leader with a violin, that set his band on fire. A little while before he died he tried change of air, by the kind permission of Messrs. Gatti, and he helped me down at Liverpool. He entered a small orchestra of good musicians that had become languid. He waked them up directly, and they played such fine music and so finely that the *entr'acte* music became at once a feature of the entertainment. A large theatre used to ring nightly with the performance of fifteen musicians only; and the Lancashire lads, who know what is good, used to applaud so loudly and persistently that Mr. Ellis had to rise nightly in the orchestra and bow to them before the curtain could be raised.

Then I repeat that there must be something wrong in the scale of remuneration, when such a man works for many years and dies in need, without improvidence. In all other professions there are low rewards and high rewards. On what false principles does such a man as Ellis receive the same pittance as a mediocre leader, who doses a play with tremolo, and "hurries," and plays you dead with polkas between the acts, and, though playing to a British audience, rarely plays a British melody but to destroy it by wrong time, wrong rhythm, coarse and slovenly misinterpretation, ploughing immortal airs, not playing them?

I respectfully invite the Press over this sad grave, to look into these matters—to adopt the habit of decomposing all the complex effects of a theatre; to ignore nobody, neither artist nor mechanic, who affects the public; to time the carpenters' delays on a first night and report them to a second; to time the author's lines, and report their time to a minute; to criticise as an essential part of the performance the music, appropriate or inappropriate, intelligent or brainless, that accompanies the lines and action; and not even to ignore the quality and execution of the *entr'acte* music. A thousand people have to listen to it three-quarters of an hour, and those thousand people ought not to be swindled out of a part of their money by the misinterpretation of Italian overtures, or by the everlasting performance of polkas and waltzes. These last are good musical accompaniments to the foot, but to seated victims they are not music, but mere rhythmical thumps. There is no excuse for this eternal trash, since the stores of good music are infinite.

If the Press will deign to take a hint from me, and so set themselves to decompose and discriminate, plays will soon be played quicker on a first night, and accomplished artists like Edwin Ellis will not work hard, live soberly, and die poor. Meantime, I do not hesitate to ask the public to repair in some degree the injustice of fortune. Millions of people have passed happy evenings at the Adelphi Theatre. Thousands have heard Mr. Ellis accompany *The Wandering Heir* and between the acts play his "Songs without Music" at the Queen's.   I ask them to believe me that this deserving and unfortunate musician caused much of their enjoyment though they were not conscious of it at the time.   Those spectators, and all who favour me with their confidence in matters of charity, I respectfully invite to aid the Theatrical and Musical Professions in the effort they are now making to save from dire destitution the widow and children of that accomplished artist and worthy man.—I am, sir, yours respectfully,

CHARLES READE.

DEATH OF WINWOOD READE

FROM THE "DAILY TELEGRAPH," APRIL 26, 1876.

WE regret to announce the death of Mr. Winwood Reade, well-known as an African traveller and correspondent, and by many works of indubitable power. This remarkable man closed, on Saturday last, April 24, a laborious career, cheered with few of Fortune's smiles. As a youth he had shown a singular taste for natural science. This, however, was interrupted for some years by University studies, and afterwards by an honest but unavailing attempt to master the art of Fiction, before possessing sufficient experience of life. He produced, however, two or three novels containing some good and racy scenes, unskilfully connected, and one ("See-Saw") which is a well-constructed tale. He also published an archæological volume, entitled "The Vale of Isis." The theories of M. Du Chaillu as to the power and aggressive character of the gorilla inflamed Mr. Reade's curiosity and awakened his dormant genius. He raised money upon his inheritance, and set out for Africa fully equipped. He hunted the gorilla persistently, and found him an exceedingly timorous animal, inaccessible to European sportsmen in the thick jungles which he inhabits. Mr. Reade then pushed his researches another way. On his return he published "Savage Africa," a remarkable book, both in matter and style.

After some years, devoted to general science and anonymous literature, he revisited that Continent—"whose fatal fascinations," as he himself wrote, "no one having seen and suffered, can resist," and this time penetrated deep into the interior. In this expedition he faced many dangers quite alone, was often stricken down with fever, and sometimes in danger of his life from violence, and once was taken prisoner by cannibals. His quiet fortitude and indomitable will carried a naturally feeble body through it all, and he came home weak, but apparently uninjured in constitution. He now published two volumes in quick succession — " The Martyrdom of Man," and the " African Sketchbook "—both of which have met with warm admiration and severe censure. Mr. Reade was now, nevertheless, generally recognised by men of science, and particularly by Dr. Darwin and his school. In November 1873 he became the *Times'* Correspondent in the Ashantee war, and, as usual, did not spare himself. From this, his third African expedition, he returned a broken man. The mind had been too strong for the body, and he was obliged to halt on the way home. Early in this present year, disease, both of the heart and lungs, declared itself, and he wasted away slowly but inevitably. He wrote his last work, " The Outcast," with the hand of death upon him. Two zealous friends carried him out to Wimbledon, and there, for a day or two, the air seemed to revive him ; but on Friday night he began to sink, and on Saturday afternoon died, in the arms of his beloved uncle, Mr. Charles Reade.

The writer thus cut off in his prime entered life with excellent prospects ; he was heir to considerable estates, and gifted with genius. But he did not live long enough to inherit the one or to mature the other. His whole public career embraced but fifteen years ; yet in another fifteen he would probably have won a great name, and cured himself, as many thinking men have done, of certain obnoxious opinions, which laid him open to reasonable censure, and also to some bitter personalities that were out of place, since truth can surely prevail without either burning or abusing men whose convictions are erroneous but honest. He felt these acrimonious comments, but bore them with the same quiet fortitude by help of which he had endured his sufferings in Africa, and now awaited the sure approach of an untimely death at home. Mr. Reade surpasses most of the travellers of his day in one great quality of a writer—style. His English, founded on historical models, has the pomp and march of words, is often racy, often picturesque, and habitually powerful yet sober ; ample yet not turgid. He died in his 37th year.

CREMONA FIDDLES

FROM THE " PALL MALL GAZETTE."

FIRST LETTER

August 19th, 1872.

UNDER this heading, for want of a better, let me sing the four-stringed instruments, that were made in Italy from about 1560 to 1760, and varnished with high-coloured yet transparent varnishes, the secret of which, known to numberless families in 1745, had vanished off the earth by 1760, and has now for fifty years baffled the laborious researches of violin makers, amateurs, and chemists. That lost art I will endeavour to restore to the world through the medium of your paper. But let me begin with other points of connoisseurship, illustrating them as far as possible by the specimens on show at the South Kensington Museum.

The modern orchestra uses four-stringed instruments, played with the bow; the smallest is the king; its construction is a marvel of art; and, as we are too apt to underrate familiar miracles, let me analyse this wooden paragon, by way of showing what great architects in wood those Italians were, who invented this instrument and its fellows at Brescia and Bologna. The violin itself, apart from its mere accessories, consists of a scroll or head, weighing an ounce or two, a slim neck, a thin back, that ought to be made of Swiss sycamore, a thin belly of Swiss deal, and sides of Swiss sycamore no thicker than a sixpence. This little wooden shell delivers an amount of sound that is simply monstrous; but, to do that, it must submit to a strain, of which the public has no conception. Let us suppose two Claimants to take opposite ends of a violin-string, and to pull against each other with all their weight; the tension of the string so produced would not equal the tension which is created by the screw in

23

raising that string to concert pitch. Consider, then, that not one but four strings tug night and day, like a team of demons, at the wafer-like sides of this wooden shell. Why does it not collapse? Well, it would collapse with a crash, long before the strings reached concert pitch, if the violin was not a wonder inside as well as out. The problem was to withstand that severe pressure without crippling the vast vibration by solidity. The inventors approached the difficulty thus: they inserted six blocks of lime, or some light wood; one of these blocks at the lower end of the violin, one at the upper, and one at each corner—the corner blocks very small and tri-angular; the top and bottom blocks much larger, and shaped like a capital D, the straight line of the block lying close to the sides, and the curved line outwards. Then they slightly connected all the blocks by two sets of linings; these linings are not above a quarter of an inch deep, I suppose, and no thicker than an old penny piece, but they connect those six blocks and help to distribute the resistance.

Even so the shell would succumb in time; but now the inventor killed two birds with one stone; he cunningly diverted a portion of the pressure by the very means that were necessary to the sound. He placed the bridge on the belly of the violin, and that raised the strings out of the direct line of tension, and relieved the lateral pressure at the expense of the belly. But as the belly is a weak arch, it must now be strengthened in its turn. Accordingly, a bass-bar was glued horizontally to the belly under one foot of the bridge. This bass-bar is a very small piece of deal, about the length and half the size of an old-fashioned lead pencil, but, the ends being tapered off, it is glued on to the belly, with a spring in it, and supports the belly magically. As a proof how nicely all these things were balanced, the bass-bar of Gasparo da Salo, the Amati, and Stradiuarius, being a little shorter and shallower than a modern bass-bar, did admirably for their day, yet will not do now. Our raised concert pitch has clapped on more tension, and straightway you must remove the bass-bar even of Stradiuarius, and substitute one a little longer and deeper, or your Cremona sounds like a strung frying-pan.

Remove now from the violin, which for two centuries has endured this strain, the finger-board, tail-piece, tail-pin and screws—since these are the instruments or vehicles of tension, not materials of resistance—and weigh the violin itself. It weighs, I suppose, about twenty ounces; and it has fought hundredweights of pressure for centuries. A marvel of construction, it is also a marvel of sound ; it is audible farther off than the gigantic pianoforte, and its tones in a master's hand go to the heart of man. It can be prostituted to the performance of difficulties, and often is; but that is not its fault. Genius can make your very heart dance with it, or your eyes to fill; and Niel Gow, who was no romancer, but only a deeper critic than his fellows, when being asked what was the true test of a player, replied, "A MON IS A PLAYER WHEN HE CAN GAR HIMSEL' GREET WI' HIS FIDDLE."

Asking forgiveness for this preamble, I proceed to inquire what country invented these four-stringed and four-cornered instruments ?

I understand that France and Germany have of late raised some pretensions. Connoisseurship and etymology are both against them. Etymology suffices. The French terms are all derived from the Italian, and that disposes of France. I will go into German pretensions critically, if any one will show me as old and specific a German word as viola and violino, and the music composed for those German instruments. "Fiddle" is of vast antiquity; but pear-shaped, till Italy invented the four corners, on which sound as well as beauty depends.

THE ORDER OF INVENTION.—Etymology · decides with unerring voice that the violoncello was invented after the violono or double-bass, and connoisseurship proves by two distinct methods that it was invented after the violin. 1st, the critical method : it is called after the violon, yet is made on the plan of the violin, with arched back and long inner bought. 2nd, the historical method : a violoncello made by the inventors of the violin is incomparably rare, and this instrument is disproportionately rare even up to the year 1610. Violino being a derivative of viola would seem to indicate that the violin followed the tenor ; but this taken alone is dangerous ; for viola is not only a specific term for the tenor, but a generic name that was in Italy a hundred years before a tenor with four strings was made. To go then to connoisseurship—I find that I have fallen in with as many tenors as violins by Gasparo da Salo, who worked from about 1555 to 1600, and not quite so many by Gio Paolo Maggini, who began a few years later. The violin being the king of all these instruments, I think there would not be so many tenors made as violins, when once the violin had been invented. Moreover, between the above dates came Corelli, a composer and violinist. He would naturally create a crop of violins. Finding the tenors and violins of Gasparo da Salo about equal in number, I am driven to the conclusion that the tenor had an unfair start—in other words, was invented first. I add to this that true four-stringed tenors by Gasparo da Salo exist, though very rare, made with only two corners, which is a more primitive form than any violin by the same maker appears in. For this and some other reasons, I have little doubt the viola preceded the violin by a very few years. What puzzles me more is to time the violon, or, as we childishly call it (after its known descendant), the double-bass. If I was so presumptuous as to trust to my eye alone, I should say it was the first of them all. It is an instrument which does not seem to mix with these four-stringed upstarts, but to belong to a much older family—viz., the viole d'amore, da gamba, &c. In the first place it has not four strings; secondly, it has not an arched back, but a flat back, with a peculiar shoulder, copied from the viola da gamba; thirdly, the space between the upper and lower corners in the early specimens is ludicrously short. And it is hard to believe that an eye, which had observed the graceful proportions of the tenor and violin, could be guilty of such a wretched little inner-bought as you find in a double-bass of Brescia. *Per contra*, it must be admitted, first, that the sound-hole of a Brescian double-bass seems copied from the four-stringed tribe, and not at all from the elder family; secondly, that the violin and tenor are instruments of melody or harmony, but the violon of harmony only. This is dead against its being invented until after the instruments to which it is subsidiary. Man invents only to supply a want. Thus, then, it is. First, the large tenor, played between the knees; then the violin, played under the chin; then (if not the first of them all) the small double-bass; then, years after the violin, the violoncello; then the full sized double-bass; then, *longo intervallo*, the small tenor, played under the chin.

However, I do not advance these conclusions as infallible. The highest evidence on some of these points must surely lie in manuscript music of the sixteenth century, much of which is preserved in the libraries of Italy; and if Mr. Hatton or any musician learned in the history of his art will tell me for what stringed instruments the immediate predecessors of Corelli, and Corelli at his commencement, marked their compositions, I shall receive the communication with gratitude and respect. I need hardly say that nothing but the MS. or the *editio princeps* is evidence in so nice a matter.

The first known maker of the true tenor, and probably of the violin, was Gasparo da Salo. The student who has read the valuable work put forth by Monsieur Fétis and Monsieur Vuillaume might imagine that I am contradicting them here; for they quote as "luthiers"—antecedent to Gasparo da Salo —Kerlino, Duiffoprugcar, Linarolli, Dardelli, and others. These men, I grant you, worked long before Gasparo da Salo; I even offer an independent proof, and a very simple one. I find that their genuine tickets are in Gothic letters, whereas those of Gasparo da Salo are in Roman type; but I know the works of those makers, and they did not make tenors nor violins. They made instruments of the older family, viole d'amore, da gamba, &c. Their *true* tickets are all black-letter tickets, and not one such ticket exists in any old violin, nor in a single genuine tenor. The fact is that the tenor is an instrument of unfixed dimensions, and can easily be reconstructed out of different viole made in an earlier age. There are innumerable examples of this, and happily the exhibition furnishes two. There are two curious instruments strung as tenors, Nos. 114 and 134 in the catalogue : one is given to Joan Carlino, and the year 1452; the other to Linaro, and 1563. These two instruments were both made by one man, Ventura Linarolli, of Venice (misspelt by M. Fétis, Venturi), about the year 1520. Look at the enormous breadth between the sound-holes; that shows they were made to carry six or seven strings. Now look at the scrolls; both of them new, because the old scrolls were primitive things with six or seven screws; it is only by such reconstruction that a tenor or violin can be set up as anterior to Gasparo da Salo. No. 114 is, however, a real gem of antiquity; the wood and varnish exquisite, and far fresher than nine Amatis out of ten. It is well worthy the special attention of collectors. It was played *upon* the knee.

There are in the collection two instruments by Gasparo da Salo worth especial notice; a tenor, No. 142, and a violono, or primitive double-bass, 199. The tenor is one of his later make, yet has a grand primitive character. Observe, in particular, the scroll all round, and the amazing inequality between the bass sound-hole and the purfling of the belly; this instrument and the grand tenor assigned to Maggini, and lent by Madame Risler, offer a point of connoisseurship worthy the student's attention. The back of each instrument looks full a century younger than the belly. But this is illusory. The simple fact is that the tenors of that day, when not in use, were not nursed in cases, but hung up on a nail, belly outwards. Thus the belly caught the sun of Italy, the dust, &c., and its varnish was often withered to a mere resin, while the back and sides escaped. This is the key to that little mystery. Observe the scroll of the violono 199! How primitive it is all round : at the back a flat cut, in front a single flute, copied from *its true parent,* the viola da gamba. This scroll, taken in conjunction with the size and other points, marks an instrument considerably anterior to No. 200. As to the other double-basses in the same case, they are assigned by their owners to Gasparo da Salo, because they are double purfled and look older than Cremonese violins; but these indicia are valueless; all Cremòna and Milan double-purfled the violon as often as not; and the constant exposure to air and dust gives the violono a colour of antiquity that is delusive. In no one part of the business is knowledge of work so necessary. The violoni 201–2–3, are all fine Italian instruments. The small violon, 202, that stands by the side of the Gasparo da Salo, 199, has the purfling of Andreas Amatus ; the early sound-hole of Andreas Amatus ; the exquisite corners and finish of Andreas Amatus; the finely cut scroll of Andreas Amatus; at the back of scroll the neat shell and square shoulder of Andreas Amatus; and the back, instead of being made of any rubbish that came to hand, after the manner of Brescia, is of true fiddle wood, cut the bastard way of the grain, which was the taste of the Amati ; and, finally, it is varnished with the best varnish of the Amati. Under these circumstances, I hope I shall not offend the owner by refusing it the inferior name of Gasparo da Salo. It is one of the brightest gems of the collection, and not easily to be matched in Europe.

SECOND LETTER

August 24th, 1872.

Gio Paolo Maggini is represented at the Kensington Museum by an excellent violin, No. 111, very fine in workmanship and varnish, but as to the model a trifle too much hollowed at the sides, and so a little inferior to some of his violins, and to the violin No. 70, the model of which, like many of the Brescian school, is simple and perfect. (Model as applied to a violin, is a term quite distinct from outline.) In No. 70 both belly and back are modelled with the simplicity of genius, by even gradation, from the centre, which is the highest part, down to all the borders of the instrument. The world has come back to this primitive model after trying a score, and prejudice gives the whole credit to Joseph Guarnerius, of Cremona. As to the date of No. 70, the neatness and, above all, the slimness of the sound-hole, mark, I think, a period slightly posterior to Gasparo da Salo. This slim sound-hole is an advance, not a retrogression. The gaping sound-holes of Gasparo da Salo and Maggini were their one great error. They were not only ugly; they lessened the ring by allowing the vibration to escape from the cavity too quickly. No. 60, assigned to Duiffoprugcar and a fabulous antiquity, was made by some 'prentice hand in the seventeenth century; but No. 70 would adorn any collection, being an old masterpiece of Brescia or Bologna.

THE SCHOOL OF CREMONA.—Andreas Amatus was more than thirty years old, and an accomplished maker of the older viole, when the violin was invented in Brescia or Bologna. He does not appear to have troubled his head with the new instrument for some years; one proof more that new they were. They would not at first materially influence his established trade; the old and new family ran side by side. Indeed it took the violin tribe two centuries to drive out the viola da gamba. However, in due course, Andreas Amatus set to work on violins. He learned from the Brescian school the only things they could teach a workman so superior—viz., the four corners and the sound-hole. This Brescian sound-hole stuck to him all his days; but what he had learned in his original art remained by him too. The collection contains three specimens of his handiwork: Violin 202, Mrs. Jay's violin — with the modern head — erroneously assigned to Antonius and Hieronymus; and violoncello No. 183. There are also traces of his hand in the fine tenor 139. In the three instruments just named the purfling is composed in just proportions, so that the white comes out with vigour; it is then inlaid with great neatness. The violoncello is the gem. Its outline is grace itself: the four exquisite curves coincide in one pure and serpentine design. This bass is a violin soufflé; were it shown at a distance it would take the appearance of a most elegant violin; the best basses of Stradiuarius alone will stand this test. (Apply it to the Venetian master-

29

piece in the same case.) The scroll is perfect in design and chiselled as by a sculptor; the purfling is quite as fine as Stradiuarius: it is violin purfling, yet this seems to add elegance without meanness. It is a masterpiece of Cremona, all but the hideous sound-hole, that alone connects this master with the Brescian school.

His sons Antonius and Hieronymus soon cured themselves of that grotesque sound-hole, and created a great school. They chose better wood and made richer varnish, and did many beautiful things. Nevertheless, they infected Italian fiddle-making with a fatal error. They were the first SCOOPERS. Having improved on Brescia in outline and details, they assumed too hastily that they could improve on her model. So they scooped out the wood about the sound-holes and all round, weakening the connection of the centre with the sides of the belly, and checking the fulness of the vibration. The German school carried this vice much further, but the Amati went too far, and inoculated a hundred fine makers with a wrong idea. It took Stradiuarius himself fifty-six years to get entirely clear of it.

The brothers Amati are represented in this collection, first by several tenors that once were noble things, but have been cut on the old system, which was downright wicked. It is cutting in the statutory sense, viz., cutting and maiming. These ruthless men just sawed a crescent off the top, and another off the bottom, and the result is a thing with the inner bought of a giant and the upper and lower bought of a dwarf. If one of these noble instruments survives in England uncut, I implore the owner to spare it; to play on a £5 tenor, with the Amati set before him to look at while he plays. Luckily the scrolls remain to us; and let me draw attention to the scroll of 136. Look at the back of this scroll, and see how it is chiselled—the centre line in relief, how sharp, distinct, and fine; this line is obtained by chiselling out the wood on both sides with a single tool, which fiddle-makers call a gauge, and there is nothing but the eye to guide the hand.

There are two excellent violins of this make in the collection—Mrs. Jay's, and the violin of Mr. C. J. Read, No. 75. This latter is the large pattern of those makers, and is more elegant than what is technically called the grand Amati, but not so striking. To appreciate the merit and the defect of this instrument, compare it candidly with the noble Stradiuarius Amatisé that hangs by its side, numbered 82. Take a back view first. In outline they are much alike. In the details of work the Amati is rather superior; the border of the Stradiuarius is more exquisite; but the Amati scroll is better pointed and gauged more cleanly, the purfling better composed for effect, and the way that purfling is let in, especially at the corners, is incomparable. On the front view you find the Amati violin is scooped out here and there, a defect the Stradiuarius has avoided. I prefer the Stradiuarius sound-hole *per se*; but, if you look at the curves of these two violins, you will observe that the Amati sound-holes are in strict harmony with the curves; and the whole thing the product of one original mind that saw its way.

Nicholas Amatus, the son of Hieronymus, owes his distinct reputation to a single form called by connoisseurs the Grand Amati. This is a very large violin, with extravagantly long corners, extremely fine in all the details. I do not think it was much admired at the time. At all events, he made but few, and his copyists, with the exception of Francesco Rugger, rarely selected that form to imitate. But now-a-days these violins are almost worshipped, and, as the collection is incomplete without one, I hope some gentleman will kindly send one in before it closes. There is also wanting an Amati bass, and, if the purchaser of Mr. Gillott's should feel disposed to supply that gap, it would be a very kind act. The Rugger family is numerous; it is represented by one violin (147).

Leaving the makers of the Guarnerius family—five in number—till the last, we come to Antonius Stradiuarius. This unrivalled workman and extraordinary man was born in 1644, and died in December, 1737. There is nothing signed with his name before 1667. He was learning his business thoroughly. From that date till 1736 he worked incessantly, often varying his style, and always improving, till he came to his climax, represented in this collection by the violins 83 and 87, and the violoncello 188.

He began with rather a small, short-cornered violin, which is an imitation of the small Amati, but very superior. He went on, and imitated the large Amati, but softened down the corners. For thirty years—from 1672 to 1703—he poured forth violins of this pattern; there are several in this collection, and one tenor, 139, with a plain back but a beautiful belly, and in admirable preservation. But, while he was making these Amatisé violins by the hundred, he had nevertheless his fits of originality, and put forth an anomaly every

81

now and then; sometimes it was a very long, narrow violin with elegant drooping corners, and sometimes, in a happier mood, he combined these drooping corners with a far more beautiful model. Of these varieties No. 86 gives just an indication; no more. These lucid intervals never lasted long, he was back to his Amatis next week. Yet they left, I think, the germs that broke out so marvellously in the next century. About the year 1703 it seems to have struck him like a revelation that he was a greater man than his master. He dropped him once and for ever, and for nearly twenty years poured forth with unceasing fertility some admirable works, of which you have three fine examples, under average wear, hard wear, and no wear—90, 92, 91. Please look at the three violins in this order to realise what I have indicated before— that time is no sure measure of events in this business. Nevertheless, in all these exquisite productions there was one thing which he thought capable of improvement—there was a slight residue of the scoop, especially at the lower part of the back. He began to alter that about 1720, and by degrees went to his grand model, in which there is no scoop at all. This, his grandest epoch, is represented by the Duke of Cambridge's violin, Mr. Arkwright's, and M. le Comte's: this last has the additional characteristic of the stiffer sound-hole and the wood left broad in the wing of the sound-hole. One feature more of this his greatest epoch: the purfling, instead of exactly following the corner, is pointed across it in a manner completely original. He made these grand violins and a bass or two till about 1729; after that the grand model is confined to his violins, and the details become inferior in finish. Of this there is an example in No. 84, a noble but rough violin, in parts of which certain connoisseurs would see, or fancy they saw, the hand of Bergonzi, or of Francesco or Homobuono Stradiuarius. These workmen undoubtedly lived, and survived their father a few years. They seem to have worked up his refuse wood after his death; but their interference with his work while alive has been exaggerated by French connoisseurs. To put a difficult question briefly: their theory fails to observe the style Stradiuarius was coming to even in 1727; it also ignores the age of Stradiuarius during this his last epoch of work, and says that there exists no old man's work by Stradiuarius himself; all this old man's work is done by younger men. However, generalities are useless on a subject so difficult and disputed. The only way is to get the doubtful violins or basses and analyse them, and should the Museum give a permanent corner to Cremonese instruments, this Francesco and Homobuono question will be sifted with examples. The minutiæ of work in Stradiuarius are numerous and admirable, but they would occupy too much space and are too well known to need discourse. His varnish I shall treat along with the others. A few words about the man. He was a tall, thin veteran, always to be seen with a white leathern apron and a nightcap on his head ; in winter it was white wool, and in summer white cotton. His indomitable industry had amassed some fortune, and "rich as Stradiuarius" was a byword at Cremona, but probably more current among the fiddle-makers than the bankers and merchants. His price towards the latter part of his career was four louis d'or for a violin ; his best customers Italy and Spain. Mr. Forster assures us on unimpeachable authority that he once sent some instruments into England on sale or return, and that they were taken back, the merchant being unable to get £5 for a violoncello. What ho ! Hang all the Englishmen of that day who are alive to meet their deserts ! However, the true point of the incident is, I think, missed by the narrators. The fact is that then, as now, England wanted old Cremonas, not new ones. That the Amati had a familiar reputation here and probably a ready market can be proved rather prettily out of the mouth of Dean Swift. A violin was left on a chair. A lady swept by. Her mantua caught it and knocked it down and broke it. Then the witty Dean applied a line in Virgil's Eclogue—

"Mantua væ miseræ nimium vicina Cremonæ."

This was certainly said during the lifetime of Stradiuarius, and proves that the Cremona fiddle had a fixed reputation ; it also proves that an Irishman could make a better Latin pun than any old Roman has left behind him. Since I have diverged into what some brute calls anec-dotage let me conclude this article with one that is at all events to the point, since it tells the eventful history of an instrument now on show.

THE ROMANCE OF FIDDLE-DEALING.—Nearly fifty years ago a gaunt Italian called Luigi Tarisio arrived in Paris one day with a lot of old Italian instruments by makers whose names were hardly known. The principal dealers, whose minds were narrowed, as is often the case, to three or four makers, would not deal with him. M. Georges Chanot, younger and more intelligent, purchased largely, and encouraged him to return. He came back next year with a better lot ; and yearly increasing his funds, he flew at the highest game ; and in the course of thirty years imported nearly all the finest specimens of Stradiuarius and Guarnerius France possesses. He was the greatest connoisseur that ever lived or ever can live, because he had the true mind of a connoisseur and vast opportunities.   He ransacked Italy before the tickets in the violins of Francesco Stradiuarius, Alexander Gagliano, Lorenzo Guadagnini, Giofredus Cappa, Gobetti, Morgilato Morella, Antonio Mariani, Santo Maggini, and Matteo Benti of Brescia, Michael Angelo Bergonzi, Montagnana, Thomas Balestrieri, Storioni, Vicenzo Rugger, the Testori, Petrus Guarnerius of Venice, and full fifty more, had been tampered with, that every brilliant masterpiece might be assigned to some popular name.   To his immortal credit, he fought against this mania, and his motto was " *A tout seigneur tout honneur.*"   The man's whole soul was in fiddles.   He was a great dealer, but a greater amateur.   He had gems by him no money would buy from him. No. 91 was one of them.   But for his death you would never have cast eyes on it.   He has often talked to me of it ; but he would never let me see it, for fear I should tempt him.

Well, one day Georges Chanot, Senior, who is perhaps the best judge of violins left, now Tarisio is gone, made an excursion to Spain, to see if he could find anything there.   He found mighty little.   But, coming to the shop of a fiddle-maker, one Ortega, he saw the belly of an old bass hung up with other things.   Chanot rubbed his eyes, and asked himself, was he dreaming? the belly of a Stradiuarius bass roasting in a shop-window !   He went in, and very soon bought it for about forty francs.   He then ascertained that the bass belonged to a lady of rank.   The belly was full of cracks ; so, not to make two bites of a cherry, Ortega had made a nice new one.   Chanot carried this precious fragment home and hung it up in his shop, but not in the window, for he is too good a judge not to know the sun will take all the colour out of that maker's varnish.   Tarisio came in from Italy, and his eye lighted instantly on the Stradiuarius belly. He pestered Chanot till the latter sold it him for a thousand francs, and told him where the rest was.   Tarisio no sooner knew this than he flew to Madrid.   He learned from Ortega where the lady lived, and called on her to see it.   "Sir," says the lady, "it is at your disposition."   That does not mean much in Spain.   When he offered to buy it, she coquetted with him, said it had been long in her family ; money could not replace a thing of that kind, and, in short, she put on the screw, *as she thought,* and sold it him for about four thousand francs. What he did with the Ortega belly is not known—perhaps sold it to some person in the tooth-pick trade. He sailed exultant for Paris with the Spanish bass in a case. He never let it out of his sight. The pair were caught by a storm in the Bay of Biscay. The ship rolled; Tarisio clasped his bass tight, and trembled. It was a terrible gale, and for one whole day they were in real danger. Tarisio spoke of it to me with a shudder. I will give you his real words, for they struck me at the time, and I have often thought of them since—

"AH, MY POOR MR. READE, THE BASS OF SPAIN WAS ALL BUT LOST."

Was not this a true connoisseur? a genuine enthusiast? Observe! there was also an ephemeral insect called Luigi Tarisio, who would have gone down with the bass: but that made no impression on his mind. *De minimis non curat Ludovicus.*

He got it safe to Paris. A certain high priest in these mysteries, called Vuillaume, with the help of a sacred vessel, called the glue-pot, soon re-wedded the back and sides to the belly, and the bass being now just what it was when the ruffian Ortego put his finger in the pie, was sold for 20,000 fr. (£800).

I saw the Spanish bass in Paris twenty-two years ago, and you can see it any day this month you like; for it is the identical violoncello now on show at Kensington, numbered 188. Who would divine its separate adventures, to see it all reposing so calm and uniform in that case—*"Post tot naufragia tutus."*

THIRD LETTER

August 27th, 1872.

"THE Spanish bass" is of the grand pattern and exquisitely made: the sound-hole, rather shorter and stiffer than in Stradiuarius's preceding epoch, seems stamped out of the wood with a blow, so swiftly and surely is it cut. The purfling is perfection. Look at the section of it in the upper bought of the back. The scroll extremely elegant. The belly is a beautiful piece of wood. The back is of excellent quality, but mean in the figure. The sides are cut the wrong way of the grain; a rare mistake in this master. The varnish sweet, clear, orange-coloured, and full of fire. Oh, if this varnish could but be laid on the wood of the Sanctus

Seraphin bass ! The belly is full of cracks, and those cracks
have not been mended without several lines of modern varnish
clearly visible to the practised eye.

Some years ago there was a Stradiuarius bass in Ireland. I
believe it was presented by General Oliver to Signor Piatti.
I never saw it; but some people tell me that in wood and
varnish it surpasses the Spanish bass. Should these lines
meet Signor Piatti's eye, I will only say that, if he would
allow it to be placed in the case for a single week, it would
be a great boon to the admirers of these rare and noble pieces,
and very instructive. By the side of the Spanish bass stands
another, inferior to it in model and general work, superior to
it in preservation, No. 187. The unhappy parts are the wood
of the sides and the scroll. Bad wood kills good varnish.
The scroll is superb in workmanship; it is more finely cut at
the back part than the scroll of the Spanish bass; but it is
cut out of a pear tree, and that abominable wood gets uglier
if possible under varnish, and lessens the effect even of first-
class work. On the other hand, the back and belly, where
the varnish gets fair-play, are beautiful. The belly is incomparable. Here is the very finest ruby varnish of Stradiuarius,
as pure as the day it was laid on. The back was the same
colour originally, but has been reduced in tint by the friction
this part of a bass encounters when played on. The varnish
on the back is chipped all over in a manner most picturesque
to the cultivated eye; only *it must go no farther*. I find on
examination that these chips have all been done a good many
years ago, and I can give you a fair, though of course not an
exact, idea of the process. Methinks I see an old gentleman
seated sipping his last glass of port in the dining-room over a
shining table, whence the cloth was removed for dessert. He
wears a little powder still, though no longer the fashion; he
has no shirt-collar, but a roll of soft and snowy cambric round
his neck, a plain gold pin, and a frilled bosom. He has a
white waistcoat—snow-white like his linen : he washes at
home—and a blue coat with gilt buttons. Item, a large fob
or watch-pocket, whence bulges a golden turnip, and puts
forth seed, to wit a bunch of seals and watch-keys, with perhaps a gold pencil-case. One of these seals is larger than the
others : the family arms are engraved on it, and only important letters are signed with it. He rises and goes to the
drawing-room. The piano is opened; a servant brings the
Stradiuarius bass from the study; the old gentleman takes it
and tunes it, and, not to be bothered with his lapels, buttons

his coat, and plays his part in a quartet of Haydn or a symphony of Corelli, and smiles as he plays, because he really loves music, and is not overweighted. Your modern amateur, with a face of justifiable agony, ploughs the hill of Beethoven and harrows the soul of Reade. Nevertheless, my smiling senior is all the time bringing the finest and most delicate varnish of Stradiuarius into a series of gentle collisions with the following objects :—First, the gold pin ; then the two rows of brass buttons ; and last, not least, the male chatelaine of the period. There is an oval chip just off the centre of this bass ; I give the armorial seal especial credit for that : *" À tout seigneur tout honneur."*

Take another specimen of eccentric wear : the red Stradiuarius kit 88. The enormous oval wear has been done thus : —It has belonged to a dancing-master, and he has clapped it under his arm fifty times a day to show his pupils the steps.

The Guarnerius family consisted of Andreas, his two sons Petrus and Joseph, his grandson Petrus Guarnerius of Venice, and Joseph Guarnerius, the greatest of the family, whom Mons. Fétis considers identical with Guiseppe Antonio, born in 1683. There are, however, great difficulties in the way of this theory, which I will reserve for my miscellaneous remarks.

Andreas Guarnerius was the closest of all the copyists of the Amati ; so close, indeed, that his genuine violins are nearly always sold as Amati. Unfortunately he imitated the small pattern. His wood and varnish are exactly like Amati ; there is, however, a peculiar way of cutting the lower wing of his sound-holes that betrays him at once. When you find him with the border high and broad, and the purfling grand, you may suspect his son Petrus of helping him, for his own style is petty. His basses few, but fine. Petrus Guarnerius of Cremona makes violins prodigiously *bombés*, and more adapted to grumbling inside than singing out ; but their appearance magnificent : a grand deep border, very noble, sound-hole and scroll Amatisé, and a deep orange varnish that nothing can surpass. His violins are singularly scarce in England. I hope to see one at the Exhibition before it closes.

Joseph, his brother, is a thorough original. His violins are narrowed under the shoulder in a way all his own. As to model, his fiddles are *bombés* like his brother's ; and, as the centre has generally sunk from weakness, the violin presents a great bump at the upper part and another at the lower. The violin 97 is by this maker, and is in pure and perfect condition ; but the wood having no figure, the beauty of the varnish is not appreciated. He is the king of the varnishers. He was the first man at Cremona that used red varnish oftener than pale, and in that respect was the teacher even of Stradiuarius. When this maker deviates from his custom and puts really good hare-wood into a violin, then his glorious varnish gets fair-play, and *nothing can live beside him*. The other day a violin of this make with fine wood, but undersized, was put up at an auction without a name. I suppose nobody knew the maker, for it was sold on its merits, and fetched £160. I brought that violin into the country ; gave a dealer £24 for it in Paris.

He made a very few flatter violins, that are worth any money.

Petrus Guarnerius, the son of this Joseph, learned his business in Cremona, but migrated early to Venice. He worked there from 1725 to 1746. He made most beautiful tenors and basses, but was not so happy in his violins. His varnish very fine, but paler than his father's.

Joseph Guarnerius, of Cremona, made violins from about 1725 to 1745. His first epoch is known only to connoisseurs ; in *outline* it is hewed out under the shoulder like the fiddles of Joseph, son of Andrew, who was then an old fiddle-maker ; but the *model* all his own ; even, regular, and perfect. Sound-hole long and characteristic, head rather mean for him ; he made but few of these essays, and then went to a different and admirable style, a most graceful and elegant violin, which has been too loosely described as a copy of Stradiuarius ; it is not that, but a fine violin in which a downright good workman profits by a great contemporary artist's excellences, yet without servility. These violins are not longer nor stiffer in the inner bought than Stradiuarius : they are rather narrow than broad below, cut after the plan of Stradiuarius, though not so well, in the central part, the sound-holes exquisitely cut, neither too stiff nor too flowing, the wood between the curves of the sound-holes *remarkably broad*. The scroll grandiose, yet well cut, and the nozzle of the scroll and the little platform. They are generally purfled through both pegs, like Stradiuarius ; the wood very handsome, varnish a rich golden brown. I brought three of this epoch into the country ; one was sold the other day at Christie's for £260 (bought, I believe, by Lord Dunmore), and is worth £350 as prices go. This epoch, unfortunately, is not yet represented in the collection.

The next epoch is nobly represented by 93, 94, 95. All these violins have the broad centre, the grand long inner bought, stiffish yet not ungraceful, the long and rather upright sound-hole, but well cut ; the grand scroll, cut all in a hurry, but noble. 93 is a little the grander in make I think; the purfling being set a hair's-breadth farther in, the scroll magnificent; but observe the haste—the deep gauge-marks on the side of the scroll; here is already an indication of the slovenliness to come: varnish a lovely orange, wood beautiful; two cracks in the belly, one from the chin-mark to the sound-hole. 94 is a violin of the same make, and without a single crack; the scroll is not quite so grandiose as 93, but the rest incomparable; the belly pure and beautiful, the back a picture. There is nothing in the room that equals in picturesqueness the colours of this magnificent piece: time and fair-play have worn it thus; first, there is a narrow irregular line of wear caused by the hand in shifting, next comes a sheet of ruby varnish, with no wear to speak of; then an irregular piece is worn out the size of a sixpence; then more varnish; then, from the centre downwards, a grand wear, the size and shape of a large curving pear; this ends in a broad zigzag ribbon of varnish, and then comes the bare wood caused by the friction in playing, but higher up to the left a score of great bold chips. It is the very beau-ideal of the red Cremona violin, adorned, not injured, by a century's fair wear. No. 95 is a roughish specimen of the same epoch, not so brilliant, but with its own charm. Here the guage-marks of impatience are to be seen in the very border, and I should have expected to see the stiff-throated scroll, for it belongs to this form.

The next epoch is rougher still, and is generally, but not always, higher built, with a stiff-throated scroll, and a stiff, quaint sound-hole that is the delight of connoisseurs; and such is the force of genius that I believe in our secret hearts we love these impudent fiddles best—they are so full of *chic*. After that, he abuses the patience of his admirers; makes his fiddles of a preposterous height, with sound-holes long enough for a tenor; but, worst of all, indifferent wood and downright bad varnish—varnish worthy only of the Guadagnini tribe, and not laid on by the method of his contemporaries. Indeed, I sadly fear it was this great man who, by his ill example in 1740–45, killed the varnish of Cremona. Thus—to show the range of the subject—out of five distinct epochs in the work of this extraordinary man we have only one and a half, so to speak, represented even in this noble collection—the greatest by far the world has ever seen. But I hope to see all these gaps filled, and also to see in the collection a Stradiuarius violin of that kind I call the dolphin-backed. This is a mere matter of picturesque wear. When a red Stradiuarius violin

is made of soft velvety wood, and the varnish is just half worn
off the back in a rough triangular form, that produces a
certain beauty of light and shade which is in my opinion the
ne plus ultra. These violins are rare. I never had but two
in my life. A very obliging dealer, who knows my views,
has promised his co-operation, and I think England, which
cuts at present rather too poor a figure in respect of this
maker, will add a dolphin-backed Stradiuarius to the collection before it is dispersed.

CARLO BERGONZI, if you go by gauging and purfling, is of
course an inferior make to the Amati ; but, if that is to be
the line of reasoning, he is superior to Joseph Guarnerius.
We ought to be in one story ; if Joseph Guarnerius is the
second maker of Cremona, it follows that Carlo Bergonzi is
the third. Fine size, reasonable outline, flat and even model,
good wood, work, and varnish, and an indescribable air of
grandeur and importance. He is quite as rare as Joseph
Guarnerius. Twenty-five years ago I ransacked Europe for
him—for he is a maker I always loved—and I could obtain
but few. No. 109 was one of them, and the most remarkable,
take it altogether. In this one case he has really set himself
to copy Stradiuarius. He has composed his purfling in the
same proportions, which was not at all his habit. He has
copied the sound-hole closely, and has even imitated that
great man's freak of delicately hollowing out the lower wood-
work of the sound-hole. The varnish of this violin is as fine in
colour as any pale Stradiuarius in the world, and far superior
in body to most of them ; but that is merely owing to its rare
preservation. Most of these pale Stradiuariuses, and especially Mrs. Jay's and No. 86, had once varnish on them as
beautiful as is now on this *chef-d'œuvre* of Carlo Bergonzi.

Monsieur Fétis having described Michael Angelo Bergonzi
as a pupil of Stradiuarius, and English writers having blindly
followed him, this seems a fit place to correct that error.
Michael Angelo Bergonzi was the son of Carlo ; began to
work after the death of Stradiuarius, and imitated nobody
but his father—and him vilely. His corners are not corners,
but peaks. See them once you never forget them ; but you
pray Heaven you may never see them again. His ticket
runs, " Michael Angelo Bergonzi figlio di Carlo, fece nel
Cremona," from 1750 to 1780. Of Nicholas, son of Michael
Angelo, I have a ticket dated 1796, but he doubtless began
before that and worked till 1830. He lived till 1838, was
well known to Tarisio, and it is from him alone we have

learned the house Stradiuarius lived in. There is a tenor by Michael Angelo Bergonzi to be seen at Mr. Cox, the picture-dealer's, Pall Mall, and one by Nicholas, in Mr. Chanot's shop, in Wardour Street. Neither of these Bergonzi knew how their own progenitor varnished any more than my housemaid does.

STAINER, a mixed maker. He went to Cremona too late to unlearn his German style, but he moderated it, and does not scoop so badly as his successors. The model of his tenor, especially the back, is very fine. The peculiar defect of it is that it is purfled too near the border, which always gives meanness. This is the more unfortunate, that really he was freer from this defect than his imitators. He learned to varnish in Cremona, but his varnish is generally paler than the native Cremonese. This tenor is exceptional: it has a rose-coloured varnish that nothing can surpass. It is lovely.

SANCTUS SERAPHIN.—This is a true Venetian maker. The Venetian born was always half-Cremonese, half-German. In this bass, which is his uniform style, you see a complete mastery of the knife and the guage. Neither the Stradiuarius nor the Amati ever purfled a bass more finely, and, to tell the truth, rarely so finely. But oh! the miserable scroll, the abominable sound-hole! Here he shows the cloven foot, and is more German than Stainer. Uniformity was never carried so far as by this natty workman; one violin exactly like the next; one bass the image of its predecessor. His varnish never varies. It is always slightly opaque. This is observed in his violins, but it escapes detection in his basses, because it is but slight, after all, and the wonderful wood he put into his basses, shines through that slight defect and hides it from all but practised eyes. He had purchased a tree or a very large log of it; for this is the third bass I have seen of this wonderful wood. Now-a-days you might cut down a forest of sycamore and not match it; those veteran trees are all gone. He has a feature all to himself; his violins have his initials in ebony let into the belly under the broad part of the tail-piece. This natty Venetian is the only old violin maker I know who could write well. The others bungle that part of the date they are obliged to write in the tickets. This one writes it in a hand like copper-plate, whence I suspect he was himself the engraver of his ticket, which is unique. It is four times the size of a Cremonese ticket, and has a scroll border composed thus:—The sides of a parallelogram are created by four solid

lines like sound-holes; these are united at the sides by two
leaves and at the centre by two shells. Another serpentine
line is then coiled all round them at short intervals, and within the parallelogram the ticket is printed :—

Sanctus Seraphin Utinensis,
Fecit Venetiis anno 17—.

THE MIGHTY VENETIAN.—I come now to a truly remarkable
piece, a basso di camera that comes modestly into the room
without a name, yet there is nothing except No. 91 that
sends such a thrill through the true connoisseur. The outline is grotesque but original, the model full and swelling but
not bumpy, the wood detestable; the back is hare-wood,
but without a vestige of figure; so it might just as well be
elm : the belly, instead of being made of mountain deal
grown on the sunny side of the Alps, is a piece of house
timber. Now these materials would kill any other maker;
yet this mighty bass stands its ground. Observe the fibre of
the belly; here is the deepest red varnish in the room, and
laid on with an enormous brush. Can you see the fibre
through the thin varnish of Sanctus Seraphin as plainly as
you can see the fibre through this varnish laid on as thick as
paint? So much for clearness. Now for colour. Let the
student stand before this bass, get the varnish into his mind,
and then walk rapidly to any other instrument in the room
he has previously determined to compare with it. This will
be a revelation to him if he has eyes in his head.

And this miracle comes in without a name, and therefore
is passed over by all the sham judges. And why does it
come without a name? I hear a French dealer advised those
who framed the catalogue. But the fact is that if a man
once narrows his mind to three or four makers, and imagines
they monopolise excellence, he can never be a judge of old
instruments, the study is so wide and his mind artificially
narrowed. Example of this false method: Mr. Faulconer
sends in a bass, which he calls Andreas Guarnerius. An
adviser does not see that, and suggests "probably by Amati."
Now there is no such thing as "*probably* by Amati," any
more than there is probably the sun or the moon. That
bass is by David Tecchler, of Rome; but it is a masterpiece;
and so, because he has done better than usual, the poor
devil is to be robbed of his credit, and it is to be given, first
to one maker *who is in the ring*, and then to another, *who is in
the ring*. The basso di camera, which, not being in the ring,

42

comes without a name, is by Domenico Montagnana of Venice, the greatest maker of basses in all Venice or Cremona except one. If this bass had only a decent piece of wood at the back, it would extinguish all the other basses. But we can remedy that defect. Basses by this maker exist with fine wood. Mr. Hart, senior, sold one some twenty years ago with yellow varnish, and wood striped like a tiger's back. Should these lines meet the eye of the purchaser, I shall feel grateful if he will communicate with me thereupon.

I come now to the last of the Goths, thus catalogued, No. 100, " Ascribed to Guarnerius. Probably by Storioni."

Lorenzo Storioni is a maker who began to work at Cremona about 1780. He has a good model but wretched spirit varnish. Violin No. 100 is something much better. It is a violin made before 1760 by Landolfo of Milan. He is a maker well known to experienced dealers who can take their minds out of the ring, but, as the *writers* seem a little confused, and talk of two Landulphs, a Charles and a Ferdinand, I may as well say here that the two are one. This is the true ticket :—

> Carolus Ferdinandus Landulphus,
> fecit Mediolani in via S. Margaritæ, anno 1756.

Stiff inner bought really something like Joseph Guarnerius ; but all the rest quite unlike : scroll very mean, varnish good, and sometimes very fine. Mr. Moore's, in point of varnish, is a fine specimen. It has a deeper, nobler tint than usual. This maker is very interesting, on account of his being absolutely the last Italian who used the glorious varnish of Cremona. It died first at Cremona ; lingered a year or two more at Venice ; Landolfo retained it at Milan till 1760, and with him it ended.

In my next and last article I will deal with the varnish of Cremona, as illustrated by No. 91 and other specimens, and will enable the curious to revive that lost art if they choose.

FOURTH LETTER

August 31*st*, 1872.

THE fiddles of Cremona gained their reputation by superior tone, but they hold it now mainly by their beauty. For thirty years past violins have been made equal in model to the *chef-d'œuvres* of Cremona, and stronger in wood than Stradiuarius, and more scientific than Guarnerius in the thicknesses. This class of violin is hideous, but has one quality in perfection —Power; whilst the masterpieces of Cremona eclipse every new violin in sweetness, oiliness, crispness, and volume of tone as distinct from loudness. Age has dried their vegetable juices, making the carcass much lighter than that of a new violin, and those light dry frames vibrate at a touch.

But M. Fétis goes too far when he intimates that Stradiuarius is louder as well as sweeter than Lupot, Gand, or Bernardel. Take a hundred violins by Stradiuarius and open them; you find about ninety-five patched in the centre with new wood. The connecting-link is a sheet of glue. And is glue a fine resonant substance? And are the glue and the new wood of John Bull and Jean Crapaud transmogrified into the wood of Stradiuarius by merely sticking on to it? Is it not extravagant to quote patched violins as beyond rivalry in all the qualities of sound? How can they be the loudest, when the centre of the sound-board is a mere sandwich, composed of the maker's thin wood, a buttering of glue, and a huge slice of new wood?

Joseph Guarnerius has plenty of wood; but his thicknesses are not always so scientific as those of the best modern fiddle-makers; so that even he can be rivalled in power by a new violin, though not in richness and sweetness. Consider, then, these two concurrent phenomena, that for twenty-five years new violins have been better made for sound than they ever were made in this world, yet old Cremona violins have nearly doubled in price, and, you will divine, as the truth is, that old fiddles are not bought by the ear alone. I will add that 100 years ago, when the violins of Brescia and of Stradiuarius and Guarnerius were the only well-modelled violins, they were really bought by the ear, and the prices were moderate. Now they are in reality bought by the eye, and the price is enormous. The reason is that their tone is good but their appearance inimitable; because the makers chose fine wood and laid on a varnish highly coloured, yet clear as crystal, with this strange property—it becomes far more beautiful by time and usage: it wears softly away, or chips boldly away, in such forms as to make the whole violin picturesque, beautiful, various, and curious.

To approach the same conclusion by a different road—No. 94 is a violin whose picturesque beauty I have described already; twenty-five years ago Mr. Plowden gave £450 for it.

It is now, I suppose, worth £500. Well, knock that violin down and crack it in two places, it will sink that moment to the value of the " violon du diable," and be worth £350. But collect twenty amateurs all ready to buy it, and, instead of cracking it, dip it into a jar of spirits and wash the varnish off. Not one of those customers will give you above £40 for it ; nor would it in reality be worth quite so much in the market. Take another example. There is a beautiful and very perfect violin by Stradiuarius, which the *Times*, in an article on these instruments, calls La Messie. These leading journals have private information on every subject, even grammar. I prefer to call it—after the very intelligent man to whom we owe the sight of it—the Vuillaume Stradiuarius. Well, the Vuillaume Stradiuarius is worth, as times go, £600 at least. Wash off the varnish, it would be worth £35 ; because, unlike No. 94, it has one little crack. As a further illustration that violins are heard by the eye, let me remind your readers of the high prices at which numberless copies of the old makers were sold in Paris for many years. The inventors of this art undertook to deliver a new violin, that in usage and colour of the worn parts should be exactly like an old and worn violin of some favourite maker. Now, to do this with white wood was impossible ; so the wood was baked in the oven or coloured yellow with the smoke of sulphuric acid, or so forth, to give it the colour of age ; but these processes kill the wood as a vehicle of sound ; and these copies were, and are, the worst musical instruments Europe has created in this century ; and, bad as they are at starting, they get worse every year of their untuneful existence ; yet, because they flattered the eye with something like the light and shade and picturesqueness of the Cremona violin, these pseudo-antiques, though illimitable in number, sold like wildfire ; and hundreds of self-deceivers heard them by the eye, and fancied these tinpots sounded divinely. The hideous red violins of Bernardel, Gand, and an English maker or two, are a reaction against those copies ; they are made honestly with white wood, and they will, at all events, improve in sound every year and every decade. It comes to this, then, that the varnish of Cremona, as operated on by time and usage, has an inimitable beauty, and we pay a high price for it in second-class makers, and an enormous price in a fine Stradiuarius or Joseph Guarnerius. No wonder, then, that many violin-makers have tried hard to discover the secret of this varnish ; many chemists have given days and nights of anxious study to it.

More than once, even in my time, hopes have run high, but only to fall again. Some have even cried Eureka! to the public: but the moment others looked at their discovery and compared it with the real thing, "inextinguishable laughter shook the skies." At last despair has succeeded to all that energetic study, and the varnish of Cremona is sullenly given up as a lost art.

I have heard and read a great deal about it, and I think I can state the principal theories briefly, but intelligibly.

1. It used to be stoutly maintained that the basis was amber; that these old Italians had the art of infusing amber without impairing its transparency; once fused, by dry heat, it could be boiled into a varnish with oil and spirit of turpentine, and combined with transparent yet lasting colours. To convince me, they used to rub the worn part of a Cremona with their sleeves, and then put the fiddle to their noses, and smell amber. Then I, burning with love of knowledge, used to rub the fiddle very hard and whip it to my nose, and not smell amber. But that might arise in some measure from there not being any amber there to smell. (N. B.—These amber-seeking worthies never rubbed the *coloured* varnish on an old violin. Yet their theory had placed amber there.)

2. That time does it all. The violins of Stradiuarius were raw, crude things at starting, and the varnish rather opaque.

3. Two or three had the courage to say it was spirit varnish, and alleged in proof that if you drop a drop of alcohol on a Stradiuarius, it tears the varnish off as it runs.

4. The far more prevalent notion was that it is an oil varnish, in support of which they pointed to the rich appearance of what they call the bare wood, and contrasted the miserable hungry appearance of the wood in all old violins known to be spirit varnished—for instance, Nicholas Gagliano, of Naples, and Jean Baptiste Guadagnini, of Piacenza, Italian makers contemporary with Joseph Guarnerius.

5. That the secret has been lost by adulteration. The old Cremonese and Venetians got pure and sovereign gums, that have retired from commerce.

Now, as to theory No. 1.—Surely amber is too dear a gum and too impracticable for two hundred fiddle-makers to have used in Italy. Till fused by dry heat it is no more soluble in varnish than quartz is; and who can fuse it? Copal is inclined to melt, but amber to burn, to catch fire, to do anything but melt. Put the two gums to a lighted candle, you will then appreciate the difference. I tried more than one chemist in the fusing of amber; it came out of their hands a dark brown opaque substance, rather burnt than fused. When really fused it is a *dark olive green, as clear as crystal.* Yet I never knew but one man who could bring it to this, and he had special machinery, invented by himself for it; in spite of which he nearly burnt down his house at it one day. I believe the whole amber theory comes out of a verbal equivoque; the varnish of the Amati was called amber to mark its rich colour, and your *à priori* reasoners went off on that, forgetting that amber must be an inch thick to exhibit the colour of amber. By such reasoning as this Mr. Davidson, in a book of great general merit, is misled so far as to put down powdered glass for an ingredient in Cremona varnish. Mark the logic. Glass in a sheet is transparent; so if you reduce it to powder it will add transparency to varnish. Imposed on by this chimera, he actually puts powdered glass, an opaque and insoluble sediment, into four receipts for Cremona varnish.

But the theories 2, 3, 4, 5 have all a good deal of truth in them; their fault is that they are too narrow, and too blind to the truth of each other. IN THIS, AS IN EVERY SCIENTIFIC INQUIRY, THE TRUE SOLUTION IS THAT WHICH RECONCILES ALL THE TRUTHS THAT SEEM AT VARIANCE.

The way to discover a lost art, once practised with variations by a hundred people, is to examine very closely the most brilliant specimen, the most characteristic specimen, and, indeed, the most extravagant specimen—if you can find one. I took that way, and I found in the chippiest varnish of Stradiuarius, viz., his dark red varnish, the key to all the varnish of Cremona, red or yellow. (N.B.—The yellow always beat me dead, till I got to it by this detour.) There is no specimen in the collection of this red varnish so violent as I have seen; but Mr. Pawle's bass, No. 187, will do. Please walk with me up to the back of that bass, and let us disregard all hypotheses and theories, and use our eyes. What do we see before us? A bass with a red varnish that chips very readily off what people call the bare wood. But never mind what these echoes of echoes call it. What *is* it? It is not bare wood. Bare wood turns a dirty brown with age. This is a rich and lovely yellow. By its colour and its glassy gloss, and by disbelieving what echoes say and trusting only to our eyes, we may see at a glance it is not bare wood, but highly varnished wood. This varnish is evidently oil, and contains a gum. Allowing for the tendency of oil to run into the wood, I should say *four coats of oil varnish :* and this they call the bare wood. We have now discovered the first process : a clear oil varnish laid on the white wood with some transparent gum not high coloured. Now proceed a step further; the red and chippy varnish, what is that? "Oh, that is a varnish of the same quality but another colour," say the theorists No. 4. "How do you know?" say I. "It is self-evident. Would a man begin with oil varnish and then go into spirit varnish?" is their reply. Now observe, this is not humble observation, it is only rational preconception. But if discovery has an enemy in the human mind, that enemy is preconception. Let us then trust only to humble observation. Here is a clear varnish without the ghost of a chip in its nature ; and upon it is a red varnish that is all chip. Does that look as if the two varnishes were homogeneous? Is chip precisely the same thing as no chip? If homogeneous, there would be chemical affinity between the two. But this extreme readiness of the red varnish to chip away from the clear marks a defect of chemical affinity between the two. Why, if you were to put your thumbnail against that red varnish, a little piece would come away directly. This is not so in any known case of oil upon oil. Take old Forster, for instance ; he begins with clear oil varnish ; then on that he puts a distinct oil varnish with the colour and transparency of pea-soup. You will not get his pea-soup to chip off his clear varnish in a hurry. There is a bass by William Forster in the collection a hundred years old ; but the wear is confined to the places where the top varnish MUST go in a played bass. Everywhere else his pea-soup sticks tight to his clear varnish, being oil upon oil.

Now, take a perfectly distinct line of observation. In varnishes oil is a diluent of colour. It is not in the power of man to charge an oil varnish with colour so highly as the top varnish of Mr. Pawle's bass is charged. And it must be remembered that the clear varnish below has filled all the pores of the wood ; therefore the diluent cannot escape into the wood, and so leave the colour undiluted ; if that red varnish was ever oil varnish, every particle of the oil must be there still. What, in that mere film so crammed with colour? Never! Nor yet in the top varnish of the Spanish bass, which is thinner still, yet more charged with colour than any topaz of twice the thickness. This, then, is how Antonius Stradiuarius varnished Mr. Pawle's bass.—He began with three or four coats of oil varnish containing some common gum. He then laid on several coats of red varnish, made by simply dissolving some fine red unadulterated gum in spirit; the spirit evaporated and left pure gum lying on a rich oil varnish, from which it chips by its dry nature and its utter want of chemical affinity to the substratum. On the Spanish bass Stradiuarius put not more, I think, than two coats of oil varnish, and then a spirit varnish consisting of a different gum, less chippy, but even more tender and wearable than the red. Now take this key all round the room, and you will find there is not a lock it will not open. Look at the varnish on the back of the " violon du diable," as it is called. There is a top varnish with all the fire of a topaz and far more colour; for slice the deepest topaz to that thinness, it would pale before that varnish. And why? 1st. Because this is no oily dilution; it is a divine unadulterated gum, left there undiluted by evaporation of the spirituous vehicle. 2nd. Because this varnish is a jewel with the advantage of a foil behind it; that foil is the fine oil varnish underneath. The purest specimen of Stradiuarius's red varnish in the room is, perhaps, Mr. Fountaine's kit. Look at the back of it by the light of these remarks. What can be plainer than the clear oil varnish with not the ghost of a chip in it, and the glossy top varnish, so charged with colour, and so ready to chip from the varnish below, for want of chemical affinity between the varnishes? The basso di camera by Montagnana is the same thing. See the bold wear on the back revealing the heterogeneous varnish below the red. *They are all the same thing.* The palest violins of Stradiuarius and Amati are much older and harder worn than Mr. Pawle's bass, and the top varnish not of a chippy character : yet look at them closely by the light of these remarks, and you shall find one of two phenomena—either the tender top varnish has all been worn away, and so there is nothing to be inferred one way or other, or else there are flakes of it left; and, if so, these flakes, however thin, shall always betray, by the superior vividness of their colour to the colour of the subjacent oil varnish, that they are not oil varnish, but pure gum left there by evaporating spirit on a foil of beautiful old oil varnish. Take Mrs. Jay's Amatisé Stradiuarius; on the back of that violin towards the top there is a mere flake of top varnish left by itself; all round it is nothing left but the bottom varnish. That fragment of top varnish is a film thinner than gold leaf; yet look at its intensity; it lies on the fine old oil varnish like fixed lightning, it is so vivid. It is just as distinct from the oil varnish as is the red varnish of the kit. Examine the Duke of Cambridge's violin, or any other Cremona instrument in the whole world you like; it is always the same thing, though not so self-evident as in the red and chippy varnishes. The Vuillaume Stradiuarius, not being worn, does not assist us in this particular line of argument; but it does not contradict us. Indeed, there are a few little chips in the top varnish of the back, and they reveal a heterogeneous varnish below, with its rich yellow colour like the bottom varnish of the Pawle bass. Moreover, if you look at the top varnish closely you shall see what you never see in a new violin of our day; not a vulgar glare upon the surface, but a gentle inward fire. Now that inward fire, I assure you, is mainly caused by the oil varnish below; the orange varnish above has a heterogeneous foil below. That inward glow is characteristic of all foils. If you could see the Vuillaume Stradiuarius at night and move it about in the light of a candle, you would be amazed at the fire of the foil and the refraction of light.

Thus, then, it is. The unlucky phrase "varnish of Cremona" has weakened men's powers of observation by fixing a preconceived notion that the varnish must be all one thing. THE LOST SECRET IS THIS. THE CREMONA VARNISH IS NOT A VARNISH, BUT TWO VARNISHES; AND THOSE VARNISHES ALWAYS HETEROGENE-OUS: THAT IS TO SAY, FIRST THE PORES OF THE WOOD ARE FILLED AND THE GRAIN SHOWN UP BY ONE, BY TWO, BY THREE, AND SOME-TIMES, THOUGH RARELY, BY FOUR COATS OF FINE OIL VARNISH WITH SOME COMMON BUT CLEAR GUM IN SOLUTION. THEN UPON THIS OIL VARNISH, WHEN DRY, IS LAID A HETEROGENEOUS VARNISH, VIZ., A SOLUTION IN SPIRIT OF SOME SOVEREIGN, HIGH COLOURED, PELLUCID, AND, ABOVE ALL, TENDER GUM. Gum-lac, which for forty years has been the mainstay of violin-makers, must never be used; not one atom of it. That vile, flinty gum killed varnish at Naples and Piacenza a hundred and forty years ago, as it kills varnish now. Old Cremona shunned it, and whoever employs a grain of it, commits wilful suicide as a Cremonese varnisher. It will not wear; it will not chip; it is in every respect the opposite of the Cremona gums. Avoid it utterly, or fail hopelessly, as all varnishers have failed since that fatal gum came in. The deep red varnish of Cremona is pure dragon's blood; not the cake, the stick, the filthy trash, which, in this sinful and adulterating generation, is retailed under that name, but the tear of dragon's blood, little lumps deeper in colour than a carbuncle, clear as crystal, and fiery as a ruby. Unadulterated dragon's blood does not exist in commerce west of Temple Bar; but you can get it by groping in the City as hard as Diogenes had to grope for an honest man in a much less knavish town than London. The yellow varnish is the unadulterated tear of another gum, retailed in a cake like dragon's blood, and as great a fraud. All cakes and sticks presented to you in commerce as gums are audacious swindles. A true gum is the tear of a tree. For the yellow tear, as for the red, grope the City harder than Diogenes. The orange varnish of Peter Guarnerius and Stradiuarius is only a mixture of these two genuine gums. Even the milder reds of Stradiuarius are slightly reduced with the yellow gum. The Montagnana bass and No. 94 are pure dragon's blood mellowed down by time and exposure only.

A violin varnished as I have indicated will look a little better than other new violins from the first; the back will look nearly as well as the Vuillaume Stradiuarius, but not quite. The belly will look a little better if properly prepared; will show the fibre of the deal better. But its principal merit is that, like the violins of Cremona, it will vastly improve in beauty if much exposed and persistently played. And that improvement will be rapid, because the tender top varnish will wear away from the oily substratum four times as quickly as any vulgar varnish of the day will chip or wear. We cannot do what Stradiuarius could not do—give to a new violin the peculiar beauty that comes to heterogeneous varnishes of Cremona from age and honest wear; but, on the other hand, it is a mistake to suppose that one hundred years are required to develop the beauty of any Cremona varnishes, old or new. The ordinary wear of a century cannot be condensed into one year or five, but it can be condensed into twenty years. Any young amateur may live to play on a magnificent Cremona made for himself, if he has the enthusiasm to follow my directions. Choose the richest and finest wood; have the violin made after the pattern of a rough Joseph Guarnerius; then you need not sandpaper the back, sides, or head, for sandpaper is a great enemy to varnish; it drives more wood-dust into the pores than you can blow out. If you sandpaper the belly, sponge that finer dust out, as far as possible, and varnish when dry. That will do no harm, and throw up the fibre. Make your own linseed oil—the linseed oil of commerce is adulterated with animal oil and fish oil, which are non-drying oils—and varnish as I have indicated above, and when the violin is strung treat it regularly with a view to fast

51

wear; let it hang up in a warm place, exposed to dry air, night and day. Never let it be shut up in a case except for transport. Lend it for months to the leader of an orchestra. Look after it, and see that it is constantly played and constantly exposed to dry air all about it. Never clean it, never touch it with a silk handkerchief. In twenty years your heterogeneous varnishes will have parted company in many places. The back will be worn quite picturesque; the belly will look as old as Joseph Guarnerius; there will be a delicate film on the surface of the grand red varnish mellowed by exposure, and a marvellous fire below. In a word, you will have a glorious Cremona fiddle. Do you aspire to do more, and to make a downright old Cremona violin? Then, my young friend, you must treat yourself as well as the violin; you must not smoke all day, nor the last thing at night; you must never take a dram before dinner and call it bitters; you must be as true to your spouse as ever you can, and, in a word, live moderately, and cultivate good temper and avoid great wrath. By these means, *Deo volente*, you shall live to see the violin that was made for you and varnished by my receipt, as old and worn and beautiful a Cremona as the Joseph Guarnerius No. 94, beyond which nothing can go.

To show the fiddle-maker what may be gained by using as little sandpaper as possible, let him buy a little of Maunder's palest copal varnish; then let him put a piece of deal on his bench and take a few shavings off it with a carpenter's plane. Let him lay his varnish directly on the wood so planed. It will have a fire and a beauty he will never quite attain to by scraping, sandpapering, and then varnishing the same wood with the same varnish. And this applies to harewood as well as deal. The back of the Vuillaume Stradiuarius, which is the finest part, has clearly not been sandpapered in places, so probably not at all. Wherever it is possible, varnish after cold steel, at all events in imitating the Cremonese, and especially Joseph Guarnerius. These, however, are minor details, which I have only inserted, because I foresee that I may be unable to return to this subject in writing, though I shall be very happy to talk about it at my own place to any one who really cares about the matter. However, it is not every day one can restore a lost art to the world; and I hope that, and my anxiety not to do it by halves, will excuse this prolix article.

CHARLES READE.

THE STORY OF THE BOAT RACE OF 1872

To the Editor of the "Observer"

This great annual race has become a national event. The rival crews are watched by a thousand keen eyes from the moment they appear on the Thames; their trials against time or scratch crews are noted and reported to the world; criticism aud speculation are unintermittent, and the Press prints two hundred volumes about the race before ever it is run.

When the day comes England suspends her liberties for an hour or two, makes her police her legislators; and her river, though by law a highway, becomes a race-course; passengers and commerce are both swept off it not to spoil sacred sport; London pours out her myriads; the country flows in to meet them; the roads are clogged with carriages and pedestrians all making for the river; its banks on both sides are blackened by an unbroken multitude five miles long; on all the bridges that command the race people hang and cluster like swarming bees; windows, seats, balconies are crammed, all glowing with bright colours (blue predominating), and sparkling with brighter eyes of the excited fair ones.

The two crews battle over the long course under one continuous roar of a raging multitude. At last—and often after fluctuations in the race that drive the crowd all but mad—there is a puff of smoke, a loud report, one boat has won, though both deserve; and the victors are the true kings of all that mighty throng; in that hour the Premier of England, the Primate, the poet, the orator, the philosopher of his age, would walk past unheeded if the stroke oar of the victorious boat stood anywhere near.

To cynics and sedentary students all this seems childish,

and looks like paying to muscle a homage that is never given by acclamation to genius and virtue.

But, as usual, the public is not far wrong; the triumph, though loud, is evanescent, and much has been done and endured to earn it. No glutton, no wine-bibber, no man of impure life could live through that great pull; each victor *abstinuit venere et vino, sudavit et alsit.*

The captain of the winning boat has taught Government a lesson; for in selecting his men he takes care of Honour, and does not take care of Dowb, for that would be to throw the race away upon dry land; but the public enthusiasm rest on broader and more obvious grounds than these. Every nation has a right to admire its own traits in individuals, when those traits are honourable and even innocent. England is not bound to admire those athletes, who every now and then proclaim their nationality by drinking a quart of gin right off for a wager; but we are a nation great upon the water, and great at racing, and we have a right to admire these men, who combine the two things to perfection. This is the king of races, for it is run by the king of animals working, after his kind, by combination, and with a concert so strong, yet delicate, that for once it eclipses machinery. But, above all, here is an example, not only of strength, wind, spirit, and pluck indomitable, but of pure and crystal honour. Foot-races and horse-races have been often sold, and the bettors betrayed; but this race never—and it never will be. Here, from first to last, all is open, because all is fair and glorious as the kindred daylight it courts. We hear of shivering stable-boys sent out on a frosty morning to try race-horses on the sly, and so give the proprietors private knowledge to use in betting. Sometimes these early worms have been preceded by earlier ones, who are watching behind a hedge. Then shall the trainer whisper one of the boys to hold in the faster horse, and so enact a profitable lie. Not so the University crews; they make trials in broad daylight for their own information; and those trials are always faithful. The race is pure, and is a strong corrective annually administered to the malpractices of racing. And so our two great fountains of learning are one fount of honour, God be thanked for it! So the people do well to roar their applause, and every nobleman who runs horses may be proud to take for his example these high-spirited gentlemen, who nobly run a nobler creature, for they run themselves. The recent feature of this great race has been the recovery of Cambridge in 1870 and 1871, after nine successive defeats; defeats the more remarkable that up to 1861 Oxford was behind her in the number of victories. The main cause of a result so peculiar was that system of rowing Oxford had invented and perfected. The true Oxford stroke is slow in the water but swift in the air; the rower goes well forward, drops his oar clean into the water, goes well backward, and makes his stroke, but, this done, comes swiftly forward all of a piece, hands foremost. Thus, though a slow stroke, it is a very busy one. Add to this a clean feather, and a high sweep of the oars to avoid rough water, and you have the true Oxford stroke, which is simply the perfection of rowing, and can, of course, be defeated by superior strength or bottom; but, *cæteris paribus*, is almost sure to win.

Nine defeats were endured by Cambridge with a fortitude, a patience, and a temper that won every heart, and in 1870 she reaped her reward. She sent up a crew, led by Mr. Goldie—who had been defeated the year before by Darbishire's Oxford eight—and coached by Mr. Morrison. This Cambridge crew pulled the Oxford stroke, or nearly, drove Oxford in the race to a faster stroke that does not suit her, and won the race with something to spare, though stuck to indomitably by Darbishire and an inferior crew. In 1871 Oxford sent up a heavy crew, with plenty of apparent strength, but not the precision and form of Mr. Goldie's eight. Cambridge took the lead and kept it.

This year Oxford was rather unlucky in advance. The city was circumnavigable by little ships, and you might have tacked an Indiaman in Magdalen College meadow; but this was unfavourable to eight-oar practice. Then, Mr. Lesley, the stroke, sprained his side, and resigned his post to Mr. Houblon, a very elegant oarsman, but one who pulls a quick stroke, not healthy to Oxford on Father Thames his bosom. Then their boat was found to be not so lively as the Cambridge boat built by Clasper. A new boat was ordered, and she proved worse in another way than Salter's. In a word, Oxford came to the scratch to-day with a good stiff boat, not lively, with 20lb. more dead weight inside the coxswain's jacket, and with a vast deal of pluck and not a little Hemiplegia. The betting was five to two against her.

Five minutes before the rivals came out it was snowing so hard that the race bade fair to be invisible. I shall not describe the snow, nor any of the atmospheric horrors that made the whole business purgatory instead of pleasure. I take a milder revenge ; I only curse them.

Putney roared ; and out came the Dark Blue crew ; they looked strong and wiry, and likely to be troublesome attendants. Another roar, and out came the Light Blue. So long as the boats were stationary one looked as likely as the other to win.

They started. Houblon took it rather easy at first ; and Cambridge obtained a lead directly, and at the Soap Works was half a length ahead. This was reduced by Mr. Hall's excellent steering a foot or two by the time they shot Hammersmith Bridge. As the boats neared Chiswick Eyot, where many a race has changed, Oxford gradually reduced the lead to a foot or two ; and if this could have been done with the old, steady, much-enduring stroke, I would not have given much for the leading boat's chance. But it was achieved by a stroke of full thirty-nine to the minute, and neither form or time was perfect. Mr. Goldie now called upon his crew, and the Clasper boat showed great qualities ; it shot away visibly, like a horse suddenly spurred ; this spurt proved that Cambridge had great reserves of force, and Oxford had very little. Houblon and his gallant men struggled nobly and unflinchingly on ; but, between Barnes Bridge and Mortlake, Goldie put the steam on again, and increased the lead to about a length and a half clear water. The gun was fired, and Cambridge won the race of 1872.

In this race Oxford, contrary to her best traditions, pulled a faster stroke than Cambridge ; the Oxford coxswain's experience compensated for his greater weight. The lighter coxswain steered his boat in and out a bit, and will run some risk of being severely criticised by all our great contemporaries —except *Zig-Zag*. As for me, my fifty summers or fifty winters—there is no great difference in this island of the blessed, they are neither of them so horrible as the spring— have disinclined me to thunder on the young. A veteran journalist perched on the poop of a steam vessel has many advantages. He has a bird's-eye view of the Thames, and can steer Clasper's boat with his mind far more easily than can a youngster squatted four inches above the water, with eight giants intercepting his view of a strange river, and a mob shouting in his ears like all the wild beasts of a thousand forests.

Mr. Goldie has done all his work well for months. He chose his men impartially, practised them in time, and finally rowed the race with perfect judgment. He took an experimental time, and finding he could hold it, made no premature call upon his crew. He held the race in hand, and won it from a plucky opponent without distressing his men needlessly. No man is a friend of Oxford, who tells her to overrate accidents, and underrate what may be done by a wise President before ever the boats reach Putney. This London race was virtually won at Cambridge. Next year let Oxford choose her men from no favourite schools or colleges, lay aside her prejudice against Clasper, and give him a trial ; at all events, return to her swinging-stroke, and practise till not only all the eight bodies go like one, but all the eight rowlocks ring like one ; and the spirit and bottom that enabled her to hang so long on the quarter of a first-rate crew in a first-rate boat will be apt to land her a winner in the next and many a hard-fought race.

CHARLES READE.

BUILDERS' BLUNDERS

To the Editor of the "Pall Mall Gazette"

FIRST LETTER

Sir,—Amidst the din of arms abroad and petty politics at home, have you a corner for a subject less exciting, but very important to Englishmen? Then let me expose that great blot upon the English intellect, the thing we call A HOUSE, especially as it is built in our streets, rows, and squares.

To begin at the bottom—the drains are inside and hidden; nobody knows their course. A foul smell arises: it has to be groped for, and half the kitchen and scullery floors taken up —blunder 1. Drains ought to be outside: and, if not, their course be marked, with the graving tool, on the stones, and a map of the drains deposited with a parish officer; overlying boards and stones ought to be hinged, to facilitate examination. Things capable of derangement should never be inaccessible. This is common sense; yet, from their drains to their chimneypots, the builders defy this maxim.

The kitchen windows are sashes, and all sash-windows are a mistake. They are small; they ought to be as large as possible. The want of light in kitchens is one of the causes why female servants—though their lot is a singularly happy one—are singularly irritable. But, not to dwell on small errors, the next great blunder in the kitchen is THE PLASTER CEILING.

The plaster ceiling may pass, with London builders, for a venerable antiquity that nothing can disturb, but to scholars it is an unhappy novelty, and, in its present form, inexcusable. It was invented in a tawdry age as a vehicle of florid ornamentation; but what excuse can there be for a *plain* plaster ceiling? Count the objections to it in a kitchen. 1. A kitchen is a low room, and the ceiling makes it nine inches lower.   2. White is a glaring colour, and a white ceiling makes a low room look lower.   3. This kitchen ceiling is dirty in a month's wear, and filthy in three months, with the smoke of gas, and it is a thing the servants cannot clean. 4. You cannot hang things on it.

Now change all this : lay out the prime cost of the ceiling, and a small part of its yearly cost, in finishing your joists and boards to receive varnish, and in varnishing them with three coats of good copal.   Your low room is now nine inches higher, and looks three feet.   You can put in hooks and staples galore, and make the roof of this business-room useful; it is, in colour, a pale amber at starting, which is better for the human eye than white glare, and, instead of getting uglier every day, as the plaster ceiling does, it improves every month, every year, every decade, every century.   Clean deal, under varnish, acquires in a few years a beauty oak can never attain to.   So much for the kitchen.

The kitchen stairs, whether of stone or wood, ought never to be laid down without a protecting nozzle.   The brass nozzle costs some money, the lead nozzle hardly any : no nozzle can be dear ; for it saves the steps, and they are dearer. See how the kitchen steps are cut to pieces for want of that little bit of forethought in the builder.

We are now on the first floor.   Over our heads is a blunder, the plaster ceiling, well begrimed with the smoke from the gasalier, and not cleanable by the servants : and we stand upon another blunder ; here are a set of boards, not joined together.   They are nailed down loose, and being of green wood they gape : now the blunder immediately below, the plaster ceiling of the kitchen, has provided a receptacle of dust several inches deep.   This rises when you walk upon the floor, rises in clouds when your children run ; and that dust marks your carpet in black lines, and destroys it before its time.   These same boards are laid down without varnish ; by this means they rot, and do not last one-half, nor, indeed, one-quarter, of their time.   Moreover, the unvarnished boards get filthy at the sides before you furnish ; and thus you lose the cleanest and most beautiful border possible to your carpet. So the householder is driven by the incapacity of the builder to pitiable substitutes—oil cloth, Indian matting, and stained wood, which last gets uglier every year, whereas deal boards varnished clean improve every year, every decade, every century.—I am, Sir, yours very truly,   CHARLES READE.

SECOND LETTER

Sir,—When last seen I was standing on the first floor of the thing they call a house, with a blunder under my feet—un-varnished, unjoined boards; and a blunder over my head —the oppressive, glaring, plaster ceiling, full of its inevitable cracks, and foul with the smoke of only three months' gas. This room has square doors with lintels. Now all doors and doorways ought to be arched, for two reasons—first, the arch is incombustible, the lintel and breast-summer are combustible; secondly, the arch, and arched door, are beautiful; the square hole in the wall, and square door, are hideous.

Sash Windows.

This room is lighted by what may be defined "the un-scientific window." Here in this single structure you may see most of the intellectual vices that mark the unscientific mind. The scientific way is always the simple way; so here you have complication on complication : one-half the window is to go up, the other half is to come down. The maker of it goes out of his way to struggle with Nature's laws: he grapples insanely with gravitation, and therefore he must use cords, and weights, and pulleys, and build boxes to hide them in—he is a great hider. His wooden frames move up and down wooden grooves open to atmospheric influence. What is the consequence? The atmosphere becomes humid; the wooden frame sticks in the wooden box, and the unscientific window is jammed. What ho! Send for the CURSE OF FAMILIES, the British workman! Or one of the cords breaks (they are always breaking)—send for the CURSE OF FAMILIES to patch the blunder of the unscientific builder.

Now turn to the scientific window; it is simply a glass door with a wooden frame; it is not at the mercy of the atmosphere; it enters into no contest with gravitation; it is the one rational window upon earth. If a small window, it is a single glass door, if a large window, it is two glass doors, each calmly turning on three hinges, and not fighting against God Almighty and his laws, when there is no need.

The scientific window can be cleaned by the householder's

servants without difficulty or danger, not so the unscientific window.

How many a poor girl has owed broken bones to the sash-window! Now-a-days humane masters, afflicted with unscientific windows, send for the CURSE OF FAMILIES whenever their windows are dirty; but this costs seven or eight pounds a year, and the householder is crushed under taxes enough without having to pay this odd seven pounds per annum for the nescience of the builder.

We go up the stairs—between two blunders: the balusters are painted, whereas they ought to be made and varnished in the carpenter's shop, and then put up; varnished wood improves with time, painted deteriorates. On the other side is the domestic calamity, foul wear, invariable, yet never provided for; furniture mounting the narrow stairs dents the wall and scratches it; sloppy housemaids paw it as they pass, and their dirty gowns, distended by crinoline, defile it.

What is to be done then?. Must the whole staircase be repainted every year, because five feet of it get dirty, or shall brains step in and protect the vulnerable part?

The cure to this curse is chunam; or encaustic tiles, set five feet high all up the stairs. That costs money! Granted; but the life of a house is not the life of a butterfly. Even the tiles are a cheap cure, for repeated paintings of *the whole surface* mighty soon balance the prime cost of the tiles set over a small part.

The water-closet has no fireplace. That is a blunder. Every year we have a few days' hard frost, and then, without a fire in the water-closet, the water in the pan freezes, the machinery is jammed, and the whole family endure a degree of discomfort, and even of degradation, because the builder builds in summer and forgets there is such a thing as winter.

The drawing-room presents no new feature; but the plaster ceiling is particularly objectionable in this room, because it is under the bedrooms, where water is used freely. Now if a man spills but a pint of water in washing or bathing, it runs through directly and defiles the drawing-room ceiling. Perhaps this blunder ought to be equally divided between the ceiling and the floor above, for whenever bedroom floors shall be properly constructed they will admit of buckets of water being sluiced all over them; and, indeed, will be so treated, and washed as courageously as are sculleries and kitchens only under the present benighted system.

61

I pass over the third floor, and mount a wooden staircase, a terrible blunder in this part of the house, to the rooms under the roof. These rooms, if the roof was open-timbered, would give each inmate a great many cubic feet of air to breathe; so the perverse builder erects a plaster ceiling, and reduces him to a very few cubic feet of air. This, the maddest of all the ceilings, serves two characteristic purposes; it chokes and oppresses the poor devils that live under it, and it hides the roof; now the roof is the part that oftenest needs repairs, so it ought to be the most accessible part of the house, and the easiest to examine from the outside and from the inside. For this very reason Perversity in person hides it; whenever your roof or a gutter leaks, it is all groping and speculation, because your builder has concealed the inside of the roof with that wretched ceiling, and has made the outside accessible only to cats and sparrows, and the "curse of families." N.B.—Whenever that curse of families goes out on that roof to mend one hole, he makes two. Why not? thanks to the perverse builder you can't watch him, and *he has got a friend a plumber.*

We now rise from folly to lunacy; the roof is half perpendicular. This, in a modern house, is not merely silly, it is disgraceful to the human mind; it was all very well before gutters and pipes were invented: it was well designed to shoot off the water by the overlapping eaves: but now we run our water off by our gutters and pipes, and the roof merely feeds them; the steep roof feeds them too fast, and is a main cause of overflows. But there are many other objections to slanted roofs, especially in streets and rows:

1st. The pyramidal roof, by blocking up the air, necessitates high stacks of chimneys, which are expensive and dangerous.

2nd. The pyramidal roof presses laterally against the walls, which these precious builders make thinner the higher they raise them, and subjects the whole structure to danger.

3rd. It robs the family of a whole floor, and gives it to cats and sparrows. I say that a five-storey house with a pyramidal roof is a five-storey house, and with a flat roof is a six-storey house.

4th. It robs the poor cockney of his country view. It is astonishing how much of the country can be seen from the roofs of most London streets. A poor fellow who works all day in a hole, might smoke his evening pipe, and see a wide tract of verdure—but the builders have denied him that;

they build the roof for cats and the "curse of families," they do not build it for the man whose bread they eat.

5th. It robs poor families of their drying-ground.

6th. This idiotic blunder, slightly aided by a subsidiary blunder or two, murders householders and their families wholesale, destroys them by the most terrible of all deaths—burning alive.

And I seriously ask you, and any member of either House, who is not besotted with little noisy things, to consider how great a matter this is, though no political squabble can be raised about it.

Mind you, the builders are not to blame that a small, high house is, in its nature, a fire-trap. This is a misfortune inseparable from the shape of the structure and the nature of that terrible element. The crime of the builders lies in this, that they make no intelligent provision against a danger so evident, but side with the fire not the family.

Prejudice and habitual idiocy apart, can anything be clearer than this, *that, as fire mounts and smoke stifles, all persons who are above a fire ought to be enabled to leave the house by way of the roof, as easily and rapidly as those below the fire can go out by the street door.*

Now what do the builders do? They side with fire; they accumulate combustible materials on the upper floors, and they construct a steep roof most difficult and dangerous to get about on, but to the aged and infirm impossible. Are then the aged and infirm incombustible? This horrible dangerous roof the merciless wretches make so hard of access that few are the cases, as well they know by the papers, in which a life is saved by their hard road. They open a little trap-door—horizontal, of course; always go against God Almighty and his laws, when you can; that is the idiot's creed. This miserable aperture, scarcely big enough for a dog, is bolted or padlocked. It is seven feet from the ground. Yet the builder fixes no steps nor stairs to it; no, get at it how you can. What chance has a mixed family of escaping by this hole in case of fire. Nobody ever goes on that beastly pyramid except in case of fire; and so the bolt is almost sure to be rusty, or the key mislaid, or the steps not close; and, even if the poor wretches get the steps to the place, and heave open the trap, in spite of rust and gravitation, these delays are serious; then the whole family is to be dragged up through a dog-hole, and that is slow work, and fire is swift and smoke is stifling.

A thousand poor wretches have been clean murdered in my time by the builders with their trap-door and their pyramidal roof. Thousands more have been destroyed, as far as the builders were concerned; the firemen and fire-escape men saved them, in spite of the builders, by means which were a disgrace to the builders.

But in my next, Sir, I will show you that in a row of houses constructed by brains not one of those tragedies could ever have taken place.—I am, Sir, yours very truly,

CHARLES READE.

THIRD LETTER

SIR,—It is a sure sign a man is not an artist, if, instead of repairing his defects, he calls in an intellectual superior to counteract them. The fire-escape is creditable to its inventor, but disgraceful to the builders. They construct a fire-trap without an escape ; and so their fellow-citizens are to cudgel their brains and supply the builders' want of intelligence and humanity by an invention working *from the street.* The fire-escape can after all save but a few of the builders' victims. The only universal fire-escape is—THE RATIONAL ROOF.

To be constructed thus: Light iron staircases from the third floor to top floor and rational roof. Flat roof, or roofs, metal covered, with scarcely perceptible fall from centre. Open joists and iron girders, the latter sufficiently numerous to keep the roof from falling in, even though fire should gut the edifice. An iron-lined door, surmounted by a skylight; iron staircase up to this door, which opens rationally on to the rational roof. Large cistern or tank on roof with a force-pump to irrigate the roof in fire or summer heats. Round the roof iron rails set firm in balcony, made too hard for bairns to climb, and surmounted by spikes. Between every two houses a partition gate with two locks and keys complete. Bell under cover to call neighbour in fire or other emergency.

Advantages offered by " *the* RATIONAL *roof* : "—

1. High chimney stacks not needed.

2. Nine smoking chimneys cured out of ten. There are always people at hand to make the householder believe his chimney smokes by some fault of construction, and so they gull him into expenses, and his chimney smokes on—because

it is not thoroughly swept. Send a faithful servant on to the rational roof, let him see the chimney-sweep's brush at the top of every chimney before you pay a shilling, and good-bye smoking chimneys. Sweeps are rogues, and the irrational roof is their shield and buckler.

3. The rails painted chocolate and the spikes gilt would mightily improve our gloomy streets.

4. Stretch clothes' lines from spike to spike, and there is a drying-ground for the poor, or for such substantial people as are sick of the washerwomen and their villainy. These heartless knaves are now rotting fine cambric and lace with soda and chloride of lime, though borax is nearly as detergent and injures nothing.

5. A playground in a purer air for children that cannot get to the parks. There is no ceiling to crack below.

6. In summer heats a blest retreat. Irrigate and cool from the cistern: then set four converging poles, stretch over these from spike to spike a few breadths of awning; and there is a delightful tent and perhaps a country view. If the Star and Garter at Richmond had possessed such a roof, they would have made at least two thousand a year upon it, and perhaps have saved their manager from a terrible death.

7. On each roof a little flagstaff and streamer to light the gloom with sparks of colour, and tell the world is the master at home or not. This would be of little use now; but when once the rational roof becomes common, many a friend could learn from his own roof whether a friend was at home, and so men's eyes might save their legs.

8. In case of fire, the young and old would walk out by a rational door on to a rational roof, and ring at a rational gate. Then their neighbour lets them on to his rational roof, and they are safe. Meantime, the adult males, if any, have time to throw wet blankets on the skylight and turn the water on to the roof. The rational roof, after saving the family which its predecessor would have destroyed, now proceeds to combat the fire. It operates as an obstinate cowl over the fire; and, if there are engines on the spot, the victory is certain. Compare this with the whole conduct of the irrational roof. First it murdered the inmates; then it fed the fire; then it collapsed and fell on the ground floor, destroying more property, and endangering the firemen.—I am, yours very truly, CHARLES READE.

FOURTH LETTER

Sir,—The shoe pinches all men more or less; but, on a calm survey, I think it pinches the householder hardest.

A house is as much a necessary of life as a loaf; yet this article of necessity has been lately raised to a fancy price by the trade conspiracies of the building operatives—not so much by their legitimate strikes for high wages as by their conspiring never to do for any amount of wages an honest day's work—and the fancy price thus created strikes the householder first in the form of rent. But this excessive rent, although it is an outgoing, is taxed as income; its figure is made the basis of all the imperial and parochial exactions, that crush the householder. One of these is singularly unfair; I mean "the inhabited house duty." What is this but the property tax rebaptized and levied over again, but from the wrong person? the property tax is a percentage on the rent, levied in good faith, from the person whom the rent enables to pay that percentage; but the inhabited house duty is a similar percentage on the rent, levied, under the disguise of another name, from him whom the rent disables.

In London the householder constantly builds and improves the freehold: instantly parochial spies raise his rates. He has employed labour, and so far counterbalanced pauperism; at the end of his lease the house will bear a heavier burden; but these heartless extortioners they bleed the poor wretch directly for improving parochial property at his own expense. At the end of his lease the rent is raised by the landlord on account of these taxed improvements, and the tenant turned out with a heavier grievance than the Irish farmer; yet he does not tumble his landlord, nor even a brace of vestrymen. The improving tenant, while awaiting the punishment of virtue, spends twenty times as much money in pipes as the water companies do, yet he has to pay them for water a price so enormous, that they ought to bring it into his cisterns, and indeed into his mouth, for the money.

He pays through the nose for gas.

He bleeds for the vices of the working classes; since in our wealthy cities, nine-tenths of the pauperism is simply waste and inebriety. He often pays temporary relief to an improvident workman, whose annual income exceeds his own, but who will never put by a shilling for a slack time.

In short, the respectable householder of moderate means is so ground down and oppressed that, to my knowledge, he is on the road to despondency and ripening for a revolution.

Now, I can hold him out no hope of relief from existing taxation; but his intolerable burden can be lightened by other means; the simplest is to keep down his bill for repairs and decorations, which at present is made monstrous by original misconstruction.

The irrational house is an ANIMAL WITH ITS MOUTH ALWAYS OPEN.

This need not be. It arises from causes most of which are removable; viz., 1st, from unscientific construction; 2nd, plaster ceilings; 3rd, the want of provision for partial wear; 4th, the abuse of paint; 5th, hidden work.

Under all these heads I have already given examples. I will add another under head 3. The dado or skirting board is to keep furniture from marking the wall; but it is laid down only one inch thick, whereas the top of a modern chair overlaps the bottom an inch and a half. This the builders do not, or will not, observe, and so every year in London fifty thousand rooms are spoiled by the marks of chair-backs on the walls, and the owners driven to the expense of painting or papering sixty square yards, to clean a space that is less than a square foot, but fatal to the appearance of the room.

Under head 4 let me observe that God's woods are all very beautiful; that ONLY FOOLS ARE WISER THAN GOD ALMIGHTY; that varnish shows up the beauty of those woods, and adds a gloss; and that house-paint hides their beauty. Paint holds dirt, and does not wash well; varnish does. Paint can only be mixed by a workman. Varnish is sold fit to put on. Paint soon requires revival, and the old paint must be rubbed off at a great expense, and two new coats put on. Varnish stands good for years, and, when it requires revival, little more is necessary than simple cleaning, and one fresh coat, which a servant or anybody can lay on. 5. Hidden work is sure to be bad work, and so need repairs, especially in a roof, that sore tried part; and the repairs are the more expensive that the weak place has to be groped for.

I have now, I trust, said enough to awaken a few householders from the lethargy of despair, and to set them thinking a little and organising a defence against the extraordinary mixture of stupidity and low instinctive trade cunning of which they are the victims: for a gentleman's blunders hurt himself, but a tradesman's blunders always hurt his customers. And this is singularly true of builders' blunders; they all tend one way—to compel the householder to be always sending for the builder, or that bungling rascal the plumber, to grope for his hidden work, or botch his bad work, or clean his unscientific windows, or whitewash his idiotic ceilings, or rub his nasty unguents off God's beautiful wood, and then put some more nasty odoriferous unguents on, or put cowls on his ill-cleaned chimneys; or, in short, to repair his own countless blunders at the expense of his customer.

Independently of the murderous and constant expense, the bare entrance into a modest household of that loose, lazy, drunken, dishonest drink-man and jack-man, who has the impudence to call himself "the British workman," though he never did half a day's real work at a stretch in all his life, is a serious calamity, to be averted by every lawful means.— I am, Sir, yours faithfully, CHARLES READE.

WHO IS HE?

To the Editor of the "Daily News"

Sir,—Your correspondent "Facing both Ways," complains that a trial, which lasted 101 days, has only revealed to him that the Tichborne Claimant is not Tichborne; who the man really is remains obscure. I think, sir, your correspondent makes his own difficulty; he overrates direct evidence, though this very trial has shown its extreme fallibility, and underrates circumstantial evidence. This is an illusion; circumstantial evidence avails to convict a man of a murder no human eye has witnessed; and *à fortiori* it avails to identify a pseudo-Tichborne with the man he really is. The proof of his identity lies in a number of circumstances, heterogeneous, and independent of each other, yet all pointing to one conclusion, and all undeniable, and indeed not denied. Now it is a property of such coincidences, that, when they multiply, the proof rises, not on a scale of simple addition, but in a ratio so enormous that at the sixth coincidence we get to figures the tongue may utter, but the mind cannot realise. In cases of murder I have never known a treble coincidence, pointing to one man as the murderer, fail to result in a conviction. But in the Tichborne case the barefaced coincidences, all pointing to the Tichborne Claimant as Arthur Orton, are not less than seven; and to these you may add one of superlative importance, viz., the coincidence of character. Character is the key to men's actions, and it is clear that Arthur Orton, when quite a youth, was instinctively inclined towards an imposture of the same kind, though not the same degree, that a jury has fixed upon the Tichborne Claimant. This youth, though "Begot by butchers, and by butchers bred," did yet hold his haughty head high out in Brazil, and boasted of some lofty origin or other. If your correspondent will only take a sheet of paper and write down, in separate paragraphs, all the undisputed coincidences, and then add the coincidence of character, and then add to that the circumstance that no other Arthur Orton could be found to go into the witness-box and say, "I am Arthur Orton," though those four words would have been worth fifty thousand pounds to the Claimant and his bondholders, he will see before him such an array of heterogeneous proofs, all radiating to one centre, as no recorded trial ever elicited before. Now, the naturalists have laid down a maxim of reasoning in such cases which every lawyer in England would do well to copy into his notebook: "The true solution is that which reconciles all the indisputable facts." Apply this test to the theories that the Claimant is Castro, is Doolan, is Morgan; those theories all dissolve before that immortal piece of wisdom like hailstones before the midsummer sun. In the same way—to use a favourite form in Euclid—it can be proved that no other person except Arthur Orton is the Tichborne Claimant. Is this uncertainty? What, then, of all we believe—either human or divine—is certain?—I am, Sir, yours faithfully, CHARLES READE.

ALBERT TERRACE, KNIGHTSBRIDGE,
   March 18, 1872.

THE
DOCTRINE OF COINCIDENCES

To the Editor of "Fact"

FIRST LETTER

Sir,—In reply to your query—it is true that after the trial at Nisi Prius, where "the Claimant" was Plaintiff, but before his trial at Bar as Defendant, I pronounced him to be Arthur Orton, and gave my reasons.

These you now invite me to repeat. I will do so; only let me premise that I am not so vain as to think I can say anything essentially new on this subject, which has been fully discussed by men superior to me in attainments.

It so happens, however, that those superior men have always veiled a part of their own mental process, though it led them to a just conclusion: they have never stated in direct terms their major premiss, or leading principle. This is a common omission, especially amongst Anglo-Saxon reasoners; but it is a positive defect, and one I do think I can supply. But before we come to the debatable matter, I fear I must waste a few words on the impossible—namely, that this man is Roger Charles Tichborne.

Well, then, let those who have not studied the evidence and cross-examination, just cast their eyes on this paper and see a sample of what they must believe, or else reject that chimera.

That Roger Tichborne was drowned with thirty more, yet reappeared years after, all alone, leaving at the bottom of the sea all his companions, and certain miscellaneous articles, viz.:—

1. His affection for his mother, his brother, and others.
2. His handwriting.
3. His leanness.
4. His French.
5. His love of writing letters to his folk.

6. His knowledge of Châteaubriand, and his comprehension of what the deuce he, Roger Tichborne, was writing about when he put upon paper—before his submersion—that he admired René, *and gave his reasons.*

7. His knowledge of the Tichborne estates, and the counties they lay in.

8. His knowledge of his mother's Christian names.

9. His knowledge of his beloved sweetheart's face, figure, and voice.

10. His tattoo marks, three inches long.

11. His religion.

12. Five years of his life. These five years lay full fathom five at the bottom of the ocean hard by No. 10, when this aristocratic Papist married a servant girl in a Baptist chapel, and was only thirty years old, as appears on the register in his handwriting, which is nothing like Tichborne's. Along with this rubbish we may as well sweep away the last invention of weak and wavering intellects, that the Claimant is no individual in particular, but a sort of solidified myth, incarnate *alias,* or obese hallucination.

And now having applied our besoms to the bosh, let us apply our minds to the debatable. Since he is not dead Castro, nor dead Tichborne, nor live *Alias,* who is he? Here then to those, who go with me so far, I proceed to state the leading principle, which governs the case thus narrowed, and —always implied, though unfortunately never stated—led our courts to a reasonable conclusion. That principle is .

THE PROGRESSIVE VALUE OF PROVED COINCIDENCES ALL POINTING TO ONE CONCLUSION.

Pray take notice that by *proved* coincidences I mean coincidences that are—

1. Not merely seeming, but independent and real.

2. Either undisputed, or indisputable.

3. Either extracted from a hostile witness, which is the highest kind of evidence, especially where the witness is a deliberate liar; or

4. Directly sworn to by respectable witnesses in open court, and then cross-examined and not shaken—which is the next best evidence to the involuntary admissions of a liar interested in concealing the truth.

Men born to be deceived like children may think these precautions extravagant; but they are neither excessive nor new: they are sober, true, and just to both the parties in every mortal cause; they have been for ages the safeguard of all great and wary minds; and neither I nor any other man can lay down any general position of reasoning, that will guide men aright, who are so arrogant, so ignorant, or so weak, as to scorn them.

On the other hand, if your readers will accept these safeguards, the general principle I have laid down will never deceive them; it will show them who the Claimant is, and it will aid them in far greater difficulties, and more important inquiries; for, like all sound principles of reason, it is equally applicable to questions of science, literature, history, or crime.—I am, Sir, yours faithfully,   CHARLES READE.

SECOND LETTER

SIR,—A single indisputable coincidence raises a presumption that often points towards the truth.

A priori what is more unlikely than that the moon, a mere satellite, and a very small body, should so attract the giant earth as to cause our tides? Indeed, for years science rejected the theory; but certain changes of the tide coinciding regularly with changes of the moon wore out prejudice, and have established the truth. Yet these coincident changes, though repeated *ad infinitum*, make but one logical coincidence.

On the other hand, it must be owned that a single coincidence often deceives. To take a sublunary and appropriate example, the real Martin Guerre had a wart on his cheek; so had the sham Martin Guerre. The coincidence was genuine and remarkable: yet the men were distinct. But mark the ascending ratio—see the influence on the mind of a double coincidence—when the impostor with the real wart told the sisters of Martin Guerre some particulars of their family history, and reminded Martin's wife of something he had said to her on their bridal night, in the solitude of the nuptial chamber, this seeming knowledge, coupled with that real wart, struck her mind with the force of a double coincidence; and no more was needed to make her accept the impostor, and cohabit with him for years.

Does not this enforce what I urged in my first letter as to the severe caution necessary in receiving alleged, or seeming, or manipulated coincidences, as if they were proved and real ones? However, I use the above incident at present mainly to show the ascending *power* on the mind of coincidences when received as genuine.

I will now show their ascending *value* when proved in open court and tested by cross-examination.

A. was found dead of a gunshot wound, and the singed paper that had been used for wadding lay near him. It was a fragment of the *Times*. B.'s house was searched, and they found there a gun recently discharged, and the copy of the *Times*, from which the singed paper aforesaid had been torn ; the pieces fitted exactly.

The same thing happened in France with a slight variation ; the paper used for wadding was part of an old breviary, subsequently found in B.'s house.

The salient facts of each case made a treble coincidence. What was the result ? The treble coincidence sworn, cross-examined, and unshaken, hanged the Englishman, and guillotined the Frenchman. In neither case was there a scintilla of direct evidence ; in neither case was the verdict impugned.

I speak within bounds when I say that a genuine double coincidence, proved beyond doubt, is not twice, but two hundred times, as strong, as one such coincidence, and that a genuine treble coincidence is many thousand times as strong as one such coincidence. But, when we get to a fivefold coincidence real and proved, it is a million to one against all these honest circumstances having combined to deceive us.

As for a sevenfold coincidence not manipulated, nor merely alleged, but fully proved, does either history, science, literature, or crime offer one example of its ever misleading the human mind ? Why, the very existence of seven independent and indisputable coincidences, all pointing to one conclusion, is a rarity so great, that, in all my reading, I hardly know where to find an example of it except in the defence that baffled this claimant at Nisi Prius.

Now, on that occasion, the parties encountered each other plump on various lines of evidence. There were direct recognitions of his personal identity by respectable witnesses, and direct disavowals of the same by respectable witnesses, just as there were in the case of the sham Martin Guerre, who brought thirty honest disinterested witnesses to swear he was the man he turned out not to be.

With this part of the case I will not meddle here, though I have plenty to say upon it.

But both parties also multiplied coincidences : only some of these were real, some apparent, some manipulated, some honest and independent, some said or sworn out of court by liars, who knew better than venture into the witness-box with them ; some proved by cross-examination, or in spite of it. We have only to subject this hodge-podge of real and sham to the approved test laid down in my first letter, and we shall see daylight; for the Claimant's is a clear case, made obscure by verbosity, and conjecture in the teeth of proof!

A. He proved in court a genuine coincidence of a corporeal kind—viz., that Roger Tichborne was in-kneed, with the left leg turned out more than the right, and the Claimant was in-kneed in a similar way.

This is a remarkable coincidence, and cross-examination failed to shake it.

But when he attempted to prove a second coincidence of corporeal peculiarities like the above, which, being the work of nature, cannot be combated, what a falling off in the evidence.

B. They found in the Claimant a congenital brown mark on the side ; but they could only assert or imagine a similar mark in Tichborne. No *vivâ voce* evidence by eye-witnesses to anything of the sort.

C. They proved, by Dr. Wilson, a peculiar formation in the Claimant; but instead of proving by some doctor, surgeon, or eye-witness a similar formation in Tichborne, they went off into wild inferences. The eccentric woman, who kept her boy three years under a seton, had also kept him a long time in frocks ; and the same boy, when a moody young man, had written despondent phrases, such as, in all other cases, imply a dejected *mind*, but here are to be perverted to indicate a malformed *body*, although many doctors, surgeons, and nurses knew Tichborne's body, and not one of all these ever saw this malformation which, in the nude body, must have been visible fifty yards off. In short, the coincidences B. and C. were proved incidences with unproved " Co's."

Failing to establish a double coincidence of congenital features or marks, the Claimant went off into artificial skin-marks.

Examples : Roger had marks of a seton ; the Claimant showed marks of a similar kind.

Roger had a cut at the back of his head, and another on his wrist. So had the Claimant.

Roger had the seams of a lancet on his ankles. The Claimant came provided with punctures on the ankle.

Roger winked and blinked. So did the Claimant.

Then there was something about a mark on the eyelid ; but on this head I forget whether the Claimant's witness ever faced cross-examination. Nor does it very much matter, for all these artificial coincidences are rotten at the core : unlike the one true corporeal coincidence the Claimant proved, they could all be imitated ; and, as regards the ankles, imitation was reasonably suspected in court, for the Claimant's needle-pricks were unlike the seam of a lancet, and were not applied to the ankle pulse, as they would have been, by a surgeon, on lean Tichborne, in whom the saphena vein would be manifest, and even the ankle-pulse perceptible, though not in a fair, fat, and false representative. Then the seton marks were stiffly disputed, and the balance of medical testimony was that the Claimant's marks were not of that precise character.

These doubtful coincidences were also encountered by direct dissidences on the same line of observation. Roger was bled in the temporal artery, and the Claimant showed no puncture there. Roger was tattooed with a crown, cross, and anchor by a living witness, who faced cross-examination, and several witnesses in the cause saw the tattoo marks at various times ; and it was no answer to all this positive evidence to bring witnesses who did not tattoo him, and other witnesses who never saw the tattoo marks. The pickpocket, who brought twenty witnesses that did not see him pick a certain pocket, against two who did, was defeated by the intrinsic nature of evidence. I shall ask no person to receive any coincidence from me that was so shaken and made doubtful, and also neutralised by dissidences, as the imitable skin-marks in this case were. But the Claimant also opened a large vein of apparent coincidences in the knowledge shown by him at certain times and places of numerous men and things known to Roger Tichborne. These were very remarkable. He knew private matters known to Tichborne and A, to Tichborne and B, to Tichborne and C, &c., and he knew more about Tichborne than either A, B, C, &c., individually knew. It is not fair nor reasonable to pooh-pooh this. But the defendants met this fairly ; they said these coincidences were not arrived at by his being Tichborne, but by his pumping various individuals who knew Tichborne : and they applied fair and sagacious tests to the matter.

They urged as a general truth that Tichborne in Australia would have known just as much about himself, his relations, and his affairs as he subsequently knew in England. And I must do them the justice to say this position is impregnable. Then they went into detail and proved that when Gibbs first spotted the Claimant at Wagga-Wagga, he was as ignorant as dirt of Tichborne matters; did not know the Christian names of Tichborne's mother, nor the names of the Tichborne estates, nor the counties where they lay. They then showed the steps by which his ignorance might have been partly lessened and much knowledge picked up; they showed a lady, who longed to be deceived, and all but said so, putting him by letter on to Bogle—Bogle startled, and pumped—the Claimant showing the upper part of his face in Paris to the lady who wanted to be deceived, and, after recognition on those terms, pumping her largely; then coming to England with a large stock of fact thus obtained, and in England pumping Carter, Bulpitt, and others, searching Lloyd's, &c.

2. Having proved the gradual *growth of knowledge in the Claimant between Wagga-Wagga and the Court of Common Pleas*, they took him in court with all his acquired knowledge, and cross-examined him on a vast number of things well-known to Tichborne. Under this test, for which his preparations were necessarily imperfect, he betrayed a mass of ignorance on a multitude of things familiar to Roger Tichborne, and he betrayed it not frankly as honest men betray ignorance, or oblivion of what they have once really known, but in spite of such fencing, evading, shuffling, and equivocating, as the most experienced have rarely seen in the witness-box. Personating a gentleman he shuffled without a blush; personating a collegian, he did not know what a quadrangle is. The inscription over the Stonyhurst quadrangle, "Laus Deo," was strange to him. He thought it meant something about the laws of God. He knew no French, no Latin. He thought Cæsar was a Greek: and, when a crucial test was offered him, which, if he had been Tichborne, he would have welcomed with delight, and turned the scale in his favour, when a thoughtful comment by Roger Tichborne on the character of René was submitted to him, and he was questioned about this René, he was utterly flabbergasted. He wriggled and writhed, and brazened out his ignorance, but it shone forth in spite of him. He was evidently not the man who had tasted Châteaubriand, and written a thoughtful comment on René. His mind was not that mind any more than his handwriting was that handwriting."

To judge this whole vein of coincidences, and their neutralising dissidences, the jury had now before them three streams of fact.

1. That at Wagga-Wagga the Claimant knew nothing about Tichborne more than the advertisements told him.

2. That in England he knew an incredible number of things about Tichborne.

3. That in England he took Mrs. Towneley for Roger's sweetheart, and even at the trial was ignorant of many things Tichborne could not be ignorant of.

NOW, IN ALL CASES, WHERE THERE ARE SEVERAL FACTS INDISPUTABLE, YET SEEMINGLY OPPOSED, SCIENCE DECLARES THE TRUE SOLUTION TO BE THAT WHICH, SETTING ASIDE THE DOUBTFUL FACTS, RECONCILES ALL THE INDISPUTABLE FACTS.

This maxim is infallible.

The good sense of the jury led them to this solution as surely as science would have led a jury of Huxleys and Tyndalls to it; and they decided that the coincidences were remarkable but manipulated, the knowledge astonishing but acquired, the ignorance an inevitable residue, which only Tichborne could have escaped. They saw a small pump working in Australia, a large pump working in Paris, a huge pump working in England, but a human, and therefore finite, pump after all, as proved in court by examination of the Radcliffes, Gosford, and others; and above all, by cross examination of the Claimant, which last is the highest evidence.

So much for the single genuine coincidence of the knees, and the manipulated coincidences of artificial skin-marks, and acquired knowledge, relied on for the Claimant.

At this stage your readers should ask themselves two questions—

1st. Is not history printed experience; and ought experience to be printed in vain?

Did not the real wart, and the simulated knowledge, and the thirty direct witnesses of the sham Martin Guerre, anticipate the broad outline of this Claimant's case?

2nd. As regards the coincidences, which were not only open to the charge of manipulation, but also neutralised by dissidences, are they mighty enough to convince any candid mind that a fat, live person—who slaughtered bullocks and married a housemaid, and swore in the box without a blush that he had lied, like a low fellow, to his friend and benefactor, Gibbs, and that he well knew, and had loved, and after the manner of the lower orders seduced a lady (though he afterwards took Mrs. Towneley for her), and still following the lower orders, blasted her reputation—was the lean, dead aristocrat, Tichborne, who went down in the *Bella*, with all hands, not one of whom has reappeared, and died, as he had lived, the delicate, loyal lover of the chaste Kate Doughty —and a gentleman—and a man of honour?

I will now show, in contrast, the *indisputable* coincidences, which, converging from different quarters, all point to one conclusion—that the Claimant is Arthur Orton, of Wapping.— I am, Sir, yours faithfully, .CHARLES READE.

THIRD LETTER

SIR,—I now venture to hope that all I have written will seem silly to fanatics, and that unprejudiced minds will grant me—

1. That, where there are indisputable facts and doubtful ones, the true solution is that which ignores the doubtful, and reconciles all the indisputable, facts.

2. That two coincidences are a hundred times as strong as one, and five coincidences a million times as strong as one; and so on in a gigantic ratio as the coincidences multiply.

3. That coincidences, like other circumstances, must rest on legal evidence, and that there is a scale of legal evidence, without which a man would be all at sea in any great trial, since such trials arise out of a conflict of evidence. I indicated this scale in my first letter; but as it is not encountered, but ignored in all the replies I have seen, I will amplify and enforce it.

THE SCALE OF EVIDENCE.

A. A written affidavit, not cross-examined, is " PERJURY MADE EASY."

B. A written affidavit, signed by a person who could carry his statement into open Court, but does not, is PER-JURY DECLARED : for, when a man's actions contradict his words, it is his words that lie.

C. In open Court the lowest kind of evidence is the evidence in chief of the plaintiff, or defendant.

D. The highest evidence is the admission, under cross-examination, of the plaintiff, or defendant.

E. The next highest is the evidence in chief of disinterested persons, not shaken by cross-examination.

These rules were not invented by me, nor for me nor against the Claimant. They are very old, very true, and equally applicable to every great trial—past, present, and to come.

Yet you have a correspondent, in whose mind this scale of

evidence has no place; he gravely urges that the bestial *ignorance* of the Tichborne estates, and the bereaved woman's name he called his mother, shown by the Claimant at Wagga-Wagga, in his very will, a solemn instrument, *by which he provided for his own wife, and expected child*, was not real, as forsooth all his *knowledge* was, but feigned in order to humbug his protector without a motive, *and bilk his own wife out of her sole provision, and sole claims on the Tichborne property ;* and for this self-evident falsehood your correspondent's authority is the evidence of the Claimant himself, a party in the suit, and a party interested in lying, and throwing dust in the eyes of simpletons, who cannot see a church by daylight if some shallow knave *says* it is a pigeon-house.

It was almost as childish to reply to me with the evidence of Moore. What evidence ? Why, he never ventured into court.

Mr. Moore is a humbug, who wrote down a romance, and —fled. Catch him carrying his tale into the witness-box, and being cross-examined out of fiction's fairy realm into one of Her Majesty's jails! See scale of evidence B. These two great instruments of evidence, men and circumstances, re-semble each other in this, that men do not lie without a motive, and circumstances never have a motive, and therefore never lie, though man may misinterpret them. And it is the beauty of true coincidences that in them circumstance pre-ponderates, and man plays second fiddle. A coincidence often surprises even deceitful men into revealing the truth : for a coincidence is two facts pointing to one conclusion; and the effect of the first fact is seldom seen till the second comes, and then it is too late to tamper effectually with the pair.

You will see this pure and unforeseeing character running through most of the coincidences I now lay before you.

1. It was proved that Tichborne was in-kneed and dead, and that the Claimant and Arthur Orton are in-kneed and alive.

2. Disinterested witnesses swore that Arthur Orton was unusually stout at twenty, and was called at Wapping " bul-locky " Orton. Later in his life, Australian witnesses, who knew him, described him as uncommonly lusty. The Claimant's figure is described in similar terms by all the Australian wit-nesses who knew him. Now, many a lean youth puts on fat between thirty-five and forty, but lean, active men do not very often fatten from twenty to thirty. This, therefore, is a coincidence, though a feeble one.

3. Arthur Orton, born September 13th, 1832, was the youngest son of George Orton, a shipping butcher, and an

importer of Shetland ponies. He used to ride the ponies from the Dundee steamers, and so got a horseman's seat; for they are awkward animals to ride, if you take them like that, one after another, raw from the Shetland Isles. When full grown, but under age, he slaughtered and dressed sheep and bullocks for his father.

The Claimant in Australia lived by riding, and slaughtering, and dressing beasts. On this point, his own evidence agrees with that of every witness who knew him. And when he came up the Thames in the *Cella* to personate Tichborne, he asked the pilot what had become of Ferguson, the man who used to be pilot of the Dundee boats. All this taken together is rather a strong coincidence. It may seem weak; but apply a test. To whom does all this, as a whole, apply? The riding—the slaughtering—and the spontaneous interest in an old Dundee pilot? To Castro? To Tichborne? To any *known* man not an Orton?

4. In 1848, Arthur Orton, aged 16, sailed to Valparaiso, and subsequently, in June 1849, made his way to Melipilla. He was young, fair, the only English boy in the place, and the good people took to him. He made friends with Dona Hayley, wife of an English doctor, and with Thomas Castro and his wife, and many others. They were very kind to him in 1849 and '50, particularly Dona Hayley, and in these gentle minds the kindly feeling survived the lapse of time, and his long neglect of them. Not foreseeing in 1850 his little game in 1866, Arthur Orton told Dona Hayley he was the son of Orton, the Queen's butcher, and as a child had played with the Queen's children. Not being a prophet, all this bounce at that date went to aggrandise Orton. He spoke of Arthur's sisters by name, and Dona Hayley, twenty years after, remembered the names with slight and natural variations. The wife of Thomas Castro was called at Melipilla Dona Natalia Sarmiento; but this English boy, knowing her to be the wife of Castro, used to call her Mrs. Castro.

This seems to have amused Dona Hayley, and she noted it. This boy was not Castro, for Castro was an elderly Spaniard, kind to this boy on the spot, and at the time. He was not Tichborne, for Tichborne was in England till late in 1852. Tichborne's *alibi* during Arthur Orton's whole visit to Melipilla is proved by a cloud of witnesses, and his own writing, and is, indeed, admitted; he sailed late in 1852, and reached Chili in 1853. Arthur Orton was back in England, June 1851.

Now so much of this as respects Arthur Orton is the first

branch of a pure, unforeseen coincidence. The second branch is this—The Claimant on the 28th August 1867 wrote from his solicitor's office, 25 Poultry, to prepare the good Melipillians for a new theory—that Arthur Orton, seventeen years old to the naked eye, was not Castro—(that cock might fight in Hobart Town, but not in Melipilla); not Castro, but Tichborne, age 23. He wrote to Thomas Castro, complained he was kept out of his estates, and begged to be kindly remembered to Don Juan Hayley, to Clara and Jesusa, to Don Ramon Alcade, Dona Hurtado, to Senorita Matilda, Jose Maria Berenguel, and his brother, and others, in short to twelve persons besides Castro himself. One of the messages has *per se* the character of a coincidence. "My respects to Dona Natalia Sarmiento, or, as I used to call her, Mrs. Castro."

Thomas Castro, to whom this was sent, being in confinement as a lunatic, his son Pedro Castro replied in a letter full of kindness, simple faith, and a desire to serve his injured friend. His letter carries God's truth stamped on it. His replies to the kind messages accord with our sad experience of time and its ravages. "His father bereft of reason, his mother —dead this fourteen months. Dona Hayley's recollection of the boy perfect, and she is ready to serve him, and depose to the truth. But the doctor's memory gone through intemperance, Dona Jesusa dead." "Don Jose Maria Berenguel is not so called, his name is Don Francesco Berenguel. He is established at Valparaiso." Then the writer goes on to say what had become of the other friends inquired after by the Claimant. One of them he specifies in particular as taking fire at the Claimant's letter, and remembering all about him, and desirous to serve him, he himself being animated by the same spirit, tells him that Dona Francesca Ahumada retains a lock of his hair, which he suggests the Claimant might turn to account: and so he might if he had been Tichborne. In the same spirit he warns him that his enemies had an agent at Melipilla hunting up data to use against him.

The correspondence thus begun continued in the same spirit. The whole coincidence is this: The Claimant stayed a long time at Melipilla in 1849 and 1850, and called himself Arthur Orton, and proved himself Arthur Orton, by giving full details of his family, and left Chili in 1850, during all which time an *alibi* is proved for Tichborne, but none can be proved nor has ever been attempted, for Arthur Orton. On the contrary, a *non alibi* was directly proved for him. He was traced from Wapping to Valparaiso, and Melipilla, in 1848. His stay there till 1850 was proved, and then he was traced in 1850 into the *Jessie Miller,* and home to Wapping in 1851 just as he had been traced out—by ships' registers and a cloud of witnesses.

The coincidence rests on the two highest kinds of evidence, the Claimant's written admission, and the direct evidence of respectable witnesses unshaken by cross-examination (see scale of evidence), and it points to the Claimant as Arthur Orton.

Those who can see he is not Tichborne, but are deceived by the falsehoods of men into believing he is not Orton, should give special study to this coincidence ; for here the Claimant is either Tichborne or Orton.   No third alternative is possible. At Melipilla, in 1850, he was either Orton, who was there, aged 17, or Tichborne, who was in England, aged 23.

5. There was, for some years, a bulky man in Australia riding and breaking horses, slaughtering and dressing beasts. His name—Castro—appears when that of Orton disappears. The two men seem to differ in name but not in figure and occupation.   And no witness ever came into the witness-box and swore that he had ever seen these two portly butchers in two different skins.   In 1867 the Claimant explained this phenomenon.

In his letter to Thomas Castro he wrote thus :—" And another strange thing I have to tell you, and I have no doubt you will say I took a great liberty on myself, that is to say, I took and made use of your name, and was only known in Australia by the name of Thomas Castro.   I said also I belonged to Chili."   He adds, however, an assurance that he had never disgraced him as a horseman.   This coincidence proves that whenever we meet in Australia a bulky butcher, stock-keeper, horse-breaker, &c., called Thomas Castro, of Chili, that means the Claimant, and also means Arthur Orton, of Melipilla.

And Arthur Orton of Melipilla is Arthur Orton of Wapping.

6. This sham Castro, sham Chilian, sham aristocrat, &c., married, as people do nine times in ten, into his own class, a servant girl who could not write her name.   She made her mark.   He forged a friend's name.   Apparently he did not foresee he was going to leave off shamming Castro and begin shamming Tichborne, a stiff Papist ; so he got married by a dissenting minister, and in signing the register, described himself as thirty years old.

Castro was, say sixty ; Tichborne was thirty-six.   Who was thirty ?

Arthur Orton of Wapping.

7. It was the interest of Gibbes this man should be Tichborne. His wishes influenced his judgment. He inclined to think he was the right man. But some things staggered him; in particular the man's want of education. Gibbes told him frankly that seemed inconsistent. Then the Claimant, to get over that, told Gibbes that in childhood he had a nervous affection which checked his education. He then described this affection so correctly that Gibbes said, " Bless me, that is St. Vitus's dance." " Yes," said the Claimant, " that is what they used to call it."

This solution eased Gibbes' mind, and he sat down and, honestly enough, sent an account of the conversation to Lady Tichborne's agent; he wrote it to serve the plaintiff, not foreseeing the turn that revelation of the truth would take.

Coming home in the *Rachaia* there was some document or other to be read out, and the passengers confided this to the Claimant as a person claiming the highest rank. He blundered and made a mess of it, and showed his ignorance so that suspicion was raised, and one Mr. Hodson put it point-blank to him— " You a baronet, and can't read !" Then the Claimant told him he had been afflicted in his boyhood with St. Vitus's dance, and could not learn his letters.

It was afterwards proved by a surgeon and a multitude of witnesses that at ten years of age Arthur Orton had been frightened by a fire, and afflicted with St. Vitus's dance, and that this had really checked his education, and that the traces of it had remained by him for years; and that, in fact, he was sent to sea in hopes of a cure. This coincidence is very strong. Observe—it is not confined to the disease; but to the time of life, and its effect on a boy's education.

No doubt a third man neither Tichborne nor Orton might have St. Vitus's dance as a little boy, and so be made a dunce, in spite of great natural ability. There is not above a hundred thousand to one against it; but coming after coincidences 4, 5, and 6, which clear away Castro and all other mere vapours, and confine the question to Tichborne or Orton, have I not now the right to say, Tichborne, by admission of all the witnesses on both sides, never had St. Vitus's dance; Arthur Orton undisputably had St. Vitus's dance; the Claimant, to account for his ignorance, spontaneously declared at different times, and to different people, that he had been afflicted with St. Vitus's dance, and this coincidence points to the Claimant as Arthur Orton of Wapping ?—Yours obediently,   CHARLES READE.

THE DOCTRINE OF COINCIDENCES

FOURTH LETTER

Sir,—I will ask those who have done me the honour to keep my last letter, to draw a circle on a sheet of paper, the larger the better, and to draw seven radii from its centre across the line of circumference to the edge of the paper; then upon those extended radii, and between the circle and the edge of the paper, I will ask them to write in small letters a short epitome of each coincidence, or a few words recalling what they consider its salient feature.

Those who will do me the honour to take the trouble, and so become my fellow-labourers in logic, will not repent it. It will, I think, assist them, as it has assisted me, to realise how vast an area both of territory and of multifarious evidence is covered at the circumference by these seven coincidences, which nevertheless converge to one central point, no bigger than a pin's head, viz., that this Claimant, who has owned himself a sham Castro of Chili, but clings to his other alias, Tichborne, is Arthur Orton of Wapping.

8. From the day the *Bella* foundered to the day Gibbes spotted the Claimant, a period of thirteen or fourteen years, Roger Tichborne never wrote a line to his mother or his brother, or any relation or friend. This is accounted for rationally and charitably by his being dead at the bottom of the ocean.

No, says the Claimant, I was alive all the time, and let my mother and my brother and my sweetheart think I had died horribly, cut off in my prime.

The animal never realised that he was both drawing upon human credulity, and describing a monster and a beast. What was it that so blinded his most powerful understanding? From 1852 to 1865 Arthur Orton never wrote a line to Wapping. He let the father who reared him, the mother who bore him, go to their graves without one little word to say their son was alive. Not a line to brother, sister, or sweetheart. This unnatural trait being absent in Tichborne till he was drowned, and present in the Claimant by his own confession, and in Arthur Orton by a pyramid of evidence, is a startling coincidence of a new class. The unnatural heart of the Claimant is the unnatural heart of Arthur Orton.

9. In 1852 Arthur Orton went out to Hobart Town with two Shetland ponies in the *Middleton*.

Subsequently, as the Claimant swore, he was for years at Boisdale and Dargo, slaughtering and riding, &c., in the service of Mr. W. Foster, and under the name of Castro, the Chilian. Foster's widow confirmed most of this, and produced her account-books for 1854, 55, 56, 57, and 58, with full details of the Claimant's service during a part of that time; but she knew him as Arthur Orton, and he figured as Arthur Orton all through the books, and the name of Castro did not occur in *any* of these books. The books were dry account-books written in Australia, with a short-sighted view to the things of the place and the time, and not in prophetic anticipation of a London trial, that lay hid in the womb of time.

Not to multiply coincidences unfairly, I am content to throw in here, that on a page of a book produced by this Australian witness, was written as follows :—

DARGO, 11*th March* 1858.

" I, Arthur Orton, &c.," vowing vengeance, in good set terms, on some persons who had wronged him.

The witness had no doubt this was written by her servant, the Claimant, whom, by-the-bye, she recognised in court as her Arthur Orton ; and two judges compared the handwriting with the Claimant's, and declared positively they were identical. Now, the judges try so many questions of handwriting, and examine so many skilled witnesses, that they become great experts in all matters of this kind ; and as they are judges who—unlike other European judges—can and do disagree, I think their consent on this matter, though not sworn evidence, is very convincing to any candid mind. However, I have no wish to press this part of the coincidence separately, or unduly ; but I do say that, taken altogether, No. 9 is a most weighty coincidence.

10. A pocket-book was produced at the trial with miscellaneous entries by the Claimant, artfully inserted to identify him with Tichborne. That being the object, it is unfortunate that he wrote down as follows :—*La Bella*, R. C. Tichborne arrived at *Hobart Town*, July 4, 1854. Because at the trial he said he landed at Melbourne.

The person who landed at *Hobart Town* was Arthur Orton in the *Middleton*. In this same book he wrote—Rodger Charles Tichborne, and Miss Mary Anne Loader, 7 Russell's

Buildings, High Street, Wapping. Now, here are three things Roger Tichborne was ignorant of:

1. That his name was Rodger.
2. That Mary Anne Loader existed.
3. That she lived at 7 Russell's Buildings, High Street, Wapping.

Now, who on earth was this, that landed, not at Melbourne, but Hobart Town, and knew so little about Roger Tichborne, and so much about Mary Anne Loader?

Who could it be but Mary Anne Loader's quondam sweetheart, whose letters, written in the Claimant's handwriting, and signed Arthur Orton, she brought into Court, and identified the man himself as her own sweetheart, Arthur Orton?

That identification would be valueless by itself, in this special line of argument, but the entry in the pocket-book by the Claimant's own hand makes it a coincidence.

11. At Wagga-Wagga the Claimant, being called upon to play the part of Tichborne, made a will, and appointed executors, to wit "John Jarvis, Esq., of Bridport, Dorsetshire, and my mother, Lady Hannah Frances Tichborne." Failing either of them, he appointed Sir John Bird, of Hertfordshire. As guardian of his children, he appointed his friend Gibbes; and failing him, Mr. Henry Angell. Now when all this was looked into by the other side, the Claimant's aristocratic friend, Sir John Bird, was found to be a myth. That aristocrat existed, like the Claimant's own pretensions to aristocracy, in the Claimant's imagination; but the plebeians were real men: friends of Tichborne? Of course not. Jarvis and Angell were old friends of Arthur Orton. When this was discovered, the Claimant pretended these plebeian executors were suggested to him by Arthur Orton; but Arthur Orton was not on the spot, except in the skin of the Claimant; out of that skin neither Gibbes nor any witness saw him at Wagga-Wagga when that will was drawn. At the trial Angell recognised the Claimant as his old acquaintance, Arthur Orton, and that evidence confirms a coincidence which was already very striking.

12. The Claimant came home, asked after Ferguson, Arthur Orton's old friend, as he steamed up the river, and at last got to Ford's Hotel with his wife.

It was Christmas Day, a cold evening, and he was in the bosom of his family, which people do not leave for strangers on Christmas night. What does he do? Gets up, leaves his family and the Christmas fire, and goes off all alone in a four-wheel?

Where to ?

To Tichborne ?

To some place where the Tichborne family could be heard of ?

No; to Wapping.

He gets to the Globe, Wapping, finds Mrs. Johnson, who keeps the house, and her mother who had once kept it.

The Claimant walks in, orders a glass, and talks about the Ortons and their neighbours, showing so much more knowledge than any stranger in the neighbourhood could have possessed, that Mrs. Fairhead looked at him more keenly, saw a likeness to old George Orton, and said, " Why, you must be an Orton."

Such is the attraction of Wapping that he goes down there again next day and sees a Mrs. Pardon, who also observes his likeness to the Ortons. He passes himself off not as Tichborne, who never could be a friend of Orton's, but as a Mr. Stephens, who might, if he existed, except as an alias.

He does not attempt the Tichborne lie at Wapping, any more than the Castro lie at Melipilla.

The portrait of his own wife and child, which he gave as a portrait of Arthur Orton's wife and child, and the other curious details are pretty well known, and I have no wish to go too far into debatable matter. Take the indisputable part only of this twelfth coincidence and read it with its eleven predecessors.

13. There were remarkable coincidences between the spelling and the handwriting of the Claimant and Arthur Orton. This is a part of the subject I cannot properly do justice to. I can only select from the mass of evidence the Chief Justice submitted to the jury. The Claimant writes the word receive receve, so does Arthur Orton ; also anythink and nothink for anything and nothing, a mistake peculiar to the lower orders. They also spell Elizabeth Elisaberth. " Few " they spell fue; "whether" "weather." The pronoun I they both write i, after the manner of the lower orders. But as this is not merely a coincidence but a vein of coincidences which it would take columns to explain, I prefer to refer the candid reader to the masterly dissection of handwriting that took place at the last trial, and the Chief Justice's most careful analysis of it.

14. At the first trial there were heavy sums at stake, and a wide belief in the Claimant, and a romantic interest in him.

The Claimaint's friends would have given hundreds of

pounds to any seaman, who would come into the box and prove he sailed in the *Bella* on her last trip. We all know Jack tar; give him his month's pay, and he is as ready to sail to the port of London as to any other, and readier to sail to London for £300 and his month's pay than to any other port for his month's pay alone. Yet not one of these poor fellows could be got alive to London for the first trial. Why not? Creation was raked for witnesses, and with remarkable success. Why could not one of these seamen be raked for love or money into the witness-box of the Common Pleas? Was it because money will not draw men from the bottom of the sea, or was it because the trial was in London, and a large sum of money awaited them *there* for expenses? Who does not see that, had the trial been at Melbourne, these fabulous seamen would have been heard of, not at Melbourne, but in London or some other port ten thousand miles off, where they could have been talked about in far away Melbourne, but never shown to a Melbourne jury.

Well, the real inability, and pretended unwillingness, of those poor seamen to come to London and get two or three hundred pounds apiece, is matched by the real inability, and fictitious unwillingness, of Arthur Orton to show his face in London except in the skin of the Claimant. The two non-appearances makes one coincidence.

The Claimant, who knows better than any other man, declared Arthur Orton to be alive in 1866; and in Australia; and from that time a hundred thousand eyes have been looking for him in the Colony, yet nobody can find him there alive, or get legal evidence of so marked a man's decease.

At the first trial seven or eight thousand pounds were waiting for him, just to show his person in the witness-box in any man's skin but the Claimant's.

Yet he held aloof, and by his absence killed the Claimant's case at Nisi Prius.

At the criminal trial there were still a thousand pounds or two waiting for this needy butcher.

Yet he never came into the witness-box, and his absence killed the Claimant's defence.

Imbeciles are now after all these years invited to believe he kept away on both occasions merely because he had committed some crime in Australia. This is bosh. *There is no warrant out against Arthur Orton in Australia.* And if suspected of a crime there, he was clearly safer in England than there.

Had he appeared at either trial, his evidence would have been simply this. " I am Arthur Orton, son of George Orton : my brothers are so-and-so, my sisters are so-and-so. You can confront them with me."

Outside this straight line hostile counsel could not by the rules of the court cross-examine so narrow and inoffensive a deponent; or if they did he need not answer them. No judge in England would fail to tell him so. But the truth is that there was never a counsel against him, who would have made matters worse by a wild cross-examination. They would have thrown up their Orton case that moment, and merely persisted that the Claimant was not Tichborne. Only as they had committed themselves to both theories, his evidence would have been death to one, and sickness to the other.

The Claimant and his counsel knew all this, yet they made no effort to show Arthur Orton to either jury, though there was money enough to tempt him into the witness-box a dozen times over.

The only real difficulty was to show him at Nisi Prius except in the skin of the plaintiff, and to show him at the Central Criminal Court except in the skin of the defendant. Years have rolled on, but that difficulty remains insuperable. Even now Arthur Orton's appearance out of the Claimant's skin would shake one limb of the verdict, and also create revulsion of feeling enough to relieve the Claimant of his second term of imprisonment. But neither pay, nor the money that is still waiting for him, nor the public acclamations that he knows would hail him, can drag Arthur Orton to light except in the skin of the defendant. And so it will be till sham Castro, sham Stephens, sham Tichborne, and real Orton all die at one and the same moment in the skin of the Claimant. After all these years and all these reasons for appearing, no man—whatever he may pretend—really believes in his heart that Arthur Orton will ever appear to us except in the skin of the Claimant.

15. I forgot to note in its place a remarkable coincidence. After several interviews with Gibbes and some correspondence with Lady Tichborne, but whilst his knowledge of Tichborne affairs was still very confined, it was thought advisable by his friends that the Claimant should make a statutory declaration. He made one accordingly in the character of Roger Tichborne, and by this time he had learned the date of Roger's birth, and landed him at Melbourne, June 24th, 1854. But, being still ignorant when

Roger sailed on his last voyage, viz., 1st March 1853, and in *La Pauline*, he declared as follows :—

"I left England in the *Jessie Miller*, 28th November 1852." Now, in point of fact Arthur Orton sailed—while Tichborne was at Upton—in the *Middleton ;* but he sailed 28th November 1852, which is a coincidence ; and the *Jessie Miller* is a ship unknown to Roger Tichborne, but well known to Arthur Orton, for he sailed in her from Valparaiso in 1851.

Subsequently, having declared he was picked up at sea by the *Osprey,* and carried into Melbourne, he was asked for the name of his principal benefactor, the captain, and of the other kind souls who had saved him, fed him, &c., for three months, and earned his eternal gratitude ; all he could recall was Lewis Owen or Owen Lewis. Now Arthur Orton's ship, the *Middleton,* contained two persons, one Lewis and one Owen. So here we find him dragging into his "voyages imaginaires" of Tichborne, true particulars of two voyages by Arthur Orton.

Your readers, especially those who have paid me the compliment of drawing the circle with radii converging to one centre, can now fill the interstices of those radii, and so possess a map of the fifteen heterogeneous, and independent, coincidences converging from different quarters of the globe, and different cities, towns, and streets, and also from different departments of fact, material, moral, and psychological, towards one central point, that this man is Arthur Orton. Then, if you like, apply the exhaustive method, of which Euclid is fond in his earlier propositions. Fit the fifteen coincidences on to Roger Tichborne if you can. If this is too impossible, try them on Castro the Chilian, or Stephens, the man who dropped down on Wapping from the sky.

You will conclude with Euclid, "in the same way it can be proved that no other person except Arthur Orton is the true centre of this circle of coincidences."

My subject proper ends here ; but with your permission I will add a short letter correcting the false impression conveyed to the judges by defendant's counsel, that the famous Irish case of James Annesley was a precedent favourable to the Claimant. I will also ask leave to comment upon the question whether the extreme term of imprisonment under the Act ought to be inflicted, and also that term repeated ; for false oaths sworn by the same individual in the course of a single litigation.—I am, yours faithfully,

CHARLES READE.

SUPPLEMENTAL LETTER

SIR,--The ordinary features of a trial are repeated *ad infinitum;* but now and then, say once in a hundred remarkable trials, comes an intellectual phenomenon—

There is at the disposal of the plaintiff's counsel, or the defendant's, a friendly witness, whose evidence to some vital point ought to carry far more weight, if believed, than any other person's evidence: yet that friendly witness is not called. Let a vital point of the case be matter of direct and absolute knowledge to A, but only matter of strong belief or conviction to B, C, and D, A is then, as regards that vital matter, the principal witness, and all B, C, and D can do is to corroborate in a small degree the higher evidence of A. Then, if A is not called, this suppression casts utter discredit upon the inferior witnesses, who are called, and upon the whole case.

The reason is obvious to all persons acquainted with litigation.

Verdicts are obtained, and, above all, *held,* by the evidence alone. Witnesses are not allowed to go into the box without consent of counsel. Counsel are consulted behind the scenes as to what witnesses are necessary to the case, and may be safely shown to the jury, and trusted to the ordeal of cross-examination. If then an able counsel withholds his principal witness from the jury, he throws dirt upon his own case; but he is not the man to throw dirt upon his own case, *except to escape a greater evil.*

Now, what greater evil than throwing dirt upon his case can there be?

Only one—his principal witness is always the very witness who may kill his case on the spot, either by breaking down under cross-examination, or in some other way, which a wary counsel foresees.

Therefore, when either suitor through his counsel does not call his principal witness, the case is always rotten. History offers no example to the contrary, and only one apparent example, which better information corrected.

In fact, whenever with evidence against him, an able counsel dares not call his principal witness, the court might save time and verbiage by giving the verdict against him without any more palaver. Such a verdict would always stand.

You have a correspondent, who cannot see the superiority of indisputable coincidences, to "Jack swears that Jill says," and even to direct evidence contradicted by direct evidence. I will give this gentleman one more chance. Does he think that *all* judges are fools, *ex officio,* and *all* jurymen idiots by the effect of the sheriff's summons? If not, let him consult that vast experience of trials he must possess, or he would hardly have the presumption to teach me how to sift legal evidence, and let him ask himself did he ever know a judge and a jury, who went with any suitor, that dared not call his principal witness.

I know one case, but the verdict was upset. Does he know a single case? I doubt it. I will give one example out of thousands to the contrary, which I had from the lips of a very popular writer, beloved by all who knew him, the late Mr. Lever. It was a reminiscence of his youth. At some county assize in Ireland, counsel called the sort of witnesses I have defined above, as B, C, and D, but did not call witness A. The judge was a good lawyer, but not polished, having been born a peasant ; but had none the less influence with country juries for that, perhaps rather more. He objected bluntly to this as a waste of time, and said the jury would expect to see witness A, and the sooner the better.

"My Lord," says the counsel, "I must be permitted to conduct my case according to my own judgment."

The judge raised no objection; only in return he claimed *his* right, which was to read a newspaper so long as the case was so conducted.

When counsel had had their say, my lord came out of his journal, fixed his eyes on the jury, and summed up. My deceased friend gave me every syllable of his summing up, and here it is :—

THE SHORTEST SUMMING-UP ON RECORD.

The Judge : "He didn't call his principal witness. WEE-Y-WHEET!"

This WEE-Y-WHEET, hitherto written for archæological reasons "Pheugh," was a long, ploughman's whistle, with which my lord pointed his summing up, and such is the power of judicious brevity falling on people possessed of common sense, that the jury delivered their verdict like a shot against the ingenious suitor, who did not call his principal witness. It was in this same country, nevertheless, that, on the single occasion I have referred to, a jury gave the verdict to the party who did not call his principal witness.

It was the great case of Campbell Craig *versus* Richard Earl of Anglesey. Craig, in this cause, was a mere instrument. James Annesley, claiming the lands and title of Anglesey, leased a farm to Craig. Anglesey expelled Craig. Craig sued Anglesey as lessee of James Annesley, and then disappeared from the proceedings. James Annesley, who had thirteen years before been kidnapped by this defendant, and sent out to the colonies, took these indirect proceedings as the son and heir of Lord and Lady Altham, to whose lands and title had succeeded, first a most respectable nobleman, the Earl of Anglesey, and, on his decease, his brother, the said Richard Annesley, both these succeeding Lord Altham in turn by apparent default of direct issue. James Annesley therefore had only to prove his legitimacy, as clearly as he proved this very defendant had kidnapped him by force—and the estates were his.

Now both parties agreed that James Annesley was the son of Lord Altham ; but the defendant said James Annesley's mother was not Lady Altham, but one Joan Landy, a servant in Lord Altham's house, who nursed him from his birth, not in Lord Altham's house, but a cabin hard by, where he was admitted to have lived with her fifteen months. There was no parish register to settle the matter, and Lady Altham, an Englishwoman, driven out of the country many years before by her husband's brutality, had died in England, and never mentioned in England that she had a son in Ireland.

The plaintiff called a cloud of second-class witnesses, but he could not be got to call Joan Landy, who had such an absolute knowledge whether the boy was her child, or her nursling, as nobody else could have.

Defendant's counsel, Prime-Sergeant Malone, one of the greatest forensic reasoners the British Empire has produced, dwelt strongly upon the plaintiff's conduct in not showing this witness to the jury.

Here is his general position—" It is a rule that every case ought to be proved by the best testimony the nature of the thing will admit, and this Joan Landy was the very best witness that could have been produced on the side of the plaintiff." He then showed this without any difficulty, and afterwards made rather an extraordinary and significant statement. " The counsel on the other side did very early in this case promise we should see her : only, as she was the person that was to wind up the case, she was to be the plaintiff's last witness, and this was the reason given for not producing her till the trial was near an end." He adds that having kept her out of court on this pretence, they now shifted their ground and professed not to call her "because she was a weak woman and might forget or be put off the thread of her story."

This last theory he exposes with that admirable logic I find in all his recorded speeches, and urges that the plaintiff's counsel were simply afraid to subject their principal witness to the ordeal of cross-examination. The three judges—for it was a trial at bar—all ignored this strong point for the defence, and the jury steered themselves through a mass of contradictory evidence by an unsafe inference—the defendant had kidnapped the boy, and therefore the defendant, who as Lord Altham's brother, must have known all about the matter, had shown by his actions that he knew him to be legitimate.

James Annesley got the verdict. But the soundness of Malone's reasoning was soon demonstrated. A bill of exceptions was tendered, and admitted, and pending its discussion, James Annesley's case was upset in a criminal trial. His impetuous friends indicted Mary Heath, a main pillar of the defence for perjury. She was ably defended, and destroyed her accuser.[1] She brought home several perjuries to some of James Annesley's witnesses, and to the whole band of them in one vital matter. They had sworn in concert that the boy was christened on a certain day at Dunmore, his godmother being Mrs. Pigot, and one of his godfathers Sergeant Cuff. Well, Mary Heath proved that Mrs. Pigot was nursing her husband with a broken leg 100 miles off, and showed by the records of the Court of Chancery that Sergeant Cuff moved the Court that very day in person, and in Dublin, 100 miles from Dunmore. After this James Annesley's case got blown more and more. The judges would not act on that verdict, and the Court of Chancery restrained him from taking fresh proceedings of a similar nature in the county Wexford. Public opinion turned dead against him. He was horse-whipped on the Curragh by the defendant, and showed his plebeian origin, by taking it like a lamb. Growing contempt drove him out of Ireland, and he lived in England upon his English connections, and fell into distress. His

[1] See *The King* v. *Mary Heath,* published in pamphlet form.

last public act was to raise a subscription at Richmond. This appears either in the *Annual Register* or the *Gentleman's Magazine* of the day—I forget which—but distinctly remember reading it in one or other of those repertories.

His successful defendant outlived him, and held the title of Anglesey, and the Irish and English estates, till his death. After that he gave some trouble, because he had practised trigamy with such skill, that the English peers could not find out who was the legitimate heir to his earldom. The Irish peers, with the help of the logical Malone, cracked the nut in Ireland, and so saved the Irish titles. In this discussion James Annesley's pretensions were referred to, *but only as an extinct matter and a warning to juries not to go by prejudice against evidence.* See the minutes of the proceedings before the Irish Lords, published at Dublin by David Hay, 1773, p. 19, and elsewhere.

It certainly is curious that both counsel for the Claimant Orton should have been ignorant how the famous case of James Annesley *terminated,* and should have cited it in support of Orton; curious that both the judges should have submitted to so singular an error.

However, there is a real parallel between the cases, though not what the learned counsel imagined. 1st. James Annesley was either an impostor or the tool of impostors, and Arthur Orton is an impostor. 2nd. James Annesley's counsel dared not call his principal witness, Joan Landy, and Arthur Orton's counsel dared not call his principal witnesses, viz., the sisters of Arthur Orton. Who, in this world, could settle the Orton question with one half the authority of these two ladies?

It was only to call them and let them look at the Claimant, and swear he was not Arthur Orton—and *stand cross-examination.*

Why was this not done? Withholding them from the jury threw dirt on all the other witnesses, who could only swear to the best of their belief, or offer reasons, not pure evidence.

The comments of Serjeant Malone on the absence of Joan Landy from the witness-box, Craig *v.* Anglesey, 322, all apply here; so does the ploughman's whistle of that sagacious judge; who economised the time of the court. It is not that the value of these ladies' evidence is not known. They have been got to sign *affidavits* that the man is not their brother. Why with this strong disposition to serve him could they not be trusted to the ordeal of an open court? Serjeant Malone put it down to dread of cross-examination. There is, however, another thing on the cards which naturally escapes a lawyer, for their minds are not prepared for unusual things.

Lord and Lady Altham were both very dark. James Annesley was fair. Now, suppose Joan Landy was fair, and otherwise like the plaintiff, whom we now know to have been her child? Annesley's counsel may have been afraid to show her to the eyes of the jury, and her son sitting in their sight, as the evidence of John Purcell shows he was.

Old George Orton is said to have marked all his children, including the Claimant, pretty strongly. Suppose these two sisters are like George Orton, and the Claimant, sworn to be like George Orton, is also like these sisters, this would be a reason for showing the public their handwriting to a statement, and not showing a jury their faces. Between this and the dread of cross-examination lies the key to the phenomenon.

He didn't call his principal witness. *Wee-y-wheet!*

Enough has been said, I hope, to reconcile men of sense to the verdicts of two juries. The sentence is quite another matter. I do not approve it, and will give my reasons in a short letter, my last upon the whole subject.—Yours faithfully,   CHARLES READE.

OUR DARK PLACES

No. I ·

GENTLEMEN,—On Friday last, a tale was brought to me that a sane prisoner had escaped from a private madhouse, had just baffled an attempt to recapture him by violent entry into a dwelling-house, and was now hiding in the suburbs.

The case was grave: the motives alleged for his incarceration were sinister; but the interpreters were women, and consequently partisans, and some, though not all, the parties concerned on the other side, bear a fair character. Humanity said, "look into the case!" Prudence said, "look at it on both sides." I insisted, therefore, on a personal interview with Mr. ——. This was conceded, and we spent two hours together: all which time I was of course testing his mind to the best of my ability.

I found him a young gentleman of a healthy complexion, manner *vif*, but not what one would call excited. I noticed however that he liked to fidget string, and other trifles between his finger and thumb at times. He told me his history for some years past, specifying the dates of several events; he also let me know he had been subject for two years to fits, which he described to me in full. I recognised the character of these fits. His conversation was sober and reasonable. But had I touched the exciting theme? We all know there is a class of madmen who are sober and sensible till the one false chord is struck. I came therefore to that delusion which was the original ground of ——'s incarceration; his notion that certain of his relations are keeping money from him that is his due.

This was the substance of his hallucination as he revealed it to me. His father was member of a firm with his uncle and others. Shortly before his death his father made a will

98

leaving him certain personalties, the interest of £5000, and, should he live to be twenty-four, the principal of ditto, and the reversion, after his mother's death, of another considerable sum.

Early last year he began to inquire why the principal due to him was not paid. His uncle then told him there were no assets to his father's credit, and never had been. On this, he admits, he wrote "abominably passionate" letters, and demanded to inspect the books. This was refused him, but a balance-sheet was sent him, which was no evidence to his mind, and did not bear the test of Addition, being £40,000 out on the evidence of its own figures. This was his tale, which might be all bosh for aught I could tell.

Not being clever enough to distinguish truth from fancy by divination, I took cab, and off to Doctors' Commons, determined to bring some of the above to book.

Well, gentlemen, I found the will, and I discovered that my maniac has understated the interest he takes under it. I also find, as he told me I should, his uncle's name down as one of the witnesses to the will. Item, I made a little private discovery of my own, viz., that —— is residuary legatee, subject to his mother's life interest, and that *all his interest* under the will goes to five relations of the generation above him should he die *intestate.*

I now came to this conclusion, which I think you will share with me, that ——'s delusion may or may not be an error, but cannot be a hallucination, since it is simply good logic founded on attested facts. For on which side lies the balance of credibility? The father makes a solemn statement that he has thousands of pounds to bequeath. The uncle assents in writing while the father is alive, but gives the father and himself the lie when the father is no longer on earth to contradict him. They say in law, "*Allegans contraria non . est audiendus.*"

Being now satisfied that the soi-disant delusion might be error but could not be aberration of judgment, I subjected him to a new class of proofs. I asked him if he would face medical men of real eminence, and not in league with madhouse doctors. "He would with pleasure. It was his desire." We went first to Dr. Dickson, who has great experience, and has effected some remarkable cures of mania. Dr. Dickson, as may well be supposed, did not take as many seconds as I had taken hours. He laughed to scorn the very notion that the man was mad. "He is as sane as we are," said Dr.

Dickson. From Bolton Street we all three go to Dr. Ruttledge, Hanover Square, and, on the road, Dr. Dickson and I agree to apply a test to Dr. Ruttledge, which it would have been on many accounts unwise to apply to a man of ordinary skill. Dr. Dickson introduced —— and me thus : "One of these is insane, said to be. Which is it ? " Dr. Ruttledge took the problem mighty coolly, sat down by me first, with an eye like a diamond : it went slap into my marrow-bone. Asked me catching questions, touched my wrist, saw my tongue, and said quietly, "This one is sane." Then he went and sat down by —— and drove an eye into him, asked him catching questions, made him tell him in order all he had done since seven o'clock, felt pulse, saw tongue : "This one is sane too." Dr. Dickson then left the room, after telling him what was ——'s supposed delusion, and begged him to examine him upon it. The examination lasted nearly half-an-hour, during which —— related the circumstances of his misunderstanding, his capture, and his escape, with some minuteness. The result of all this was a certificate of sanity ; copy of which I subjoin. The original can be seen at my house by any lady or gentleman connected with literature or the press.

"We hereby certify that we have this day, both conjointly and separately, examined Mr. —— and we find him to be in every respect of sound mind, and labouring under no delusion whatever. Moreover we entertain a very strong opinion that the said Mr. —— has at no period of his life laboured under insanity.

"He has occasionally had epileptic fits.

"(Signed)   JAMES RUTTLEDGE, M.D.
S. DICKSON, M.D.

"19 GEORGE STREET, HANOVER SQUARE,
9th August, 1858."

This man, whose word I have no reason to doubt, says the keeper of the madhouse told him he should never go out of it. This, if true, implies the absence of all intention to cure him. He was a customer, not a patient ; he was not in a hospital, but in a gaol, condemned to imprisonment for life, a sentence so awful that no English judge has ever yet had the heart to pronounce it upon a felon. —— is an orphan.

The law is too silly, and *one-sided,* and *slow,* to protect him against the prompt and daring men who are even now hunting him. But while those friends the God of the fatherless has raised him concert his defence, you can aid justice greatly by letting daylight in. I will explain why this is in my next.—I am, Gentlemen, your obedient servant,   CHARLES READE.

GARRICK CLUB,
   10th August, 1858.

No. II

GENTLEMEN,—In England "Justice" is the daughter of "Publicity." In this, as in every other nation, deeds of villainy are done every day in kid gloves; but they can only be done on the sly: here lies our true moral eminence as a nation. Our Judges are an honour to Europe, not because Nature has cut them out of a different stuff from Italian Judges: this is the dream of babies: it is because they sit in courts open to the public, and *" sit next day in the newspapers."*[1] Legislators who have not the brains to appreciate the Public, and put its sense of justice to a statesmanlike use, have yet an instinctive feeling that it is the great safeguard of the citizen. Bring your understandings to bear on the following sets of propositions in lunacy law :—First grand division—Maxims laid down by Shelford. "A. The law requires satisfactory evidence of insanity. B. Insanity in the eye of the law is nothing less than *the prolonged departure, without an adequate external cause, from the state of feeling, and modes of thinking, usual to the individual when in health.* C. The burthen of proof of insanity lies on those asserting its existence. D. Control over persons represented as insane is not to be assumed without necessity. E. Of all evidence, that of medical men ought to be given with the greatest care, and received with the utmost caution. F. The medical man's evidence should not merely pronounce the party insane, but give sufficient reasons for thinking so. For this purpose it behoves him to have investigated accurately the collateral circumstances. G. The imputations of friends or relations, &c., are not entitled to *any weight or consideration* in inquiries of this nature, but ought to be dismissed from the minds of the judge and jury, who are bound to form their conclusions from impartial evidence of

---

[1] We are indebted to Lord Mansfield for this phrase.

facts, and not to be led astray by any such *fertile sources of error and injustice."*

The second class of propositions is well known to your readers. A *relative* has only to buy two *doctors,* two surgeons, or even two of those "whose poverty though not their will consents," and he can clap in a madhouse any rich old fellow that is spending his money absurdly on himself, instead of keeping it like a wise man for his heirs; or he can lock up any eccentric, bodily-afflicted, troublesome, account-sifting young fellow.

In other words, the two classes of people, who figure as *suspected witnesses* in one set of clauses, are made judge, jury, and executioner, in another set of clauses, one of which, by a refinement of injustice, shifts the burthen of proof from the accusers to the accused in all open proceedings subsequent to his wrongful imprisonment.—Shelford, 56.

Now what is the clue to this apparent contradiction—to this change in the weathercock of legislatorial morality? It is mighty simple. The maxims, No. 1, are the practice and principle that govern what are called "Commissions of Lunacy." At these the newspaper reporters are present. No. 2 are the practice and principle legalised, where no newspaper reporters are present. Light and darkness.

Since then the Law de Lunatico has herself told us that she is an idiot and a rascal when she works in the dark, but that she is wise, cautious, humane, and honest in the light, my orphan and myself should indeed be mad to disregard her friendly hint as to her double character. This, gentlemen, is why we come to you first: you must give us publicity, or refuse us justice. We will go to the Commissioners in Lunacy, but not before their turn. We dare not abjure experience. We know the Commissioners; we know them *intus et in cute;* we know them better than they know themselves. They are of two kinds, one kind I shall dissect elsewhere; the rest are small men afflicted with a common malady, a commonplace conscience.

These soldiers of Xerxes won't do their duty if they can help it; if they can't, they will. With them justice depends on Publicity, and Publicity on you. Up with the lash!!

I am now instructed by him who has been called mad, but whose intelligence may prove a match for theirs, to propose to his enemies to join him in proving to the public that their convictions are as sincere as his. The wording of the challenge being left to me, I invite them to an issue, thus:—

" My lads, you were game to enter a dwelling-house kept by women, and proposed to break open a woman's chamber-door, till a woman standing on the other side with a cudgel, threatened 'to split your skulls,' and that chilled your martial ardour.

> " Vos etenim juvenes animum geritis muliebrem
> Ila virago viri.

" And now you are wasting your money (*and you will want it all*) dressing up policemen, setting spies, and, in short, doing the Venetian business in England; and all for what? You want our orphan's body. Well, it is to be had without all this dirty manœuvring, and silly small treachery. Go to Jonathan Weymouth, Esq., of Clifford's Inn. He is our orphan's solicitor, duly appointed and instructed; he will accept service of a writ *de lunatico inquirendo*, and on the writ being served, Mr. Weymouth will enter into an undertaking with you to produce the body of E. P. F. in court, to abide the issue of a daylight investigation. If you prove him mad, you will take him away with you; if you fail to make him out mad before a disinterested judge, at all events you will prove yourselves to be honest, though somewhat hard-hearted men and *women.*"

Should this proposal be accepted, the proceedings of our opponents will then assume a respectability that is wanting at present, and in that case these letters will cease. *Sub judice lis erit.*—I am, Gentlemen, your obedient servant,

CHARLES READE.

No. III

GARRICK CLUB, *October.*

GENTLEMEN,—My last letter concluded by inviting the person, who had incarcerated my orphan on the plea of insanity, to prove that, whether mistaken or not, he was sincere. No such evidence has been offered. He has therefore served a writ upon this person, and will proceed to trial with all possible expedition, subject of course to the chances of demurrer, or nonsuit.[1]

---

[1] Individually I entertain no apprehension on this score. The constitutional rights of Englishmen are safe in the hands of the present judges; and trial by jury, in a case of this character, is one of those rights—provided, of course, the proper Defendant has been sued.

It would not be proper to say more, *pendente lite*. But, some shallow comments having been printed elsewhere, it seems fair that those Editors, who had the humanity, the courtesy, and, let me add, the intelligence, to print my letters, should possess this proof that their columns have not been trifled with by their obliged and obedient servant,

CHARLES READE.

No. IV

" Cunctando restituit rem."

GENTLEMEN,—When, four months ago, I placed my orphan under the wing of the law, I hoped I had secured him that which is every Englishman's right, a trial by judge and jury; and need draw no further upon your justice and your pity. I have clung to this hope in spite of much sickness of heart, month after month; but at last both hope and faith are crushed in me, and I am forced to see, that without a fresh infusion of publicity, my orphan has no reasonable hope of getting a public trial, till he shall stand with his opponents before the God of the fatherless. I do not say this merely because his trial has been postponed, and postponed, but because it has been thrice postponed on grounds that can be reproduced three hundred times just as easily as thrice, unless the light of publicity is let in.

Let me premise that the matters I have to relate are public acts, and as proper for publication and criticism as any other judicial proceedings, and that they will make the tour of Europe and the United States in due course. When the day of trial drew near in November last, defendant's attorney applied to have trial postponed for a month or two, for the following sole reason:—He swore, first, that a Mr. 3 Stars, dwelling at Bordeaux, was a witness without whom defendant could not safely proceed to trial; and he swore, second, that said 3 Stars had written to him on the 18th November, that, owing to an accident on the railway, he was then confined to his room, and had little hope of being able to leave Bordeaux under a month. No. 1, you will observe, is legal evidence; but No. 2 is no approach towards legal evidence. Nothing is here sworn to but the fact that there exists an unsworn statement by a Mr. 3 Stars. On this demi-semi-affidavit, unsupported by a particle of legal evidence, a well-meaning judge, in spite of a stiff remonstrance, postponed the trial, nominally for one month, really for two months. I fear my soul is not so candid as the worthy judge's, for on the face of this document, where he saw veracity, I saw disingenuousness, stand out in *alto relievo*. So I set the French police upon Mr. 3 Stars, and received from the Prefect of La Gironde an official document, a copy of which is enclosed herewith. By it we learn, first, that the accident or incident was not what plain men understand by an accident on a railway. The man hurt a leg getting down from a railway carriage just as he might from his own gig. Second, that it was not quite so recent as his suppression of date might lead a plain man to presume, but was three weeks old when he wrote as above; third, that he must have been well long before the 9th of December, for, writing on that day, the Prefect describes him as having made frequent excursions into Medoc since his incident. Unfair inaccuracy once proved in so important a statement, all belief is shaken. In all human probability, Mr. 3 Stars was convalescent on the 18th November, viz., three weeks after his railway incident. But it is certain he was *well* on or about the 1st December, and that, consequently, he could with ease have attended that trial, which his statement that he could not move till about 18th December caused to be put off for two months. What man who knows the world can help suspecting that the arbitrary period of a month was arranged between him and the attorney, not so much with reference to the truth as to the sittings of the Court at Westminster upon special jury cases?

So much for abjuring the experience of centuries, and postponing an alleged lunatic's trial for two months, upon indirect testimony that would be kicked out of a County Court in a suit for a wheelbarrow : hearsay stuccoed, nursery evidence ; not legal evidence.

Well, gentlemen, the weary months crawled on, and the lame, old, broken-winded, loitering beldame, British justice, hobbled up to the scratch again at last. Mr. 3 Stars was now in England. That sounded well. But he soon showed us that—

> "Cœlum non animam mutant qui trans mare currunt."

His health still fluctuated to order. Pretty well as to the wine trade ; very sick as to the Court of Queen's Bench. He comes from Bordeaux to London (and that is a good step), burning, we are told, to attend the trial at Westminster. The trial draws near : he whips off—to Hampstead ? No ;—to *Wales.* Arrived there, he writes, in due course, to his late colleague in affidavit, that he can't travel. This time the gentleman that does the interlocutory swearing for the defendant (let us call him Fabius), doubting whether the 3 Stars malady would do again by itself, associated with his " malade affidavitaire " two ladies, whom, until they compel me to write a fifth letter, I will call Mrs. Plausible and Mrs. Brand. Non-legal evidence as before. Fabius swears, not that 3 Stars is ill ; that might have been dangerous ; but that 3 Stars says he is ill : which is true. Item, that Mrs. Brand cannot cross the ditch that parts France from England, because she has had an operation performed. It turns out to have been *twelve months ago.* Item, Fabius *swears* that Mrs. Plausible *says*, the little Plausibles have all got scarlatina ; and, therefore, Fabius *swears* that Mrs. Plausible *thinks* the constitutional rights of the English people ought to remain in doubt and suspense, in the person of our orphan, till such time as the said scarlatina has left her nursery (and the measles not arrived ?), " A tout bambin tout honneur."

All which conjectural oaths, and sworn conjectures, and nursery dialectics, they took to Mr. Justice Erle, of all gentlemen in the world ; and moved to postpone the trial indefinitely. Early in the argument their counsel having, I think, gone through the schools at Oxford, took a distaste to the Irish syllogism that gleamed on his brief ; videlicet, no witness who has scarlatina can come to Westminster and stand cross-examination by Q.C. Little b, c, and d are not witnesses but have got scarlatina.

Ergo, capital A can't come to Westminster and stand cross-examination by Q.C.

Counsel threw over Mrs. Plausible and Hibernian logic generally, and stood on the 3 Stars malady, second edition, and the surgical operation that was only twelve months old. But Mr. Justice Erle declined to postpone human justice till sickness and shamming should be no more. He refused to ignore the plaintiff, held the balance, and gave them a just and reasonable delay, to enable them to examine their " malades affidavitaires " upon commission. He was about to fix Saturday, Jan. 5, for the trial. They then pleaded hard for Monday. This was referred to plaintiff's attorney, who conceded that point. Having accepted this favour, which was clearly a conditional one, and only part of the whole arrangement, they were, I THINK, bound by professional good faith not to disturb the compact. They held otherwise: they instantly set to work to evade Mr. Justice Erle's order, by tinkering the Irish syllogism. In just the time that it would take to send Mrs. Plausible a letter, and say it is no use the little Plausibles having scarlatina; you must have it yourself, madam; you had better have it by telegraph—Mrs. Plausible announces the desired malady, but not upon oath. "Scarlatina is easily said." *Il va sans dire que* they don't venture before Mr. Justice Erle again with their tinkered affidavit. They slip down to Westminster, and surprise a fresh judge, who has had no opportunity of watching the rise and progress of disease. Their counsel reads the soldered affidavit. Plaintiff's counter affidavits are then intrusted to him to read. What does he do? He reads the preamble, but burks the affidavits. The effect was inevitable. Even bastard affidavits cannot be met by rhetoric. They can only be encountered by affidavits. Judges decide, not on phrases, but on the facts before them. Plaintiff's facts being silenced, and defendant's stated, the judge naturally went with defendant, and postponed the trial. (No. 3.)

Now, gentlemen, I am the last man in the world to cry over spilled milk. I don't come to you to tinker the untinkerable past, but, for the future, to ask a limit to injustice in its worst form, trial refused.

Without your help, this alleged lunatic is no nearer the term of his sufferings; no nearer the possibility of removing that frightful stigma, which is not stigma only, but starvation; no nearer to trial of his sanity by judge and jury, than he was four months ago. True, there are now three judges who will not easily be induced to impede the course of justice in this case; but there are other uninformed judges who may be surprised into doing it general. Fabius can at any day of any month *swear* that some male or female witness *says* she wants to come into the witness-box, and can't. And so long as "Jack swears that Jill says" is confounded with legal evidence, on interlocutory motions, justice can be defeated to the end of time, under colour of postponement. Gentlemen, it is a known fact among lawyers that, in nine cases out of ten, postponement of trial has no other real object but evasion of trial by tiring out the plaintiff, or breaking his heart, or ruining him in expenses.

I see little reason whatever to doubt that this is a principal object here. Defendants have a long purse. Plaintiff is almost a pauper in fact, whatever he may be in law. Mr. 3

Stars, sworn to as an essential witness, has not seen the boy for years. How can he, therefore, be a very essential witness to his insanity at or about the period of his capture? Dr. Pillbox and Mr. Sawbones must be better cards so far: in a suit at law the evidence of insanity, like that of sanity, cannot be spread out thin over disjointed years, like the little bit of butter on a schoolboy's bread. Mr. 3 Stars may be an evidence as to figures: but then the books are to be in court subpœnâ; and nobody listens much to any of us swearing arithmetic, when a ledger is speaking. The lady I have called Mrs. Plausible, would not, in my humble opinion, go into a witness-box if she were paid a hundred pounds a minute. I mean this anything but discourteously.

I implore all just and honest men, especially those who are in the service of the State, to try and realise the frightful situation in which postponement of trial keeps an alleged lunatic. The bloodhounds are hunting him all this time. There were several men looking after him the very last day he lost his hopes of immediate trial. Suppose that, on unsubstantial grounds, and illegal evidence, time should be afforded to find him out and settle the questions of fact and law, by brute force, what complexion would these thoughtless delays of justice assume *then* in the eye of the nation; ay, and to do them justice, in the consciences of those whose credulity would have made the bloodhounds of a lunatic asylum masters of an argument that has been now for many months referred to the Lord Chief Justice of England and a special jury. Mind, the constitution has been tampered with; "habeas corpus" has been suspended by the boobies that framed the Lunacy Acts. The judges have power to impede justice, but none to impede injustice. In these peculiar cases, I am advised, they can't order a sane man out of a lunatic asylum into the witness-box. Justice hobbles, but injustice flies to its mark. I declare to you that I live in mortal terror lest some evil should befall this man, under the very wing of the court—not of course from the defendant—but from some member or members of the gang of stupid ruffians I am assured are still hanging about the skirts of the defence; men some of whom have both bloodshed and reasonshed on their hands already. My very housemaids have been tampered with to discover where "the pursuer," as the Scotch call him, is hiding and quaking. Is such an anomaly to be borne? Is a man to be at the same time run from with affidavits and chased with human bloodhounds? Is this a state of things to be *prolonged*, without making our system the scorn and laughing-stock of all the citizens and lawyers of Europe?

Fletcher *v.* Fletcher only wants realising. But some people are so stupid, they can realise nothing that they have not got in their hands, their mouths, or their bellies. This is no common case; no common situation. This particular Englishman sues not merely for damages, but to recover lost rights dearer far than money, of which rights he says he is unjustly robbed; his right to walk in daylight on the soil of his native land, without being seized and chained up for life like a nigger or a dog; his footing in society, his means of earning bread, and his place among mankind. For a lunatic is a beast in the law's eye and society's; and an alleged lunatic is a lunatic until a jury pronounces him sane.

I appeal to you, gentlemen, is not such a suitor sacred in all good men's minds? Is he not defendant as well as plaintiff? Why, his stake is enormous compared with the nominal defendant's; and, if I know right from wrong, to postpone his trial a fourth time, without a severe necessity, would be to insult Divine justice, and trifle with human misery, and shock the common sense of nations.—I am, your obedient servant,

CHARLES READE.

With this a copy is enclosed of the French Prefect's letter, and other credentials. These documents are abandoned to your discretion.

Nothing in the above letter is to be construed as assuming that the defendant has a bad case. He may have a much better one than the plaintiff. I am not asking for the latter a verdict to which he may have no right; but a trial, to which he has every right.

BORDEAUX, *le* 9 *Décembre*, 1858.

MONSIEUR,—En réponse à la lettre que vous m'avez adressée, à la date du 26 Novembre dernier, j'ai l'honneur de vous transmettre les renseignements qui m'ont été fournis sur le Sᵣ Cunliffe, sujet anglais.

Le Sᵣ Cunliffe demeure à Bordeaux, rue Corie, 43. Il est négociant en vins et parait jouir de l'estime des personnes qui le connaissent.

Il est vrai qu'un accident lui est arrivé, il y a un mois et demi, sur le chemin de fer; il est tombé en descendant et s'est blessé à une jambe; par suite il a gardé le chambre pendant quelque temps, mais aujourd'hui il parait être retabli ; vaque à ses occupations ordinaires et fait souvent des excursions dans le Médoc, à quelques lieues de Bordeaux.

Recevez, Monsieur, l'assurance de ma parfaite consideration,
Le Préfet de la Gironde,
(Signed)

A MONSIEUR CHARLES READE,
6 BOLTON ROW, MAYFAIR, LONDRES.

In spite of letter four : the trial was postponed twice more. At last it came and is reported in *The Times* of July 8, 1859. The court was filled with low repulsive faces of mad-house attendants and keepers, all ready to swear the man was insane. He was put into the witness-box, examined and cross-examined eight hours, and the defendant succumbed without a struggle. The coming damages were compounded for an annuity of £100 a year, £50 cash, and the costs.

As bearing upon this subject, my letter to the *Pall Mall Gazette* of Jan. 17, 1870, entitled "How Lunatics' Ribs get Broken," should be read. This letter is now reprinted at the beginning of *Hard Cash*.

THE RIGHTS AND THE WRONGS OF AUTHORS

To the Editor of the "Pall Mall Gazette"

FIRST LETTER

Sir,—Those, who do not bestow sympathy, have no right to ask it. But if a man for years has been quick to feel, and zealous to relieve, his neighbour's wrongs, he has earned a right to expose his own griefs and solicit redress. By the same rule, should a class, that has openly felt and tried to cure the wrongs of others, be deeply wronged itself, that class has a strong claim to be heard. For the public and the State to turn a deaf ear would be ungrateful, and also impolitic; it would be a breach of the mutual compact that cements society, and tend to discourage the public virtue of that worthy class, and turn its heart's milk to gall.

Now, the class "authors" may be said to rain sympathy. That class has produced the great Apostle of Sympathy in this age; and many of us writers follow in his steps, though we cannot keep up with his stride. In the last fifty years legislation and public opinion have purged the nation of many unjust and cruel things; but who began the cure? In most cases it can be traced to the writer's pen, and his singular power and habit of sympathising with men whose hard case is not his own. Accordingly, in France and some other countries this meritorious and kindly class is profoundly respected, and its industry protected as thoroughly as any other workman's industry. But in Great Britain and her colonies, and her great offshoot, the class is personally undervalued, and its property too often pillaged as if it was the production of an outlaw or a beaver. The notorious foible of authors is disunion; but our wrongs are so bitter, that they have at last driven us, in spite of our besetting infirmity, into a public league for protection,[1] and they drive me to your columns for sanctuary. I ask leave to talk common sense, common justice, common humanity, plain arithmetic, and plain English, to the Anglo-Saxon race, about the property of authors—a theme which has hitherto been rendered unintelligible to that race by bad English, technical phrases, romantic pettifogging, cant, equivoques, false summing, direct lies, roundabout sentences, polysyllables, and bosh. Do not fear that I will abuse the public patience with sentimental grievances. I have lived long enough to see that each condition of life has its drawbacks, and no class must howl whenever the shoe pinches, or the world would be a kennel, sadly sonorous in the minor key. I will just observe, but in a cheerful spirit, that in France the sacred word " Academy " means what it meant of old—a lofty assemblage of writers and thinkers, with whom princes are proud to mingle; and that in England the sacred word is taken from writers and thinkers, and bestowed with jocular blasphemy upon a company of painters and engravers, most of them bad ones; that the great Apostle of Sympathy, when dead, is buried by acclamation in Westminster Abbey, but is not thought worthy of a peerage while living, yet a banker is, who can show no title to glory but a lot of money; that what puny honours a semi-barbarous but exceeding merry State bestows on the fine arts are given in direct ratio to their brainlessness—music, number one; painting, number two; fiction, the king of the fine arts, number nothing;—that authors pay the Queen's taxes and the parochial rates, and yet are compelled to pay a special and unjust tax to public libraries, while painters, on the contrary, are allowed to tax the public full fifteen thousand pounds a year for leave to come into a public shop, built with public money, and there buy the painters' pictures. All these are Anglo-Saxon humours, that rouse the contempt of the Latin races, but they cannot starve a single author and his family; so we leave them to advancing civilisation, political changes, and the ridicule of Europe.

But insecurity of property is a curse no class can endure, nor is bound to endure. It is a relic of barbarism. Every nation has groaned under it at some period; but, while it lasted, it always destroyed happiness and goodness. It made fighting and bloodshed a habit, and criminal retaliation a form

---

[1] The Association to Protect the Rights of Authors, 28 King Street, Covent Garden.

of justice. Insecurity of property saps public and private morality ; it corrupts alike the honest and the dishonest. It eggs on the thief, and justifies the pillaged proprietor in stealing all round, since in him theft is but retribution. Under this horrible curse there still groans a solitary class of honest, productive workmen, the Anglo-Saxon *author*, by which word I mean the writer, who receives no wages, and therefore his production becomes his property, and his sole means of subsistence. To make his condition clear to plain men, I will place him in a row with other productive workmen and show the difference :—

1. His own brother, the Anglo-Saxon writer for wages, is never robbed of a shilling. He has the good luck not to be protected by feeble statutes, but by the law of the land at home and abroad.

2. His first cousin, the Latino-Celtic author, has his property made secure by the common law of his nation, and efficient statutes, criminal as well as civil.

3. The painter, the cabinet-maker, the fisherman, the basket-maker, and every other Anglo-Saxon workman, who uses his own or open materials, and, receiving no wages, acquires the production, has that production secured to him for ever by the common law with criminal as well as civil remedies.

Only the Anglo-Saxon author has no remedy against piracy under the criminal law, and feeble remedies by statute, which, as I shall show, are sometimes turned from feeble to null by the misinterpretations of judges, hostile (through error) to the spirit and intention of the statute. The result of this mess is that the British author's property is pillaged at home ten times oftener than any other productive workman's property ; that in Australia he is constantly robbed, though his rights are not as yet publicly disputed ; that in Canada he is picked out as the one British subject to be half-outlawed ; and that he is fully and formally outlawed in the United States, though the British writer for wages is not outlawed there, nor the British mechanical inventor, nor the British printers—these artisans are paid for printing in the United States a British author's production—nor the British actor ; he delivers in New York for five times as many dollars as his performance is worth those lines which the British author has created with five times his labour and his skill, yet that author's remuneration is outlawry.

Unjust and cruel as this is, the other Anglo-Saxon authors are still worse used, especially the American author. He suffers the same wrongs we do, and a worse to boot. Our home market is not seriously injured by American piracy, but his home market is. The remuneration of the established American author is artificially lowered by the crushing competition of stolen goods; and as for the young American author, however promising his genius, he is generally nipped in the bud. I can give the very process. He brings the publisher his manuscript, which represents months of labour and of debt, because all the time a man is writing without wages the butcher's bill and baker's are growing fast and high. His manuscript is the work of an able novice; there are some genuine observations of American life and manners, and some sparks of true mental fire; but there are defects of workmanship: the man needs advice and practice. Well, under just laws his countryman, the publisher, would nurse him; but, as things are, he declines to buy, at ever so cheap a rate, the work of promise, because he can obtain gratis works written with a certain mechanical dexterity by humdrum but practised English writers. Thus stale British mediocrity, with the help of American piracy, drives rising American genius out of the book market. Now, as the United States are not defiled with any other trade, art, or business, in which an American can be crushed under the competition of stolen goods, the rising author, being an American, and therefore not an idiot, flings American authorship to the winds, and goes into some other trade, where he is safe from foul play. At this moment many an American, who, under just laws, would have been a great author, is a second-rate lawyer, a second-rate farmer, or a third-rate parson: others overflow the journals, because there they write, not for property, but wages, and so escape from bad statute law to the common law of England and the United States. But this impairs the just balance of ephemeral and lasting literature. It creates an excess of journalists. This appears by four tests—the small remuneration of average journalists; the prodigious number of native journals compared with native books; the too many personalities in those too many journals; and the bankruptcy of 800 journals per annum. Now I am ashamed to say all this injudicious knavery had its root in England. It was here the words were first spoken and written which, being thoughtlessly repeated by statesmen, judges, writers of law-books, and now and then by publicists, have gradually deluded the mind and blunted the conscience of the Anglo-Saxon. That great race is inferior to none in common sense, respect for property, small as well as great, and impartial justice. To be false to all these, its characteristic and most honourable traits, it must be under some strong delusions. I will enumerate these, and show that they have neither truth, reason, common law, nor antiquity to support them; and I hope, with God's help and the assistance of those able men I may convince, to root them out of the Anglo-Saxon mind, and so give the Anglo-Saxon conscience fair play. CHARLES READE.

SECOND LETTER

SIR,—The four main delusions that set the public heart against authors' rights are :—

1. THE ÆTHERIAL MANIA.—That an author is a disembodied spirit, and so are his wife and children. That to refuse an unsalaried fisherman an exclusive title to the fish he has laboured for in the public sea would starve the fisherman and his family; but the same course would not starve the unsalaried author, his wife, and his children. Those little imps may seem to cry for bread; but they are squeaking for ideas. The ætherial mania intermits, like every other. Its lucid intervals coincide with the visits of the rent-gatherer, the tax-gatherer, and the tradesmen with their bills. On these occasions society admits that an author is a solid, and ought to pay or smart; but returns to æther when the funds are to be acquired, without which rent, taxes, and tradesmen cannot be paid, nor life, far less respectability, sustained. No Anglo-Saxon can look the ætherial crotchet in the face and not laugh at it. Yet so subtle and insidious is Prejudice, that you shall find your Anglo-Saxon constantly arguing and acting as if this nonsense was sense : and, pray believe me, the most dangerous of all our lies are those silly, skulking falsehoods which a man is ashamed to state, yet lets them secretly influence his mind and conduct. Lord Camden, the great enemy of authors in the last century, was an example. Compel him to look the ætherial mania in the face, and his good sense would have revolted. Yet, dissect his arguments and his eloquence, you will find they are both secretly founded on the ætherial mania, and stand or fall with it.

2. AN HISTORICAL FALSEHOOD.—That intellectual property is not founded on the moral sense of mankind, nor on the

common law of England, but is the creature of modern statutes, and an arbitrary invasion of British liberty. This falsehood is as dangerous as it looks innocent. It crosses the Atlantic, and blunts the American conscience : and it even vitiates the judicial mind at home. It works thus down at Westminster. The judges there hate and despise Acts of Parliament. They make no secret of it ; they sneer at them openly on the judgment-seat, filling foreigners with amazement. Therefore, when once they get into their heads that a property exists only by statute, that turns their hearts against the property, and they feel bound to guard common law liberties against the arbitrary restrictions of that statute. Interpreted in this spirit, a statute, and the broad intention of those who framed it, can be baffled in many cases that the Legislature could not foresee, of which I shall give glaring examples.

3. That the laws protecting intellectual property enable authors to make more money than they deserve, and that piratical publishers sell books, not for love of lucre, but of the public, and for half the price of copyrighted books. I will annihilate this falsehood, not by reasoning, but by palpable facts and figures.

4. The worst delusion of all is, that what authors, and the Legislature, call intellectual property is neither a common law *property* nor a *property* created by statute, but a *monopoly* created by a statute.

This confusion of ideas, unknown to our ancestors, and at variance with the distinctive terms they used, was first advanced by Mr. Justice Yates in the year 1769. He repeated it eight times in Millar *v.* Taylor; and, indeed, without it his whole argument falls to the ground. The fallacy has never been exposed with any real mental power, and has stultified senatorial and legal minds by the thousand. It was adopted and made popular by Macaulay in the House of Commons, February 14, 1841. He was on a subject that required logic ; he substituted rhetoric, and said striking things. He said, " Copyright is monopoly, and produces all the effects the general voice of mankind attributes to monopoly." In another part of his rhetoric he defined copyright " a tax on readers to give a bounty to authors ; " and this he evidently thought monstrous, the remuneration to producers in general not being an item that falls on the public purchaser ; but where he learned *that*, only God, who made him, knows. In another part he stigmatised copyright as " *a monopoly in books.*" He did not carry out these conclusions

honestly. Holding them, it was his duty to advocate the
extinction of intellectual property; but, if his conclusions
were weak, his premises were deadly. He took a poisoned
arrow out of the custody of a few pettifoggers, and put it
into the hands of ten thousand knaves and fools; where the
respected word " property " had stood for ages, he and the
pettifogger Yates, whom he echoed, set up the hated word
" monopoly." " Rank weeds do grow apace; " this fallacy
spread swiftly from the Senate to the bar, from the bar to the
bench. I have with my own ears heard the Barons of the
Exchequer call copyright a monopoly; nor is the expression
confined to that court; it is adopted by writers of law-books,
and so infects the minds of the growing lawyers. But only
consider the effect—Here is a property the great public never
reads about nor understands, and is therefore at the mercy of
its public teachers. It hears the mouthpieces of law, and the
mouthpieces of opinion, declare from their tribunals that the
strange, unintelligible property called by the inhuman and
unintelligible name of " copyright " is a monopoly. The
public has at last got a word with a meaning. It knows
what monopoly is, knows it too well. This nation has groaned
under monopolies, and still smarts under their memory. It
abhors the very sound, and thinks that whoever baffles a
monopoly sides with divine justice and serves the nation.
Therefore to call an author's property a monopoly is to make
the conscience of the pirate easy, and even just men apathetic
when an author is swindled; it is to prejudice both judges
and juries, and prepare the way to false verdicts and disloyal
judgments. I pledge myself to prove it is one of the stupidest
falsehoods that muddleheads ever uttered, and able but unguarded men ever repeated. I undertake to prove this to the
satisfaction of the Anglo-Saxon race, and of all the honest
lawyers who have been decoyed into the error, and have
delivered it as truth from the judgment-seat this many a year.
At present I will only say that if any statesman or practical
lawyer, or compiler of law-books, who either by word of
mouth or in print has told the public " copyright " is a
" monopoly," dares risk his money on his brains, I will meet
him on liberal terms. I will bet him a hundred and fifty
pounds to fifty copyright is not a monopoly, and is property.
All I claim is capable referees. Let us say Lord Selborne,
Mr. Robert Lowe, and Mr. Fitzjames Stephen, if those gentlemen will consent to act. I offer the odds, so I think I have
a right to demand discriminating judges. If any gentle-

man takes up this bet I will ask him to do it publicly by letter to the *Pall Mall Gazette,* and we will then proceed to deposit the stakes, &c.*

From all these cruel delusions I draw one comfort : perhaps authors are not hated after all, but only misunderstood; and, if we can enlighten the mind of statesmen, lawyers, and the public, we may find the general heart as human to us as ours has always been to our fellow-citizens, and they don't deny it.

The two great properties of authors are "copyright," or the sole right of printing and reprinting for sale the individual work a man has honestly created, and "stage-right," or the sole right of representing the same for money on a public stage. The men who violate these rights have for ages been called pirates. The terms "copyright" and "stage-right" are our calamities. They keep us out of the Anglo-Saxon heart by parting us from its language. France calls them both by one name, "*les droits d'auteurs ;*" and it is partly the long use of this human phrase that has made France so just and humane to authors. Warned by this experience, I pause in alarm before these repulsive words, that stand like a bristling wall between us and manly sympathy ; and I implore the reader of these letters to be very intelligent, to open his mind to evidence that under these unfortunate and technical words lie great human realities; that both rights mean *property,* and that to infringe either property has just the same effect on an author as to rob his house ; but to infringe them habitually by defect of law or judicial prejudice is far more fatal; the burglar only takes an author's superfluities, but the unchecked pirate takes his house itself, and, indeed, his livelihood :

> "You take my house, when you do take the prop
> That doth sustain my house ; you take my life,
> When you do take the means whereby I live."

I do earnestly beg the reader, then, in the name of wisdom, justice, humanity, and Christianity, not to be baffled by a miserable husk where there is really a rich kernel ; not to let the technical appearance of two words divert him from a serious effort to comprehend the rights and the wrongs of those men, living, whose insensible remains he worships when dead. In face of eternal justice the dead and the living author are one man ; the dead is an author who was alive yesterday ; the living is an author who will be dead to-morrow.

* No person has ever ventured to encounter Mr. Reade, and risk his money on his opinion that copyright is a monopoly.

In a word, then, take away or mutilate either of the properties so unfortunately named, and you remove the sole check of piracy; but, piracy unchecked, the ruin and starvations of authors, and the extinction of literature follow as inevitably as sunset follows noon. To give the reader a practical insight into this, I will select literary piracy, or infringement of copyright, and show its actual working. The composition is the true *substance* of a book; the paper, ink, and type are only the *vehicles*. The volumes combine the substance and the vehicles, and are the joint product of many artisans, and a single artist, the author. The artisans, to wit, the paper-makers, compositors, pressmen, and binders are all paid, whether the book succeeds or fails. To go from the constructors to the sellers, you find the same distinction; the retail bookseller takes the enormous pull of 25 per cent. on every copy, yet the failure of the work entails no loss on him—unless he overstocks himself—because he is paid out of the gross receipts. But the author and the publisher take their turn last, and can only be paid out of profits. Where there is a loss it must all fall on author or publisher, or both. Now, books not being so necessary to human life as food or clothing, publishing is a somewhat speculative trade. It is calculated that out of, say, ten respectable books, about half do not pay their expenses, and of the other five four yield but a moderate profit both to author and publisher, but that the tenth may be a hit and largely remunerative to publisher and author, supposing those two to share upon fair terms. But here comes in the pirate. That caitiff does not print from manuscripts nor run risks. He holds aloof from literary enterprise till comes the rare book that makes a hit. Then he and his fellows rush upon it, tear the property limb from jacket, and destroy the honest shareholders' solitary chance of balancing their losses. The pirate who reprints from a proprietor's type, and reaps gratis the fruit of the publisher's early advertisements, and does not pay the author a shilling, can always undersell the honest author or the honest publisher, who pays the author, and buys publicity by advertising, and sets up type from manuscript, which process costs more than reprinting. This reduces the honest author's and publisher's business to two divisions: the unpopular books— often the most valuable to the public—by which they lose money or gain too little to live and pay shop, staff, &c.; and the popular book, by which they would gain money, but cannot, because the pirates rush in and share, and undersell,

119

and crush, and kill.   I appeal to all the trades and all the arts if any trade or any art ever did live, ever will live, or can live, upon such terms?   The trade—all commercial enterprise requires capital, and all genuine capital is timorous and flies from insecure property.   The art—to produce popular books requires, as a rule, such intelligence and capacity for labour, as need not starve for ever, but can go in the course of a generation, and after much individual misery, from literature to some easier profession.   Therefore, piracy drives out both capital and brains, and marks out for ruin the best literature, and would extinguish it if not severely checked.   This is evident, but it does not rest on speculation.   History proves it.   Piracy drove Goldoni out of Italy, where he was at the top of the tree, into France, and made him end his days a writer of French pieces for the one godlike nation that treated a pirate like any other thief, and a foreign author like a French author; piracy extinguished an entire literature in Belgium; piracy, A.D. 1875, stifles a gigantic literature in the United States; piracy for a full century has lowered the British and American drama three hundred per cent.; A.D. 1694, the protection afforded to copyright by the licensing Acts being removed, literary piracy obtained a firm footing in England for a time.   What followed?   In a very few years a handful of hungry pirates reduced both authors and respectable publishers to ruin, them, and their families.   This was sworn and proved before Queen Anne's Parliament, and stands declared and printed in their Copyright Act, A.D. 1709.   Those collected examples of honest artists and traders ruined by piracy are hidden for a time in the Record Office; but there are many sad and public proofs that piracy can break an honest trader's heart, or an honest workman's. I will select two out of hundreds.   The ill-fated scholar we call Stephanus was not only ruined but destroyed, mind and body, by a piratical abridgment.   He found the Greek language without a worthy lexicon.   He spent twenty years compiling one out of the classical authors.   It was and is a gigantic monument of industry and learning.   He printed it with his own press and rested from his labours; he looked at his Colossus with honest pride, and boasted on the title-page, very pardonably,

"Me duce plana via est, quæ salebrosa fuit."

What was his reward?   A man, who had eaten his bread for years as a journeyman printer, sat down, and without any real labour, research, or scholarship, produced in one volume an abridgment of the great lexicon. With this the miscreant undersold his victim, and stopped his sale, and ruined him. In his anguish at being destroyed by his own labour stolen, the great scholar and printer went mad, and died soon after.

The composer of our National Anthem surely deserved a crust to keep body and soul together. Well, piracy would not let him have one. His immortal melodies sold for thousands of pounds, but the pirate stole it all and never gave the composer a farthing. At eighty years of age he hung himself in despair to escape starvation. The old cling to life—goodness knows why; it is very rare for a man of eighty to commit suicide; but when an inventor sees brainless thieves rich by pillaging his brains, and is gnawed by hunger as well as the heart's agony and injustice too bitter to bear, what wonder if he curses God and man, and ends the intolerable swindle how he can. The malpractice, which could murder the composer of our National Anthem, has surely some little claim to national disgust, and the legal restraints upon that malpractice to a grain of sympathy. Well, its only restraints upon earth are not justice nor humanity—it mocks at these —but copyright and stage-right, whose ugly sound pray forgive, and listen to their curious history.

CHARLES READE.

THIRD LETTER

SIR,—The Greeks and Romans and Saxons had no printing press, and no theatres taking money at the doors. It is idle to search antiquity, or even mediæval England, for copyright, or stage-right, or my right to my Cochin China hen and every chick she hatches. " Bonæ legis est ampliare jura ; " common law, old as its roots are, has at every period of its existence expanded its branches, because its nature is the reverse of a parliamentary enactment, and is such as permits it to apply old principles to new contingencies ; to bloodhounds, potatoes, straw-paper, the printing press, each as they rise. Copyright and stage-right, and many other recent rights, grew out of two old principles of common law ; and these laid hold of the printing press and the theatre *as soon as they could and how they could.* The first old principle is this: Productive and unsalaried labour, if it clash with no property, creates a property. All the uncaught fish in the sea belong to the public. Yet every caught fish comes to hand private property, because productive labour, when it clashes with no precedent title, creates property at common law.

The second old principle is this. Law *abhors* divestiture, or forfeiture of property. From time immemorial the law of England has guarded property against surmises and surprises by defining the terms on which it will permit divestiture. They are two—" consensus " and " delictum ; " that is to say, " clear consent " and "long neglect," *each to be proved before a jury.*

By the first principle—viz., that productive labour not clashing with property creates property—a writer or his pay-master acquires the sole right to print the new work for sale. All lawyers out of Bedlam go thus far with me.

By the second the proprietor acquires nothing at all ; he merely retains for ever that sole right to print which he has acquired by productive labour—unless, indeed, he divests himself by " clear consent " or "long neglect," to be proved before a jury.

Transfer to another individual is " clear consent." To leave a printed book fifty years out of print might possibly be "delictum," or long neglect—*if a jury should so decide*—and that would make the right common. But to print and reprint one's own creation is to exercise the exclusive right, and exercise is the opposite of " delictum : " it is the very course the common law has prescribed from time immemorial to keep alive an exclusive right when once acquired.

So much for the governing principles. Now for their operation.

No French nor Dutch jurist disputes that intellectual pro-perty was the product of his national law, though afterwards regulated by statutes ; and that alone is a reply to the meta-physical sophists who argue *à priori* that common law could not recognise a property so subtle. However, a little fact is worth a great deal of sophistical conjecture. So let us examine fact, and candidly. In England the early history of the property has to be read subject to a just caution ; we must assign no judicial authority to unconstitutional tribunals, but only glean old facts from them, and that discreetly. From the infancy of printing till the year 1640, an Englishman could neither print his own book honestly nor his neighbour's dishonestly without a license from the Crown. Its principal agent in this iron rule was the Star Chamber, a tribunal whose deeds and words are not worth the millionth of a straw *judicially.* But, as *historical* evidence, especially on any matter irrelevant to its vices, its records are as valuable to a modern as any other ancient official memoranda of current events. The original word for "copyright" was "copy," and the Star Chamber used this word in very early times. This proves a bare fact, that copyright existed of old in printed books, and that, under the Tudor Sovereigns, it was an antiquity; since it had even then lived long enough to take the technical name "copy," whereas literary *monopolies* granted by the Crown were invariably and with just discrimination called "patents;" and "stage-right," whose existence (in unprinted dramas) by common law, at this time, is not doubted by any English lawyer, had no name at all, direct nor roundabout.

The Stationers' Company was first chartered in 1556. In 1558 they enter copyrights under the names of their proprietors, and the entries continue in an unbroken series until 1875. In 1582 there are entries with this proviso, that the Crown license to print should be void, if it be found that the copyright belonged to another person. This shows how Englishmen, when not corrupted by pettifoggers, gravitate towards law and the sanctity of property. The Stationers' Company was chartered by the Crown, and invested with some unconstitutional powers; yet in a very few years they make the Royal license bow to a precedent title of proprietorship, that could in 1582 have no foundation but in common law.

In 1640 the Star Chamber was abolished, and for a while everybody printed what he liked; thereupon, as free opinions differ, some wrote against the Parliament. Straight the two Houses of Parliament took a leaf out of the book of Kings, and passed an ordinance forbidding any work to be printed without a formal license; and then, as pirates, relieved of the licenser, had begun their game, the same ordinance forbade printing without the consent of the owner of the copyright, on pain of forfeiture of the books to the owner of the copyright. Thus the Commonwealth, in protecting copyright, went a step beyond the monarchical Governments that preceded it: which please make a note of, Brother Jonathan.

November 1644, Milton published his famous defence of unlicensed printing, and attacked that portion of the aforesaid ordinance, which infringed common-law liberties; but he sanctioned very solemnly that portion which protected common-law rights. That great enthusiast for just liberty used these words, "the just retaining of each man his several 'copy' (copyright), which God forbid should be gainsaid."

Anno 1662. Act 13 and 14 Charles II. prohibited printing

any book without consent of the *owner*, upon pain of certain forfeitures, half to the King, half to the *owner*. This statute followed the wording of the Republican ordinance. I need hardly say that in any Act of Parliament " owner " means the " legal owner," not the claimant of an impossible or even doubtful right. Under this statute a leading case was tried, that might be entitled Property *v.* Monopoly. " Streater " held what our ancestors with a scientific precision their muddle-headed descendants have lost till this day called a " patent." He was law patentee, *i.e.*, he had from the Crown a sole right to print law reports, and *that*, Messrs. Yates and Macaulay, was "*a monopoly in books*" if you like. Streater reprinted Judge Croke's reports. Roper sued Streater, proving his own legal ownership by purchase of Croke's copyright from Croke's executor. Roper's title was at common law, for the statute of Charles II. never pretended to confer ownership ; it only protected the existing legal owner by special remedies. Streater (Monopoly) pleaded the King's grant ; Roper (Property) demurred. This brought the question of law before the full Court of Common Pleas. It was given for the plaintiff against the King, by judges who were removable at the will of the Sovereign, and more inclined to stretch a point for him than against him. Opposed to a Royal grant, had Roper's title at law been doubtful, they would have swept him out of court with a besom.

Successive licensing Acts protected the common-law owner of copyright until 1694, when the last Act expired ; but as another was threatened for five years, a dread hung over piracy. This being removed in 1699, the pirates went to work with such fury that the proprietors of copyright began to cry out, and in 1703 petitioned Parliament for protection. For six weary years they besieged hard hearts and apathetic ears. One of the petitions survives, and therein the petitioners, though it was their interest to exaggerate their case, and say they had no remedy at law, do, on the contrary, *admit* there is a remedy at common law. But they say it is inadequate—that in an action on the case the jury will give no more damages than can be proved, and how can a thousand piratical copies be traced all over the country ? " Besides, the defendant is always a pauper," &c. &c., cited from the journals of the House.

In 1709 the Legislature took pity on authors and honest publishers, and passed an Act, the words of which and their contemporaneous interpretation are necessarily the last great link in the history of copyright, before that creature of the common law became the nursling of statutes. The preamble of a statute is not law, but history : it relates antecedent facts, and declares the cause and motives of the enactment to follow. Instead of comments I put italics :—

" Whereas printers, booksellers, and others have *of late* frequently taken the *liberty* of printing, reprinting, and publishing books and other writings, without the consent of the authors, or *proprietors,* to their very great detriment, and too often to the ruin of them and their families—for preventing therefore such *practices* for the future, be it enacted " —8th Anne, cap. 19, sec. 1.

In the body of the Act thus prefaced, the old word "copy" for "copyright" is used six times in the sense it had been used for ages, and, so far from inventing even a new protection to old copyright, as dreamers fancy, the Act, in that respect also, is a servile imitation of the various licensing Acts. As the Monarchical licensing Acts, and the Republican ordinances, found *owners* and *proprietors* of *"copy"* so this Act finds *proprietors* of " *copy,"* and, as the Republican and Monarchical Acts protected the existing owners or proprietors of " copy " by *confiscation of the piratical* books, so this Act protects the existing *proprietors* of " *copy,"* by *confiscation of the piratical* books ; and, to any man with an eye in his mind, this deliberate imitation of preceding Acts, that had recognised " copyright " at common law, and protected it by penalties, is not only a recognition of the *property,* but a recognition of the recognitions and the penalties. Dreamers always confound dates ; they forget that many of the Parliament men A.D. 1709 had themselves in person passed a licensing Act. Even the one apparent novelty—the curtailing clause—was a bungling attempt to arrive in another way at the temporary feature, which was the characteristic of the licensing Acts. The bill, we know, went into Committee an Act protecting property *for ever* by penalties. In Committee it encountered old members, and these, with a servile double imitation of the licensing Acts, *which were penal, and only passed for a term,* fixed an imitation term to the imitation penalties, but so unskilfully that, by the grammatical sense of their words, they shortened the days of the sacred everlasting property itself. Subject to a saving clause, which afterwards proved too obscure and feeble to combat the spoliation clause, they fixed a term—of a book already printed, twenty-one years ; of a book to be printed, fourteen years ; but fourteen more should the author survive the first term.

Such to a reader of this day, when the application of the

lying term "monopoly" has blunted the understanding and the conscience, is the apparent sense of the statute. But you must remember that in 1709 the word "monopoly" had never been applied to "copyright" by any human creature : and so rooted was all common-law property, and the sense of its inviolability, in the English mind, that neither the laymen nor the lawyers of Queen Anne's generation read the statute as curtailing the sacred property. Honest Englishmen, not blinded by cant, know no difference of sanctity in *property*. From a hovel to a palace it is equally sacred. Curtailment of an Englishman's *property* is spoliation *in futuro*, and spoliation, without a full equivalent, is a public felony Englishmen were slow to suspect the State of. Queen Anne's Parliament sat at Westminster, not Newgate ; and therefore the curtailing clauses were interpreted to apply to the new penalties, not to a thing so inviolable as the ancient property. Authors continued, *after this* statute, to assign their copyright for ever, and publishers to purchase them for ever, just as they did before the statute ; and, for forty years at least, while the contemporaneous exposition of the statute was still warm, equity judges, *who had conversed with members of both Houses that passed the Act, and with lawyers who had framed it*, and had means of knowing the mind of Parliament that we can never have, granted relief by injunction to several plaintiffs, who by the lapse of time had no legal claim to any benefit from the statute, but only from the precedent common-law right.

In 1769—Millar *v.* Taylor—the judges of the King's Bench, by a majority of three to one, decided that Queen Anne's statute had not curtailed the ancient right, but, like its models, the licensing Acts, had supported it by penalties, which expired in a few years, leaving the bare right protected only by action upon the case, as it was before the statute.

This decision stood for five years. But all those five years the lying word "monopoly," launched by the dissentient judge in Millar *v.* Taylor, was undermining the property.

February 9, 1774, on an appeal from the Court of Chancery in Donaldson *v.* Becket, the House of Peers directed the judges at common law to reply to three questions, which may be thus condensed :—

1. Had an author the sole right at common law to print his MS. ?

2. If so, did he lose his exclusive right by printing ?

3. Did the statute of Queen Anne curtail this right, and confine it entirely to the times and other conditions specified ?

On the first question the judges, including Lord Mansfield, were nine to three, on the second, eight to four against the forfeiture, and on the third, six to six.

But Lord Mansfield, whose great learning left little room in his mind for so small a trait as pluck, withheld his voice, without changing his mind, and made the numbers appear to be—on the first question eight to three, on the second seven to four, on the third six to five. Pursuing the same delicate course in the House of Peers itself, he sacrificed the biggest thing on earth, and that is justice, to an extremely pretty, but small, thing, etiquette; whereas Lord Camden, who for known reasons hated authors, and hated Lord Mansfield, laid aside not only etiquette, but judicial gravity, and ranted and canted without disguise, as counsel for the pirates, and so stole a majority (of lay lords, not lawyers), whose judgment, however, went only to this, that the statute had *curtailed* the everlasting common-law right.

Thus these lucky knaves, the pirates, got a sham majority of the judges to defy the contemporaneous and continued interpretation of a statute sixty years old—a malpractice without precedent in our courts—and—anomaly upon anomaly—to curtail so sacred a thing as an Englishman's property. Unfortunately their good luck did not stop there; though they were defeated upon the first and second questions, yet the Anglo-Saxon muddlehead now interprets their bastard victory on the first question, into a victory on the second question, where they were overpowered by numbers, and crushed by weight, Mansfield and Blackstone being in the majority, and in the minority three comic judges, Eyre, Perrot, and Adams, who held in the teeth of all the cases that an author has not, by common law, the sole right to *print his own manuscript*. Now the metaphysical muddleheads, led by Yates, had the same contempt for these three comic judges, their allies, that Mansfield and Blackstone had for their allies and them. So then the majority who said—" No, copyright at common law is not forfeited by its lawful exercise," for law abhors forfeiture—were agreed in principle; but the minority were only agreed to say, " Copyright in printed books did not exist at common law." They could not agree *why*. The only *principle* the metaphysical judges, and the comic judges, held in common, was " a labefactation of all principle," viz., a resolution to outlaw authors *per fas et nefas*. But the Anglo-Saxon addlepate, unable to observe, and therefore unable to discriminate, contemplates, with his mooning, lack-lustre eye, a consistent majority, led by the only judges Europe recognised as jurists, and a minority, composed of trumpery little obscure judges at war with each other; and, in the teeth of this treble majority, by numbers, weight, and unanimity, says copyright was declared by the judges a creature of statutes.

Not so, my friend and jackass. A great majority of the judges, led by giants, and agreeing in principle, overpowered a small and discordant minority of judicial dwarfs, and declared copyright in printed books a creature of the common law, and a nursling of statutes.

Looking at the conduct of its first nurse, in 1709, the latter term is doubly appropriate; for, when a nurse is not the mother, she is the very woman to overlie the bantling, and *shorten its days.*

Thus from 1700–1709, authors and their assignees suffered such lawless devastation of their property and undeserved ruin as no other citizens ever endured at that epoch of civilisation; and in 1774 the same favourite victims of injustice suffered two such wrongs, judicial and legislatorial, as would, had they fallen on any powerful class of citizens, have drenched the land in blood, have set the outlawed proprietors killing pirates like rats, and imperilled the House of Lords, both as a tribunal and a branch of the Legislature. And this is the right way to measure public crimes; for, though it is safer to trample unjustly on the worthy and the weak than on the strong, it is not a bit more just, and it is not so much more expedient as it looks; for every dog gets his day.

The judicial wrong.—The judges are the constitutional interpreters of statutes, and their interpretations are law. Precedent rules our courts like iron. When judges, who sit near the time of an Act, interpret it in open court by judgments, and so precedents of interpretation accumulate, the chain of practical interpretations becomes law, and immutable; especially if the Act so interpreted came after a right at common law and recognised it. Never, since England was a nation, has sixty years' interpretation of a statute been upset, except to injure *authors.* Sixty years' interpretation of Queen Anne's statute, had the interpretation been *injurious* to authors, would have stood as immovable as the walls of Westminster Hall. Not one English judge would have listened either to reason, or to principle, or to grammar, or to all three, against a chain of precedents, had those precedents been *injurious* to authors. Every lawyer knows this is so, and that the answer of the judges to an innovating author would have been, "We do not make interpretations of old statutes; we find them in the cases. *Have you a case, Mr. Author?*"

The House of Lords was not itself in this matter. Besides the excess of lay peers, there were two elements that vitiated its judgment. 1st. Lord Mansfield withheld his vote. That was monstrous. In the tribunal whence there is no appeal, if the most capable judge withholds his voice, the majority is a delusion. I don't say his silence was without precedent. But the other side flung precedent to the winds. 2nd. Lord Camden, one of the judges, was corrupt. A man may be corrupted with other things than bribes. This lawyer was corrupted by his passions. He hated authors for blackballing him at their club, and he hated Lord Mansfield for being a greater lawyer than himself. Lord Mansfield was silent, yet Camden spoke *at* him all through; and he spoke on the judgment-seat, not as judges speak who are trying to be just, but as counsel play with claptrap on the prejudices of a jury—and what were the lay lords but a jury! He, who had never worked his brain for reputation only, but also for money, money for pleading causes, money for doing justice on the Bench, pension-money for having judged cases and been paid at the time, he had the egotism and the impudence to urge that "Glory is the sole reward of authors, and those who desire it scorn all meaner views. Away, then," says canting Camden, "with the illiberal avarice that, at sixty or seventy years of age, still seeks a return from books written at thirty or forty. No, let the aged author take his tottering limbs and his grey hairs to an almshouse or starvation; *I*'m all right: *I*'ve got a pension." With such justice, such unselfishness, such humanity as this, well wrapt in rant and omnipotent cant, he bribed Lord Noodle and Lord Doodle—judges in virtue of their titles—to annul a chain of true judicial precedents, to pillage the property of their intellectual superiors, and doom their declining days to poverty and degradation. Why not? The villainy could not recoil on any one of the perpetrators: the lay judges had all got land from their sires, a property, the title to which is generally impure, but it cannot be curtailed, and the pensioned pettifogger was kept in affluence by the State he no longer worked for; that State, which does not pension retired *authors,* and therefore was all the more bound to secure to their old age the property—for creating which they receive neither salaries nor pensions—against pilfering pirates, metaphysical muddleheads, romantic pettifoggers, canting pensioners, and all the other egotists, dunces, and knaves, who, possessing the lower intellect, hate the highest intellect, and grudge it a long lease of its own poor, little, insufficient freehold, held by ten thousand times the purest title law can find on sea or land — Creation.

The legislatorial wrong.—The nation cried shame at the judicial robbery of authors and their assigns. The House of Commons, which is the representative of the country in Parliament, wasted no time, but proceeded to cure the wrong by fresh legislation. They brought in a bill restoring the common-law right apart from the statutory penalties. It was carried by a large majority. But in the Upper House it encountered Lord Camden. To be sure, matters were changed now : justice and humanity no longer asked him to resign his new, but grammatical, interpretation of an old statute. They bowed to his new interpretation, and merely asked him to legislate accordingly : to rectify the unhappy misunderstanding by a fairer and more humane enactment. No ! the cruel legislator retained the perverse malignity of the passionate judge ; he met all the petitions of the sufferers, and all the assignments for ever of literary property, that had been made in good faith, with a *falsehood*—that copyright is a monopoly—and with the same rant and cant he had defiled the judgment-seat with in Donaldson v. Becket. He wrought upon the passions and the illiterate prejudices of a House, which was not the enlightened assembly it is now ; justice in the person of Lord Mansfield once more sat mumchance, apathetic, cowardly, dumb, despising secretly the romantic injustice, the pseudo-metaphysical idiocy, the rant and cant, and misplaced malevolence, he should have got up and throttled, like a man ; unfortunate authors !—the foibles of your friends, the vices of your enemies, all tended by some gravitation of injustice to weigh down the habitual victims ; and so a small majority of the peers was got to overpower a large majority of the Commons, and the sense and humanity of the nation.

Upon this, authors and honest publishers fell into deep dejection, and resigned all hope of justice during their enemy's lifetime. After his death the House of Peers became more human ; they seemed to admit, with tardy regret, that Lord Camden had misled them a *little;* that an author, after all, was not an old wild beast, but an old man ; and so they gave him back his stolen property for his whole life, and for twenty-eight years at least.

That remorse did not decline, but grew as civilisation advanced. In 1842, Parliament, advised by lawyers worthy of the name, passed a nobler bill. They gave the lie direct to Mr. Justice Yates and Lord Camden, by formally declaring copyright to be *property* (Act 5 and 6 Victoria, cap. 45, sect. 25), and they postponed the statutory dissolution of this sacred and declared *property* for forty-two years at least, and seven years after the author's death.

But for Macaulay's rhetoric, and his popular cry "Monopoly," Parliament would have refunded us our property for sixty years: and that may come as civilisation and sound views of law advance. For, in this more enlightened century, the progress of intellectual property keeps step with advancing civilisation and sound views of trade. Accordingly in 1838 there was a faint attempt at international justice to authors, and in 1851 other nations began really to comprehend what France, the leading nation in this morality, had always seen, that the nationality of an author does not affect his moral claim to a property in his composition. But that question includes international stage-right, and must follow its legal history; which, however, will not detain us long from the main topic of these letters. CHARLES READE.

FOURTH LETTER

SIR,—Stage-right is a term invented by me, and first printed in a book called "The Eighth Commandment." The judges of the Common Pleas accepted it from me when I argued in person the question of law, that arose out of the first count in Reade *v.* Conquest. The term was necessary. Truth and legal science had not a fair chance, so long as the fallacious phrase "Dramatic Copyright" infested the courts and the books: its use, by counsel and judges, had created many misunderstandings, and one judicial error, Cumberland *v.* Planché. Language has its laws, which even the learned cannot violate with impunity: adjectives can qualify a substantive, but cannot change its substance; "Dramatic Copyright" either means the exclusive right of printing a playbook, or it means nothing: but, since the word "Copyright" covers the exclusive right of printing a play book, "Dramatic Copyright" does really mean nothing. It is an illogical, pernicious phrase, and, if any lawyer will just substitute the word "Stage-right," he will be amazed at the flood of light the mere use of a scientific word will pour upon the fog that at present envelops history and old decisions, especially Coleman *v.* Wathen, Murray *v.* Elliston, and Morris *v.* Kelly, leading cases.

Stage-right, or the sole right of an author to produce and reproduce his *unprinted* dramas on the stage, is allowed by lawyers to have been a common-law right up to the date of 3 Will. IV. This admission shortens discussion. Henslowe's Theatre was exceptional: in his days and Shakespeare's most theatres were managed thus: established actors were the shareholders, and obtained plays on various terms; if an author was a member of the sharing company, he was paid by his share of the profits. The non-sharing author received a sum, or the overplus of a certain night, or both. The stage-right of an author vested in the company upon the common-law principle that the paymaster of a production is its proprietor. To this severe equity we owe a literary misfortune; several hundred plays, many of them masterpieces, were kept out of print, and have been lost. The plays of Jonson, Fletcher, Shakespeare, and others, were confined to the theatre until well worn. Messrs. Pope, Warburton, and Jonson had not the key to Shakespeare's business, and wrote wildly—that he neglected his reputation, did not think his works worth printing, and, thanks to his flightiness, his lines come down to us more corrupt than the text of Velleius Paterculus: but the truth is, other plays were kept out of print as long as his were, and his text is by no means the only corrupt one of that day; and what those fine fellows call his flightiness was good sense and probity. He valued reputation, as all writers do. But he valued it at its value. The man wrote poems as well as plays, and did the best thing possible with both: of a poem the road to a little fame and profit was the printing press; of a play the way to great fame and profit was the theatre; readers were very few, playgoers numerous beyond belief; observe, then, his good sense—he prints his *poems* in 1594, almost as soon as he can afford to do it: of his *plays* he prints a few, one at a time, and never till each play has been well worn in the theatre. Observe his probity; he was a sharing author, and his fellow shareholders had an equitable lien on his plays. To gratify his vanity by wholesale publication of his plays would have been unfair to them. This is connected with my subject thus—In his will, particular as it is, he did not bequeath his plays to any one.

Therefore, *primâ facie* they would go to his residuary legatee. But they did not go to her. Created by a shareholder in the Globe, and handsomely paid for year by year, they remained, by current equity, the property of the theatre. The shareholders kept them to the boards for seven years after his death, and then printed them. His first editors, Hemming and Condell, had been his joint shareholders in the Globe. Now observe how the men of that day commented by anticipation on the romantic cant of recent pettifoggers, that centuries ago if any one printed a MS., he resigned all the rights he held while it was in MS.! The copyright in Shakespeare's plays—it was not violated at all. The stage-right—it was not violated for some years after the plays were printed; but, as printing and publishing plays facilitate dramatic piracy, though they do not make it honest, some companies plucked up courage in 1627, and began to perform Shakespeare's dramas from the printed book. Then the holders of the stage-right went to the licenser of plays, and he stopped the company of the Red Bull Theatre in that act of piracy. See " Collier's Annals of the Stage," vol. ii. p. 8. The Chamberlain's decision, in this matter, is of no legal value; but it shows historically that the moral sense and equity, which in the present day govern stage-right and copyright, were not invented by recent Parliaments; and the proof is accumulative, for ten years later—namely, in 1637—another Chamberlain is found acting on the same equity, and in terms worth noting. On application from the shareholders of the Cockpit in Drury Lane, the Chamberlain gave solemn notice to other companies not to represent certain plays, twenty-four in number, which " did all and every of them *properly,* and *of right,* belong to that company," and he " requires all masters and governors of playhouses, and all others whom it concerns, to take notice and forbear to impeach the said William Bieston (who represented the shareholders of the Cockpit) in the premises." Of these twenty-four plays some were in MS., and some printed. The notice is worded by a lawyer, and the declared object is to protect *property.* Malone in Prolegomena to Shakespeare, vol. iii. p. 158.

Soon after this the theatres were closed; and that made the readers of plays a hundred, where one had been, and deranged for ever the equitable custom that prevailed before the Civil War. As soon as the theatre reopened, dramatists made other and better terms, and those terms were uniform; they never sold their manuscripts out and out to the theatre; from

1662 to 1694 they divided their stage-right from their copy-right; they took from the theatre the overplus of the third night, generally at double prices, and they always sold the copyright to the booksellers. *Testibus* Downes, Pepys, Malone, Collier, and many others.

The following figures can be relied on :—Stage-right.—In 1694 Southerne obtained another night, the sixth. In 1705 Farquhar obtained a third night, the ninth, and authors held these three nights about a century. Dryden, under the one-night system, used to receive for stage-right about £100, and for copyright £20–£25. But his plays were not very popular. Southerne, for " The Fatal Marriage," A.D. 1694, stage-right two nights' overplus, £260, copyright £36. Rowe's " Jane Shore," stage-right three nights, copyright £50, 15s. Rowe's " Jane Grey," stage-right three nights, copyright £75. Southerne's " Spartan Dame," stage-right not known, copyright £120, A.D. 1719. Cibber's " Non-Juror " and Smythe's " Rival Modes," stage-right three nights each, copyright a hundred guineas apiece from Book-seller Lintot. Fenton's " Marianne," stage-right and copy-right, total £1000, A.D. 1723. " George Barnwell," by Lillo, stage-right the overplus of three nights, copyright £105. This copyright Lillo assigned to Bookseller Gray and his heirs *for ever*, on the 25th of November 1735. The assign-ment is to be seen to this day, printed in full, in the edition of 1810. Dr. Young's " Busiris," stage-right three nights, copy-right £84. Lintot. Copyright alone of Addison's " Drummer " (failed at the time on stage), £50. Dr. Young's " Revenge," stage-right large, copyright £50. " Beggar's Opera," stage-right £1600, copyright £400. " Polly," by the same author, representation stopped by the Chamberlain, copyright £1200. This proves little ; it was published by subscription. " The Brothers," by Dr. Young, stage-right and copyright £1000, the proportions not ascertained. " The Follies of a Day," by Holcroft, stage-right £600, copyright £300. " Road to Ruin," stage-right £900, copyright £400. Goldsmith's " Good-natured Man," stage-right £300, copyright £200. " She Stoops to Conquer," stage-right £500, copyright £300.

Now the other branch of fiction had but one market, copy-right: yet the copyright of a story in prose or verse was less valuable than the copyright of a play. Milton's " Paradise Lost " was sold in 1657 for £5 per edition, which was rather less than the copyright of a play in 1662, and 80 per cent. less than the stage-right. Defoe did not receive £105 for

" Robinson Crusoe." Pope's " Rape of the Lock," first edition,
£7. Second edition, £15. Dr. Johnson's " Irene," a very
bad play, brought him £315. " Rasselas," an exquisite tale,
only £100 ; and his true narratives, and best work, " The
Lives of the Poets," only £200. Goldsmith's " Vicar of
Wakefield " only £60, which compare with the copyrights of
Goldsmith's plays ; that were nevertheless less remunerative
than his stage-rights. Of the two properties in a play, both
so largely remunerated, neither could have been an empty
sound ; book-copyright, far less valuable, was, we know,
secure ; nor is it credible that the stage-right was legally
dissolved, if the author went into print ; otherwise, the
managers would have objected to the dramatist going into
print, and the managers were clearly masters of the situation.

Macklin v. *Richardson*—A.D. 1770.—Macklin, author of a
MS. farce, used to play it, but never printed. Richardson
took it down shorthand from the actor's lips, and printed it.
Macklin filed an injunction. Defendant tried the reasoning
of Mr. Justice Yates : " Plaintiff had flown his bird ; had
given his ideas to the public, and no member of the public
could be restrained from doing what he liked with them."
This piece of thieves' cant failed, and the injunction was
made perpetual. This is a pure copyright case ; stage-right
never entered the discussion. Coleman *v.* Wathen, and
Murray *v.* Elliston, were neither copyright, nor stage-right,
but bastard cases, where the wrong plaintiff came into court.
They arose out of an imperfect vocabulary. "Words are the
counters of wise men, but the money of fools," says Lord
Bacon : the sole right of printing being represented by a
good hard substantive, any mind could realise that right, but
the sole right of representation not being represented by a
substantive, the soft heads of little lawyers could not realise
its distinct existence and heterogeneous character. One has
only to supply the substantive, stage-right, and the fog flies.

Coleman v. *Wathen.*—O'Keefe wrote a play ; by this act
he created two properties assignable to distinct traders—a
common-law right, stage-right ; and a statutory right, copyright. He assigned the copyright to Coleman in terms that
could not possibly convey the stage-right. Wathen played
the play piratically at Richmond. This was an infraction of
O'Keefe's stage-right, but not of Coleman's copyright : yet
bad legal advisers sent not O'Keefe, but Coleman, into court
as plaintiff. Coleman produced in court an assignment of
copyright, and sued under the Act of Parliament for breach

of it : but that statutory right had never been infringed. As for the stage-right, it never came into court at all ; it stayed outside with O'Keefe and the common law.

Murray v. *Elliston.*—The same error. Lord Byron, by writing "Sardanapalus," created stage-right at common law, and copyright by statute. He assigned the copyright to Murray. He could have assigned the stage-right to Morris. By not assigning it to anybody he retained it. "Expressum facit cessare tacitum." Elliston played "Sardanapalus." If Murray had been well advised, he would have sent off a courier to Lord Byron, and obtained an assignment of the common-law right of representation. Instead of that, this assignee of the copyright went to Eldon, and asked him to restrain a piracy upon the author's stage-right, which was actually at that moment the author's property and not Murray's. Now it is sworn in the Blue-book of 1832 that Lord Eldon never refused an injunction to a *manager* who had purchased a stage-right. But of course when not a manager, but a *publisher*, the assignee of a statutory *copyright*, came to him to restrain an infringement of common-law *stage-right*, he declined to interfere, and sent the plaintiff to Westminster. The judges decided against this plaintiff, but did not give their reasons. That is very unusual ; but how could they give their reasons ?· The poor dear souls had not got the words to explain with. Existing language was a mere trap. They had got one word for two distinct properties : so they very wisely avoided their vehicle of confusion, language, and *acted* the just distinction they could not *speak* for want of a substantive. There is no reason to suppose that they would have denied the title of a theatrical manager armed with an assignment of the stage-right in "Sardanapalus." There was a side question of abridgment in Murray *v.* Elliston, but that was for a jury. The judges had nothing to do with that : what they denied was Murray's right to bring an action ; and they were right : he was no more the plaintiff than my grandmother was.

Morris v. *Kelly.*—This is the only stage-right case in the books. Morris, manager of the Haymarket Theatre, was not a dealer in copyrights, but stage-rights. He produced, not an assignment of O'Keefe's copyright, as Coleman had done, but good *primâ facie* evidence that he had purchased O'Keefe's stage-right. The very same judge, who declined to assist the assignee of Byron's copyright in a case of piratical representation, granted an injunction with downright alacrity when the assignee of O'Keefe's stage-right stood before him. The play, whose performance was thus restrained, had been in print ever so long. Therefore, the theory that under the common law stage-right exists in a MS., but expires if the play is printed, received no countenance from that learned and wary judge, Lord Eldon. I knew the plaintiff, Morris: he was a most respectable man ; he has sworn before Parliament that Lord Eldon constantly granted injunctions in support of a manager's stage-right. Morris's evidence is incidentally confirmed by "Godson on Patents:" he mentions an injunction, Morris v. Harris, which is not reported.

The sworn deposition of Morris, and the support given to it by the two recorded cases, Morris v. Kelly, and the unreported case mentioned by Godson, would be meagre evidence, if opposed; but there is nothing at all to set against that evidence—not a case, not a dictum ; and it accords with the prices of plays, play-books, and story-books in prose and verse, for 150 years, 1657–1810. Stage-right, therefore, in unprinted plays was, by admission, a creature of the common law and the natural product of common justice : the immense publicity given to the author's ideas by representation did not justify the public in carrying away the words to represent them in another theatre. Printing a play would greatly facilitate piracy : but the power to misappropriate is not the right to misappropriate. That printing a play could actually forfeit so heterogeneous a property as stage-right is a conjecture. What little evidence there is runs against the forfeiture. Up to the Commonwealth, the Chamberlain, *alleging property*, stopped violation of stage-right in plays, whether they were printed or not. After the Restoration we have only the evidence of prices for 150 years, and Lord Eldon's judgment. He protected stage-right after publication, and his is the only judicial decision that touches stage-right at common law, either in MSS. or play-books.

If, therefore, we are to go by impartial principles of law and the best direct evidence we can get, and superior weight of judicial authority, speaking *obiter* in Donaldson v. Becket, and *ad rem* in Morris v. Kelly, stage-right in MSS., and even in printed plays, was like copyright, a creature of common sense, common justice, and common law ; but, like copyright, is now a nursling of statutes, thanks to a sudden onslaught by pirates. For, if law be ever so clear, but carry no penalty for breach, property is the sport of accident ; so, on the close of the war in 1815, monopoly and piracy fell upon the dramatist, and destroyed him. Two theatres got the sole right to play legitimate pieces in London, and this made the author their slave. They robbed him of his three nights' overplus, and threw him a few pounds for a drama worth thousands. As to the provincial theatres, a single pirate drove all the dramatists clean out of them. Here is a copy of his public advertisement—and please observe it is unprinted plays he pirates wholesale : —" Mr. Kenneth, at the corner of Bow Street, will supply any gentleman with any manuscript on the lowest terms " — and here is an example : — Mr. Douglas Jerrold gives evidence to the Parliamentary Commission, Blue-book, p. 156 :—" ' The Rent Day ' was played in the country a fortnight after it was produced at Drury Lane, and I have a letter in my pocket in which a provincial manager said he would willingly have given me £5 for a copy, had he not before paid £2 for it to some stranger" (meaning Kenneth). The method of this caitiff is revealed in another quarter. "Kenneth went to the theatre with a shorthand writer, who took the words down and the *mise-en-scène*. He had copyists ready at home to transcribe, and the stolen goods were on their way to the provincial theatres in a few hours." But the London theatres also pirated the author. Moncrieff deposed that he produced "Giovanni," a musical piece, at a minor theatre. Drury Lane, one of the two theatres that had a monopoly in legitimate pieces, sent into Surrey, stole this illegitimate piece, and played it in the teeth of the author. The manager made thousands by it, and brought out Madame Vestris in it, and she made thousands. It was only the poor author that was swindled for enriching both manager and actor. That victim of ten thousand wrongs dared not resist this piece of scoundrelism ; the managers would have excluded him altogether from the market, narrowed by monopoly.

But piracy has also its indirect effects. Even honest people will not give much for a property they see others stealing. By "The Rent Day" the theatre cleared twenty thousand pounds ; but the author only £150 ; and for "Black-eyed Susan," which saved Manager Elliston from bankruptcy and made him flourish like a green bay-tree, the author received only £60 ; whereas the actor, Cooke, who played a single part in it, cleared £4000 during its first run, and afterwards made a fortune out of it in the country theatres, which did not pay the author at all.

The Commissioners proceeded fairly. They heard the authors relate their wrongs, the monopolists defend their monopolies, and the pirates prove their thefts pure patriotisms *as usual :* and they reported to Parliament a deep decline of the British drama, and denounced as its two causes, the monstrous monopoly of the managers, and the insecurity of the author's property; on the latter head these are their instructive words : " A dramatic author at present is subjected to indefensible hardship and injustice, and the disparity of the protection afforded to his labours, when compared *even with that granted to authors in any* other branch of *letters,* seems alone sufficient to divert the ambition of eminent and successful writers from that department of intellectual exertion."

Thereupon Parliament, in the interest of justice and sound national policy, took away from the two patent theatres their wicked monopoly, and secured the property of a dramatist by a stringent enactment. The last link in the evidence is the statute itself. 3 & 4 Will. IV. did not create a property; it found one; and it found a law, but ineffectual. The title, which is evidence, when not contradicted in the body of an Act, runs thus :—" An Act to *amend* the laws relating to dramatic literary *property.*" Then, as to the Act itself, it protects the dramatist so sharply, that if Parliament had been creating a right, they would certainly have fixed a term. But they respected the common-law right they were nursing, and left it perpetual ; and this, *to my personal knowledge,* they did because of the growing disgust to the spoliation authors had suffered from preceding Parliaments. What this Parliament thought was, that stage-right existed for ever in *unprinted dramas ;* and they laboured to extend the right to its just consequences, and protect it *for ever* by special provisions. When the right had been a statutory right for ten years, it got curtailed ; but Parliament, that took it from the common law, did not curtail it.

This is the mere legal history of two sacred properties up to the dates when Parliament, after profound consideration, and full discussion at wide intervals, did, without haste, or prejudice, or any of those perturbing influences with which Lord Camden corrupted the Peers in his day, declare both these properties to be not monopolies, but personal properties. The full statutory definition amounts to this—" they are personal properties, so sacred during the term of their statutory existence, that they carry a main feature of real property ; the very proprietor cannot convey them to another, by word of mouth : and indeed a bare licence to print, or to perform in a theatre, concurrently with the proprietor, is void, unless given in writing." This distinct recognition of property was a return, in principle, to the common law, and the principle was too just and healthy not to grow and expand. Exceptional law is bad law, and stands still. Good law is of wide application, and therefore grows.

When one nation takes wider views of justice or durable policy than other nations, we do not say like our forefathers, "That nation is hare-brained." We say, nowadays, "That nation is *before* the rest;" implying that we shall be sure to follow, soon or late : and we always do. France saw thirty years ago that children must not be starved, and so murdered, by adulterated milk. She enlisted science ; detected, fined, imprisoned the adulterators, and made them advertise their own disgrace in several journals. She was not mad, nor divine ; she was human, but ahead. Prussia saw long ago that the minds of children must be protected, like their other reversionary interests. If, therefore, parents were so wicked as to bring children into the world and not educate them, she warned, she fined, she imprisoned the indulgent and self-indulgent criminals. She was before other nations, that is all. England was the first to see free trade. She was before the rest of Europe, that is all. France saw, ages ago, that if A creates by labour a new intellectual production, and B makes one of its vehicles, the paper, and C and D set up, and work, the type, which is another vehicle, and print the sheets, and E (the publisher) sells the intellectual production, together with its vehicles, in volumes to F (the retail book-seller), and F sells them to the public, all these workers and traders must be remunerated in some proportion to what they contribute ; and that the nationality either of A, B, C, D, E, or F is equally irrelevant ; and it is monstrous to pick out A, whose contribution to the value is the largest, and say, *You* are a foreigner, and therefore you can claim neither property, nor wages, nor profit in France, though the smaller contributors, B, C, D, E, and F, have a right to be remunerated, *whether they are foreigners or not.* French jurists, with the superior logic of their race, saw this years ago, and in 1851 we all began to follow the leading nation, according to our lights : and they were blinkers ; because we were not Latins, but Anglo-Saxons : God has not made us jurists ; so the devil steps in, whenever we are off our guard, and makes us pettifoggers.

I am going to ask brother Jonathan a favour. I want him to cast a side glance, but keen—as himself—at what passed between France and England from 1851-1875 inclusively, and then ask himself honestly whether the European things I shall relate do not appeal to his own sense of justice and true public policy. The United States of America can teach us, and have taught us, many things. We can teach them a few things; not that we are wiser, but that we are older. Age alone brings certain experiences. In the United States Piracy says, " I will get you a constant supply of good cheap books and dramas: it is your interest to encourage me, and not to foster literary poverty." Piracy says this in the United States, and is believed. Why not? It looks like a self-evident truth. But piracy *has* said this in Europe many times, and in many generations, and in many countries, and *has* been believed, and believed, and believed. But European nations have, by repeated trials, at sundry times, and in divers places, found out whether what piracy says is a durable truth, or a plausible lie. Thus what in America is still a matter of intelligent conjecture, has become, in Europe, a matter of absolute, proved, demonstrated certainty; and, on this account, I ask American statesmen for the first time in their lives to bring the powers of their mind really to bear on the European facts I shall relate, and am ready to depose to on oath either before an American Congress or a British Parliament.

CHARLES READE.

FIFTH LETTER

SIR,— INTERNATIONAL COPYRIGHT AND STAGE-RIGHT, A.D. 1851–52.

It is instructive to look back and see how this great advance in justice and public policy was received by different classes.

1. The managers of our theatres, and the writers of good French pieces into bad English ones, showed uneasiness and hostility.

2. The British publishers, dead apathy. M. Paguerre, President of the " Cercle de la Libraire," came to London to invite their hearty co-operation ; " but found them indifferent except as regards America. To the moral bearings of the question they appeared tolerably callous."—*Athenæum*, September 20, 1851. This was afterwards proved by the prodigious silence of their organs. On this, the greatest literary event of modern times, the *Quarterly Review*, the *Edinburgh*, the *British Quarterly*, *London and Westminster*, *Blackwood*,

Fraser, the *New Monthly, North British, Christian Observer, Eclectic Review, Dublin Review, Dublin University Review,* delivered no notice nor comment, not one syllable. They shut out contemporary daylight, and went on cooking the stale cabbage of small old ages by the light of a farthing candle.

3. This phenomenal obtuseness was not shared by the journals and weeklies. The journalists, though they have little personal interest in literary property, being remunerated in a different way, uttered high and disinterested views of justice and public policy. They welcomed the treaty unanimously. Accept a few articles as index to the rest. *Examiner,* 1851, November 29; 1852, January 24, September 4, October 30. *Leader,* 1851, November 15, November 29. *Sunday Times,* December 7, 1851. *Era,* same date. *Critic,* 1851, March 15, February 2, 1852. The *Times,* 1851, November 19 and November 26; also December 1, page 4, column 6. *Illustrated London News,* 1851, May 24. *Literary Gazette,* 1851, May 24, July 5, November 15, November 22, December 13. *Athenæum,* 1851, January 18, March 15 and 29, June 7, August 2, September 20, November 22. *Art Journal,* 1851, September and November. The *New York Literary World,* March 1851. It would be agreeable to my own feelings to go through these articles; they bristle with hard facts proving that piracy upon foreigners is a mere blight on literature, and *a special curse to the nation the pirate lives in.* But, perhaps, a reader or two, like those St. Paul calls noble, will search the matter, and to save time, the rest may believe me, writing with the notes before me. I will, however, select a good specimen. A letter from Cologne, by an old observer of piratical translations in Germany, states that thirty years before date, good translations of Scott came into the German market; Bulwer followed, then Dickens. They were read with avidity; so, not being property, rival translations came out by the dozen. This cut down the profits, and the rival publishers were obliged to keep reducing the pay of the translators—till at last it got to £6 for translating 3 vols. Act 1.

Act 2. Bad translations, by incompetent hands, bad type, bad paper: valueless as literature; yet, by English reputation and cheapness, under-selling the German inventor. Death to the German novelist; a mere fraud on the German public —bad translations being *counterfeit coin* — and no good to any German publisher, because they all tore the speculation to rags at the first symptom of a sale. *Literary Gazette,* November 15, 1851.

The *Times*, November 26, 1851, supported the proposed treaty in a leader, taking the higher ground of morality, justice, and humanity, but omitting sound national policy. The leader contains such observations as these :—"Intellectual produce has been the only description of goods excluded from equitable conditions of exchange."——"Genius has been outlawed. The property it should have owned has, by the comity of nations, been treated as the goods of a convicted felon." After giving examples of French, English, and American genius pillaged, the writer goes on thus :— "Still worse, copies were multiplied at a cheap rate in Brussels, and disseminated all over the Continent."—— "There has long existed a profound immorality of thought with regard to the productions of genius."——"How short-sighted the policy has been, the example of Belgium evinces. The effect of its habitual piracy has simply been the extinction of literary genius throughout Belgium."

The *Illustrated London News*, May 24, 1851, welcomed international justice, and put the logic of international larceny rather neatly :—"An English book was treated like any other commodity produced by skill and industry, and so was a foreigner's watch; but not a foreigner's book."

In a word, the British journalists, all those years ago, showed rare enlightenment, and personal generosity; for there are no writers more able, and indeed few so surprising to poor Me, as the first-class journalist, whose mind can pour out treasures with incredible swiftness, and at any hour, however unfavourable to composition; bed-time to wit, or even digestion-time. Yet these remarkable men, in their business sacrifice personal reputation, and see it enjoyed by moderate writers of books: this would sour a petty mind, and the man would say, like Lord Camden, "Let authors be content with the reputation they gain; and what is literary property to *me* ? *I* have no stake in it." But these gentlemen showed themselves higher-minded than Lord Camden; they silenced egotism, and rose unanimously to the lofty levels of international justice, and sound policy; and it would ill become me, and my fellows, in Great Britain and America, to forget this good deed, or to pass it by without a word of gratitude and esteem.

4. With less merit, because we were interested, every author worthy of the name hailed the new morality with ardour. The American authors in particular conceived hopes that justice and sound policy would cross a wider water, than the ditch, which had hitherto obstructed the march of justice in

Europe; and they organised a club to support the movement, with Mr. Bryant for president.

I myself had glorious hopes I now look back on with bitter melancholy. I was one of the very few men who foresaw a glorious future for the British drama. It was then so thoroughly divorced from literature, and so degraded, that scholars in general believed it could never again rear its head, which once towered above all nations. But I was too well read in its previous fluctuations, and, above all, in their *causes*, to mistake a black blight on the leaves for a decayed root. England is by nature the most dramatic country in the world; piracy, while it lasts, has always been able to overpower nature, and always will; but, piracy got rid of, nature revives. The condition of the theatre, in 1851, was this—a province of France, governed by English lieutenants, writers without genius, petty playwrights, public critics, who could get their vile versions of a French play publicly praised by the other members of their clique. The manager was generally an actor thirsting for this venal praise. If he produced an original play, he was pretty sure not to get it; but, by dealing with the clique for stolen goods, he secured an article that suited him to a T; it was cheap, nasty, praised. The first-class theatres, whose large receipts qualified them to encourage the British inventor, barred him out with new French plays, or old English ones—anything they could steal; yet they could spend £80 a night for actors and singers.

Haymarket Theatre, 1851. Opened with Macready's fare-wells. Began its *pieces*, February 4, with " Good for Nothing" (French); February 6, " Presented at Court " (French); March 3, " Don Cæsar de Bazan " (French); March 8, "Othello;" March 25, "Tartuffe" (French); March 27, " Make the Best of It" (French); April 21, "Arline" (a piratical burlesque of an English opera); May 3, " Retired from Business " (English, *perhaps*); May 26, " Crown Diamonds " (French); June 18, "The Cadi" (French); June 23, "John Dobbs" (French); June 24, Mr. Hackett, an American actor, in Falstaff, &c.; July 1, " Grimshaw, Bagshaw, and Bradshaw" (French); July 7, " Son and Stranger " (German); August 13, "The Queen of a Day" (I don't know whether original or French); August 21, " His First Champagne " (French); "Tartuffe" and "The Serious Family " (both French); September 10, "Grandmother Grizzle" (French); October 11, "La Sonnambula" (Italian), " Grandmother Grizzle " (French), and " Grimshaw," &c.; October 14, " Sonnambula" and " Mrs.

White" (French); November 17, "Charles the Second" (French), "God save the King"—a Jacobite song, the words and treble by Henry Carey, the bass by Smith (Carey sang "God Save King James" till the tide turned against the Stuarts, and carried this melody with it, lines and all)—"Rough Diamond" (French); November 18, "The Ladies' Battle ' (French); November 25, "The Two Bonnycastles" (French); November 26, "The Beggar's Opera" (Old English); December 9, "The Man of Law" (French); December 2, "The Princess Radiant" (doubtful).

The Lyceum. January 1 to March 24, "King Charming" (French story dramatised), and farces; March 24, "Cool as a Cucumber" (French); April 21, "Queen of the Frogs" (French fairy tale); May 20, "Only a Clod" (French); June 4, "Court Beauties" (French); October 2, "Game of Speculation" (French), "Forty and Fifty" (French), "Practical Man" (English, I think); December 26, "Prince of Happy Land" (French story dramatised). This is no selection, but the whole business of these first-class London theatres, and a true picture of the drama in the City of Shakespeare.

I comprehended the entire situation, and saw that the new treaty was a godsend, and might give England back her drama, if supported heartily. I visited France, and many of her dramatists; we hailed the rising sun of justice together, and, as good words without deeds are rushes and reeds, I gave Auguste Maquet £40 for his new drama, "Le Château de Grantier."

The promised Act of Parliament came out. Alas!—what a disappointment! A penny dole, clogged with a series of ill-natured conditions. It was like a mother's conscience compelled to side with a stranger against the child of her heart—"Oh, they all tell me he is a blackguard; but he is such a darling." It was full of loopholes for the sweet pirate: full of gins, and springes, and traps for authors and honest traders.

International Copyright.—The State sells to the foreign author the sole right of translation and sale in England, for a petty period, on cruel conditions. 1. He must notify on the title-page of the original work that he reserves the right of translation. 2. He must register the original work at *our Stationers' Hall*—a rat-hole in the City—and deposit a copy gratis within three months after first publication. 3. Must publish authorised translation in England within one year. 4. Must register that translation, and deposit a copy in our rat-hole, within a certain time—15 & 16 Vict. cap. 12. In short, the State is "alma mater" to the rascal, "injusta noverca" to the honest trader.

The poor wretch, protected after this fashion, glares and trembles, and says to himself, " Incedo per ignes." The first stipulation is reasonable, and *all-sufficient ;* the rest are utterly superfluous, vexatious, oppressive, *ill-natured.* If the foreign author and his assignee escape by a miracle all these gins, springes, and author-traps, the State secures them for five years only what was their own for ever *jure divino, and by the law of France,* and by the universal human law of productive, unsalaried labour, without any gins, springes, or ill-natured, catchpenny conditions whatever.

International stage-right, 15 & 16 Vict. cap. 12.

Stipulations 1, 2, and 4, same as above.

3. Must *publish* the authorised translation in England within *three months* of registering original play, &c.

In this clause, and indeed in No. 2, you see the old unhappy confusion of stage-right with copyright. Why, in the name of common sense, is the dramatist, because he objects to be swindled in a *theatre,* to be compelled to *publish ?* Publication is not a dramatist's market. There is no sale for a play-book in England nowadays. How can the poor wretch afford to translate and *publish a translated play,* of which the public would not take six copies, though he should spend £100 advertising ? Such imbecile legislation makes one's blood boil. Was ever so larcenous a tax on honesty ? It is a pecuniary premium on Theatrical Piracy ; that kind of pirate does not print ; he merely steals and sells to the Theatre ; so his "alma mater," and our "injusta noverca," does not persecute *him* with any tyrannical and irrelevant tax applicable to *copyright,* but not to *stage-right.* It only bleeds the everlasting victim, the honest author.

But there was worse behind. When the victim of ten thousand wrongs has been bled out of all the money it costs to publish an unsaleable translation, and has escaped the gins, springes, author-traps, and probity-scourges, and looks for his penny dole, his paltry five years' stage-right, then he is encountered with a perfidious proviso.

" Nothing herein contained shall be so construed as to prevent fair imitation or adaptation to the English stage of any dramatic piece or musical composition published in any foreign country, but only of piratical translations."

Now, the English theatre has seldom played a translation ;

the staple piracy from 1662 to 1852, and long after, was by altering the names of men and places from French to English, shortening and vulgarising the dialogue, and sometimes combining two French pieces, and sometimes altering the sex of a character or two; sometimes, though very rarely, adding a character, as Mawworm in "The Hypocrite" adapted from "Tartuffe." But whether servile or loose, the versions from French pieces were *adaptations*, not honest translations; and all the more objectionable, since here a dunce gratifies his vanity as well as his dishonesty, and shams originality, which is a fraud on the English public as well as on the French writer; moreover, it is the adaptation swindle that turns French truths into English lies. The Legislature, therefore, appeared to say this:—"The form of piracy most convenient to the English dramatic pirate seems to be not direct reproduction; but colourable piracy. We will profit by that experience. We will compel the honest dealer to translate literally; we will put the poor devil to the expense of *publishing* his literal translation. No manager will ever play his literal translation. However, to make sure of that, we now legalise piracy in the established and fashionable form of fair adaptation or imitation."

This, after one's experiences of the Anglo-Saxon pettifogger, seemed to reveal that animal at work defiling the scheme of the Latin jurists, and ensnaring his favourite victim, an author's property: and so it turned out to be. We soon learned how the trick had been done: a piratical manager had employed a piratical writer to crawl up the backstairs of the House of Commons, and earwig Lord Palmerston, and get this proviso inserted to swindle the French dramatist. The Minister, I need hardly say, did not realise what a perfidy he was lending himself to, and the French Government had no chance of divining the swindle, because this thief's cant of "fair adaptations and imitations" is entirely English; the Frenchmen did not even know what the words meant, nor are they translateable; "imitations faites de bonne foi" has quite a different sense from "fair imitations;" and how could they suspect that a great nation, treating with them on professedly higher views of national justice than had heretofore prevailed, could hold out its right hand to receive protection of its main intellectual export—magazines, reviews, histories, biographies, novels—yet with its left hand slyly filch away the main intellectual export of the nation it was dealing with, in time of peace and in declared amity?

History, thank God, offers few examples of such turpitude. But why? It is only because legislators, in protecting any other class of property, are never so weak as to take advice of pirates—a set of God-abandoned miscreants, whose advice to us, and to you, Brother Jonathan, and to any other nation on the globe, is always a compound of Newgate and Bedlam.

When the French did find the Satanic juggle out, they concealed neither their disgust nor their contempt. They reminded each other that their fathers had used a certain phrase, " Perfide Albion," which we had treated as a jest. Was it such a jest after all? Could we discover a more accurate epitaph for this piece of dastardly juggling?

Here is a distich they applied :—

> "Comptez donc sur les traités signés par le mensonge,
> Ces actes solennels *avec art* preparés ; "

and here a quatrain on the " fair imitations " that our Legislature protected and secured *gratis* as soon as ever it had decoyed the poor honest gull into the expense of publishing the translation that no creature could try to read nor theatre would play :—

> "Quoiqu'en disent certains railleurs,
> J'imite, et jamais je ne pille.
> Vous avez raison, Monsieur Drille :
> Oui, vous imitez—les voleurs."

The Satanic proviso that disgraced us in the eyes of a noble nation recoiled, as it always does and always will, Brother Jonathan, upon the nation that had been inveigled into legalising piracy. It postponed the great British drama for another quarter of a century. Colourable piracy of French pieces being legalised instead óf crushed, drove the native dramatist off the boards. *The shops* were limited by monopoly (6 and 7 Victoria), and piracy enabled a clique of uninventive writers to monopolise *the goods*. If, by a miracle, a genuine dramatist got a play played, then piracy punished him in another way. The price was not a remuneration, but a punishment of labour and skill. I saved a first-class theatre from bankruptcy with a drama. I received only £110 ; and the last ten pounds I had to county-court the manager for ; gratitude is too good a thing to waste on that etherial vapour, yclept an author. For " Masks and Faces," a comedy which has survived a thousand French pieces, and more, Mr. Taylor and I received £150. In France it would have been £4000.

For " Two Loves and a Life," a drama that has been played throughout Anglo-Saxony, and is played to this day, we received £100. In France it would have been worth £5000. The reason is, a manager was—through bad legislation—a fence, or receiver of stolen goods, and he would only pay fence's prices even to inventors. I am known, I believe, as a novelist; but my natural gift was for the drama : my greatest love was for the drama; yet the Satanic proviso, and the colourable piracy it inflicted on the nation, drove me off the boards, and many other men of similar calibre. I beg attention to this, not as a personal wrong ; in that light I should be ashamed to lay it before the English and American public, but as one of a thousand useful examples, that nature gives way before piracy. Able men always did, and always must, turn from their natural market, choked, defiled, and lowered, by piracy, to some other less congenial business, where there is fair play. This is how American literature is even now depopulated. I invite evidence from American authors.

The Satanic proviso injured the drama. A French truth, I repeat, may be an English lie ; and, as the adapter puts English names of men and places to French pieces, this happened eternally. The maids and wives presented on the English stage were called Mrs. and Miss ; but the situations and sentiments were French. Thus the women of England were habitually misrepresented. Now the public gets tired of a shop that keeps selling false pictures of familiar objects.

The Satanic proviso injured our drama in a third way. Property never blocks the theatre ; piracy always. " The Courier of Lyons " was played in nearly every London theatre, one year, 1855 ; and made the theatre unpopular by monotony. " The Corsican Brothers " was played in every London theatre without exception, and in many of them at the same time. In the drama's healthy day each theatre played its own pieces. But, under the hoof of piracy, variety is crushed : in one month, viz., May 1852, the Princess's Theatre played " The Corsican Brothers," Surrey Theatre " Corsican Brothers," Haymarket " O Gemini ! "—a burlesque on the subject, and Olympic " Camberwell Brothers." Adelphi, which had played " The Corsican Brothers," was playing " The Queen of the Market " (" La Dame de la Halle "); Strand, " The Lost Husband " (" La Dame de la Halle "); Lyceum, " Chain of Events " (" La Dame de la Halle "). As for " Don Cæsar de Bazan," that piece entirely blocked the first-class London theatres for months; and I, who write these lines, fled to Paris, where "Don Cæsar" was property, merely to get away from the doomed city, where "Don Cæsar," not being property, had become a monotony-scourge, and an emptier of theatres into music-halls, public-houses, and Baptist chapels.

In 1859, though I had left the theatre in despair, I still thought it my duty to combat the Satanic proviso for the benefit of the nation and of other dramatists, whom it would otherwise stifle, as it had me. I wrote a book denouncing it on the two grounds of justice and public policy, and I appealed, in that book, to the commercial probity and good sense of the House of Commons, and the sense of honour in legal matters which resides, theoretically, in the bosom of the Peers. I sowed good seed, and it fell among stones. I hope for better luck this time. But were I sure to fail, and fail, as long as I live, I would still sow the good seed, that cannot wholly die ; for it is truth immortal.

There being, at that time, a great outcry against American piracy, I publicly denied that the United States had ever been guilty of any act so dishonest, disloyal, and double-faced, as Great Britain had committed by treating with France for international rights, and contriving, under cover of that treaty, to steal the main intellectual property of that empire ; and I offered to bet £70 to £40 this was so. "The Eighth Commandment," p. 156. I refer to that now, because it is a fair proof I am one who can hold the balance between my native country and the United States ; and such I think are the men to whom that great Republic should lend an ear ; for such men are somewhat rare ; they have some claim to be called citizens of the world, and are as incapable of deliberate injustice as sham patriots are incapable either of national justice or national wisdom.

In 1866 I was examined, before the House of Commons, by Mr. Goschen, and cross-examined by members rather hostile to my views. I answered 150 questions, most of them judiciously put; and full a third of them bore on the effects of national piracy in *injuring the nation that pirates*. Cross-examination trebles the value of evidence ; and therefore I recommend it with some confidence to the study of those, who care enough for the truth in these matters, to prefer the sunlight of experience to that Jack-o'-lantern, *à priori* reasoning. I have no time to quote more than one answer :—" If you strike out that clause (the Satanic proviso), I pledge you my honour as a gentleman that you will see a great drama arise in England." (Report of the Select Committee on Theatrical Licences. Price 3s. 8d. Index 9d. Hansard, Great Queen Street, London.)

1875.—Parliament has rescinded the Satanic proviso, and thereby laid the first stone of a great British drama, as time will show.

Between 1852 and 1875 I felt, with many others, that the American Legislature is cruel and unjust to authors; but I have never urged it with any spirit, because my noble ardour was chilled by a precept of the highest possible authority— to say nothing of its morality and good sense. I think it runs to this effect, errors excepted: "Take out first the beam that is in thine own eye, and then shalt thou see clearly to take out the mote in Brother Jonathan's eye."

Now this year, Parliament having at last taken the beam out of my eye, I do see my way to address a remonstrance to that great nation, which hangs aloof from modern progress, and selects for hatred, contempt, and outlawry, while living, those superior men, whose dead bones it worships.

CHARLES READE.

SIXTH LETTER

SIR,—INTERNATIONAL COPYRIGHT WITH AMERICA:—The question has been mooted for forty years, and various British Governments have made languid movements towards obtaining justice for British and American authors. These have failed; languor often does: so now faint-hearted souls say, "Oh, it is no use: you might as well appeal to the Andes against snow, or to a hog in his neighbour's garden for clemency to potatoes, as ask the Americans for humanity to British authors."

Before I can quite believe this, they must write out of my head, and my heart, that this American people, torn by civil war, and heartsore at what seemed our want of principle and just sympathy, sent over a large sum of money to relieve the British cotton-spinners, whom that war, and their own imprudent habits, had brought low. Moreover, I can never despair of a cause, because it has been bungled forty years. There is a key to every lock; and if people will go on trying the wrong keys for forty years that is no proof that the right key will fail for forty more. To find the right key, we must survey—for the first time—the whole American situation. It comprises five parties : the judges—the Legislature—the authors—the publishers—the people.

The *judges*—what, in speaking to a Frenchman, we call the law of England, is, in America, the common law of both countries; our common ancestors grew it: the American colonists carried it in their breasts across the Atlantic; and it has the same authority in the States as here : it bows to legislative enactments ; but, wherever they are silent, it is the law of the land. An American lawyer, who cites it with the reverence it really deserves, does not pay *us* any compliment. He is going back to the wisdom and justice of his own ancestors. Now Congress not having meddled with *international* copyright or stage-right, an English author's copyright in New York, A.D. 1875, is what it was in London before the statute of Queen Anne, and his stage-right what it was before 3 & 4 William IV.

Half our battle is won in the courts; for the American judges concede to an English author stage-right in unprinted dramas. "Keene *v.* Wheatley ;" 9 American Law Reg. 23. "Crowe *v.* Aitken ;" 4 Am. Law Review, 23, and other cases.

And they concede copyright in unpublished manuscripts ("Palmer *v.* de Witt," &c.).

If, under the latter head, they tied the sole right of printing to the paper and handwriting of the manuscript, our case would be hopeless. But they disown this theory, and give a British author the *incorporeal right*, that is, the sole right to print his composition, *though the pirate may be in as lawful possession of a copy as is the public purchaser of a printed book.* I shall now prove that full international copyright is included in that admission.

There are three theories of copyright at common law :—
The washerwoman's theory.
The lawyer's theory.
The mad sophist's theory.

THE WASHERWOMAN'S THEORY.—That there can be no incorporeal property at common law. An author's manuscript is property. If another misappropriates it, and prints the words, that is unlawful ; but the root of the offence is misappropriating the material object, the author's own written paper. Thus, if a hen is taken unlawfully, to sell the eggs she lays after misappropriation *is* unlawful.

The lawyer's and the sophist's theory both rest on a fundamental theory opposed to the above, viz., that an author's mental labour, intellectual and physical, creates a mixed property, words on paper; that the words are valuable as vehicles of ideas, and are a property distinct from the paper; and only the author has a right to print them under any circumstances. Examples :—Pope wrote letters to various people : they paid the postage ; the paper, and the inked forms of the letters, became theirs, and ceased to be Pope's. Curll possessed this corporeal property lawfully. Yet Pope restrained the printing. " Pope v. Curll."

Lord Clarendon gave a written copy of the famous history to a friend. That gentleman's son inherited it. Had Lord Clarendon's heir misappropriated this written paper, he could have been indicted, and sent to gaol. Yet, when the lawful possessor of the transcript sent it to press, with the words on it not written by the author's hand, but conveying the author's ideas, Lord Clarendon's heir sued him, nearly a century after the history was composed, and obtained heavy damages. " Duke of Queensberry v. Shebbeare." There are many other cases, including " Macklin v. Richardson," and " Palmer v. De Witt," lately tried in New York. But this peculiar position in " Queensberry v. Shebbeare " is the best to scrutinise. A is the lawful possessor, by inheritance, of a transcript. B is the author's heir. If B steals A's transcript he can be *indicted;* if A prints his own transcript, he violates the pure incorporeal copyright of B, and cannot be indicted, but can be sued on the case for violation of a property as incorporeal and detached from paper and all other material substance as any that was confirmed to an author by Queen Anne's statute, or the Acts of Congress *in re.*

THE LAWYER'S THEORY.—When an author exerts this admitted incorporeal right, by printing and publishing, a new party enters, the public purchaser ; he acquires new rights, which have to be weighed against the author's existing right strengthened by possession ; for the author has created a large material property under his title, which would be destroyed as property if his copyright was forfeited by publication.

How our ancestors dealt with this situation is a simple matter of history ; therefore we distrust speculation entirely and go by the legal evidence.

THE MAD SOPHIST'S THEORY rejects with us the washerwoman's theory, and concedes that an author has, at common law, intellectual property, or copyright, thus abridged—he has the sole right, under any circumstances whatever, to print his unprinted words. But, when he publishes, he sells the volumes without reserve; he cannot abridge his contract with the reader and retain the sole right under which he printed. He has abandoned his copyright by the legal force of his act, and this is so self-evident that the sophist *declines to receive evidence against it.* Whether copyright in printed books existed before Queen Anne's Act, he decides in a later age, whose modes of thinking are different, by *à priori* reasoning, and refuses to inquire how old the word " copy " is, or what is meant under the Tudor and Stuart Princes, in acts of State, licensing Acts, and legal assignments, or to look into the case of " Roper *v.* Streater," " Eyre *v.* Walker," or any other legal evidence whatever.

This was the ground taken by Justice Yates in " Millar *v.* Taylor." He founded a school of copyright sophists, reasoning *à priori* against a four-peaked mountain of evidence. He furnished the whole artillery of falsehood, the romantic and alluring phrases " a gift to the public," &c., the equivoques, and confusions of ideas, among which the very landmarks of truth are lost to unguarded men.

Since it is this British pettifogger who, in the great Republic, stands between us and the truth—between us and law—between us and morality—between us and humanity —between us and the eighth commandment of God the Father—between us and the golden rule of God the Son, Judge Yates becomes, like Satan, quite an important equivocator, and I must undeceive mankind about Judge Yates and his fitness to rule the Anglo-Saxon mind.

In " Millar *v.* Taylor," the case that has given Judge Yates so great a temporary importance in England and America, the main question was a simple historical fact: did copyright in printed books, which preceded legislation in France and Holland, also precede in England a certain enactment called Queen Anne's statute? No *à priori* reasoning was needed here. The Latin jurists used none to ascertain the identical fact in their own country, and, therefore, with no better evidence than we have, they are *unanimous.* We are divided by *à priori* reasoning on fact.

In " Millar *v.* Taylor " two modes of searching truth encountered each other on the narrow ground, each party rejecting the washerwoman's theory, and admitting pure copyright, but disputing whether in England it was forfeited by publication.

One method is by *à priori* reasoning, and was the method of the Greek sophists and mediæval schoolmen.

The other is by observation and evidence, and is the method of Lord Bacon and his pupils.

Scholars sometimes permit themselves to talk as if the former method was universal in the ancient world. That statement is excessive. Plain men, in their business, anticipated the Baconian method thousands of years ago, as the jury in "Millar *v.* Taylor" followed it. The Greek sculptors anticipated it, and their hands reached truth, while the philosophers, their contemporaries, were roaming after their will-o'-the-wisp,

"And found no end in wandering mazes lost."

There was the pity of it; those who, by learning, leisure, and ability, were most able to instruct mankind, were enticed by bad example and the arrogance of the intellect, into *à priori* reasoning, and diverted from docile observation; and so they fell into a system that kept the sun out and the door shut.

The other system, in 250 years, has enlightened that world which lay in darkness.

To test the systems, take any period of 400 years before Lord Bacon, and estimate the progress of the world in knowledge and useful discoveries. Then take the 250 years after Lord Bacon. I vary the figures, out of justice, to allow for increased population.

Lord Bacon was the saviour of the human intellect. He discouraged plausible conjecture, or *à priori* reasoning, and taught humble, close observation. Thereby he gave the key of the heavens to Newton, and the key of nature and her forces to the physical investigator, and the prying mechanic. Man began to cultivate the humble but wise faculty of observation; it grew by cultivation, and taught him how to wrestle with nature for her secrets, and extort them. There is scarcely a branch of useful learning that method has not improved 500 per cent. Of course, even since Lord Bacon, prejudice has, in holes and corners, resisted observation; but the final result is sure. *À priori* reasoning bled people to death with the lancet for two centuries after Bacon; but Bacon has conquered the lancet. A handful of Jesuits will tell you that the historical query, whether one Bishop of Rome has contradicted another in faith, must not be learned from contemporary history, but evolved by internal thought a thousand years afterwards. Well, that mediæval crotchet will go and Bacon stay. And so it must be, sooner or later, with everything, copyright at common law—the national expediency of piracy—the infallibility of men with mitres—*everything*. The world has tasted Bacon. It will never eat cobwebs again for long.

To put the matter in another form—Such of our common ancestors, Brother Jonathan, as invented phrases, were nearly always acute observers. They called a prodigal "a spend-thrift," having observed how often that character dissipated the savings of another man. A quarrel, with almost divine sagacity, they called not "a difficulty," which is a brainless word, but a *misunderstanding*, and they called a madman *a man out of his senses*. Why not out of his reason? Well, they had *observed*. The madman, who did not fly at their throats, but gave them time to study him, did nothing but reason all day and not illogically; but blinded by some preconceived idea, could not see, nor hear, nor *observe*. Intelligent madmen have busy minds, and often argue speciously, but start from some falsehood contradicted by their senses. The senses are the great gates of wisdom, and to the lunatic these gates are always more or less closed by prepossession. Now events distant by space or time cannot be seen nor heard by us, but by persons present. Where they get recorded *at the time*, the senses of the eye-witnesses have spoken; and the pupil of Lord Bacon must have recourse to the senses and report of those persons. Into that evidence he peers, and even cross-examines it if he can; and he can sometimes; for, when a dead witness makes an *admission*, it has the effect and value of a truth extracted from a living witness against his will. Where contemporary evidence is abundant and mani-form, it is very reliable, and the man who opposes *à priori* reasoning, or preconceived ideas to it, IS A LUNATIC IN THE SECOND DEGREE.

I feel that I am giving a large key to unlock a small box; but small keys have failed; and Cicero says well, "Errare, falli, labi, tam turpe est quam decipi." I will, therefore, in my next give The Baconian method *v.* the method of the ancients, or Millar *v.* Taylor, showing how an English judge proved, out of the depths of his inner consciousness, that copyright at common law could not have existed, even as a waggish Oxford professor proved, by the same method, that Napoleon Bonaparte could never have existed.

CHARLES READE.

SEVENTH LETTER

SIR,—The poet Thomson, in 1729, assigned the copyright of "The Seasons" to Millar, his heirs and assigns *for ever*. In 1763 Taylor printed "The Seasons" and Millar sued him: the case, as handled, turned mainly on whether copyright in printed books was before Queen Anne's statute. This being a mixed question of law and fact, the opinion of the jury was taken upon documentary evidence, the records of Stationers' Hall, and many ancient assignments of copyright drawn up by lawyers long before the statute, and others long after it. The defendant had powerful counsel: so this evidence doubtless was sifted, and kept within the rules. The jury brought a special verdict, in which are these words—"And the said jurors, upon their oath, further say that before the reign of her Majesty Queen Anne, it was usual to purchase from authors the perpetual copyright of their books, and assign the same for valuable considerations, and to make the same the subject of family settlements." The jury here were within their province; they swore not to a matter of law, but to a custom, in which, however, lawyers at different epochs had taken a part by drawing the legal assignments. Most of this evidence has melted away, but the sworn verdict of twelve unprejudiced men of the world remains, and, by the law of England and America, overpowers and indeed *annuls*, all *judicial conjectures* in this one matter of fact. On this basis the judges discussed the *law*, and Lord Mansfield, Mr. Justice Willes, and, above all, *Mr. Justice Aston*, uttered masterpieces of learning, wisdom, close reasoning, and common sense, that the instructors of youth in Harvard, Oxford, &c., would do well to rescue from their dusty niche, and make them teachers of logic, law, and morals, in universities and schools. They built on all the rocks: 1st, on the voice of conscience; on Meum and Tuum; on the sanctity of productive labour; on the title of labourer A to the fruits of A's labour, and the *primâ facie* absence of a title in B to the fruits of A's labour *without a just equivalent*. 2nd, on the *universal admission* that an author alone has a right to print his written words, and on the legal *consequence* that by exercising this sole right and creating a large *material* property under it, he keeps the right alive, not dissolves it, since common law abhors divestiture of an admitted right, and loss of property created by invitation of law,

From these *principles* they went, 3rdly, to special *evidence,* and traced the history of the exclusive right to print published books; showed it at a remote period called by the very technical and legal name the statute adopted centuries later; proved the recognition of this right by name in proclamations and decrees, and Republican ordinances, and three parliamentary licensing Acts under three different Sovereigns prior to Queen Anne's statute; the entire absence of dissent in the old judges, and their uniform concurrence when speak they did; their *dicta in re,* and their *obiter dicta*—as that "the statute of Charles II. did not give the right (copyright), but the action:" and "of making title to a copyright," and of "a copy" being a property paramount to the King's grant, and so on—and then they cited law cases in a series, beginning with "Roper *v.* Streater," long before the statute, and continued in equity long after the statute upon titles created long before the statute, as "Eyre *v.* Walker," where the assignment of the copyright was in writing dated 1657, and "Tonson *v.* Walker," where the assignment (Milton's "Paradise Lost") was dated 1667: "Motte *v.* Falkner," &c. They also cited the preamble, or historical preface, of the statute itself, and other matters. This reveals the Baconian method, and the true legal method, which goes by principles resting on large induction, and applicable to all citizens, impartially; and by the best direct evidence accessible. Against the Washerwoman's theory they cited "Pope *v.* Curll," and "Queensberry *v.* Shebbeare." Judge Yates accepted, though rather sullenly, "Pope *v.* Curll," and "Queensberry *v.* Shebbeare," and, in stating his own theory, forswore the washerwoman. He admitted that, before the statute, if any person printed an author's words without his express consent to print them, he acted unlawfully, *although he came by them by legal means, as by loan or devolution.* The word "devolution" he used expressly to keep within "Queensberry *v.* Shebbeare" (4 Burroughs, 2379).

But from that point he parted company with the judges and the jury, and undertook to prove, out of the depths of his inner consciousness, that the incorporeal right, which in "Queensberry *v.* Shebbeare," prevailed against sixty years' lawful possession of a written copy, could not *possibly* have continued against five minutes' lawful possession of a *printed* copy:—(*risum teneatis, amici*).

Yates.—"Goods must be capable of possession, and have some visible substance; for, without that, nothing is capable of actual possession." "Nothing can be an object of property which has not a corporeal substance," &c. This proposition repeated about six times.

"The author's unpublished manuscript is corporeal. But after publication by the true proprietor, the mere intellectual ideas in a book are totally incorporeal, and therefore incapable of any distinct separate possession ; they can neither be *"seized, forfeited, nor possessed,"* &c., and this discovery he repeated often, and rang the changes. "Can the sentiments themselves, apart from the paper, be taken in execution for a debt ? In case of treason, can they be forfeited ? If they cannot be seized, the sole right of publishing them cannot be confined to the author. There can be no property where there can be no forfeiture," &c. &c.

Behold the lunatic in the second degree ! His senses, if he had not been out of them, revealed that copyright in printed books existed by law while he spoke, and yet that ideas were incorporeal, and could not be *seized* nor *forfeited;* nor the sentiments taken in execution. The nature of ideas throughout creation was the same before and after Queen Anne's little trumpery statute ; yet here is a lunatic in the second degree, who either says Queen Anne's Parliament had repealed God Almighty in this particular, or says nothing at all ; for the sole point in dispute is, Did copyright in printed books exist amongst English human beings, before Queen Anne's statute, as it did amongst French human beings, before any special enactment—or did it exist in written works only ? Who but a lunatic in the second degree cannot see that the sole right of printing unpublished ideas is the very same property in *the ideas* as the sole right of reprinting the same ideas, and that all publication can do is to let in another claimant to the right of printing, viz., the public purchaser.

As to all his "galimatias" that there can be no property detached from a visible substance—the fool has gone and blundered into THE WASHERWOMAN'S THEORY, and blundered out of the insane sophist's. The insane sophist began with disowning the washerwoman. *She,* poor wretch, is contradicted not only by "Roper v. Streater," but by "Queensberry v. Shebbeare" and "Pope v. Curll," the cases Yates admits. But Lord Mansfield collared the insane sophist and would-be washerwoman on this, and literally pulverised his washerwoman's twaddle, with fifteen sledge-hammer sentences beginning thus :—"It has all along been

159

expressly admitted," and ending "under a commission of bankruptcy."

I do not cite the pulverising paragraphs, because there is no need. Yates's attempt to smuggle in the washerwoman's theory under the insane sophist's is self-evident, and has failed utterly; for to "Pope *v.* Curll," and "Queensberry *v.* Shebbeare," are since added "Macklin *v.* Richardson," and "Palmer *v.* De Witt," both death-blows to the washerwoman's theory. *Palmer* v. *De Witt.*—Robertson, English dramatist, wrote a comedy, "Caste," and played it all over England, but did not publish. He assigned the copyright, and stage-right, at common law, to Palmer, an American citizen. De Witt published "Caste" in New York. Palmer sued him, and the case was settled, by judgment for Palmer, who was, in law, the English author. (New York Court of Appeals, Feb. 27, 1872.) The judgment lies before me. There was no violation whatever of the manuscript. Nothing was misappropriated but the naked right to print and publish a composition, to which enormous publicity has been given by twenty prompt copies and fifty sets of parts, and representation in fifty theatres at least. Therefore this American Court of very high authority has gone with Lord Mansfield, and other great lawyers, and swept the very mainstay of Judge Yates's sophistry away for ever.

This narrows the question to forfeiture, or non-forfeiture, by publication, of copyright at common law. Now this *soi-disant* forfeiture, Queen Anne's Parliament treat, in the preamble, or historical prelude, as a *malpractice*, a violation of property; they say it is *unjust—cruel—*and *new;* which is pre-statutory evidence in the statute itself. Yates gives Queen Anne's Parliament the lie, and undertakes to prove, out of the depths of his inner consciousness, that this malpractice was—at the very moment when Parliament denounced it, and prepared, in imitation of *preceding* Acts, to *punish* it as a *misdemeanour—just, reasonable,* and *old.* Having set this very Parliament above the Creator, he now sets it below Yates. However, his argument runs thus: he says that we authors put forward ideas and sentiments, as the direct object of property at common law in old times, and insult common sense and justice in pretending that we could publish our ideas, yet reserve the right of printing those ideas for publication. This is plausible, and paves the way for his romantic phrases that have intoxicated ordinary minds, such as "the act of publication, when voluntarily done by the author himself, is virtually and necessarily a *gift to the public.*" Then handling it no longer as a donation but under the head of implied contracts, which is a much sounder view of the author's sale to the public purchaser, he says, neatly enough, the seller delivers it without restriction, and the buyer receives it without stipulation. Then he jumps to this droll inference :—" Nothing less than legislative power can restrain the use of anything." This, however, is a purely chimerical distinction ; the common law was founded partly on *Royal statutes*, largely conceived, and resembling maxims ; and limited uses are not altogether unknown to it ; every river is a highway, over which the public can pass, and even bathe in it, without infringing property ; but not always fish ; and a right of way obtained by use, or leased to the churchwardens, under which the public can lead its cow across a freeholder's field, gives no right to graze her *upon the path ;* and, if I let the public into my tea-garden at sixpence a head to eat all the fruit they can, no express stipulation is required to reserve the fruit *trees.* Moreover, Yates's position is too wide ; it lets in other nations ; now the French and Dutch common law give it the lie direct in copyright itself ; so, if we must reason *à priori*, the chances are fifty to one the English common law gave it the lie too.

But this is our direct reply—for the multiplying power of the press is so unique, it excludes all close comparisons—so far from claiming a property in ideas, that is the very thing the holders of copyright at common law did not claim. That is the claim of the patentees alone, as I shall show in the proper place.

So far from ideas becoming incorporeal after publication, &c., which statement of Yates's is a " galimatias," and an idiotic confusion ; ideas are incorporeal only at a period long antecedent to publication—viz., while they lie in the author's mind.

An author connects his ideas with matter once, and for ever, when he embodies them in a laboured sequence of words marked by his hand on paper. These written words are matter, by collocation, laboured sequence, and the physical strokes of a pen with a black unguent ; matter, as distinct from the paper as gas is from the pipe, and, though they *convey* mental ideas, the written words themselves are not so fine a material as gas, which yet is measured and sold by the foot. The phrase " intellectual labour " is an *équivoque* and a snare that has deluded ten thousand minds. It applies somewhat loosely to study; but an author's *productive labour* is only one species of skilled labour; it is physical, plus intellectual, labour, and those compositions which led to common-law rights were the result of long, keen labour, intellectual and physical, proved to be physical by the vast time occupied —whereas thought is instantaneous—and by shortening the life of the author's body, through its effects on the blood-vessels of the brain, which are a part, not of the mind but of the body. The said vessels get worn by an author's productive labour, and give way. This, even in our short experience, has killed Dickens, Thackeray, and perhaps Lytton. The short life of authors in general is established by statistics. See Neison's "Vital Statistics."

The words are the *material vehicle* of the ideas; the paper is the material vehicle of the words.

The author has, by admission of Yates, the sole right to do as follows, and does it:—He takes the written words, which are the vehicle of his ideas, to the printing compositor, and the compositor takes printed letters identical with the author's, though differing a little in shape—but that is a mere incident of the day; in the infancy of printing they were identical in shape, only worse formed—he sets the letters in formes, and passes them to the pressman. For this the compositor charges say £28. With the pressman, and not with the compositor, who is *a copyist for the Press*, begins the Press. Now comes the mechanical miracle which made copyright necessary and inevitable; the Press can apply *different* sheets to the *same* metal letters conveying the composition; thus a thousand different paper volumes are created in which the letters and the author's composition are *one*, but the volumes of paper a *thousand*. The volumes are now ready, *but not issued*: and I beg particular attention to the author's admitted position at common law one moment before publication. He has still, by law (Yates assenting), the sole right to print, and publish; he has created, *for sale*, a thousand volumes, under an exclusive legal right to create volumes *for sale*: he has added to his original legal right three equities:—1st, priority of printing, which is nothing against a legal title, but something against a rhapsodical title; 2nd, the peculiar expense of setting up type from written words; 3rd, occupancy; and the equitable right to sell again the thousand volumes, a large material property created under an exclusive legal title founded on morality and universal law, and conceded by Judge Yates. For the force of occupancy added to title, see Law, *passim ;* and for the force of the above special equity, see " Sweet *v.* Cator."

Well, the *man in possession* of the legal right, and *also* of the additional equities, and *also* of the material volumes, now does a proper and rational act, by which the public profits confessedly, an act such as no man was ever lawfully punished for ; he publishes, or sets in circulation, his one composition contained in many paper vehicles. He sells each volume say for six shillings to the trade, eight shillings to the public reader. What he intends to sell to the public reader for eight shillings, is—paper and binding, two shillings ; printers' work, sixpence ; useful or entertaining knowledge, *alias* his own labour, four shillings ; the right of using the ideas in many ways, of even plagiarising and printing them re-worded, and also the right of selling again the very thing the purchaser bought—the one material volume with its mental contents. *Primâ facie,* the contract, so understood, is not an unjust one to the buyer, nor an extortionate one for the seller. His profit, on these terms, does not approach the retail trader's, who, in practice, is the seller to the public, *yet forfeits nothing by the sale.* Now it is a maxim of the common law, that where two interpretations of a contract, express or implied, are possible, one that gives no great advantage to either party, and the other that gives a *monstrous* advantage to one party, the fairer interpretation is to be preferred, since men, meeting in business, are *presumed by the law to exchange equivalents ;* and this rule, established by cases, applies especially where a whole class of contracts is to be interpreted. Please observe that the ground I am upon, viz., of implied contracts, was selected by Yates, and I ask which interpretation, Yates's or ours, agrees with the undisputed common-law doctrine of equivalents ?

The purchase of books is a lottery. But there are a host of prizes. Lord Bacon's works gave the public purchaser a great deal more than a thousand million pounds' worth of knowledge and power ; yet he made no extra charge to justify a claim on his copyright founded on purchase of his volumes. The great books balance the little : and the buyer has the choice. Colonel Gardiner was converted in an afternoon, from vicious courses, not by a vision, but a duodecimo ; and that is a fact attested by Jupiter Carlyle. I didn't find it in my intestines, where Yates looks for facts. Many men, about the very time of " Millar *v.* Taylor," ascribed the salvation of their souls to a copy of Doddridge's " Rise and Progress of Religion in the

Soul." If a pupil of Yates, before purchase of Doddridge, that would be a great improvement in a reader's prospects— for 8s. Besides, after he has been converted from Yates's reading of the 8th of Anne, to Doddridge's reading of the 8th of Moses, and his soul saved, &c., he can lend or sell the volume. Then why pillage Doddridge for un-Yatesing him, and saving his soul dirt cheap? Find me the party to any other contract, who can eat his cake, yet sell it afterwards, like the honest purchaser of a good volume.

CHARLES READE.

EIGHTH LETTER

SIR,—The next intellectual article the insane sophist opposes to evidence is vituperation, or mendacity trading upon popular prejudice. "It is a monopoly opposed to the great laws of property," &c., repeated ten times. Now gauge his logic. He says: 1. The sole right of printing a man's own composition is a perpetual property at common law. 2. If the proprietor exerts that perpetual right lawfully, to the benefit of himself and the community, and law, mistaking him for a felon, divests him of it, the good citizen forfeits his *property*. 3. If law declines to abjure its abhorrence of forfeitures, and does not divest him of his sacred property, the sacred *property* becomes *monopoly*. How? by bare retention? by non-forfeiture? by continuation? Did ever continuation or non-forfeiture of a property metamorphose that property into a monopoly? So then if my hen and her chickens run upon a common, and law, having imbibed a spite against feathered property, lets the public in to scramble for them, I can scramble with the lot, but lose my *property* in my hen and chickens. But if law declares they are mine still, though my blind confidence has made it very easy to pirate them, then my *property* in *my* hen and *my* chickens becomes a monopoly—which word means the sole right to sell *any* hens or *any* chickens whatever. Is this a lunatic, or a liar?—or both?

I have no theory of my own about monopoly. I merely apply settled truths that idiots repeat like cuckoos but cannot apply. Monopoly is defined in the law-books, and justly defined, to be "an exclusive right to sell any *species* of merchandise"—" genus quoddam mercaturæ."

Property is a wider right over a narrower object. It is the

sole right of keeping, destroying, leasing, or selling, not a *species* of merchandise, but only that individual *specimen* of merchandise, or those individual specimens, which happen to be the man's own by law. One well-known historical feature of monopoly is that it was the creature of Royal prerogative ; another that it has always clashed in trade with undoubted property. In this kingdom are now no literary monopolies, but there is one dramatic monopoly, viz., the exclusive right of the licensed managers to represent any play whatever— yours, mine, or theirs (6 & 7 Victoria). But literary monopolies infested the ages Anachronist Yates misrepresents ; and those men of the common law he underrates—and they were great masters of logic compared with him—always called them by their right name, "Patents." Under Henry VIII., one Saxton had the sole right to sell printed maps and charts, and, under Elizabeth, Tallis and Bird, to sell music. Both were vetoes on a species—nature, monopoly—name, a *patent*—root, prerogative. The owners of copyright groaned publicly, again and again, under these infractions of their property by prerogative patents ; and, after the second revolution, when prerogative was staggering under repeated blows, literary property, or copyright, took a literary patent or monopoly boldly by the throat, in "Roper v. Streater." Streater, *law patentee*, had, from the Crown, the sole right to sell law reports *by whomsoever written*. This was monopoly —an exclusive right to sell a *species* of literary composition. Roper bought of Judge Croke's executor the copyright or sole right to reprint Judge Croke's reports, and line his trunk with them or sell them—which is property.

And this muddlehead Yates could look with his moon-calf's eye at "Roper v. Streater," yet call literary property in a man's own (by purchase) printed composition, a monopoly, even when he saw literary monopoly and literary property cheek by jowl in a court of law—fighting each other as rival suitors—and the monopoly in a *species* of books declaring its nature, its distinctive title, "patent," and its root in prerogative ; and the literary property declaring its nature, its distinctive title, copyright, and its root in common law. So that, in "Roper v. Streater," the plaintiff gives Yates the lie on behalf of property ; the defendant gives him the lie on behalf of monopoly ; and the judges give him the lie in the name of the common law, when he calls copyright in a man's own printed book " *a monopoly contrary to the great laws of property.*" In my very first letter I offered the statesmen and lawyers

Yates has gulled with this fallacy a bet of £150 to £50 a man's copyright in his own printed book is *property*, and not *monopoly;* yet of all the men who are so ready to swindle authors at home and abroad out of a million pounds by means of this pettifogger's lie, not one has had the honesty nor the manhood to risk £50 *of his own against* £150 *of an author's*, upon the lie. I hope the world will see through this, and loathe it, and despise it, as I do.

To sum up the bag of moonshine.—To any man who has read history at its sources, as Mansfield and Blackstone did, Yates's whole picture of old England is like an historical novel written by an unlettered girl. She undertakes, like him, to present antiquity; and what she does portray is the little bit of her own age she has picked up, its thoughts and phrases. Under the Tudors and the Stuarts her characters are impregnated with modern views of liberty, and rhapsodise accordingly: they have even a smattering of "political economy" and let you know it; and they say "the Sabbath"—"illusions"—"developments"—"to burke an inquiry"—"the fact of my being so and so," meaning "the circumstance of my being so and so,"—and her counsel address the jury for a criminal, and you may thank your stars if Lady Jane Grey does not lay down her Longinus (of whom there was not a copy in the kingdom) and waltz with the Spanish Ambassador. The sentiments and the phrases Judge Yates ascribes to men under the Tudors, the Stuarts, the Commonwealth, and the Dutchman, are all pure anachronisms, quite as barefaced to any scholar as those in a virgin's novel. Old England never personified "the public," as Yates fancies it did, and "Fur Publicola," or the patriot thief of copyright, was yet unborn. The men who built seven gables to one house, and breakfasted on ale, had no such extravagant anticipations of liberty as to despoil private property in its sacred name. Indeed "copy" was a word oftener used than "liberty," under James I., and even when liberty began to struggle, it was against power in high places, not property in low ones. It cut down prerogatives; it did not run away with fig-trees because the proprietor sold it the *figs.* The tall talk, the bombastical mendacity, "publication of a *volume* being a *gift* of the *copyright* to the *public*"—"a property in ideas," &c., all this rhapsodical rubbish emanated from romantic pettifoggers, gilding theft, at a known date—namely, between 1740 and 1765, and the ideas were not a month older than the varnish, for they were all invented, not by judges, but by *counsel* for the defence of post-statutory piracies. Find me this slip-slop defiling the mouths of the old judges.

So much for *à priori* reasoning against evidence. What else was to be expected? The system of reasoning that kept the world dark for ages, it would be odd indeed if that system could not darken a single subject, and turn so small a thing as a pettifogging judge into so common a thing as a lunatic.

THE BACONIAN METHOD *v.* THE METHOD OF THE DARK AGES.

Evidence on one line may mislead, but concurrent evidence never. By concurrent evidence I mean veins of evidence starting from different points, but converging to one centre. Three distinct coincidences, pointing to one man as a murderer, have always hanged him in my day. I have many examples noted. Almost the greatest concurrence of heterogeneous evidence *on any historical fact whatever,* is that which proves copyright at law in printed books before Queen Anne; which also proves an Englishman has full copyright in the United States.

First let me ask—What is A WORD? The insane sophists seem to fancy it is a thing, or else air. It is neither. It is defined, and justly, by the logicians, "the current sign of an established thing." It can never precede the thing signified. We all know the word-making process; for we have all seen it. There was no word more wanted than "telegram," yet it was not coined till years after the thing signified. I saw the verb "to burke" created. It was coined about six months after Burke, who smothered folk for the anatomists, was hung; but it took years to penetrate the kingdom. When a word gets to be used by different classes, governing and governed, that is the voice of the nation, and its currency shows the thing to be full-blown and long-established. It is simply idiotic to look, with moon-calf eye, at an ancient popular word, and bay the moon with conjectures that no ancient thing was signified.

Heads of the evidence against forfeiture of copyright by publication.

1. The word "copy" from the Tudor Princes to Queen Anne's statute, and in the statute, and after the statute, always used to signify the sole right of printing before and after publication. That alone bars Yates's theory that publication dissolves the property.

2. The ancient use of this technical word in *disconnected*

things and *places*, yet always to denote property and occupation.
Example *A.*—Entries of sales and transfers of copyright, from
1558 to 1709, at Stationers' Hall, by occupiers. Proviso in
1582 that where the king had licensed any individual to
print, the licence should nevertheless be void, if the copyright
belonged to another. *B.*—Recognition of " copy " as property
in Acts of the Star Chamber, and Republican ordinances, both
valid as *historical evidence,* and in the licensing acts of Parliament 13 & 14 Charles II., 1 James II., c. 7, 4 William and
Mary, c. 24, which are evidence, and something more, since,
in all these, Royal Parliaments, having the same powers as
Queen Anne's, protected, by severe penalties, that very property at law in published books which Yates divines out of
his inside had expired by publication. Either these licensing
Acts were copyright Acts—which is absurd—or they protected
copyright as it existed for ever at common law. Here " copy,"
or " copyright," might very well imitate Des Cartes, and say,
" Protegor; ergo sum." *C.*—Use of the old word " copy,"
in Queen Anne's statute. The first statute on any matter
is written under the common law. Even this truism has
escaped the babblers on copyright. In Queen Anne's Act,
the word " copy " is used six times in its common-law sense ;
and it is first applied, viz., in sect. 1, not to manuscripts on the
eve of publication, but to printed books; and the preference
antiquity had for the printed book over the MS. is here
continued ; twenty-one years the minimum term to a published book, fourteen to a MS. on the eve of publication. Is
that how Yates talks about the MS. and the book ? *D.*—
Recognition of the word, and thing, in business. Public and
notorious sales of ancient copyrights, some of them famous :
" The Whole Duty of Man ;" Dryden's copyrights, both
dramatic and epic ; Milton's, Southern's, Rowe's, and *some* of
Defoe's, Swift's, and Addison's. *E.*—Several assignments of
" copy " for ever, that now survive only in the verdict of the
jury, " Millar *v.* Taylor." A vast number drawn after the
statute upon the perpetual common-law right : one, referred
to in a former letter, survives in print, " George Barnwell,"
ed. 1810. *F.*—The use of the word " by lawyers " in these
pre-statutory agreements, also in the declaration " Ponder *v.*
Bradyl," an action on the case brought for piratical printing
of " The Pilgrim's Progress," " of which "—so runs the plaint
—" the plaintiff was, and is, the true proprietor ; whereby
he lost the profit and benefit of his ' copy.' " This brief and
technical statement of the grievance is not like a pleader

groping his way by periphrasis to a doubtful right. The pleader is on a beaten track.

3. The terms on which Milton leased the copy of " Paradise Lost " to Simmons, in 1667. £5 for the first edition, £5 for the second edition, £5 for the third. (See Todd's " Life of Milton.") This contradicts Yates, and his theory of forfeiture by publication, as precisely as A *can* contradict B *in advance.* When the liar speaks first, true men can fit the contradiction to the lie, in terms ; but, when the honest men speak first, the liar can evade their direct grip, by choice of terms ; for he has the last word. Put yourself in the place of Simmons ; if you were a publisher, and publication forfeited copyright, would you agree to give an author *the very same sum* for the second edition, and the third, *as for the first* ? I am quite content to refer Simmons's treaty with Milton to Messrs. Harper & Co., Messrs. Osgood, Ticknor & Co., Messrs. Appleton & Co., Messrs. Sheldon & Co., New York publishers. They shall decide between Yates and me. Mr. Justice Yates says Simmons's was an agreement with Milton, under the common law, for the mere sale of early sheets, and I say Mr. Justice Yates is a romancer. Now multiply this evidence by a hundred. *We* only know this business (Milton and Simmons) through the accidental celebrity of the book ; but the jury, in 1769, had a pile of examples before them.

4. The subsequent history of " Paradise Lost." Paid by Simmons to John Milton £5 in 1667. In 1669, £5 for the second edition. In 1674, £5 for the third edition, paid to Milton's widow. In 1680, sale of the copyright, for £8, Dame Milton to Simmons. Simmons, in two years, sold the copyright to Aylmer for £25 ; and Aylmer, 1683, sold half to Tonson, and, in 1690, the other half for a considerable sum. Soon after that a vast public sale set in ; yet Tonson held the copyright undisturbed. The temptation was strong ; but so was the common law. It was never pirated till 1739, seventy-two years after first publication. It was no sooner pirated than Tonson moved the court. It had no protection under the Act. That protection expired in 1731. A judge, who was a ripe lawyer before Queen Anne's statute, and knew the precedent common-law right, restrained the piracy at once under the common law, " Tonson *v.* Walker."

Legal History—1667–1710, protected by common law alone, and never pirated. 1710–1731, protected by common law and statute. 1732 to 1774, by common law only. Protected by injunction, 1739, and again in 1751.

5. The verdict of the special jury in "Millar *v.* Taylor." They were not men blinded by any preconceived notion; they were twelve men of the world; they sifted the evidence, and found disjunctively that it was "usual, before Queen Anne, to purchase from authors perpetual copyrights, *and* to assign the same from hand to hand, *and* to make them the subject of family settlements:" all those disjunctive findings are equally good against the public claimant, unless Yates can prove it was also the custom before Queen Anne to settle Bagshot Heath, and Wimbledon Common, and ten turnpike roads upon son Dick, with a mortgage to nephew Tom, and a remainder to cousin Sal. His legal objection that custom short of immemorial cannot make a legal title is specious. But *he forgets;* the root of our title is not in anything so short as what lawyers call immemorial custom. Our title is *acquired* by productive labour, and is personal property—a legal right six times as old as the British nation. The narrow question of fact the jury dealt with was this—was it usual for the act of publication to dissolve in one moment the perpetual right Judge Yates admits, a right acquired not by custom, if you please, but by productive labour and universal law? For its modest office of *interpreter* of law, applied to so narrow a matter as non-forfeiture of an admitted right, the custom of two hundred years (solidified by a law case or two), and contradicted by no elder nor concurrent custom, is more than sufficient—"consuetudo interpres legum." The special jury were educated men; impartial men; sworn men; many men; unanimous men; Yates was one unsworn man, with a bee in his bonnet. The twelve jurors were the constitutional tribunal, chosen of old by the Kingdom, and still chosen by the great Republic to try such issues. The one Yates was, as respects this issue, an unconstitutional tribunal appointed by himself, and no more sworn to try that issue than Dr. Kenealy was sworn to try the issue in the "Queen *v.* Baker."

The verdict of that jury is *law;* and the usage of the kingdom for ages before Queen Anne is proved to be non-forfeiture by publication, and proved on evidence since dispersed; and therefore PROVED TO THE END OF TIME.

6. The preamble of the statute. This is pre-statutory evidence, and Yates says it accords with his views. The

reader shall judge. I will draw a preamble honestly embody-ing his views—as every candid mind shall own—and I will place it cheek by jowl with Queen Anne's prelude.

PREAMBLE À LA YATES.	PREAMBLE OF THE ACT 8TH ANNE.
Whereas, for the greater en-couragement of writers and other learned men, to produce laborious and useful books of lasting benefit to mankind, it is expedient to restrict, for certain times, and under certain conditions, that just liberty, which the subjects of this realm have hitherto enjoyed, of reprinting and publishing all such works as by publication have become common property; be it enacted, &c.	Whereas printers, booksellers, and other persons, have of late fre-quently taken the liberty of print-ing, reprinting, and publishing books, and other writings, with-out the consent of the authors, or proprietors, of such books and writings, to their very great detri-ment and too often to the ruin of them and their families; for preventing therefore such prac-tices for the future, be it en-acted, &c.

I make no comment. I but invite ripe men to inspect this as intelligently as girls do Sir Octopus. Eyes and no eyes have muddled copyright long enough.

7. Law cases. *A.*—"Roper *v.* Streater." King's Bench. *Alias* copyright, or literary property, *v.* monopoly.

Judgment of the whole Bench for copyright at law against monopoly and prerogative.

B.—"Roper *v.* Streater." House of Lords.

The Lords admitted perpetual copyright at law, but de-clared the king had a paymaster's claim to judge Croke's reports because he paid the judges and acquired a copyright in their decisions. Thus they smuggled him in as *proprietor at common law.* Yates's theory of forfeiture by publication never occurred to the mind of any judge, either in the King's Bench or the House of Lords.

C.—The injunctions soon after the statute. Here there are two things to be considered. 1st. A judge does not roll out of his cradle on to the woolsack. Sir Joseph Jekyl was a ripe lawyer in 1700, when "Roper *v.* Streater" was tried in the Lords. He saw the common-law right long before the statute, and went by it after the statute, and against the literal words of the statute; for they affix a term, and so could never *suggest* a new perpetual right. In 1735 he restrained a piracy on "The Whole Duty of Man," published in 1657 ("Eyre *v.* Walker").

2nd. In those days an injunction really meant "*an injunction*

to stay waste of some property not disputable at law." Where
there was a shadow of doubt at Westminster no equity judge
would ever grant an injunction. This is notorious. Consequently the injunctions granted on the perpetual common-
law right, by judges so timid, are evidence not only of their
own adhesion to the perpetual common-law right, but proves
that all the contemporary judges at Westminster concurred
tacitly. Agreeably to this Lord Mansfield distinctly declares
that the first doubt, which ever arose about the perpetual
right, was in " Tonson v. Collins ; " and the Court of Chancery,
on hearing a mere whisper of that doubt down at Westminster,
instantly refused the injunction, because of the doubt, though
they did not share it. I myself know from quite another
source that they even suspended their proceedings in " Macklin
v. Richardson " because " Millar v. Taylor " was pending in
the King's Bench. Therefore the chain of injunctions they
granted between 1735 and 1751, on the perpetual common-
law right, were *post-statutory acts by pre-statutory minds representing the whole judicial opinion of the nation before and after
the statute.*

8. Admissions.—This is the highest kind of evidence. *A.—*
Milton attacked a parliamentary licensing Act with great
spirit. When a man falls upon a measure in the heat of
controversy he is seldom nice. Yet this polemic and great
enthusiast for liberty drew the reign at private property, and
solemnly approved the constitutional clause in the Act, the
severe protection of copyright. *B.—*The petitioners to Parliament in 1703. It was their interest to make a strong case
for parliamentary interference. Yet they *admitted* they had
an action on the case against pirates, and had no fears of a
verdict; but could not get sufficient *damages,* nor enforce
them, because the pirates were paupers. The force of this
unwilling evidence has never been justly appreciated.

C. — A Legal Phenomenon. — Judge Yates had a peck at
several minor cases, but never once, in a discourse that lasted
three hours, did he dare to touch " Roper v. Streater," either
in the King's Bench or the House of Lords. Now when a
lawyer dare not call his own principal witness, we all know
fact is dead against him ; and, when he affects to ignore the
leading case against him, that means he cannot get over the
law of that case, and knows it. Of course a more honest
judge would have faced it, and. either got over it, or else
given in to it. Indeed, there is no other recorded instance in
which a dissentient puisne judge ever shirked the leading case

relied on by the chief of his court and the other puisnes in any case so fully reported as "Millar *v.* Taylor." It is phenomenal. Every practical lawyer knows in his heart what it means, and it is a game that only pays with dull or inexperienced men. To us, who know courts of law, and the tact of counsel in gliding, with a face of vituline innocence, over what they cannot encounter, it is but shallow art; for it blows the gaff; and the critic goes at once to the ignored case, to see *why it was ignored.* Well, Yates ignored "Roper *v.* Streater" because he wanted people to believe two infernal falsehoods—(1) that perpetual copyright at law in printed books did not exist before Queen Anne, and (2) that, had it existed, it would have been *a monopoly opposed to property.* Now, in both these particulars, Roper, or property, gave him the lie—Streater, or monopoly, gave him the lie—and all the judges, in both courts, gave him the lie. That is why he evaded "Roper *v.* Streater," and the unprecedented evasion is *evidence* that he knew it smashed him.

Thus "Palmer *v.* De Witt," and the other cases, backed by common sense and universal law, prove a man's perpetual incorporeal property in the fruit of his own skilled labour. That law, deviating from all its habits, divested a man of so sacred a right because he exercised it, is a chimera supported only by *à priori* reasoning and romantic phrases born about 1750, and *unknown to the old judges.* First we answer a fool according to his folly, and pull his chimera to pieces. Then we answer him not according to his folly, but on the great Baconian method. And now this is clear; either Bacon was an idiot, or Yates was an idiot. We prefer Bacon, and to go, in a matter of fact, by the general usage, and the sense of the old kingdom, sworn to on evidence by a jury, and confirmed and solidified by a chain of reported law cases, beginning before the statute and continuing by the force of common law after the statute, in a perfect catena; also the *obiter dicta* of the old judges, and their *dicta ad rem,* all which heterogeneous evidence is "uncontradicted by any usage, book, judgment, or saying." *Teste* Lord Mansfield. So then "Robertson *v.* De Witt" and the complete proof *supra* of non-forfeiture by publication at common law give us copyright in printed books in the United States. We claim it from the judges at Washington, should we be driven to fight it in that form, and meantime we appeal to their consciences to back us with the Legislature of their country. For, if Robertson, making twenty copies of "Caste," and fifty sets of parts, which is multiplication of copies in a way of trade, and handing the parts to two hundred different actors—a reading public—and delivering the words for money to about a million spectators who pay, cannot by the common law be pillaged of his sole right to print and publish, what a farce it is to pretend on *grounds of common law* that another British writer, for publishing a book and selling one hundred copies in Great Britain, can be lawfully despoiled in the United States of his sole right, in spite of Blackstone and Mansfield, and on the ground of a mere variation in the *mode* of publicity and the *way* of selling. By such reasoning law is divorced from common sense and from all ancient interpretation and usage, and from even the shadow of morality. Now law *exists*, not for the sake of law, but of morality. CHARLES READE.

NINTH LETTER

SIR,—The power of judges is often crippled by precedents, that revolt their consciences and their sense; but a Legislature is happier; the justice it sees, that it can do. Now, when literary property was first seriously discussed in the States, the question whether copyright is a property or a monopoly, a natural right or a creature of prerogative, had just been discussed in England, and the Legislature of Massachusetts read " Millar *v.* Taylor" and " Donaldson *v.* Becket," and decided between the dwarf sophist Yates, and the great lawyer Mansfield, in very clear terms. I beg particular attention to this, that Justice Yates pointed to the *title* of Queen Anne's statute, as " an Act for the encouragement of learning, by vesting the copies (copyrights) of printed books in the authors or purchasers," and said very fairly that the term " vested" implied that the right did not exist before, in the opinion of Parliament. To this Lord Mansfield replied that the *title of an Act is no part of an Act;* and that in the body of the Act the word " to *vest*" is not used, but the word " to *secure*," and that the preamble would decide the question, even if a title could be cited against the body of an Act, for the preamble is full and clear in its recognition of the then existing property.

In March 1783, the Legislature of Massachusetts gave judgment on this question of title *v.* body and preamble, as precisely as if Mansfield and Yates had referred it to them.

They passed their first Copyright Act under this title—" An Act for the purpose of *securing* to authors the exclusive right and benefit of publishing their literary productions for twenty-one years." Having elected between " vest " and " secure " in their title, they passed to the second point; and, to leave no shadow of a doubt as to their views, drew such a preamble, as even Mr. Justice Yates, who affects to misunderstand Queen Anne's preamble, could hardly twist from its meaning; and I shall be grateful to any American critic, who will do American and English authors so much justice as to inspect the comparative preambles I put together in my last and compare both with this which I now cite :—

" Whereas the improvement of knowledge, the progress of civilisation, the public weal of the community, and the advancement of human happiness, greatly depend on the efforts of learned and ingenious persons in the various arts and sciences : As the principal encouragement such persons can have to make great and beneficial exertions of this nature must depend on the legal security of the fruits of their study and industry to themselves; and, as such security is one of the *natural rights* of all men, there being no *property* more peculiarly *a man's own* than that which is produced by *the labour of his mind*, therefore to encourage learned and ingenious persons to write useful books for the benefit of mankind, Be it enacted," &c. 1 Mass. Laws, 94, ed. 1801.

The other States followed this example and these sentiments; all avoid the word " vest " and employ the word " secure," and all, or most of them, recognise the *security* of an author's property as " a right perfectly agreeable to the principles of natural justice and equity." See the excellent work on copyright of G. T. Curtis, an American jurist, p. 77.

The very idea of " monopoly " is absent from all these Acts; they emanated from men who were lovers of liberty and constitutional rights, and had shown how well they could fight for them; whereas canting Camden illustrated his peculiar views of the common law by not uttering one word of objection in the House of Lords to a parliamentary tax upon the Colonies for the benefit of England; an usurpation it would be as difficult to find in the law of England as it is easy to find copyright there.

From these sound principles of justice and national policy the Legislature of the United States has fallen away, and listened this many years to cant, and the short-sighted greed of a Venetian oligarchy sticking like a fungus on the fair trunk of the Republican tree. But I dare say not one member of Congress knows how unjust and unwise is the present state of statute law, as regards British and American authors. It is not only injustice we writhe under, but bitter, and biting, and inconsistent *partiality*.

Even little lawyers, though their mental vision is too weak to see the essential difference between patent-right and copy-right, have a sort of confused notion that copyright is a trifle more sacred, and consistent with common law, than the various and distinct monopolies, just and unjust, which the narrow vocabulary of law huddles together under the term patent-right. Yet, in this great and enlightened Republic, inter-national copyright and stage-right, *by statute*, are refused, and international patent-right established.

The distinction.is a masterpiece of partiality, immorality, and inconsistency. The patent on new substances discovered or imported is a monstrous, unconstitutional restraint of just liberty, and will be abolished whenever Legislature rises to a science. The patent of invention is salutary. It is the exclusive right to carry out and embody, by skilled labour, one or two bare and fleshless ideas, but sometimes of prodigious value to the world : oftener, of course, not worth a button.

The patent of invention is a mild monopoly in a species or sub-species of ideas ; but copyright in bare ideas does not exist. Copyright cannot arise until the bare and fleshless ideas of the author, infinitely more numerous than a patentee's, have been united with matter, and wrought out by the *mental* and *physical* labour of the writer, which *physical* labour accelerates the death of his body. An author's physical posture, when at work, is the same as a printing compositor's physical posture—see the famous portrait of Dickens at work —and his physical labour is similar, and equally bad for the body, whereas thinking and sweating at the same time are healthy. The author does the intellectual and physical labour not only of the architect or the mechanical *inventor*, but also of the *builder* or of the skilled *constructor*, and his written manuscript corresponds *not with the specification of a patent, or the plan of a house, but with the wrought article, and the built house*. The printing press adds nothing to the author's pro-duction ; it does not even alter the vehicles, but only improves them, and that only of late years, since running hand. The modern manuscript is paper with a certain laborious sequence of words marked on it in ink by skilled labour ; the book is paper with the same laborious sequence of words marked on it by mere mechanical labour taking little time. Let A read from the manuscript and B from the book, and both readers deliver the same *complete production,* corresponding with the patented or patentable article, not with the bare specification.

This object of property, the author's material web of words, has not, in itself, the value of a patentable article. Its value lies in its unique power of self-reproduction by means of the actor or the press. Mechanical articles of very moderate value are more valuable *per se* than any author's MS., but mechanical articles have no power of self-reproduction. There is no magic machine with which three quiet idiots, without an atom of constructive skill, can reproduce steam-engines, power presses, and sewing-machines. But three quiet idiots, with the printing press, can, without one grain of the original author's peculiar art, skill, and labour, reproduce exactly his whole composition, and can rob him of the entire value in his object of property, because, without the sole right of printing, his object of property has not the value of a deal shaving, whereas an article that might be patented, but is not, is worth *ninety-two per cent. of the same article patented.*

Thus the American Legislature outlaws the complete, executed, wrought out *property* of a Briton, and protects his inchoate monopoly or exclusive right to go and work upon certain bare intellectual ideas, *provided they are bare ideas applicable to mechanics.*

Take this specification to a Patent Office. "I have invented a young man and two sisters in love with him. They were amiable till he came, but now they undermine each other to get the young man; and they reveal such faults that he marries an artful jade who praised everybody."

You apply for a patent or monopoly of these bare ideas, this little sub-species of story. You are refused, not because there is no invention in the thing—there is mighty little, but there is as much as in nine patents out of ten: where is the author who could not sit on a sofa and speak *Patents?*—but because the common law, whose creature copyright is, protects in an author, not invention, but constructive labour; gives him no property in bare ideas, but only in a laboured sequence of written words which *convey* ideas, but are produced by physical and intellectual labour mixed, and are distinctly material in nature and character, though they carry an intellectual force and value.

The piratical imitation of a patented sewing-machine is only *imitation* by skilled workmen of the patentee's ideas; it is not identical *reproduction* of his wrought-out and embodied ideas, by mere mechanics working a stealing machine. To pirate a patented article you must employ the same kind of *constructive* skill the patentee, or his paid constructors employ, and then you only mimic; but to pirate an author and steal his identical work, none of an author's skill or labour is required. All the brains required to reproduce mechanically that sequence of words, which is an author's object of property, are furnished to this day by John of Gutenberg, who invented the machine by which an author lives or dies, as law protects him, or lets thieves rob him with a stealing instrument worked by mere mechanics.

So then the American Legislature protects a foreigner's *monopoly*, and steals a foreigner's *property*. The monopoly this great Republic protects is the creature of the British Crown, to which the great Republic owes nothing, and the property it outlaws is a property that arose in the breast and brain and conscience of our common ancestors. They, whose wisdom and justice founded this property in England, were just as much Americans as English, and we all sprang from those brave, just, and honest men.

To swindle poor, weak, deserving, private men of a kindred nation out of this sacred property, which our common ancestors created and venerated and defended against the Crown in " Roper *v.* Streater," as the United States defended their rights against a Parliament usurping Russian prerogatives, a property which Milton revered, whose heart was with the Pilgrim Fathers, and all just liberty whatever ; and to protect a Briton's monopoly, the mere creature of arbitrary prerogative—this double iniquity, I say, is legislation that disgraces the name of legislation and national sentiment ; it is a prodigy of injustice, partiality, and inconsistency. What ! I spend two thousand hours' labour on a composition ; to be sold it must be wedded to vehicles, paper, type, binding, and it must be advertised. I pay the paper-makers, the printers, the binders. I pay the advertisements : the retail trader takes twenty-five per cent. of my gross receipts; the publisher justly shares my profits. The book succeeds. I cross the water with it, and its reputation earned by my labour, and my advertisements ; I ask a trifling share of the profits from an American publisher, who profits by *me* as much as ever my *British* publisher did. " You ! " says he, " you are *nobody* in this business. I shall pay for the *vehicles,* but not for the *production* that *sells* the *vehicles.* I shall pay the paper-makers, and also the printers and binders, Britons or not. But I shall take *your* labour gratis, on the pretence that you are a Briton." The American public pays a dollar for the book; fifty-five cents of the value is contributed by the English author. The various labourers, who are all paid, make up the forty-five cents amongst them. He who alone contributes fifty-five per cent. is the one picked out of half-a-dozen workmen concerned to be swindled out of *every cent*, and the Legislature never even suspects that by so doing it disgraces legislature and mankind. An Englishman writes a play, mixing labour with invention. The stage carpenter contributes a petty mechanical idea suggested by the scene; he uses wavy glass at an angle under limelight to represent the water. The play crosses the Atlantic; anybody steals it for all the Legislature cares, but, if they touch my carpenter's demi-semi-invention, his bare fleshless intellectual idea of placing an old substance, glass, at an angle under another old thing, limelight—" Halte là—ne touchez pas à la Reine !" The creature of Crown Prerogative protects in New York and Boston the naked half *idea* of the British carpenter. No American glass and limelight honestly bought must be wedded to that bare idea; and the idea taken gratis. Only the *property* can be stolen—because it belongs to the everlasting victim of man's beastly cruelty and injustice; the dirty little British *monopoly* is secure. The British actor must be paid four times his British price for delivering the British author's property in a New York or Boston theatre; the fiddlers, Britons or not, for fiddling to it; the door-keepers for letting in the public to see it, &c. Only the one imperial workman, who created the production, and inspired the carpenter with his lucrative demi-semi-idea, and set the actors acting, and the fiddlers fiddling, and the public paying, and the thief of a manager jingling another man's money, is singled out of about eighty people, all paid out of his one skull, to be swindled of every cent, on the pretence that he is a Briton; but really because he is an author.

The world—wicked and barbarous as it is—affords no parallel to this. It is not the injustice of earth; it is the injustice of hell.

CHARLES READE.

179

TENTH LETTER

Sɪʀ,—I ask leave to head this letter

The Five-fold Iniquity.

The outlawry of British authors and their property is a small portion of the injustice. The British Legislature has for years offered the right hand of international justice ; it is therefore the American Legislature that robs the American author in England. That is No. 2. But the worst is behind. The United States are a stiff protectionist nation. The American chair-maker, carriage-maker, horse-breeder, and all producers whatever are secured by heavy imposts against fair competition with foreigners. Also the American publisher, and the American stationer. The tariff taxes paper, I think, and is severe on English books. But turn to the American author. He cannot write a good work by machinery; like the English author, he can only produce it by labour, intellectual and physical, of a nature proved to shorten life more or less. While he is writing it, debt must accumulate. When written, how is this laborious producer in · a protectionist nation protected ? Are imported compositions paid for like any other import, and also taxed at the ports to protect the native producer ? On the contrary, the foreign literary composition is the one thing not taxed at the ports, and also the one thing stolen. And the State, which dances this double shuffle on the author's despised body at home, robs him of his property abroad.

The enormity escapes the judgment of the American public in a curious way, which I recommend to the notice of metaphysicians. It seems that men can judge things only by measurement with similar things. But the world offers no parallel to this compound iniquity, and so, comparison being impossible, the unique villainy passes for no villainy.

I will try and remove that illusion. Let us suppose a fast-trotting breed of horses, valueless in trade without a car and harness. You must yoke the horse to car and harness, and then they run together, and are valuable ; but they don't melt together, because they are heterogeneous properties ; and so are the author's composition and its vehicles heterogeneous

180

properties ; you may mix the two, but you cannot confound them as you can flour and mustard, by mixing.

An American citizen breeds a horse, at considerable expense, for the dealers. They supply the cart and harness, and have *virtually* a monopoly in the trade.

Carts and harness, to be imported, must be bought and taxed.

But the Legislature permits the dealer and trade monopolist to steal foreign horses, and also import them *untaxed*.

How can the American breeder compete with this double iniquity ?

The analogy is strict. This is the social, political, and moral position of the American author in a protectionist nation, and he owes it to his own Legislature. *Our* Legislature offers to treat him as a man, not a beast. Now does this poor devil pay the national taxes ? He does. What for ? *The State has no claim on him.* The State has outlawed him ; has disowned his citizenship, and even his humanity. Is he expected not to take any property he can lay his hand on ? Stuff and nonsense ! *Law is only a mutual compact between man and man.* In the American author's case, the Republic, through its representatives, has dissolved that mutual compact, and broken the public faith with the individual subject. The man is now reduced to a state of nature, and may take anything he can lay his hands on. There is not a casuist, alive or dead, who will deny this. Earth offers no parallel to this quintuple iniquity. 1. British monopoly respected. 2. British property stolen. 3. American author struck out of the national system, Protection. 4. Crushed under the competition of foreign stolen goods. 5. Robbed of his natural property, and his rights of man, in England.

A property founded, as the sages of Massachusetts justly say, on the natural rights of man to the fruits of his labour, cannot be property in one country and no property in another. It can be *protected* in one country and *stolen* in another ; but it is just as much property in the country where it is stolen, as in the country where it is protected. Geographical probity—local morality—Thou shalt not steal—except from a British author out of bounds—Do unto your neighbour as you would he should do to you—unless he is a British author out of bounds—all these are vain endeavours to pass geographical amendments upon God's laws, and on the old common law, and on the great ungeographical conscience of civilised mankind. The honest man spurns these provincial frauds, plain relics of the savage ; and the pirate takes them, with a sneer, as stepping-stones to the thing withheld.

In proof of this I give a few indirect consequences of the five-fold iniquity.

1. Mutilation and forgery.—The same people that steal a foreign author's property mutilate it, and *forge his name* to what he never wrote : and they cannot be hindered, except by international copyright. *A.*—Tom Taylor and Charles Reade write a comedy called "The King's Rival." Here Nell Gwynne, a frail woman with a good heart, plays a respectable part, because her faults are not paraded, and her good qualities appear in action. The comedy concludes in the King's closet; he forgives his cousin, the Duke of Richmond, and Francis Stuart; the centre doors are thrown open, the Queen and Court appear, and the King introduces the Duke and Duchess as a newly married couple, and the curtain falls, because the suspense has ceased; and that is a good rule. The character of Nell Gwynne was admirably played, and we arranged for the actress (Mrs. Seymour) to show one hand, and a frolic face at a side curtain, unseen, of course, by the Queen and the Court, who occupy the whole background.

Our Transatlantic thief was not satisfied with this, nor with stealing our brains. He brings Nell Gwynne out of her sly corner into the very centre of the stage, and gives her a dialogue with the King, during which the Queen is mute, perhaps with astonishment. The twaddle of the speakers ends with the King inviting the company to adjourn to the playhouse, and receive another lesson from Mistress Gwynne. That lady, who in the play had shown a great deal less vanity than characterises actresses in general, now replies pedantically for the first time :—

"It is our desire, your Majesty, while we amuse, to improve the mind. Our aim is—

> By nature's study to portray most clear
> From Beaumont, Fletcher, Jonson, immortal Shakespeare,
> How kings and princes by our mimic art
> Yield their sway and applaud the actor's part.
> The Bard of Avon in that prolific age
> Traced thoughts upon the enduring page."

Is it possible ?

> " Precepts in that powerful work we find
> To improve the morals and instruct the mind.

There he holds, as 'twere, a mirror up to Nature,
Shows Scorn her own image, Virtue her own feature.
To-night, king, queen, lords, and ladies act their part,
Each prompted by the workings of the heart,
And Nelly hopes they will not lose their cause—
Nor will they—if favoured—by your applause."

This is how dunces and thieves improve writers. Though she is the King's mistress, this unblushing hussy stands in the very centre of the stage, with the King between her and his wife, the Queen of England; and though she is an actress who had delivered the lines of Shakespeare, Fletcher, and other melodious poets, she utters verses that halt and waddle, but do not scan. The five-foot line is attempted, but there are four-foot lines and six foot-lines, and lines unscannable. Now there is no surer sign of an uneducated man than not knowing how to scan verses. We detect the uneducated actor in a moment by this. Our self-imposed collaborateur forges the name of a Cambridge scholar and an Oxford scholar to a gross and stupid indelicacy, showing the absence both of sense and right feeling, and also to verses that do not scan. He lowers us, as writers and men, in the United States, which is a very educated country with universities in it; and, as these piratical books are always sent into England, in spite of our teeth, he enables the home pirate to swindle us out of our property, and also of our credit as artists, scholars, and gentlemen, at home. The humbugs who, following Yates and Camden, say an author should write only for fame, will do well to observe that, wherever our property is outlawed, our reputation and credit as artists are sure to be filched away as well. The *Publishers' Circular*, a publication singularly gentle and moderate, has had to remonstrate more than once on the double villainy of taking an historical or scientific treatise, using the British author's learning, so far as it suited, and then falsifying his conclusions with a little new matter, and *still forging his name to the whole for trade purposes.* If this is not villainy, set open the gates of Newgate and Sing-Sing, for no greater rogues than these are in any convict prison.

B.—Fitzball, an English playwright, dramatised a novel of Cooper's. Fitzball coolly reversed the sentiments, and so, without a grain of invention, turned the American inventor's genius inside out, and made him write the Briton up and the colonist down. Such villainy in time of war would make a soldier blush. What is it in time of peace? The British

Legislature is willing to put this out of any Fitzball's power.

2. Recoil of Piracy.—I have the provincial right in a comedy, " Masks and Faces." Many years ago I let the book run out of print, because I found it facilitated piratical representation. Instantly piratical copies, published in New York, were imported; and, on the most moderate calculation, the American Legislature has enabled British managers, actors, and actresses to swindle me, *in my own country*, out of eight hundred pounds iu the last fourteen years on this single property. I have stopped the piratical version by injunction. But I can only stop its sale in shops. . It penetrates into theatres like a weasel or a skunk; and no protection short of international copyright and stage-right is any protection. America saps British morality by example; British actresses are taught, by Congress, to pillage me in the States. They come over here and continue the habit the American Legislature has taught them. At this very moment I have to sue a Glasgow manager, because an English actress brought over a piratical American book of " Masks and Faces " in spite of the injunction, and they played it in Glasgow; and I can see the lady thinks it hard, since she had a *right* to pillage her countryman in the States, that she should not be allowed to pillage him also in his own country. That is how all local amendments on the eighth commandment operate. They make the whole eighth commandment seem unreasonable and inconsistent.

3. A Dublin editor pirated my story, " It is Never too Late to Mend," under the title of " Susan Merton : a Tale of the Heart." This alarmed me greatly ; it threatened a new vein of fraud on copyrights. I moved the Irish Court of Chancery at once. The offender pleaded ignorance, and produced, to my great surprise, an American paper, in which the story was actually published under the title " Susan Merton : a Tale of the Heart "—and the English author's name suppressed. So careful of an author's fame, my Lord Camden, are those superior spirits who set him an example of nobility by despising his property. " It is Never too Late to Mend " is an ideaed title. " Susan Merton " is an unideaed title. I never saw an American idiot yet, so I apprehend this ingenious customer altered the title for the worse, and suppressed my name, in order to defraud his own countrymen, by passing the thing off as a novelty in some sequestered nook of the Union. Well, this lie, on the top of the piracy, jeopardised my pro-

perty in England, and cost me a sum of money; for the defendant could not pay the costs. The piratical proprietor of two Irish newspapers paid £1 per week for a little while, and then disappeared. He went to the States no doubt. I hope he did; for there he'll meet his match.

4. "Foul Play," a drama, was produced in New York. I was on shares with Mr. Boucicault. In course of the representation there was a dispute, the grounds of which, as reported, I could not understand. However, the sheriff came on the stage with his men. There was resistance. Shots were fired, and two humble persons employed in the theatre, an old man and a boy, were wounded. I felt very sorry for these poor fellows, who had no interest in the quarrel. Also I felt half guilty, since it happened in connection with that particular play. I sent out £10 for them, to my friends Messrs. Harper: they were good enough to take charge of the matter, and saw the sufferers got it. Now I don't set up for a sweet, benevolent soul; I intended this as a fair percentage to American sufferers, to be paid out of American profits. But the Yankee in charge of the receipts deranged my arithmetic. He levanted with the receipts, and my whole commercial transaction is represented in my books by a payment of that small, but solid percentage upon—air.

The American saw the Britisher recognise our common humanity and not draw geographical distinctions; but he despised my example: for why, he had the example of his Legislature, which says, "When you catch a British author here, show your hospitality. Swindle him up hill and down dale—and then go to church and 'pray' to our common Father."

An actress calls on me from Illinois, tall, dark, graceful, handsome, and talks well, as all American ladies do. She wants a new part. Says she has been to another author, and he demanded the price down, because she was an American. Of course I put on a face of wonder at that other author; so inseparable is politeness from insincerity. I let her have "Philippa" and "The Wandering Heir" in the States for ten dollars per night, which is a mere nominal price. Subsequently two English actresses of the very highest merit and popularity asked leave to play the piece in the United States. But the Britisher stood loyal to his Illinois girl. Well, she sent me a very small sum from California. She then went to Australia, played the piece repeatedly; wrote to me eight months ago, telling me she only withheld payments because she was coming to England; and never came to England, nor made me any remittance. The part is invaluable to an actress. It has been played by three actresses in England, and in each case has proved valuable to the performer. In the United States I am done out of it as property, and done out of all returns, because I trusted an American woman in a matter of literary property.

5. My first letter announced that I considered the American author the head victim, and I even suggested how difficult it must be for a novice, even if a man of genius, to get before the public at all. I have now advices from young American authors sending me details. They say that it is very hard to get MSS. read; that, when they bring a picture of American life, it is slighted, and they are advised to imitate some British writer or other; and that, in fact, servile imitation of British styles is a young writer's best chance. But they tell me something I did not divine—that the publishers keep copying machines, and the rejected manuscript often bears the marks of the machine: and the subject-matter is, in due course, piratically used.

Look this cruel thing all round. It becomes the old to feel for the young; let me trace that poor young author's heart. He is young, and the young are sanguine: he is young, and the young are slow to suspect cold-blooded villainy and greed in men that are rich, and need not cheat to live, and live in luxury. He takes his MS. in good faith to a respectable man. He is told that it shall be read. There are delays. The poor young man, or young woman, is hot and cold by turns; but does not like to show too much impatience. However, in time, he begins to fear he is befooled. He calls, and will have an answer one way or other. Then a further short delay is required to re-peruse, or to consider. That delay is really wanted to copy the MS. by a machine. The manuscript is returned with a compliment; but the author is told he is not yet quite ripe for publication: he is paternally advised to study certain models (British), and encouraged to bring another MS. improved by these counsels. Ods Nestor! it reads like criticism, and paternal advice. The novice yields his own judgment; sighs many times if he is a male, if female has a little gentle cry that the swine earth is tenanted by are not asked to pity nor even comprehend; and the confiding American youth, thinking grey hairs and grave advice must be trustworthy, sets to work to discover the practical merit that must lie somewhere or other at the bottom of British mediocrity and "decent debility;" he never suspects that the sole charm of these mediocre models lies not in the British platitudes and rigmarole, but in the Latin word *gratis*. While thus employed he sees, one fine day, some sketches of life in California, Colorado, or what not, every fact and idea of which has been stolen from his rejected MS., and diverted from its form, and reworded, and printed; while he, the native of a mighty continent, has been sent away, for mundane instruction, to the inhabitants of a peninsula on the north coast of France. The poor novice had contributed a real, though crudish, novelty to literature, *as any American can by opening his eyes in earnest, and writing all he sees*. It was rejected for reasons that sounded well, but were all trade pretexts stereotyped these many years, though new to each novice in his turn; and now the truth comes out; it was not worth buying cheap; but it was *well worth stealing* in a nation where the Legislature plays the part of Satan and teaches men *the habit of stealing* from authors, a habit which, once acquired, is never dropped nor restrained within any fixed limits.

What must be the feelings of the poor young man, or woman, so bubbled, so swindled, and so basely robbed, because he trusted a trader well to do, and did not take him for a ticket-of-leave man turned out of Sing-Sing into a store? And now go behind the swindle, and see how the geographical amendment of the eighth commandment, and the local variation of the golden rule prepare Dives for heaven in spite of parables.

" Rob the British author of his composition, by machinery," says Congress. " We will stop his *volumes* at our ports: but we will connive at one volume passing, for the use of theft, for theft is all sanctifying; and you have but to take this one volume and wed his stolen composition to bought vehicles, for mind you must only swindle the British author; you must not swindle a Briton unless he is an author, nor an author unless he is a Briton. As for God Almighty, we have a great respect for him—in the proper place, and that is church; but out of church he has not looked into these little matters *so closely as we have*. He is addicted to general rules; and local distinctions have escaped him. We are more discriminating."

But observe the result. The publisher goes on; "Excelsior" is his motto. Taught to pillage the British author by a miraculously clever machine, the press, he invents another machine and pillages the native author. That machine is also a kind of press, and a clever one ; for, like the compositor and the press combined, it separates the author's words from his paper, and steals them with a view to wedding the cream of the composition gratis to other pieces of paper honestly bought, and selling the *bought paper* and the *stolen ideas* of the author without regard to his nationality. What does this poor boy gain by being *an American at home* ? He would be safer out of bounds. No British publisher would so abuse his confidence.

Miss Leclercq, an English actress, settled in the United States, purchased not long ago an original play of an American author. She had not played it many nights when it was stolen by means of shorthand writers, and manuscripts sold. When she came to tour the Union with her new American piece honestly paid for, she found it was valueless, being stolen and stale. No Legislature can place unnatural limits to fraud, and say to theft, " Thus far shalt thou come and no farther, and here shall thy dirty waves be stayed."

You produce a drama in England ; it is taken down short-hand for the United States. An Englishman's *unpublished play* only escapes theft or colourable piracy in the States by failure. Merit is rewarded by pillage.

But I hope enough has been shown to prove that a Legislature and its judges launch its people into illimitable fraud, when they pass geographical amendments upon the eighth commandment and the golden rule, and defile the common law with pettifogging distinctions, the fruit of corruption and sophistry, which are bad in law, grossly immoral, revolting to common sense and the conscience of all impartial men, and contradicted by the usage of the old kingdom, and the deeds, and the words, of our common ancestors.

I leave that, and go to public expediency. I shall prove the fivefold iniquity is bad public policy ; that the American reading public is between two stools ; robbed of free trade in books to swell the taxes, and robbed of a national literature, and a national drama, to gratify one of the smallest cliques in the nation ; and this without either the nation or the clique gaining *or saving* one single cent. So that the thing is suicidal kleptomania. And this I say is one of the bitterest wrongs of authors—that sooner than not pillage them, men will hurt themselves, and will cut their own throats, to wound an author.

CHARLES READE.

ELEVENTH LETTER

THE FOUR FOGS.

SIR,—Outside these letters and Mr. Reverdy Johnson's, international copyright and stage-right are shrouded in four thick fogs—legal, moral, verbal, arithmetical.

I read what is written over the water, and grope for an idea. In vain: it is all verbal and arithmetical fog.

Verbal fog *A.*—They can't get along without calling copyright and stage-right monopolies; but they dare not risk £50 to £150 upon that fallacy, and it is an irrelevant fallacy, here, since international patent-right is a monopoly : and it cannot be used to defend the American Legislature, because that Legislature, for the last hundred years, has declared copyright to be property, in the laws of the separate States and the laws of the Republic, which these ignorant citizens had better begin to read.

B.—But a more delicious piece of verbal fog is this—they say, " We shall not give up free trade in books to please the Britishers." Free trade in books, quotha ! why, it does not exist in the Union. Free trade is not freebooting. Free trade means buying and selling, unburdened by imposts. Now there is thirty per cent. duty on foreign books at the American ports, and freebooting in copyright can never supply the place of free trade, for copyright is, in money, only seven per cent. on retail prices ; and, as for stage-right, that does not take a cent from the public. The prices of an American theatre are just the same when a play is paid for or stolen. By theft of a foreigner's stage-right the American public has lost a national drama ; but it has never gained nor saved the millionth of a cent since the country was colonised.

International stage-right is not offered by those who object to international copyright. These arithmeticians draw no distinction. Against international copyright and stage-right every one of their arguments rests on the notion that the main expense of a book, or of a seat in a theatre, is the dramatist's fee, and the fee which copyright enables a book author to extort directly from the publisher and indirectly from the public purchaser. Of course, so impudent a falsehood is never stated. But why ? Statement is not the weapon of a liar, nor of a self-deceiver. Both these personages convey—insinuate—suggest—assume. They never state. Clear statement and detail are antidotes to the subtle poison of vague fallacies. But just test their public arguments, and see if you can find one which does not convey, in a fog of words and figures, that the author's fee is the main expense of a book. One salaried writer not only takes this ground, but, as piracy has deprived Americans of their own judgment, and made them provincial fog-echoes of British muddleheads, he repeats, with true provincial credulity, Macaulay's Fog Epigram, for the instruction of his countrymen. This done, and very old London fog offered to ·New York for modern sunshine, he infers fairly enough—because the *inference is his own*—that if domestic copyright is so heavy a tax on the public, a State should hesitate to extend the injustice to foreign nations. Very well, young gentleman : I have no quarrel with *you*. *If* Macaulay is right, you are right.

A second-rate rhetorician may be a babe in logic. Macaulay, in this very speech, called copyright "a monopoly in books," and that is verbal fog, as I have shown. The only monopoly in books now-a-days is a trade monopoly held by publishers, and established by custom, not law. As for copyright, it is a singularly open property ; why, every *man, woman,* and *child,* in the Republic or the Empire, who can fill a sheet of paper, can create, enjoy, and bequeath a copyright, though a minor, and in case of co-heirs it is distributable like other personal property. It is a property *bounded only by nature.*

Fog epigrams are for our amusement, not our instruction, and Macaulay's is bottled essence of arithmetical fog.

"Copyright," says he, "is a tax on readers to give a bounty to authors."

Now we will let in a gleam of arithmetical sunshine on this. Writers are human beings with stomachs. They cannot write masterpieces, as Duns Scotus copied the Bible, during the throes of starvation. They must be paid, copyright or no copyright ; and an author's copyright has a special operation on a *pirate,* but none on the *reader.* Whether an author is paid by wages or by copyright, his remuneration must equally fall on the public purchaser. Macaulay, therefore, has taken a distinction where there is no difference. The Anglo-Saxon muddlehead is always doing this. It is his great intellectual excellence, and makes him the ridicule of Europe.

However, the great vice of his fog epigram is " FRAUDULENT SELECTION." It picks out of many legitimate profits a single one, and conceals the others. If just profits on human labour,

&c., were *taxes, which they are not,* every edition of a work would represent the following taxes :—

1. The rag-picker's profit. 2. The paper merchant and his men. 3. The printer and his men. 4. The binder and his men. 5. The publisher and his staff. 6. The author. 7. The retail bookseller. 8. The advertising column. These are all taxes and bounties, as much as is the author's remuneration, be it wages or copyright. To be sure, if any one of these characters makes an *excessive* profit, compared with the others, that might be called a bounty. And that reminds me—was not Macaulay's Fog epigram preceded by another which said, "Publishers drink their wine out of authors' skulls?"

Well, if any one gets a bounty, or excessive profit, it is not the copyrighted author, and I don't think it is the publisher—epigram apart. The public result of these *copyright transactions* is this :—

The paper merchants are rich.

The printers are rich.

The binders are well to do, but few.

The publishers are well to do. But I deny that they owe that to *books.*

The authors are the poorest creators of valuable property on the face of the earth.

To descend to details. The retail dealer gets TWENTY-FIVE PER CENT. of the retail price. All that authors of books, as a class, extort by means of copyright, is SEVEN PER CENT. on the retail price, which is 10 per cent. on the publisher's net returns. So much for the comparative tax the reader pays to the author and seven more traders. Now for the bounty. This can only be ascertained by measuring the work done against the remuneration. Price of a book to the oppressed reader—say 1 dollar, or 4s. Value of the paper, printing, binding, advertisements, 45c., or thereabouts ; of the composition, 55c. Sole creator of the composition, the author ; his remuneration 7 per cent., his share of the production worth 55 per cent. Droll bounty this !! For passing the book through his hands, often on sale or return, the retailer gets 25 per cent. What the other traders and workmen get, I cannot say, nor is it necessary. Enough that they are all richer than the authors. Now compare the arithmetical fog of Macaulay, and his transatlantic echo, with this gleam of arithmetical sunshine.

The American Legislature now knows the worst. Seven

per cent. on the retail price does domestic copyright enable authors, one with another, to screw out of a book. Seven per cent. is all we expect, or hope, or *ask*, from the great Republic, and all the American author will ever get in England.

The misfortune of authors is this—they cannot, as a class, secure any remuneration at all except through copyright. But copyright effects this just end by unpopular means. It stops all sale till it secures a modest remuneration. Then men, forgetting that the stoppage of sale is not the end, but only that severe means to a just end, which the heartless dishonesty of mankind makes necessary, fall into needless fear of the tyrannical means that leads to a mild result. This sentiment it is which leads to a misgiving in the United States that international copyright would be abused to enhance the prices of English books. Americans do not really know our book trade, and are led to natural but erroneous notions of English prices by seeing the three-volume novel advertised at 31s. 6d. But the truth is we have a rotten trade for the upper ten thousand, and a healthy trade for the nation. The rotten trade is the hiring trade ; of course, it operates on books just as it does on pianofortes—it reduces the customers to a handful, and artificial prices become a necessity of that one narrow market. The 31s. 6d. is all humbug, the public does not buy a copy, the sale is confined to the libraries, and the real price is 15s. to 18s., if by a popular author, but otherwise 9s. to 12s. But it is a calamitous system, encourages the writing of rubbish, and enables the librarian, whose customers are a class born to be humbugged, to hold back the good book, and substitute the trash, with dishonest excuses, in the credulous country customer's parcel. But so far from clinging to this rotten trade, intelligent authors and publishers in this country would gladly see it done away with, and the universal habit of buying books restored : and I, for one, look to the American publishers to help us in this with their sounder system ; for under just laws, when a sound system encounters an unsound, it is always the unsound that gives way. Below the above rotten trade lies the true trade of the country—good books at moderate prices—and some books and periodicals at wonderfully small prices. These very novels, sold to the libraries at fabulous prices, are sold to the public in one volume at 6s., 5s., and 2s. At 2s. they are in boards, with an illustration outside, and a vignette.

To show what a bugbear copyright is in books of durable

sale, American publishers can't produce such a volume for 50c., by stealing the composition, as the English publishers do, paying copyright.

I submit to you specimens of cheap publications under copyright, and I challenge the American publishers to match them with cheap piratical books or papers.

However, there is nothing new under the sun. The fear that British authors or the assignees of their American copyrights might stand out for our *library prices* in the United States is an old misgiving which has had its day in England. Queen Anne's Parliament had much such a fear. Well! What did they do? Why, provided against it in a section giving a right of complaint to several great functionaries, or any one of them, and investing those dignitaries with special powers to compel the publication on reasonable terms. The precaution proved quite superfluous; for not one single human being was so perverse as to lock up a good book, or sell it at a price the public could not afford. The section was a dead letter, and is now repealed. However, if the Legislature of the United States is uneasy on this head, it is not for us, who ask a great boon, to make childish difficulties. Here is the cure in a stroke of the pen :—

"And that the price of books written by British subjects, but papered, printed, and bound in the United States, as hereinbefore enacted, may not be unduly enhanced, be it enacted that the proprietor of the copyright in any such work shall be compelled to publish, or cause the same to be published, in the United States, within the times hereinbefore specified, at a reasonable price, not exceeding the highest price that is demanded for a book of the same character, size, and quality, written by an American citizen, and published at, or about, the time; and the price of such work shall be duly notified and advertised in three journals of large circulation seven days before publication, and, should the price so advertised appear excessive, it shall be lawful for any person to lodge a complaint with . . . . . [here enumerate the functionaries], and the . . . . . on the said complainant giving security for costs and offering evidence, shall have authority to suspend the publication and hear the evidence without delay, and, if the price advertised be excessive, shall affix a just and reasonable price, provided always that in those cases where the book shall be published for the foreign proprietor by an agent being a native of the United States, the agent, or proprietor, shall be allowed to add the reasonable fee of the agent to the price of the said book." Add a clause giving various and large discretionary powers to the said judges.

If, with all these safeguards to the American public, to the stationers, and the public, international stage-right, against which no objection has ever been offered, and international copyright, both properties that belong to us by common law, are both refused to the American and British author, while international patent-right is enacted, and yields a balance of £300,000 a year, British money, to American citizens, then justice is *nothing*, fair play is *nothing*, humanity to those men living, whom the Republic worships dead, is *nothing*, and a national literature is *nothing*, and it is *nothing* for a great nation which in the heat and misery of its war, could find pity and substantial generosity for one set of British subjects, and by so doing has covered itself with glory—it is nothing, I say, for that noble nation to single out another set of British subjects less improvident, and more deserving, and make war upon those worthy, weak, and unarmed men, in time of peace.

Could I gain the ear of one Ulysses Grant, I think he would side with the weak ; and if he did the quintuple iniquity would soon fall ; for it is not so well defended as Richmond was.

CHARLES READE.

TWELFTH LETTER

SIR,—Permit me to head this short letter

THE IMPENITENT THIEF.

This is a character disapproved in Jewish history. But he has it all his own way with us in Anglo-Saxony. One of his traits is to insult those whom he pillages. He puts one hand in our pockets, and shakes the other fist in our faces. As an example I note some sneers by a Mr. Pascoe, and other professors of moral and arithmetical fog, that authors, in asking for international copyright, show an excessive love of money. That remark applies more to those who covet the property of others, than to those who only covet their own. It is a sneer that comes as ill from salaried writers, who cannot be pillaged, as it does from pensioned lawyers; and it is a heartless sneer; for they know by history—if they know anything—that authors have passed through centuries of pauperism, misery, and degradation, and have only arrived at modest competence and decent poverty. Popular authors are rare, and even *their* income does not approach that of the prosperous lawyer, divine, physician, actor or actress. There are two actors about, who have each made one hundred and fifty thousand pounds by playing a single part in two plays, for which the two authors have not received two thousand pounds. The painter has two great markets, his picture and his copyright. The author has but'one. International copyright will merely give him two, and raise him to the painter's commercial level. No author has ever left a fortune made by writing. Dickens, the sole apparent exception, was a reader and a publisher. As a rule, when a respectable author dies, either he had independent means, or the hat goes round. If authors are to be respected in Anglo-Saxony, they must not be poor; they must have better terms at home, or international copyright, to meet the tremendous advance of price in the necessaries of life. Three or four stray individuals, such as Milton and Spinosa, have been poor and dignified. But they were *raræ aves*. Dignified poverty in a class is a chimera. It never existed. The character of a class is the character of the majority in that class; now no majority has ever resisted a strong temptation, and that is why all greatly tempted classes fall as classes. Johnson knew more than Camden, and he says, " Poverty is the worst of all temptations; it is incessant, and leads, soon or late, to loss of self-respect, and of the world's respect." The hypocrite Camden demanded an author with aspiring genius and no eye to the main chance. The model he demanded crossed his path in Oliver Goldsmith; but the hypocrite Camden treated his *beau-idéal* with cold hauteur, because his *beau-idéal* was poor; the same hypocrite was to be seen arm-in-arm with Garrick, for *he* had lots of money.

Oliver Goldsmith, next to Voltaire, was the greatest genius in Europe; on the news of his death Burke burst into tears, and Reynolds laid down his brush and devoted the day to tender regrets.

I now cite a passage verbatim from the notice on Goldsmith in the " Biographia Dramatica:"—" It was at first intended to bury him in Westminster Abbey; and his pall was to have been supported by the Marquis of Lansdowne, Lord Louth, Sir Joshua Reynolds, Mr. Burke, and Mr. Garrick. But a slight inspection of his affairs showed the impropriety of incurring so great an expense. He was privately interred in the Temple burial-ground, attended by Mr. Hugh Kelly, Mr. Hawes, the Rev. Joseph Palmer, and a few coffee-house acquaintances."

If the deceased genius was poor, Reynolds, and Garrick, and the rest, were rich. *They* could have secured him the place he deserved in the national temple. But no; he was *poor:* and observe, those who were ready to lay genius in Westminster Abbey had it been wealthy, would not even follow it to the Temple Church when they found it was poor. The fact is, that great immortal genius was flung into the earth like a dog, and to this day *nobody knows where he lies.*

I now cite verbatim from the "Life of Mrs. Oldfield":— "The corpse of Mrs. Anne Oldfield was carried from her house in Grosvenor Street to the Jerusalem Chamber, where it lay in state, and afterwards to the Abbey, the pall being supported by the Lord Delawar, Lord Harvey, the Right Honourable Bubb Doddington, and other men of *ton.*"

This lady was a good actress, and had lived in open shame with Mr. Maynwaring and Brigadier Churchil, and had lots of money. Therefore this artist was buried in the Abbey, and the greater artist, Goldsmith, being pure, but poor, had the grave of a dog.

In these two extracts you see the world unmasked by its own hand, not mine. This, my Lord Camden, is that dirty world, of which you were a gilt lump. This is the real world as it is, and was, and always will be. Many authors are womanish; so they listen to the flatteries that cost nothing, and, when they find it is all humbug, they sit down and whine for a world less hollow and less hard. But authors, who are men, take the world as they find it, see its good sense at the bottom of its brutality, and grind their teeth, and swear that the public weasel shall not swindle them into that unjust poverty, which the public hog despises in an author, and would in an apostle.

CHARLES READE.

THIRTEENTH LETTER

Sir,—An egotist has been defined a man who will burn his neighbour's house down to cook himself two eggs.

If it be true that three or four American publishers are the sole obstacle to international stage-right and copyright, the definition applies, so great is the injury they do; so little, if any, the advantage to themselves. How would international stage-right injure them? Yet it is they who crush it, and demoralise theatrical business, and kill the national drama. How would even international copyright, on the conditions I have offered, injure them? It could not hurt them at present; it must improve their condition in the end. The professors of arithmetical fog call it "a present to British authors." The idiots! is it any more a boon to English than to American authors? It is a *present* to neither. On the contrary, it offers the publisher his highest remuneration for his smallest outlay. Take a popular English novel—it is not unusual to sell 120,000 copies at a dollar. Under piracy by law established, one publisher does not get the sale. Often the thing is torn to pieces; but let us limit the publication to four persons; assuming that each sells about 30,000 copies at a profit of 25 cents, that gives 7,500 dols. I admit that under international copyright 7 per cent. must be deducted for the British right. But then the publisher who pays the Briton will sell all the books. Now 120,000 copies at a profit of 25 cents minus 7 = 18 gives a total of 21,600 dollars. And here you may see the reason why copyrighted books can be sold *cheaper* than pirated books, yet yield a good profit.

Publication of *books* is in a general way a poor business. Men of enterprise and talent would not descend to it but for the great prizes. I therefore reason fairly in taking a book of large sale for trade sample; not that 120,000 copies is a very large sale in the United States; I know books that have quadrupled that figure in a year's sale.

Under international copyright the American publisher, dealing either by purchase or otherwise with British copyright, could also levy a just and moderate tariff on the 400 or 500 newspapers that now steal any popular British book. So much for the American side. But the American publisher would also, by his position and intelligence, secure many of the American copyrights in England, and, even if he contented himself with an author's percentage there, that would be at least a set-off, though it needs no set-off. But if, on the contrary, he should take the public advice I have given him, and have a place of business in London—which is the great game —all manner of lucrative combinations would arise under international copyright. That great boon would not change the nature of authors and make them, as a class, hard bargainers or even good men of business. They deserve 7 per cent. in each market, but they would not be sharp enough to get it one time in thirty.

When you add to all this that international copyright would relieve the American author of the competition of stolen goods, which is stifling him, and make the most intellectual country in the world a hotbed of intellectual productions, by which the American publishers must necessarily profit most, their opposition to international justice and public policy will, I hope, cease; for it would be egotism beyond the definition supra; it would be the blind egotism that sacrifices national honour and the clear interests of all producers, and of the public reader, to one *sham* interest.

With this letter I send one to a powerful American firm, offering them again what I offered them years ago, that, under international copyright, they shall be my London publishers, if they please, and publish my books, if they please, on the very terms I will demand of them in New York: 7 per cent. on the retail price, which is 10 per cent. on the trade sale price. As I am popular in America, and perhaps no writer under international copyright could make better bargains, and as I pass for a screw, this should tend to convince reasonable Americans that international copyright, though a great boon to authors and honest publishers on both sides the water, is not a tax upon any one. Consider—for passing my books through their hands in London I offer an American firm all I will ask in New York for having written those books; for having written those books I will ask no more in the United States than I offer them for just passing the books through their hands in London. Please bring your minds to bear on this, you that possess a mind.

So much for petty expediency and financial fog. Ought these to stand in the way of national justice, national impartiality, and a national literature? Ought classes so important as the American author, the American spectator of plays, and the American reader, to be mocked with the title of Republicans, yet misgoverned and outlawed by a Venetian oligarchy, a mere handful of short-sighted traders, clinging blindly to piracy as some men cling to drink, not that it does them an atom of good, but just because they have got into the habit?

Those mediævals whose lofty method—conjecture *v.* evidence—Sir Joseph Yates follows in copyright, discovered that witches who rode upon the whirlwind and led the storm could be arrested in their furious career by two straws placed across. When I consider with what pitiable reasons the five-fold iniquity has been defended, and is even now defended, against Mr. Reverdy Johnson, and these letters, I seem to see the men of the dark ages laying down their straws. Ah! and so you think national justice, honour, and humanity are three old beldams that will never pass your straws? I deem more nobly than you do of the nation you disgrace and mislead. The people that were in trouble yet relieved the British cotton-spinners must have a heart not bounded by the ocean; the nation that could, at a cost of blood and treasure, forego the two-legged beast of burden and make the negro a man, must have a conscience; and our turn will come, please God, though my head and heart may both have ceased to ache at man's bad logic, and man's injustice. Yes, the great Republic has raised its negro to the level of a man; it will one day admit its authors to the level of a negro.

Farewell, you four fogs, farewell you rogues and fools who made them; I leave the pettifogger who reasons *à priori* against evidence, and divines that the common law abhors forfeiture of a right—unless it is held by an *author*—and reads implied contracts as "exchange of equivalents"—unless one of the parties is an *author*, and if an author *gives* a written copy without reserve, and abandons, for eighty years, his right to publish, says that is no *gift* of the right to publish; but if, instead of laches and neglect and all that really forfeits a right, he adds possession to title and *sells* one copy to a man, says that *sale* is a *gift* of the right of publication. I leave the liars, idiots, and beasts, who reason thus against evidence, and call it law, with one remark: the greatest asses God has ever made are *little lawyers.* Your little lawyer is a man who has parted with the good sense of the layman, and has not advanced one inch towards the science of a Mansfield or a Story.

I leave the men of verbal fog, the poor addlepates, who call a man's sole right to sell his own composition "monopoly," and his sole right to sell his own hen and her chickens, his own seed and its great increase, " property ; " and call free-booting in copyright with a 30 per cent. tax on books " free trade in books."

I leave the ranting rogues, the romantic pickpockets, who say that an author is to work only for praise (against which dispraise and foul scurrility are not to weigh, of course), but that a judge and an archbishop are to work for money as well as credit—in a word, I leave the whole tribe of gorillas and chimpanzees, in whose hands I found this subject, to recommence their incurable gibbering and chattering; reason they never did, and never will. As for me, I shall take leave to rise, for a little while, above their dunghill in a fog, and speak as a man who by long study of the past has learned to divine the future, and is fit to advise nations.

1. Justice to authors is the durable policy of nations.

2. The habit of inventing is a richer national treasure than a pyramid of stolen inventions.

3. Invention is on the average the highest and hardest form of mental labour. It is the offspring of necessity, and nursed by toil.

4. Hence it follows that in whatever country invention can be appropriated by direct theft, or adaptation, or any easy process except purchase, the habit of invention is discouraged, and each act of invention undersold and the inventor punished.

5. Therefore, by pirating from foreign authors, a nation scratches the foreign author's finger, but cuts the native author's throat, and turns its own intellectual sun into a moon, and robs itself of the habit of inventing, which is a richer national treasure than a pyramid of stolen inventions. This is a universal truth : the experience of Europe in every age confirms it, and in the United States it is a special truth, for the Republic has put justice and injustice side by side, so that even a child may see which is the more enduring policy. Of international patent right the result has been rapid and re-markable. The States were behind us in invention ; they soon advanced upon us, and caught us, and now they head us far. International justice began with a trade balance in our favour ; yet now the States draw an enormous balance from Europe, and about three hundred thousand a year from Great Britain. Europe teems with the material products of American genius ; American patents print English newspapers and sew English-men's shirts ; a Briton goes to his work by American clocks, and is warmed by American stoves and cleansed by American

dust collectors; whereas my housemaid, when she dusts with a British broom, only drives it from pillar to post. In a word, America is the leading nation in all matters of material invention and construction, and no other nation rivals nor approaches her. It is "Eclipse first, and the rest nowhere."

Now do but turn an eye to the opposite experiment. What is the position in the world of the American author? Does he keep pace with the American patentee? Why, it is a complete contrast; one is up, the other is down; one leads old nations, the other follows them; one is a sun diffusing his own light over his hemisphere and ours, the other a pale moon lighted by Europe. Yet the American mechanical inventor has only the forces and materials our mechanical inventor can command; whereas the American author has larger, more varied, and richer materials than ours. Even in fiction, what new material has the English artist compared with that gold-mine of nature, incident, passion, and character—life in the vast American Republic? Here you may run on one rail from the highest civilisation to the lowest, and inspect the intervening phases, and write the scale of man. You may gather in a month amidst the noblest scenes of nature the history of the human mind, and note its progress. Here are red man, black man, and white man. With us man is all of a colour, and nearly all of a piece; there contrasts more piquant than we ever see spring thick as weeds; larger and more natural topics ring through the land, discussed with broader and freer eloquence. In the very Senate, the passions of well-dressed men break the bounds of convention; and nature and genuine character speak out in places where with us etiquette has subdued them to a whisper. Land of fiery passions and humours infinite, you offer such a garden of fruits as Molière never sunned himself in, nor Shakespeare neither. And what food for poetry and romance were the feats of antiquity compared with the exploits of this people? Fifty thousand Greeks besieged a Phrygian city, fighting for a rotten leaf; the person of an adulteress without her mind. This ten years' waste of time is a fit subject for satire; only genius has perverted it into an epic; what cannot genius do? But what is it in *itself*, and what were the puny wars of Pompey and Cæsar, compared with a civil war, where not a few thousand soldiers met on either side to set one Pompey up, one Cæsar down; but armies like those of Xerxes encountered again and again, fighting not for the possession of a wanton, nor the pride of a general, but the integrity of a nation and the rights of man. Yet the little old things sound great and the great new things sound small, *carent quia vate sacro.*

The other day man's greatest feat of labour was the Chinese wall. It is distanced. An iron road binds hemispheres together. See it carried over hill and dale, through civilised and uncivilised countries; see the buffaloes glare and snort; and the wild tribes gallop to and fro in rage and terror, as civilisation marches, with sounding tread, from sea to sea. See iron labour pierce the bowels of the mountain, and span the lake's broad bosom. It creeps; it marches; it climbs; it soars; it never halts; the savages arm, and saddle their wild steeds; they charge; they fire; they wheel about, with flaming eyes and flying arrows; but civilisation just takes its rifle in one hand and its pick in the other, and the labours of war and peace go on together, and still the mighty iron road creeps, climbs, and marches from hemisphere to hemisphere, and sea to sea.

These are the world-wide feats that touch mankind, and ought to thrill mankind. Yet they go for less than small old things done in holes and corners—*carent quia vate sacro.* For there, where the soil is so fertile, art is sterile. Few are the pens that glow with sacred fire; few great narrators; and not one great dramatist. Read the American papers—you revel in a world of new truths, new fancies, and glorious crude romance, awaiting but the hand of art; you roll in gold-dust. Read their dramas or narratives—How French! How British! How faint beside the swelling themes life teems with in this nation, that is thinking, working, speaking, living, and doing everything except writing, at a rate of march without a present rival or a past parallel beneath the sun.

The reason is nine-tenths of their heaven-born writers are nipped in the bud, snubbed, starved, and driven out of immortal literature by piracy before they can learn so profound and difficult an art. Some driven into business; some driven on to the land, which their God, in his mercy, has thrown open to the oppressed; some driven into journals that go bankrupt by the hundred.

Mr. Emerson : " There are men in this country who can put their thoughts in brass, in iron, stone, or wood ; who can build the best ships for freight, and the swiftest for ocean race. Another makes revolvers, another a power press. But scarcely one of our authors has thrown off British swaddling clothes. The great secret of the world-wide success of ' Uncle Tom ' was its novelty; it had something peculiarly American in it. The works of American authors have been smothered under English authors in the American market. Not only has the wholesale system of mal-appropriation most injuriously affected the interests of living American authors, but it has a tendency to dwarf down the original literature of the United States to a servile copyism, and to check the development of the national mind."

Piracy is a upas tree. If you really love your great Republic, and wished to see it honoured and appreciated, down with that upas tree, and you will lead the world in art as well as in mechanics. The gorillas and chimpanzees are not ashamed to say that they see no consequences of international justice, but that books will be dearer in the States. Perhaps not, and for that very reason we don't look to gorillas for prescience, or to chimpanzees for prophecy.

Of international copyright and stage-right the following are a few, and only a few, of the certain consequences :—

1. The American publishers will say, " Confound John Bull. We'll show him we can do without him." They will read American MS. with a kindlier eye. Young American authors will get a chance to learn their art by practice.

2. American publishers will have a place of business in London. Combinations will arise they never dreamt of. They will do all sorts of business with our authors and publishers, and often take the whole property in Britain, her colonies, and the States.

3. Australia, seeing so good an example, will fall into better practical arrangements both with Great Britain and the States. Waste a few years more and she will pillage us both.

4. The deep and sullen resentment British authors now feel against the American nation will give way to kindly and grateful feelings. They will go over to the States, not to fleece the natives in return, by reading poor lectures in a country of good lectures, nor yet to skim a few States with jaundiced eye and published shallow venom ; but to sojourn and study, with keen and kindly eye, the nation, best worth studying in the universal globe. From this will arise great pictures of American life with some inaccuracies.

5. Taught by foreigners their own treasures, Americans will begin to take bird's-eye views of American life, and we shall get great American narratives of all sorts, and, by-and-by, a great play or two.

6. The American women, better cultivated than other

women, reared with larger minds, and less overburdened with domestic cares, will begin to take their true place in Anglo-Saxon literature. A brilliant career awaits them.

7. Americans are mortified, and justly, at the sullen apathy of Europe and British indifference. It will soon cease when the cause ceases. They have made a bad selection; the Britons they should have outlawed are the chimney-sweeps, not the intellectual lords who guide public opinion. All they do will be noticed and criticised justly, and no nation is the worse for that.

8. International property is a bond of friendship and a security for peace and good-will. There will be in each country several persons holding property in the other, and desirous to compose differences, not inflame them; whereas the writer for wages is comparatively reckless, and has often jeopardised peace with his stings.

9. Eventually the States will produce beyond men's wildest dreams at present. Nature is rich; we are too apt to bound her by the narrow experience of our own life. Time, population, and encouragement will grow another Scott, another Cooper, another Byron, and even perhaps another Shakespeare; for, under equal rights, intellectual giants are far more likely to spring in the States than here. The studies of Bret Harte, the pastorals of Carleton, and other true gleams of genius that now come from the States are like jets of water forcing their way through a sea-wall. The gorillas and chimpanzees look at them, and say "that is all the water there is." To a higher intelligence they show how strong is nature, that any water at all can come through the barrier of bad laws. Remove the wall, and the infinite waters will flow, where now those struggling jets reveal the curbed ocean.

The true law-giver is rare. For ages senators have preferred party to mankind, and it has made them as ephemeral as gad-flies. Your Solon and Lycurgus climbed hills above the dust of strife and the mists of clique, and took a bird's-eye view of all the land. If amongst my American readers there is one senator to whom the old Republican law-giver seems a bigger, and a better, and a more enduring man than the ephemeral mouthpiece of ephemeral party, he can play the ancient law-giver on a grander field than antiquity afforded. It is not every day that a single earnest statesman can brighten the tarnished escutcheon of a great and generous Republic, and heal the deep wound of a kindred nation, cut down a five-fold iniquity and a national upas tree, lay the first stone of a mighty literature, and earn the gratitude of the greatest minds in two great countries. This would be to rise above the mob of senators, the noisy squabblers of a Congress, and them "whose talk is of bullocks." If there be such a man at Washington—and surely there must be many—let him hold out his hand and grasp true honour, not vociferous, but lasting; the arts, immortal themselves, confer immortal fame, or infamy, on friend and foe; cliques and parties come and go; but these flow on for ever; and, though no greasy palms applaud their champion, to the bray of trumpets and the flare of gas, a mild but lasting light, still brightening as justice spreads and civilisation marches, shall hover around his living head, and gild his memory when dead. The words of Reade are ended.

Sir,—I did intend to go into the domestic wrongs of authors. But, as a commission of inquiry is about to collect facts, it would be more proper, on many accounts, to postpone that matter. Besides I have already intruded too long. Be pleased to accept our thanks for the sacrifice you have made to justice; you have allowed a worthy but unpopular subject to occupy many, many columns of a popular journal, and both American and English authors owe you a deep debt of gratitude, which, unfortunately, we can only pay in words.

CHARLES READE.

LETTER TO MR. J. R. LOWELL

(UNITED STATES MINISTER)

ON INTERNATIONAL COPYRIGHT

19 Albert Gate, Knightsbridge,
September 2, 1880.

Dear Mr. Lowell,—You are good enough to desire my opinion upon a proposed Copyright Treaty between the United States and Great Britain, "the principal feature of which is the granting of Copyright, provided the book be manufactured in the country so granting it by a subject or citizen thereof within three months of its publication by the author."

To reply to this outline I must ask to dissect it ; for here in one sentence are two proposals that I consider heterogeneous, and even discordant.

Permit me then to put the matter thus :—

1. The book to be manufactured in the country granting Copyright, by a subject or citizen.

2. This to be done (and I conclude the book published) within three months, &c.

No. 1. Let us examine precisely the grievance this treaty proposes to alleviate.

An author's work which, when worth pirating, is the fruit of great labour, consists of an essential substance and a vehicle.

The substance is the composition ; the vehicle is generally paper and words written with ink.

That the composition is the substance — though puny lawyers and petty statesmen cannot see it, is shown by this —it can be sold *vivâ voce* apart from paper and written or printed words: dramatic compositions are so sold, and the first epic poem was so delivered to the public for centuries, and the Chronicles of Froissart were sold *vivâ voce* by the

206

author, and to his great profit, and no copies made till he died; and the public used to pay Dickens a much higher price for his spoken compositions, than for the same compositions papered, printed, and bound.

A printed book, or play, is only the manuscript multiplied; the composition remains the substance; the paper, print, and binding are still a mere vehicle, and not the only one; the Theatre sells the same composition with quite a different vehicle.

Now the grievance of authors against nations cultivating piracy is this—they rob the foreign workman, who produces the substance, of a book or play, yet remunerate all the workmen, *whether native or foreign*, who produce the mere vehicle. The injury is levelled at the foreign author *quâ* author, and not *quâ* foreigner.

Let a foreign author cross the water with a play and a book. Let him go into a theatre and a printing house; let him play one of those many characters he has created in his drama, and print fifty pages of his own composition, he can extort remuneration—although he is a foreigner—for both vehicles; but he can enforce none for the far more valuable substance he has created with infinitely greater, higher, and longer labour. Here then is an exceptional fraud levelled at exceptional merit, and one producing labourer picked out of a dozen for pillage, though what he produces contributes more to the aggregate value than the labour of all the other workmen concerned.

This iniquity may pay a handful of booksellers, or theatrical managers, in a nation cultivating Piracy, but it massacres the authors of that nation by the competition of stolen compositions, and it robs the nation of the habit of literary and dramatic invention, which is a greater *national treasure* than any amount of stolen compositions, since the nation which harbours pirates has to pay the full price for the vehicles, and does not get the substance or composition for nothing, any the more because its booksellers and theatrical managers do. Indeed, as to the latter, the prices are never lowered to the native public one cent, in those cases where the manager steals the drama from a foreign author.

Now proposition 1, taken singly, entirely cures the above grievance, so far as printed books are concerned.

Authors have a moral right to be paid for their compositions, in every nation where the vehicle is paid for and the combination sold, not given away; but they have no moral claim, that

I am aware of, to create and sell the *vehicle* in a distant land, and if they have no such right, still less can their native publishers—mere occasional assignees of copyright—pretend to acquire a right from authors, which authors themselves do not claim.

The United States are a protectionist nation, and it would be egotistical and childish of English authors to expect that nation to depart from its universal policy, and to make an exception in favour of authors, and their mere occasional assignees ; our cry is " no partiality !" To ask you to deviate from your universal policy would be to ask for " some partiality."

Proposition 2.—This rests on no basis of universal equity or of uniform national policy. It does not come from the mind of any American lawyer or statesman. It is one of those subtle suggestions of Piracy, with which all copyright acts are marred. Copyrights are neither meal nor meat, and therefore, like other products of high civilisation, they cannot obtain their just value on a forced sale. But three months to transact the sale of the composition and also create the vehicle is a very forced sale.

Habits are strong, and this proviso would encourage the bad habit the treaty professes to cure, instead of stimulating a good one. It would turn all the publishers, on both sides the water, into Lot's wives, hankering after dear old Piracy, and longing to put the clock on three months. By hanging back during that short period they might drive even popular authors into a corner. But the proviso would do a much worse thing than that—the rising American author, who is literally withering under the present system, and who is the victim, that needs loyal and earnest protection, far more than any British author does—would be juggled, under this proviso. For some years he must necessarily come into our market at a certain disadvantage independent of law. British publishers would either offer him one-tenth of his value or demand time to see how his book sold in the United States : and then, having gained time, would use this proviso, steal his composition, if it proved a success, or chuck him a bone instead of his just slice.

But these comments, you will understand, are levelled at the nude proviso as you have presented it to me.

If your government has foreseen that it is certain to be abused, and to render the whole treaty more or less illusory, and therefore intends to control it by some other clause, that is another matter.

If not, and the proviso has been incautiously inserted with the reasonable desire to protect the public against a foreign author's refusal to sell his copyright at all, or on reasonable terms, the whole case could be met by an additional clause giving the foreign author or proprietor the right to apply to the Judges in Banco for an extension of the term, on the ground that he had offered the copyright, or a share in it, or the use of it, but had been unable to obtain terms corresponding in any degree with his market value at home. The judges to have the right to receive written evidence, less strict than a jury would require, and to extend the term or authorise the foreign proprietor to publish through a native agent, or afford some other relief, under the vital conditions of the treaty.

Having gone deeper into the matter than I intended, I may as well volunteer a remark or two outside your queries which may be of service to the American Legislator, if he will receive it from me.

There are two great literary properties of nearly equal value and importance.

1. A man's exclusive right to print and publish the composition he has created, whether history, romance, treatise, or drama, &c.

2. His exclusive right to represent on a public stage the dramatic composition he has created.

No. 1 is called Copyright, No. 2 is called Stage-right. But, unfortunately, the Anglo-Saxon muddlehead has hitherto avoided the accurate term, stage-right, and applied, in the teeth of sense, grammar, and logic, the imbecile phrase, "dramatic copyright," to No. 2. But the phrase, "dramatic copyright," means the sole right of printing and publishing a play-book, or it means nothing at all. It cannot mean, nor be made to mean the right of representing a play. Now men are the slaves of words; and so our lawgivers and yours, having the word "copyright" dinned eternally into their ears, and never hearing the word "stage-right," are at this moment in a fool's paradise. They imagine copyright to be an all important right and stage-right an insignificant affair.

Pure chimera! stage-right is at least as important as copyright, and international morality and sound policy demand international stage-right as much as they do international copyright.

Our two nations invest their money on the following scale.

1. A vast sum daily in newspapers, of which the title is copyright; but not the contents. These protect themselves

from fatal piracy; they die a natural death every afternoon, and so escape assassination next morning.

2. A small sum, daily, in books.

3. A large sum, daily, in represented plays—one hundred thousand pounds sterling per day at the very least.

As regards 2 and 3, you will find the comparative scale indicated in the newspapers themselves; these, with unerring instinct, discover the habits of their nation. Take them through the breadth of the land, you will find they review a book now and then, but they are eternally puffing plays, and at great length.

Now by piracy of stage-right from foreigners, a nation loses its chance of that great treasure, a national drama, and does not get one cent per annum in exchange for that serious deprivation. The piratical publisher pretends he sells a book cheaper for stealing the composition. It is not true; for, if he bought the composition under a copyright act, he would sell all the copies instead of sharing the sale with other pirates; and so could sell cheaper than in the way of Piracy: but, if not true, it is plausible, and has deceived shallow statesmen by the score.

But the piratical manager of a theatre does not even *pretend* to lower his prices to the public in those cases, when he steals the composition.

There are, besides all this, two special reasons why you should propose international stage-right to the British Government, along with international copyright, and not as an after-clap, which you will have to do if you will not listen to Cassandra, better known in Knightsbridge as Charles Reade. One is, that the people most likely to give you trouble in this country, over international copyright, are the British publishers. Habitual creators of the vehicle and not of the composition and the copyright, they will naturally think it very hard they are not to be allowed to create the vehicle in the United States.

Their opposition might be serious; because, for some generations, they have been allowed to thrust themselves forward and put the authors unreasonably in the background.

To discuss with our Government the two great properties authors create, viz., stage-right and copyright, would tend to open John Bull's eyes and show him which is really the leading character in literary property, the authors, who create all the stage-rights and all the copyrights, or the publishers, who acquire by assignment about one-third of the copyrights only, and none of the stage-rights.

The second reason is that at present the American dramatic author suffers a special iniquity, by Act of Parliament, deteriorating the common law of England.

If a British author writes a drama, represents it on the stage in Great Britain, but does not publish it, and then exports it to the United States, he possesses the sole right of representation in the United States, or, at all events, in the principal States. This has been decided by your judges after full and repeated discussion.

The American dramatist, until 1842, possessed the same right under the law of England; and accordingly Macklin v. Richardson, which is the English case that protects all unpublished dramas under the common law, was lately cited with authority in the tribunals of the United States on the occasion I have referred to.

But our copyright act of 1842 poked its nose into stage-right, with which it had nothing on earth to do, and inserted an unjust, oppressive, and unreasonable clause, outlawing from stage-right all dramas not first represented in Great Britain. The framers of this, and a similar clause in the body of the act, mistook the root of an author's title. The poor souls imagined it accrues by publication or representation under an Act of Parliament, whereas it accrues earlier in time, and by an older and much higher title, viz., creation, and under the common law.

Test.—Let A. write a MS. and lend it to B. B. print and publish it, and register it at Stationers' Hall, and hand the MS. back, uninjured, without a scratch on it, to A. A. would sue B. for breach of copyright, under the common law, and B.'s parliamentary title, by publication and registration, would prove not worth a rush against the precedent title by creation and common law.

The American dramatist, therefore, is by the above clause in an act that had no need to run, like a frolicsome colt, out of copyright into stage-right, and so extend the field of its blunders, subjected to a special iniquity.

In copyright there is at present a sort of equity of fraud. Rob my authors, and I will rob your authors. But in stage-right it is pure iniquity, and the American dramatist the victim.

These are the principal reasons why I venture to advise you not to exclude international stage-right from

211

your discussion of international copyright with the British Government.

I must now apologise for my presumption—which, however, arises from good-will—and for the crude and hasty character of these comments. But I present them to one who is well able to sift the chaff from the grain, and so make the best of them.—I am, my dear Mr. Lowell, yours very sincerely,

CHARLES READE.

VICARIA

Sir,—There is a little stroke of business going to be done next Friday in the little town of Uxbridge, against which I beg to record a little protest. It is a public auction of a very small personality professedly for the benefit of the Crown; but I apprehend the proceeds will go to another branch of the revenue. This sale and the threatened appropriation of certain money which was regarded by the deceased holder as trust-money, arose out of the following circumstances: The Rev. W. Orr, a Nonconformist minister, wrote, with his own hand, August 6, 1881, a will, containing a just and proper disposition of his small property. He bequeathed £50 to New College, Hampstead; £50 in three sums to three poor Christian women who had been his housekeepers at different periods; a few of his choicest books to clerical friends; his gold watch and chain to a Miss Ellen Orr; and the balance, after payment of expenses, to a Mrs. W. Orr. But as to a sum of £300, he did not bequeath it, but directed it to be returned to Miss Sarah Peters; and he appointed a Mr. Harris his executor. Mr. Orr showed this will at various times to several persons who knew his handwriting; and its contents became public. They even reached the three poor housekeepers; and that is a sad feature of the case at present. A few days before Mr. Orr died, a dear friend of his learned that his will was not attested, and advised him to repair that omission. Mr. Orr assented, but death surprised him before he could execute his declared purpose. He died February 7, 1882, deeply mourned by his own flock and revered by all good Christians in the town of Uxbridge.

He had no relations in law. His will was attested, in fact, by half-a-dozen witnesses, but not, in law, "by two," and therefore his property lay at the mercy of what cuckoos still call " the Crown," but accuracy—if such a bird of paradise existed in England—would call " the Revenue."

However, high-minded men, acting in the name of the Crown, have of late been very shy of confiscating even in cases of felony, and as Mr. Orr was not a felon, but only a saint and an Irishman, and therefore could not, *ex vi terminorum*, be a man of business, we hoped that the Lords of the Treasury would respect his solemn wishes, since they are as clear, and clearer, than if the will had been drawn by a lawyer's clerk and signed by two witnesses.

Accordingly the matter went before the Lords of the Treasury in two forms.

1. Sarah Peters petitioned for the return of her £300, as above.

2. Mr. Harris, executor, offered to act and discharge all the debts, expenses, and legacies, if the Lords of the Treasury would forego their claim.

Miss Peters tells me she has received no reply.

Mr. Harris has heard only from the Solicitor of the Treasury, ordering an immediate sale of the property—with one exception. His vicarious Majesty, the Solicitor for the Treasury, accords to the executor the right to withhold the choice books, but not the right to withhold the gold watch and chain, which were as solemnly bequeathed to a person specified as the books were. Now, I did not expect this Imperial edict and high-minded, though illogical, distinction to be signed by the chief of that bureau, for he has valued books far more than gold from his youth up until now. But, by what I can learn, the edict is not signed by any Lord of the Treasury whatever. It is clear on the face of things that neither the petition of Miss Peters nor the proposal of Mr. Harris has been laid before the Lords of the Treasury, nor considered by responsible men. Yet prompt action is taken at once by vicarious rapacity. There is no vice in any of the individuals concerned; it is merely a vicious system. The Solicitor of the Treasury would not pounce upon this property for his personal benefit; the Lords of the Treasury will bring their understandings and their consciences to bear on the matter—after a few months or years; and will probably decide in favour, not of English law, but of Continental law and universal morality, both of which support this deceased clergyman's will written by his own hand and shown to his friends. But, meantime, this harsh auction, ordered with inconvenient and indecorous haste, over a new-made grave—this present activity of vicarious greed and dead silence as to equity to come—have shocked and revolted a thousand mourners, and cruelly disappointed the humbler legatees as well as excited some public odium. I do not wish to inflame their feelings, but to suggest their removal. Therefore, as my views are always unintelligible to the clerks and secretaries, the duffers, the buffers, and the agents, of a public office, and I can no more get a manuscript past that incarnate rampart of "vicaria" than Miss Peters or Mr. Harris can, will you kindly allow me to approach the magnates of the Treasury by the only *direct* road I know—viz., the columns of a great public journal? I think, my lords, it would be well to let the people know without delay that you intend personally to consider the question whether or not, under the peculiar circumstances, any portion of this deceased clergyman's estate, except the amount of legacy duty, shall be finally appropriated by the State ; and as regards the gold watch and chain, it is not too late to withdraw them from the coming sale ; and I hope you will concede this favour, because, if they are thrown into the melting-pot of the Treasury next Friday, for not being hexaglot bibles, it may be difficult, even should Dr. Stevenson vouchsafe his aid, to reintegrate and reconstruct the component parts so as to recover their value to the legatee. To her they are not so many ounces of jeweller's gold, but the souvenir of one who never wasted time, yet lived for eternity.—Yours faithfully,

CHARLES READE.

March 16, 1882.

HANG IN HASTE, REPENT AT LEISURE :

A SUPPRESSED INDICTMENT

To the Editor of the "Daily Telegraph"

FIRST LETTER

September 29th, 1877.

Sir,—I read with surprise and deep concern these lines in the *Daily Telegraph*, Sept. 27 :—

"The jury asked the learned judge if they could have a copy of the indictment.

"Mr. Justice Hawkins said, 'It would not help them in the least, written as it was in legal phraseology.'"

Now, if the judge had said, "Of course, gentlemen, you have as much right to examine the indictment as I have ; but I warn you it is written in a jargon you are not intended to understand, but only to pronounce on, and so hang your fellow-creatures," there would have been no harm done and a wholesome reprimand administered to the pedantic clique which words these public and terrible accusations in jargon and equivoques.

But I infer from your printed lines that the jury asked for a copy of the indictment to compare with the condensed evidence, and did not get one.

If so, the thing is monstrous, and vitiates the proceedings, creditable as they were in many respects. Consider, sir, the Crown is not above the law. The Crown, in a prosecution of this sort, comes before the jury, who are the country, in the general character of plaintiff and proceeds by indictment. That indictment is the grave and deliberate accusation which the Crown, to guard against the errors and defects of the tongue, submits *in writing* to the judge and the jury. It is a

216

legal document which the judge is bound to criticise severely, on grounds of law. It is an allegation of facts and motives the jury is equally bound to dissect severely, and compare it in every particular with the evidence. Then, if there is a legal defect in it no bigger than a pin's head, the judge can upset the case in spite of its merits; and by the same rule—whatever the egotism of the legal clique may think—if it vary from the truth in its allegations of fact or of motives, which latter are the vital part of an indictment, it is the duty of the jury to throw it over, or in certain cases to reduce the verdict. And it does so happen that in cases of alleged homicide the indictment ought always to be dissected without mercy by the jury, for here, where the Crown ought to be most accurate, it is most apt to exaggerate. The truth is, that many years ago the legal advisers of the Crown thirsted for the blood of accused persons, and framed indictments accordingly; and such is the force of precedent that even now the Crown (or some attorney's clerk we are content to call by that name) is somewhat given to equivocating, exaggerating, and alleging more than can be proved, especially in the way of motives, which are the true sting of an indictment.

Whatever bad and unreasonable custom the legal clique, in dealing with the nation, may have introduced into our courts, it is clearly the duty of the Crown Solicitor to lay before the jury, who are the country, not the copy, but twelve copies, of the indictment, before the prosecuting counsel opens his lips. The judge has no better, no other, title to a copy of the indictment than each several juryman has. As to the jargon of indictments, I have not found it so thick but that a plain man can pick out of the rigmarole the facts and motives whereof what we call "the Crown" accuses the prisoner. If it were, the matter should be looked into at once. All cliques, however respectable, are public enemies at odd times. Many years ago the country had to compel the clergy to read prayers "in a language understanded of the people." Country v. Clique. Next we had to compel a clique to give us the laws of England in English. Country v. Clique. By-and-by we had to force a clique to drop the grossest compost of bad Latin and bad French nation ever groaned under, and to give us our law pleadings in English. Country v. Clique. And now, if it is seriously asserted that the Crown attacks the lives and liberties of Britons in a language not understanded of the country, though the country has to judge both Crown and prisoner, it is time we copied ancestral wisdom, and put our foot on imbecility No. 4. Country *v.* Clique.

These, however, are after-considerations; at present I stand upon clear constitutional rights.

I understand the country demanded in open court a copy of that indictment, and did not get one.

I repeat that demand in your columns, in order that the country may see it, jargon or no jargon, and compare it with the evidence in your columns. Of course I do not address my demand to any gentleman in particular. There are several copies in existence. No doubt some just man will awake from his slumbers and send you a copy. I earnestly hope to see it printed *in extenso*. Till then I forbear all comments on the case, because the issues are not before me, any more than they were before the country at the trial.— Your faithful servant, CHARLES READE.

SECOND LETTER

October 2nd, 1877.

SIR,—It is an old saying that one fool makes many. I have, however, discovered something more—viz., that one muddle-head sometimes makes a million, if he can get a popular journal to print him. I must take the world as it is ; and in so grave and terrible a case, I dare not let your correspondent " A. B." pass unanswered.

He is a lawyer, and does not pretend to deny that the jury have as good a right to a copy of the indictment as the judge has. But he says that in a large experience of criminal trials, he never knew a judge to hand a copy of the indictment to the jury. He adds, in the roundabout style of men who do not think clearly, what really comes to this, that as the judge *talked* a great deal and well, it did not matter to the jury what the Crown *wrote*.

Now, sir, this is no answer to me. I never said the judge was bound to volunteer a copy of the indictment to the jury; I never denied the malpractice of the courts, and that the Crown Solicitor does not hand twelve copies to the jury, though it is his duty. I have never denied that twelve unguarded jurymen, new to the courts, often let the legal clique trepan them into trying a case without studying the written issues. But ignorant persons can only forego their own rights. Their ignorance does not forfeit the rights of the informed. What we have to do with is a jury which acted on their rights and their duty. They were just enough, wise enough, and wary enough, to demand, at a critical period of the trial, a copy of the very words of the Crown upon which, and not upon the judge's words, they had to say, "Guilty or not guilty." The judge put off this their just and proper demand, and gave a reason which, weighed against the wise and proper reasons of the jury and against their constitutional right, sounds almost like mere levity. By so doing, he left them to give their verdict on his own spoken words alone, and not on the written words of his Sovereign and theirs. This is the case. I think it is without precedent and vitiates the proceedings. If there is a precedent, however, it will be found and quoted. But the country will expect it to be a precedent that fits the case, without shuffling or equivocation, and meantime I hope the execution will not be hurried, but time given for the country and the Home Secretary to consider this fatal blot on the proceedings. Indeed, the matter ought to be noticed in Parliament, especially in the House of Commons.—I am, Sir, your faithful servant,

CHARLES READE.

THIRD LETTER

October 3rd, 1877.

SIR,—Mr. Abbott says the author of "It is Never too Late to Mend" is soft-hearted. Not a bit of it. He is only harder-headed than certain Englishmen. He proved in the story cited above that the honest man who kills a thief in prison contrary to law is a greater criminal than the thief. That was logic ; not compassion. Mr. Abbott now reminds us that pettifogging judges, looking too closely into indictments, have quashed them on trumpery grounds of law, in spite of evidence. This is notorious. But what is the inference ? are the *judges* not to be allowed a copy of the indictment ? He has proved *that*, or he has proved nothing; for no *jury* ever defeated justice with a quibble on the indictment. In spite of these occasional abuses, constitutional rights must not be tampered with. A judge is as much entitled to a copy of the indictment as even the jury are, who have to try the issues. What we have to do with is a new thing—the separate indictments of four persons, submitted to the judge, but not seen by the jury, though they asked for them, and the jury delivering a sort of lump verdict on unseen indictments, in which, perhaps, the Crown did not lump four very different cases in one without any discriminating words whatever. Who knows? The indictments are still suppressed. Another of your correspondents draws me out by malicious misinterpretation. He puts violent and cruel words into my mouth, and is reckless enough, with my sober lines before him, to pretend that I compare Mr. Justice Hawkins to Judge Jeffreys. Of course such unscrupulous people can compel a man to notice them. The learned judge has been my counsel, and I have profited by his abilities. I was never so unfortunate as to have him against me, in court. I hope I never shall. The jury asked by word of mouth for the indictment. He replied, without much reflection, by word of mouth. His reply was unfortunate, as many a hasty reply of my own has been, and as its effect was to deprive the jury of their constitutional rights, I think it vitiates the proceedings. As to the merits of the case, is it fair of any man to tell the public what I think when I myself have been so careful not to rush hastily into that question? As it happens, I approve some things in the learned judge's summing-up in spite of the objection taken to those particulars by others. It is only in one part of the subject I do not at present agree with him. Even then, I desire to think well before I write, for no man feels more than I do the responsibility to God and man of every one who uses the vast power of a popular journal in a case of life and death.—Yours faithfully,

CHARLES READE.

FOURTH LETTER

October 10th, 1877.

SIR,—When a woman of property is half starved by people who are eating her bread, and her husband, with his paramour, lives but one mile distant, on the money of their injured benefactress, and the victim dies covered with vermin and weighing about five stone, the wildfire of indignation will, I hope, always run through every vein of the country, and the judges share the just wrath of the gentry and of the millions who work so hard to feed their own helpless charges.

But great wrath, even when just, is still a fever of the mind, and cannot discriminate. Whilst the heart is still hot with that fire which has been so truly called "a passing frenzy" (*ira brevis furor*), the culpable ones seem criminal, the criminal ones seem monsters, and "our great revenge has stomach for them all."

I, who write these lines, am but a man recovering fast from a fever in a nation which is recovering slowly but surely. I recover fast, because, from my youth, I have been trained in a great school to reason closely and discriminate keenly, and armed with Oxford steel against the tricks and sophistries of rhetoric, against the derangement of dates (which single artifice will turn true facts into lies), against those fatal traps, equivoques in language, and against all gaps, in evidence, however small they may appear to the unwary. I grieve to say that I receive shoals of insulting letters, telling me I am a Whalleyite and a novelist, and so disqualified. This draws a few unwilling words from me to disarm prejudice. I declared against Orton in the *Daily News* before ever the Crown tried him. I then laid down the scientific principle which governs his case, the doctrine of multiplied coincidences; and, though I write novels at one time, I can write logic at another, and when I write a novel I give the public my lowest gifts, but I give them my highest when I write in a great journal upon life and death and justice. But the best thing the public, and those who govern it, can do, will be to go by things, not names, to sift my arguments as closely as I shall analyse the evidence and the hasty inferences in the greatest judicial error of modern times.

The verdict against the Stauntons and Rhodes is a hodge-podge, in which the legally criminal and the legally culpable are confounded, and both sets of legal culprits are confounded with the moral culprits, who are clear of the case by the law of England and the rules of evidence that bind the Central Criminal Court.

Few observers of mankind will deny me this, which, indeed, reads like a truism :—

Where A, B, and C confound four things, and D, on the same evidence, distinguishes them, it is a thousand to one that D is right, and A, B, and C are wrong.

The position becomes even stronger when we find that A, B, and C have been subject to several confusing influences. It may be worth while to point out the confusing processes that muddled the jury, of which processes some rise from the habitual malpractices of this particular court, and others from faults that have been imported into it for this single occasion.

Processes of Confusion.

1. The court, for its convenience, tried four dissimilar cases in the lump, and the four prisoners stood together at the bar.

2. Being near and dear to each other, and involved in one danger, they suffered and sympathised openly.

3. Twelve unguarded men looked on, and deluded by the senses, which are always stronger than the judgment in untrained minds, said to themselves, "they are all in one boat." So they were—in one family boat, not one legal boat. But the family boat being in a legal dock, these good souls took it for a legal boat directly.

4. The four separate indictments, with their curious counts, would have tended to cure this. But here the malpractices of the court came in with another process of confusion.

By the law of England the arraignment of a prisoner consists of three parts: (*a*) He is called to the bar by his name ; (*b*) the indictment is read to him, every syllable of it ; (*c*) he is invited to plead to the indictment, and no other form of words, and he has a right to plead guilty to one count, and not guilty to another count ; and, if he is legally culpable, but not criminal, it is the wisest thing he can do.

This being done by the Clerk of Arraigns, the paper that Clerk has read from becomes, from the universal practice of all our courts, the property of the jury so long as that trial lasts.

But the Clerk of Arraigns, by a modern malpractice, broke this just and necessary law, and the judge let him. So each prisoner was grossly robbed of his right to admit one count and deny another, and the jury were grossly robbed of a copy of the indictment, though the mere preliminary jury, whose responsibility is so much less, had one to study and find a true Bill on ; and though it is not merely the right but the duty of the jury, as laid down by Blackstone himself very clearly, to study the indictment very closely and to find "guilty" on one count, and "not guilty" on another, and to carry discrimination even further, for they can find guilty on one half of a divisible count and acquit upon the other.

5. Law, justice, and common sense having thus been defied by the Central Criminal Court, and the great written instru-

ment of discrimination withheld from them contrary to law, they were manipulated and confused by a rhetorician on the Bench, who picked out the highest count and ignored the others, and with gentle hand extinguished their one faint gleam of incipient discrimination, and left no doubt to the jury in a case crammed with doubts; which was unprecedented.

The result corresponded with all these co-operating processes.

The judge laid down the law that whoever has by law, or takes upon himself, the charge of a helpless person and does not give her enough to live upon is guilty of murder by omission. He did not say whoever has one-fourth of the charge, for that is not the law.

THE CHARGE.

Under this ruling, on which I have something to say hereafter, the jury on the evidence contrived to see four persons, all of whom had either by law or their own act "*the* charge" of Harriet Staunton, and all saw her pine to death and let her pine to death.

Now let all men, in whose minds the very landmarks of truth are not obliterated, look on that picture conjured up by a jury under several processes of confusion along with this picture which the evidence reveals to a discriminating eye.

Patrick Staunton, a committer of a crime, responsible for Harriet Staunton's life by a pecuniary contract with Louis. He docks her food, strikes her, terrifies and strikes his wife for interfering, &c. The evidence suggests that if the man had died in 1876, Harriet Staunton might be alive now. He comes under the judge's ruling. He had "*the* charge." This is the only committer of them all. Yet the jury can see nothing exceptional in his position. We now step down to a much lower grade of crime.

THE MERE OMITTERS.

At the head is Mrs. Patrick Staunton, a grown-up woman, experienced, and no fool. Her neglect of Harriet is *primâ facie* barbarous; but it transpires that there was conjugal influence and coercion. The woman encountered blows in defence of the victim. The deterring effect of those blows, and her pregnancy, cannot be exactly estimated; nor is it necessary. The law, already disposed to assume conjugal influence, except in an indisputable case of murder, is amply satisfied with the admissions made on this head, and she is not a criminal, but a culpable offender. Two years' imprisonment. The next omitter is Clara Brown. She slept in the same room with the victim; allowed the vermin to accumulate; saw her sufferings more than Mrs. P. Staunton: filled her own belly and let her perish; nor did she show any positive goodness of heart, as the elder woman did once or twice. I mean she never faced a blow nor got an angry word, and she never told a soul till the Crown Solicitor inspired her with higher sentiments. On the other hand, she was young, inexperienced, and stupid; and, though she saw most of the victim, never anticipated her death, which blindness in her rouses a suspicion that the whole set were much greater fools and smaller villains than they look. We now take a step in law which is as wide as the step down from the one committer to the four omitters. We go out of the house. We don't even go next door, but to another house a mile distant, where two self-indulgent adulterers were hiding themselves from Harriet Staunton and absorbed in adultery, which was made smooth by Patrick's control of the injured wife. I never knew how low the human understanding could sink till I saw a jury who could confound this situation with that of Mrs. Patrick Staunton and Clara Brown, two people living in the house where Harriet Staunton pined on the first floor. That first-floor Louis Staunton and Alice Rhodes avoided from self-indulgent motives, that are out of the case. Of these two persons, the law never had any hold on Rhodes. A mistress living in one house is not bound to provide food for a wife living in another. Rhodes is out of the case. Louis Staunton, until some day in August 1876, was deep in the case. But the judge, in order to make hostile comments on his niggardliness, let in as evidence that he made a contract with Patrick Staunton of this kind—Patrick was to receive Harriet in his own house, and receive twenty shillings per week. Louis was a mean scoundrel to offer so small a sum, but a rustic labourer and eight children live on less. It crushes the charge of murder as completely as twenty pounds a week would. It is a contract in which both contracting parties contemplated, not the death, but the indefinite life of Harriet Staunton. Its very niggardliness proves that on behalf of

Louis Staunton. A man can transfer his legal responsibility. It is done daily. The legal responsibility of Louis Staunton passed by that pecuniary contract to Patrick as much as did the responsibility of that mother, who handed her child for five shillings a week to a baby-farmer, which baby-farmer neglected the child till it died a bag of bones, and was tried by Sir James Hawkins two days after the Stauntons. (See *The Daily Telegraph*, Oct 1.) The attempts made to drag Rhodes into the case at all, and to drag Louis back into it after admission of that contract, are pure sophistry and equivocation, as I shall show in the proper place. Meantime here is the true picture.

1. Committer and criminal.

2. Culpable omitters; one condemned to die, one walking about London.

3 and 4. Two vile moral omitters clear of the crime, but relieved by the lawyers of all their ill-gotten money, defended with admirable speeches, but worse defended on the evidence than they could have defended themselves, and condemned to die.

The blunder has been brought about partly by the recent malpractices, and the inherent defects, of the Central Criminal Court, whose system is so faulty that it never gets below the surface of a case, and is the worst instrument for the discovery of truth in Europe; and partly from special vices and errors, that found their way into the case, and surprise the whole legal profession, so opposed are they to precedent, and to the best traditions, and most sober habits, of the court. These it will be my next duty to analyse closely, but I think I can hit upon a briefer method than I have been able to pursue in this letter.—Yours faithfully, CHARLES READE.

FIFTH LETTER

October 12th, 1877.

SIR,—Were I, who denounce an indiscriminating verdict upon four immoral egotists, to endorse the indiscriminating censure levelled at the judge who tried the case, I should exceed the error I condemn, for I should be morally unjust to the good, he has only been legally unjust to a portion of the bad.

I declare, then, that he had no power to prevent one of the

omitters from giving evidence against the others, whose mouths were closed by an iniquity of the law which is itself doomed to death; nor had he any right to disparage her whole evidence, but only to reject one part and sift the rest with keen suspicion; and when he directed the jury to prefer the opinion of doctors who had seen the body, to that of doctors who had not, and bade the jury observe the ugly circumstance that Harman, the doctor who had watched the post-mortem examination on behalf of the defendants, was not called for the defence, he did his duty to the jury, guided by innumerable precedents, which not only justified, but bound him. He did not make the rules of evidence: he found the rules of evidence, and very wise they are. In a word, I will not wilfully object to anything but what defies precedent, and the habits of our other judges, and every one of their predecessors, whose name their country honours.

1. The judge laid down the law thus, as affecting the only count of a suppressed indictment which he permitted the jury to try; "every person who is under a legal duty, whether such duty be imposed by the law, or imposed by contract, or by the act of taking charge, wrongfully, or otherwise, of another person, to provide the necessaries of life, every such person is criminally responsible for the culpable neglect of that duty. And if the person so neglected is, from age, insanity, health, or any other cause, unable to take care of himself, and by reason of that neglect death ensues, the crime is murder."

Now this is the law if you don't stretch it, and try to catch more fish than the law allows. It is the law as it lies in the text-books, and is there applied to a *single person, having the sole legal charge.*

But as regards these four offenders it is too broad and loose, and is not the law of England as appears in the cases to which those very text-books refer, and in fifty other cases, well known, though not reported by lawyers, but only word for word by the newspapers. These are shunned by the lawyers; they are invaluable; but then they are not published and sold by that sacred clique.

However, the cases of criminal omission, though pitiably reduced in number by that childish prejudice, are, I think, fatal to this new theory of criminal responsibility in the highest degree attaching to persons who have not the sole charge in law of the murdered person.

What will my readers think, and what will the Home Secretary think, when I tell him that to find in the books a verdict of murder by omission I must go back to *ninety-seven years*—to a time when jurymen were so used to shed blood like water by statute law that they naturally applied even the common law with a severity that is now out of date.

I, who with these eyes have seen a boy of eighteen hanged for stealing a horse, though the jury could have saved him, and the judge could have saved him with a word, am not disposed to rate beyond its value the case of "Rex *v.* Squires," on which Sir J. Hawkins, I think, relies, still less to stretch it *ad infinitum*, where the jury that hanged him restricted it so closely.

In 1790 the Crown indicted Squires and his wife for murder. They had starved a young apprentice, and beaten him cruelly. The wife, as to the beating, could not by law prove conjugal influence, for she had beaten the boy in her husband's absence, which bars that plea. The post-mortem, however, revealed starvation, and not the boy's wounds, to be the cause of death. The jury found Squires guilty of murder; but they held that Mrs. Squires had not in this, as she had in the blows, acted independently of her husband. She had not intercepted any food her husband had given her for the boy.

If this case is to be acted on in our day, at least we should not garble, and take the sanguinary half. The jury acquitted Mrs. Squires, a far worse woman than Mrs. P. Staunton, and they acquitted her logically. In a case of omission they could not convict the husband capitally but by loading him with the whole charge, and the whole criminality of a joint act. Does this case, looked into and understood, support the new theory of criminal responsibility, infinitely divisible, without diminution of guilt.

A leading case of our own day, and therefore a better guide for us, is "The Queen *v.* Bubb and Hook." Elizabeth Bubb was a widow with two children, and sister to Richard Hook's wife, deceased. Hook invited her into his house, and gave her money to keep the family. She fed and clothed her own family, and half starved the poor dead sister's. She carried her cruelty so far that the neighbours remonstrated often, but Hook looked calmly on, and did not mind. By steady degrees this fiendish woman murdered Hook's youngest child by starvation and cold. She was indicted for murder. The jury did not conceal their horror, but they used their right, and reduced the crime to manslaughter ; but, as that verdict opens the door to lenient sentences, they guarded the judge in a way that shows how wise twelve plain men can be when each of them thinks for himself. They brought it in " aggravated manslaughter." Hook was tried for manslaughter at the same assize. As he had supplied Bubb with means, there was nothing against him but his apathy and neglect of his pining child, and his turning a deaf ear to remonstrances. It was left to the jury to decide whether this was culpable neglect, or stupid neglect in a father—not an outsider, like Rhodes. They decided for stupid neglect, and acquitted Hook. Here is the same principle. They were resolved to put the saddle on the right horse, and not upon two horses. Will my readers pause, and compare the guilt of the heartless, relentless fiend Bubb—sole instigator, sole executor of a deadly deed, in spite of remonstrances—with the case of Mrs. Patrick Staunton, a wife, and under influence, who in her moments of conscience resisted the cruelty, and was over-powered.

If you divide an apple into four pieces, you have four pieces, but not four apples. If, in a case of omission, you could really divide the legal charge, and the highest criminal responsibility, the effect would not be what Sir J. Hawkins told the jury the effect would be—to subdivide and fritter away the criminal responsibility till it should escape the lash of the law, and meet no punishment but public reprobation.

Example—two Welsh parents had an imbecile girl, who professed sanctity and fasting, and the old people made their money out of her. Incredulous doctors demanded a test. Parents consented. Doctors watched night and day, and went at the first plunge much deeper than the Stauntons ; for they stopped all supplies dead short. They killed her quick amongst them. The doctors sat round her bed and saw the lamp of life burn out in eight days. Vulgar curiosity does not excuse deliberate murder. See now if by any quibbling or evasion the conduct of the parents can be taken out of murder—as the law was laid down for the Stauntons, see above —or the doctors cleared of manslaughter. Clean stoppage of food is the short cut to murder, with the goal in sight all the way.

Insufficient supply of food is an uncertain road to man-slaughter. The victim may get used to it. Luigi Cornaro achieved a vast longevity by no other means than insufficient nutriment arrived at by degrees. If divided responsibility leaves seven people equally responsible, why were not those parents and doctors all hung?

2. " Imposed by Law, or Imposed by Contract."

True. But throughout this case he withheld from the jury that when the law and lawful contract are opposed, contract prevails. In order to submit to the jury some just comments on the niggardly wretch, Louis Staunton, and the 20s. he agreed to pay Patrick to house and board his wife, he let in the paltry contract as evidence; yet he withheld from the jury the immediate legal effect of the contract. This was to give Patrick the sole charge of the wife, and the sole criminal responsibility of the highest degree.

The legal responsibility passed clean out of Louis by passing into Patrick. Had Louis failed to pay weekly, Patrick could have sued him.

Whether a responsibility originally so sacred as a husband's could not be revived partially, and in a lower form, by Louis constantly visiting his wife and actually seeing her pine away, and whether this would not make him guilty of manslaughter is another matter, and one I shall deal with under another head; but I complain that the judge withheld his legal knowledge from the jury whenever it could serve a prisoner, of which this is one example.

3. Another is his dead silence as to Mrs. P. Staunton's legal position as a wife, and the influence of her husband upon her as well as on Rhodes—an influence the law is not unwilling to assume, though of course it can be rebutted, as when Mrs. Manning was proved to be the instigator of a joint crime. But here the husband had by contract the sole legal charge, like Squires in 1790.

4. Illegal and improper evidence was admitted, such as no prisoner with his mouth closed has ever been assassinated by in my time. Clara Brown was allowed to depose to the existence of a letter written by Louis Staunton to Alice Rhodes in August 1876. That was allowable, for Rhodes admitted having received and lost a letter. But now comes the legal wrong. She was allowed to own herself a thief as regarded that particular letter, and also what the old judges called " a spoliator of evidence."

As regarded that one letter, I mean she was allowed to depose that she had burnt it wilfully, and with her own hand, and yet she was permitted to take advantage of her own suppression of the real letter, to give by memory or imagination just so many words as the Crown Solicitor, who got up the case, thought might suffice to hang Louis Staunton by an equivocation pointing to murder, and an admission of long criminal intimacy, to prove adultery before as well as after marriage. "Spoliation of evidence" does not figure much in the text-books. You must go wide and deep to find the hundreds of cases that lie behind all the older maxims of law. "Assume everything to the discredit of a spoliator of evidence" is the maxim, and the person who destroys any written document divining its importance is certainly a spoliator of evidence. But if the good, though almost obsolete, phrase be objected to, I will resign it, and stick to the substance. Why, even at Nisi Prius, if a witness, to decide a case, swore he received a letter from a party who could not be put in the box, and proved that he really had received a letter from that person of some kind or other, would he be allowed to say "I burned the letter, seeing its importance; the writer *cannot be called to contradict me, so I remember enough of the contents to win this verdict,* £50,000, *for the party who puts me in the box*"—would not the judge hesitate to let the jury's mind be prejudiced by hearing this witness's garbled quotations? If another hand had burned it, well and good; but surely not when he had burnt it himself, and so put the court entirely at the mercy of partial quotation and misquotation. I am of opinion, subject to the decision of the judges—and it is quite time they sat to review criminal cases—that this sham reproduction of a selected and garbled part of a written letter the witness had wilfully destroyed was legally inadmissible against two prisoners whose mouths were sealed.

I shall show in my next that this violation, not of some pedantic rule of evidence, but of its very fundamental principles, lets a whole vein of romantic error into the case, and shall expose generally the false system by which the order of the facts was dislocated and the facts falsified.—Yours faithfully, CHARLES READE.

I beg to acknowledge with thanks some insulting letters from people who don't sign their names, and some encouraging ones from ladies and gentlemen who do.

SIXTH LETTER

October 13th, 1877.

Sir,—In reply to reasonable comments let me say I have not put forward that branch of law which concerns the aiding and abetting any kind of murder, whether by commission or omission, because the judge did not lay that down to the jury, and he was bound to do so if that was the law he relied on.

He never treated Louis Staunton as an "accessory before the fact," which under this head of law was the only cap that could be made to fit him. He never told the jury what precise evidence the law demands against a man who has made a niggardly contract contemplating, by its very niggardliness, the indefinite life of the victim, ere a jury is to pronounce that he did "procure, counsel, command and abet," the murder of that person.

Of course no lawyer will pretend that a man living out of the house of murder can be accessory *at* the fact, or what the text-books call "a principal in the first degree;" nor will any lawyer deny that if he lives out of the house, but procures, counsels, commands, or abets the murder, *beyond doubt*, he can be an accessory *before* the fact, or a principal in the second degree. But there must be high evidence and direct evidence, and if spoken or written words are relied on they must be addressed to the very person who does the murder, and must be unequivocal. A doubtful phrase addressed to Rhodes, who took no part in the murder, is not at all the kind of evidence required by all the books and all the cases. See the word "accessory" in any text-book or report whatever.

The Facts.

In our Criminal Court, where the prisoners, the only people who really know the ins and outs of the case, are not allowed to open their lips, and correct any of the shallow guesswork that is going on about them in their astonished ears, one great abuse like that I denounced in my last letter is sure to let in many more. Clara Brown, the one witness on whom the case for the Crown really depends, was allowed by the judge to swear she had destroyed a letter, and yet to cite so much of

231

it, correctly or incorrectly, as fitted the two horns of the prosecution. That abuse led at once to another. This model witness was allowed another privilege the rules of evidence do not grant—viz., to argue the case. For this the defendants are indebted to their counsel.

He asked whether she understood the sentence about Harriet being "out of the way" to refer to her death. To this question she replied "Yes."

French counsel surprised by a prosecution would immediately have had a personal conference with the prisoners, and would have asked the girl questions that would have greatly benefited the prisoners. The jury, hearing a witness swear to an interpretation of a doubtful phrase, were not aware this was not evidence, and ought severely to be rejected from their minds. So one abuse led to another, and it is not too much to say that this imaginary letter with the witness's black-hearted interpretation is the rope that is to hang Louis Staunton.

Well, such a rope of sand has never hung an Englishman in my day. It is pitiable to see how little, if anything, that can even by courtesy be called mental power, was brought to bear by twelve men of the world on this quotation of a letter without its contents, one of the stalest frauds in the world and also in literature of every kind, especially controversial theology.

Permit me to test this imaginary extract from what was proved, I think, to be a real letter, by one or two sure methods of which I am not the inventor.

Have those twelve gentlemen counted the number of words a young servant girl swore she had remembered in their exact order for nine months or more, though she had burned the letter, and the subject had never been recalled to her mind till she fell into the hands of the prosecution?

The words are sixty-two in number.

"My own darling,—I was very sorry to see you cry when I left you. It seems as though it never must be, but there will be a time when Harriet will be out of the way, and we shall be happy together. Dear Alice, you must know how I love you by this time. We have been together two years now."

Now, sir, even if those fatal words about a time when Harriet will be out of the way were ever written without some explanatory context, I think the jury ought to have

232

been throughout solemnly warned and guarded against the illogical interpretation of them. The just rule of interpretation is that you should always prefer a literal to a vague or metaphorical interpretation. The words "out of the way" mean out of the way; they don't mean dead. A man can say "dead," and if Rhodes was projecting murder with him, why should he not have said so?

The next rule is, that you prefer the interpretation which the writer himself confesses by his own act, and the next is, that you prefer the interpretation that is first fulfilled in order of time. Now, it was Louis, the writer of the words, who took a farm soon after, settled Harriet with Patrick, and so got her out of the way, and lived in smooth adultery with Rhodes, whereas it was other people who killed Harriet Staunton, and nine months 'afterwards. But I shall now show the extract as sworn to was never written.

1st objection.—It is too long, and too short, which two traits can never meet in a genuine extract.

A. Too long for a servant girl to remember, word for word, nine months after hearing it.

B. Too short. Louis Staunton was not preparing his own prosecution. It was not on the cards of mere accident that he should furnish in sixty-two words *two equivocal* expressions — one establishing a long adulterous intercourse of which there is no corroborative proof, but the reverse, and another quibble projecting distant murder, of which there is no corroborative proof, since Harriet was well used for months after.

2. The line reminding her she had been his mistress for two years is worded by a woman, and not by Staunton or any man. Decent women like Clara Brown have a delicate vocabulary unknown to men. "We have been together," which means everything the prosecution wanted, but says nothing at all, is a woman's word for criminal connection.

3. The statement itself is not true, and from that you must argue backward against the genuineness of the quotation, since he would not say this to a girl who knew better.[1]

4. The witness could remember nothing but her lesson:

---

[1] Since this letter was written, it has been proved to be a falsehood. The criminal connection was hardly one year old.

sixty-two consecutive words, all neat and telling, and meeting the two great views of the prosecution; but, that done, a blank—a total blank; not six consecutive words. This is barefaced. Daniel Defoe would have managed better. He would have armed the witness with ten consecutive words on some matter quite foreign to the objects of the prosecution. The quotation is fabricated.

The process has nothing exceptional in it, nor is there any one to blame, except the Court, for letting in parole evidence about a written document destroyed by the witness herself.

Allow 10,000 such witnesses, and, if the case is ably prepared, you must, in the very nature of things, have 10,000 inaccurate quotations, all leaning towards the side that calls the witness.

The people who get up a prosecution have but one way of dealing with such a witness. She comes to them remembering a word here or there. She is advised to speak the truth and take time. But, as the conference proceeds, she is asked whether she happens to remember anything of such a kind ? She is very ductile, and forces her memory a bit in the direction she instinctively sees is desired. The very person who is examining her with an *ex parte* view does not see that she is so wax-like as she is.

Add a small grain of self-deception on both sides, and a mixture of truth and falsehood comes into the unwary and most inconsistent court, which stops Louis Staunton's mouth, yet lets in a worse kind of evidence than the prisoner's own, viz., this horrible hodge-podge of memory, imagination, and prompting, which, in *the very nature of things, and by the mere infirmity of the human mind, must be a lie.*

That a man should die only because he is tried in England. Bring your minds to bear on this, my countrymen. If an ignorant man, like this Staunton, is defended in a suit for fifty-one pounds, he can go into the witness-box and explain all the errors of the plaintiff, if any ; but if he is tried for his life, which is dearer to every man than all the money in the world, he is not allowed to say one word to the jury, if he has counsel. Now, in France he may speak after his counsel have done muddling his case, but here, with heartless mockery, when Ignorance all round has hanged him, he is allowed to speak—To whom ? To the judge. On what ? The nice quibbles of the law, but not on facts or motives—that being the one thing he can never do, and this being the thing he could generally do, and flood the groping Court with light, especially as to his true motives and the extenuating circumstances of his case. By this system the bloodthirsty murderer, who chooses his time, and slays swiftly in the dark, gains an advantage he cannot have in the wiser Courts of Europe. But God help the malefactor who is not an habitual criminal, or one of the deepest dye, but a mixed sinner, who has glided from folly into sin, and from sin into his first crime, and who has been fool as well as villain. His mouth is closed, and all the extenuating circumstances that mouth could always reveal are hidden with it, or, as in this case, grossly and foully perverted into aggravating circumstances.

This is very unfair. The nation will see it some day. At present what is to be done? After all, thank God, it is a free country, and one in which bad law is sometimes corrected by just men.

To all such I appeal against the rope of sand I have had to untwist in this letter.

The post has enabled me to do something more : to resist foul play and garbled quotations and those most dangerous of all lies, equivoques in language, such as "Harriet out of the way," the very kind of lies Holy Writ ascribes to Satan, and the great poets of every age have described as hellish, which they are.

I resolved to give Louis Staunton, what that den of iniquity and imbecility, the Central Criminal Court, did not give him, one little chance of untwisting that rope of sand, although he has the misfortune not to be a Frenchman. I conveyed a short letter to Mr. Louis Staunton through the proper authorities, requesting him to try and remember the entire matter of a certain letter he had unquestionably written to Alice Rhodes in August 1876, and to send it to me verbatim. Some delay took place while my letter was submitted to authorities outside the gaol, but fair play prevailed, and I now append the letter to my own, which is of less value. I send it all the same, because I have looked narrowly into that of Staunton's, and I don't see any of that self-evident mendacity I have felt it my duty to point out in the garbled quotation the rope of sand. This letter, at all events, *may* be true. For here I see youth, with its selfish vices, not looking months and months ahead, either for good or bad, but getting Harriet out of the way without a metaphor, to enjoy the sweet vice his self-indulgent soul was filled with, and not with long cold-blooded schemes of murder

235

such as belong to more hardened natures than this, who, we learn from the Crown itself, and on oath, sat down and cried because his wife upset the house. The following is

Louis Staunton's Letter.

MAIDSTONE GAOL, *October 11th*, 1877.

SIR,—I duly received your letter of the 9th inst., and now beg to reply to it. The letter in question I wrote to Alice Rhodes on or about August 17, 1876. The facts are these: I had several times promised to take Alice Rhodes down to Brighton for a week, but had been prevented from doing so. But on Saturday, August 14, Mrs. Staunton, Alice Rhodes, and myself, went down to Cudham, for the purpose of leaving Mrs. Staunton there, that we might go to Brighton on the Tuesday; but on the Monday I received a telegram to say my father was worse. My brother and myself immediately came up to London, leaving Alice Rhodes and Mrs. Staunton at Cudham. I then wrote her this letter:—

"My own Darling,—I know you will be sorry to hear that my poor dear father passed away yesterday. This is a sad blow to me, but we all have our troubles. Our trip must now be put off again. It seems as if it is not to be; but I will arrange another time to get Harriet out of the way; so you must not be disappointed. I shall have to remain down home for a few days, so Harriet had better stop down with you."

I believe I have now given you word for word what I said in this letter. I have thought well over it, and cannot remember saying anything more. What I meant by "It seems as if it is not to be," was our going to Brighton, and of getting "Harriet out of the way," that she might not know anything about it.

This is the whole truth of the letter.—I am, Sir, yours obediently, Louis Staunton.

CHARLES READE, ESQ.

The public is to understand that I deal fairly with the powerful journal which has done me the honour to allow me to express boldly my unalterable convictions. I do not write letters and say "Thus said Staunton;" I tender you his handwriting, begging you to do me the honour to keep it, and show it to few or many as you think proper. I do not lead witnesses as I think Clara Brown was led—unconsciously, no doubt. My short letter, to which this is a reply, lies in Maidstone Gaol. I can't remember what I write, like this young sinner, nor imagine what other people write—like Miss Brown *plus* an attorney's clerk. But I am sure it is a short line, just asking the man to send the truth. He looks on himself as a dying man; has no hope of saving himself; and I think he has come pretty near the truth in his letter.— Yours faithfully,   CHARLES READE.

P.S.—Now that I have opened the dumb creature's mouth, which that beastly court, the disgrace of Europe, had closed, who doubts the real meaning of the letter, and that the writer had Adultery in view, and had not Homicide.

THE LEGAL VOCABULARY

To the Editor of the "Pall Mall Gazette."

Sir,—Now those swift-footed hares, my eloquent contemporaries, have galloped over Diblanc's trial, may I ask you, in the name of humanity, to let the tortoise crawl over it with his microscopic eye? Where female culprits are to be judged, a patient drudge, who has studied that sex profoundly in various walks of life, including Diblanc's, is sometimes a surer exponent of facts than is a learned lawyer. I will keep strictly within the limits of the legal defence. The Crown used Diblanc as its witness to the killing, and this, by a rule of law which is inexorable, and governs alike a suit or an indictment, let in the prisoner's explanations *as evidence*. But there are degrees of evidence; what she said against herself was first-class evidence; what she said favourable to herself was low evidence, to be received when it is contradicted neither by a living witness nor a clear fact. I keep within this circle, traced by the judge himself, simply premising that I have seen many a prisoner acquitted on his own explanation of motives, thus made admissible, though poor, evidence, by the prosecutor.

Now did the criminal seek the victim, or the victim her? Where was the crime committed? In the kitchen. And what is the kitchen? It is a poor man's cottage on the ground-floor of a gentleman's house. No paper—no carpet—stone floor—it is made like a servant's home out of contempt; but the result of that contempt is, that the female domestic feels at home in it, soul and body. It is the servant's house, and the cook's castle and workshop. To come and insult her there galls her worse than in the gentlefolk's part. What a lady feels if a cook walks up into the drawing-room to affront her, that the cook feels if the mistress comes down into her castle to affront her. But a kitchen is something else—it is

238

an arsenal of deadly weapons, with every one of which the cook is familiar. The principal are—a hatchet to chop wood, a rolling-pin, a steel to sharpen knives, a cleaver, an enormous poker, a bread knife, carving knife, &c. Into this cook's castle and arsenal of lethal weapons comes Diblanc's mistress on a Sunday forenoon, when even a cook is entitled to a little bit of peace and some little reduction of her labour, if possible, and gives an inconsiderate order. The cooks says there's no need for that; dinner is not till seven. This offends the mistress, and she threatens to discharge her on the spot. The cook says she will go directly if her month's wages are paid her. " No," says the mistress, " I will keep you your time ; but I will make you suffer." Here there is a lacuna ; but the climax was that the mistress called this poor hard-working woman, in her castle and workshop, a prostitute, and dwelt upon the epithet. Then the cook, goaded to fury, took, not one of the murderous weapons close at hand, but sprang at her mistress's throat, and griped it with such fury that she broke the poor creature's jaw and throttled her on the spot, and probably killed her on the spot, whatever she may have said to the contrary. The deed done, the criminal is all amazement, vacillation, and uncertainty in word and deed. Her deeds : She carries the body wildly here and there ; she puts a rope round its neck in a mad attempt to pass the act off for suicide ; she resolves on flight ; she has not the means ; she casts her eyes round, and sees the safe with money in it ; she breaks it open, and takes enough for her purpose ; she does not pillage ; she steals the means of flight ; she robs in self-defence. Her words : " I leave for Paris this evening." Then a horror falls on her like a thunderclap. " No, I shall never see Paris again, not even my parents." Is there nothing human in this sudden cry of a poor savage awaking to her crime ? " I shall try to leave for America." So, then, she goes out intending to sail to America, and goes just where she does not mean to go—to Paris. She gets there, and instantly pays a just debt with the money she no longer needed to save her life. In other words, she is no more a real thief than a real murderer, as the common-sense of mankind understands the words. With the light thus reflected by her subsequent conduct, all vacillation and inability to carry out a design, I return to the homicide and its true interpretation.

Fact goes by precedent as well as law, and, strange to say, lawyers, those slaves of precedent, often forget this. Now, what does experience or precedent teach us with regard to the murder of adults by adults? Is the open hand the weapon murder selects? It is the weapon cold-blooded robbery has often selected *to avoid murder.* But is it the weapon murder has often selected? Certainly not. But Diblanc's defence rests on far stronger ground. The point of her defence is this: *She stood in an arsenal of deadly weapons, and yet avoided them, and used the non-lethal weapon—her bare hands—being maddened to fury and burning for revenge, but not positively intending to murder either before the attack or at the moment of the attack.* These facts, minutely examined, tear the theory of "premeditation" up by the roots; but you cannot tear that theory up by the roots without displacing the theory of "intention," and letting in the defendant's evidence that she did not intend to kill Madame Riel. And this brings me naturally to the nature and extent of the provocation that stung her to fury.

Mr. Baron Channell says that no mere words can by provocation reduce wilful killing to manslaughter. Granted; but I think this applies only to killing with lethal weapons. Where two things combine—where A receives a foul provocation in language from B, and, avoiding the lethal weapons close to his hand, kills B with the bare hand, I think the jury have a right to call that manslaughter if they please. A calls B a liar; B knifes him. Murder. B calls C a liar; C fells him with a blow, and kills him. Manslaughter. Oh, but throttling is worse than striking. Ay, worse in a man, but not in a woman, because women do not fight with the fist; they *always* go at each other with the claws, and no murder done one time in a thousand. If we are to judge women we really must not begin by being pig-headed idiots, and confounding them entirely, mind and limbs, with men. The truth is, language contains no word with which a man can strike a man to the heart, in his own person, as a woman can strike a woman with a word. It is at once stupid and cruel the way in which this poor creature's provocation has been slurred over. The evidence is all in favour of her continence. When out of place in Paris she fell in debt directly; a plain proof labour was her only way of getting bread. Here in London it comes out that her wages were everything to her. She wanted to go, but could not for want of a little money. Why, her very strength, about which so much twaddle has been uttered, was not the strength of the individual, it was only the strength that comes to women of her age by an honourable, laborious, and continent life. And is it a small thing that to such a woman, working in her kitchen for her bread, another woman, whose life was not laborious and honourable like hers, should come and say, You are a prostitute. "Facile judicat qui pauca considerat." We must consider not the insult only, but the quarter whence it came; and we shall find the utmost limits of verbal provocation have been reached in Diblanc's case. The time—Sunday morning, when the world gets peace, and even cooks hope for it. The place —her own kitchen. The insult—the most intolerable the mind can conceive; and *a lie*. The result—honest labour and continence used none of the lethal weapons at hand, but took luxury and foul-mouthed slander by the throat. Luxury's arm was pithless against insulted labour and continence, and a crime was consummated, when between two working women there would only have been a fight.

It is the misfortune of women that few men, except one or two writers of fiction, can put themselves in a woman's place, and so qualify themselves to judge her in these obscure cases. But let me put a man, as nearly as I can, in this woman's place. A man is with his wife, whom he loves as dearly as Diblanc loves herself. Another man comes and calls that woman a prostitute to her face and his; there's a hatchet on one side of the husband, a carving knife on the other. The husband takes neither, but seizes the slanderer by the throat and squeezes the life out of him. Would that man be indicted for murder? I doubt it. Would Baron Channell ask a conviction for murder? I doubt it. If he did, no jury in England would convict. Yet here the provocation is purely verbal, and the killing identical with Diblanc's.

Let me now, without blaming any living person, draw the attention of public men to the stereotyped trickery and equivocation by means of which the death of Marguerite Diblanc has been compassed—in theory; for she is not to die, I conclude. Some lawyer, in the name of a humane Sovereign, draws a bloodthirsty, exaggerated indictment, and says Diblanc slew Madame Riel wilfully and with malice aforethought. The evidence contradicts the malice and the afore-thought, which are the very sting of the indictment, and the jury demur. "Oh, let that flea stick in the wall," says the judge, "we don't go by Johnson's Dictionary here; 'afore-thought,' that means 'contemporaneous' in our vocabulary, and 'malice' means rage, passion, anything you like—*except malice, of course*. All you have got to do is to disregard the terms of the indictment, and if she killed the woman at all say she killed her with malice aforethought." The jury, who are generally novices and easily overcome by the picture of a gentleman thatched with horsehair, assent with reluctance, and recommend the prisoner to mercy, thereby giving their verdict the lie: for if the indictment was not an impudent falsehood and their verdict another she would be a most unfit subject for mercy. This bastard verdict which says "Yes" with a trumpet and "No" with a penny whistle being obtained by persuasion, the judge goes coolly back to Dr. Johnson, whom he has disowned for a time in order to get a verdict, and condemns the woman to death for having killed her fellow-creature with malice aforethought, as Johnson understands the words. But, as he too knows it is all humbug, and a verbal swindle invented by dead fools and forced upon him, he takes measures to refer it to a layman called the Home Secretary, who is to find straight-forwardness, sense, manhood, and, above all, English for the whole lot.

Now, sir, I agree with the writer of your able article of the 15th of June, that the way out of this is to enlarge, purify, and correct the legal vocabulary. The judges are in a hole. With two words—"manslaughter" and "murder"—they are expected to do the work of three or four words; and how can they? It is impossible. Enlarge this vocabulary, and the most salutary consequences will flow in. Sweep away "manslaughter," which is an idiotic word meaning more than murder in etymology, and less in law, and divide unlawful killing into three heads—homicide, wilful homicide, murder. Then let it be enacted that henceforward it shall be lawful for juries to understand all words used in indictments, declarations, pleadings, &c., in their plain and grammatical sense, and to defy all other interpretations whatever. Twelve copies of every indict-ment ought to be in the jury box, and every syllable of those indictments proved whether bearing on fact or motive, or else the prisoner acquitted. Neither the Crown nor the private suitor should be allowed to exaggerate without smarting for it in the verdict, just as in the world overloaded invective recoils upon the shooter.—I am, Sir, yours faithfully,

CHARLES READE.

MAGDALEN COLLEGE, OXFORD,
June 17th, 1872.

COLONEL BAKER'S SENTENCE

To the Editor of the "Daily Telegraph"

Sir,—A great many journals and weeklies have told the public that an English judge has passed too lenient a sentence on Colonel Baker because he belongs to the upper classes. Some have added that the same judge had inflicted a severe sentence on certain gas stokers, and so we have a partial judge upon the bench. This is a grave conclusion, and, if true, would be deplorable. You would yourself regret it, and therefore will, I am sure, permit me to show you, by hard facts, that all this is not only untrue, but the exact opposite of the truth in every particular. Fact 1. The proceedings against Baker commenced with an application for delay and a special jury. Here was an opportunity to favour him. The judge rejected the application, and he was tried by a common jury. 2. On the trial the prosecuting counsel attacked him with a severity that is now unusual, and used a false comparison to lead the jury farther than the evidence warranted. 3. In contrast to this, Baker was defended with strict moderation. In France the accused speaks as well as his counsel, but in England his own mouth is closed, and we must assume instructions and give him the credit or discredit due to his line of defence. Now, there was a point in the plaintiff's evidence which to my mind is womanly and charming, but still, before a common jury, Mr. Hawkins could have done almost what he liked with it. It appeared that when the young lady was on the doorstep she told her assailant he must hold her or she would fall. They little know the power of counsel who doubt that, by a series of sly ironical questions on this point, the case could have been weakened by ridicule, and the plaintiff tortured. Since the lower orders have been dragged into this, it should be considered that every one of them would have so defended himself, except those who had got rid of the case before by shoving the girl off the step instead of holding her. "That is the sort of men *they* are." My brilliant contemporaries know nothing about them. How should they, being in an exalted sphere? 4. The common jury cleared him of a criminal assault, and found him guilty of an indecent assault. My brilliant contemporaries hanker after the higher issue, and would like to see it in the judgment, though it was not in the verdict. But that would be to juggle with the constitutional tribunal, and be inexcusable in a judge. 5. Mr. Justice Brett dwelt on the enormity of the offence, and admitted only one palliating circumstance—viz., that the culprit, when he found the lady would risk her life sooner than be insulted, came to his senses, and showed a tardy compunction. This was so ; and Colonel Baker's line of defence before the magistrates and before the court entitled him to this small palliation. 6. Witnesses were called to character, with a view to mitigating punishment. Now, when a culprit of the lower orders can do this effectually, it always reduces punishment—sometimes one half, or more. Were it to go for nothing where a gentleman has committed his first public crime, there would be gross partiality in favour of the lower orders, and an utter defiance of precedent. 7. The punishment inflicted was a fine, £500, and a year's imprisonment as a first-class misdemeanant. My brilliant contemporaries think that a poor man would have been much worse punished. Now let us understand one another. Do they mean a poor man who had so assaulted a lady, or a poor man who had so assaulted a poor woman? Their language only fits the latter view. Very well, then. My brilliant contemporaries have eaten the insane root that takes the reason prisoner. Every day in the year men of the lower orders commit two thousand such assaults upon women of the lower orders, and it is so little thought of that the culprits are rarely brought to justice at all. When they are, it is a police magistrate, and not a jury, the women apply to. It is dealt with on the spot by a small fine or a very short imprisonment. Colonel Baker, had he been a navvy, would have got one month. My brilliant contemporaries go to their imagination for their facts. I, poor drudge, go to one out of twenty folio notebooks in which I have entered, alphabetically, the curious facts of the day for many a year. The fines for indecent assaults range from five pounds to twenty. Amongst the examples is one that goes far beyond Baker's case, for the culprit had recourse to chloroform. I call this a criminal assault. The magistrate, however, had a doubt, and admitted the culprit to bail. At the expiration of the bail the Lucretia in humble life walked into the court on Tarquin's arm, and begged to withdraw the plaint. She had married him in that brief interval. And that, O too imaginative contemporaries, " is the sort of *women they* are." The magistrate scolded them both, and said it was collusion to defeat the law. He lacked humour, poor man. When a lady or a gentleman is one of the parties that immediately elevates the offence. I have a case in my list that resembles Baker's in some respects. It was a railway case—the offender a gentleman, the plaintiff a respectable milliner. This was dealt with at quarter sessions; fine £200, no imprisonment. In Craft's case the parties were reversed. Craft, a carpenter, at Farringdon, kissed by force the daughter of a neighbouring clergyman. She took him before a jury, and he got six months. But her Majesty remitted three months of this sentence.

I am informed there was a case the other day, and a bad one—punishment two months. But I will not be sure, for I have not seen it. Of this I am absolutely sure, that Baker's sentence is severe beyond all precedent. His fine is more than double the highest previous fine. His imprisonment, if not shortened, will be four times the term of Craft's, and about twelve times what, if the female had been in humble life, a blackguard by descent and inheritance would have got, and he is both fined and imprisoned. I think it most proper a gentleman should be more severely punished for so heinous an offence. But it is not proper that facts should be turned clean topsy-turvy, and the public humbugged into believing that the lower order of people are treated more severely in such cases, when, on the contrary, they are treated with gross partiality; still less is it proper that these prodigious errors of fact should be used to cast a slur upon the just reputation of a very sagacious, careful, and independent judge. To drag the gas stokers' case into this question is monstrous. Law has many branches, and a somewhat arbitrary scale of punishments that binds the judges more or less. As a rule it treats offences against the person more lightly than offences against property—ay, even when marks of injury have been left upon the person for months. Now, the law of England abhors conspiracy, and Mr. Justice Brett found the law; he did not make it, nor yet did his grandfather. The gas stokers' sentence had nothing on earth to do with their birth and parentage. They were representative men—the ringleaders of a great conspiracy, and the only offenders nailed in a case where our gaols ought to have been filled with the blackguards. It was a heartless, egotistical, and brutal conspiracy; its object a fraud, and its instrument a public calamity. The associated egotists inflicted darkness on a great city during the hours of traffic. They not only incommoded a vast public cruelly; they also added to the perils of the city, and most likely injured life and limb. The judge who punished these deliberate and combined criminals severely was the mouth-piece of an offended and injured public, and not of any clique whatever; for no clique monopolises light nor can do without it, least of all the poor. He gave his reasons at the time, and the press approved them, as anybody can see by turning to the files. To these facts, sir, I beg to add a grain of common sense. What is there in a British colonel to dazzle a British judge? The judge is a much greater man in society and in the country; and in court he is above the Princes of the Blood, for he represents the person and wields the power of the Sovereign. Class distinctions do not much affect the judges of our day. They sit too high above all classes. One or two of them, I see, share the universal foible, and truckle a little to the press. If a modern judge is above that universal weakness, he is above everything but his conscience and his God. Perhaps my brilliant contemporaries have observed that solitary foible in our judges, and are resolved that Mr. Justice Brett shall not overrate their ability to gauge his intellects or his character. If that was their object, they have written well.

CHARLES READE.

August 30th, 1875.

PROTEST AGAINST THE MURDER
AT LEWES GAOL

To the Editor of the "Daily News"

Sir,—I claim the right of a good citizen to disown, before God and man, a wicked and insane act just committed in the name of the country, and therefore in mine, unless I publicly dissent.

An Englishman named Murdock was killed yesterday at Lewes by the ministers of the law, for a crime the law of England does not visit with death. The crime was manslaughter. It is not possible that even an English judge could so mistake the law as really to take the man's crime for murder. It was destitute, not of one, two, or three, but of all the features that the law requires in murder. On the other hand, it had all the features that distinguish manslaughter. There was no murderous weapon—there was no weapon at all ; no premeditation, no personal malice. The act was done in the confusion, hurry, and agitation of a struggle, and that struggle was commenced, not by the homicide, but the victim.

As respects the animus at the time, it is clear the violence was done *alio intuitu;* the prisoner was fighting, not to kill but to escape ; and that he never from first to last aimed at killing appeared further by his remaining in the neighbourhood, and his surprise and ignorance of his victim's death. In a word, it was manslaughter in its mildest form. I have seen a boy of eighteen hanged for stealing a horse. It was a barbarous act, but it was the law. I have seen a forger hanged. It was cruel, but it was the law. But now, for the first time (while murderers are constantly escaping the law), I have seen an English head fall by the executioner in defiance of the law. I

248

wash this man's blood from my hands, and from my honourable name. I disown that illegal act, and the public will follow me. I cannot say to-day where the blame lies, and in what proportions; but I will certainly find out; and as certainly all those concerned in it *populo respondebunt et mihi.*

CHARLES READE.

STARVATION REFUSING PLENTY

To the Editor of the "Daily Telegraph"

Sir,—The journals recorded last week the death by starvation of a respectable sempstress. Now, the death by starvation of a single young working woman is a blot upon civilisation and a disgrace to humanity. It implies also great misery and much demi-starvation in the class that furnishes the extreme example. The details in this case were pitiable, and there were some comments in the *Daily Telegraph* well adapted to make men feel and think even if they never knew hunger personally. They have set me thinking for one, and I beg to offer my thoughts. I have observed, in a general way, that the world is full of live counterparts, by which I mean people that stand in need of other people, who stand equally in need of them; only these two live counterparts of the social system cannot find each other out. Distance and ignorance keep them apart. Of late the advertisement sheet has done much to cure that, and is an incalculable boon to mankind. But as there are counterpart individuals, so there are counterpart classes, and I shall ask your assistance to bring two of these classes together and substitute for starvation repletion. I see before me, say, two thousand honest, virtuous, industrious young women, working hard and half starved; and I see before me at least twenty thousand other women holding out plenty in both hands, and that plenty rejected with scorn by young women of very little merit, or, if not rejected, accepted only under vexatious and galling conditions imposed by the persons to be benefited.

Aid me then, Sir, to introduce to a starving class an oppressed and insulted and pillaged class which offers a clean healthy lodging and no rent to pay, butcher's meat twice a day, food at all hours, tea, beer, and from £12 to £18 a year pocket-money, in return for a few hours of healthy service per day. To speak more plainly, domestic servants have become rare, owing to wholesale and most injudicious exportation; and although their incapacity in their business has greatly increased—especially the incapacity of cooks—they impose not only higher wages, but intolerable conditions. The way the modest householder is ground down by these young ladies is a grievance too large to be dealt with under this head, and will probably lead to a masters' and mistresses' league. Suffice it here to say that full forty thousand domestic servants are now engaged yearly in London on written characters, and thirty thousand without a character; and I speak within bounds when I say that there are good places by the dozen open to any respectable sempstress. There are mistresses by the thousand who, in the present dearth of good and civil servants, would try a respectable novice. A respectable sempstress has always half a character, for she is trusted with materials and does not steal them; and the oppressed mistresses in question would forgive a few faults in housework at first starting in a woman who could compensate them by skill with the needle—no mean addition to a servant's value. I now turn to the sempstresses. Why do they sit hungry to the dullest of all labour, and hold aloof from domestic service, at a time when ladies born are beginning to recognise how much better off is the rich housemaid than the poor lady? I suspect the sempstresses are deluded by the words, "liberty" and "wages." They think a female servant has no liberty, and that her principal remuneration is her "wages."

I address myself to these two errors. Οὐκ ἔστιν ὅστις, ἐστ' ἀνήρ ἐλεύθερος. Our liberty is restrained by other means than bolts and bars. It is true that a female servant cannot run into the streets whenever she likes. But she sometimes goes on errands and takes her time. She slips out eternally, and gets out one evening at least every week. Then, as to wages, the very word is a delusion as far as she is concerned. Her wages are a drop in the ocean of her remuneration. She comes out of a single room, where she pigs with her relations, and she receives as remuneration for her services a nice clean room all to herself, the market price of which, and the actual cost to her employer, is at least 6s. per week, and the use of a kitchen, and in some cases of a servants' hall, which is worth 2s. per week, and the run of other bright and healthy rooms. In the crib where she pigged with her relations, she often had a bit of bacon for dinner, and a red herring for supper.

In the palace of cleanliness and comfort she is promoted to, she gets at least four meals a day, and butcher's meat at two of them. This, at the present price of provisions, is 16s. per week, which is more than an agricultural labourer in the Southern counties receives wherewith to keep a wife and seven children. But, besides this, she gets a shilling a week for beer, and from a shilling to eighteenpence for washing. Besides all this she has from twelve to eighteen pounds in hard cash, with occasional presents of money and dress. The wages of her class have been raised when they ought to have been lowered. The mechanic's wages are justly raised, because the value of money depends upon the value of the necessaries of life. These have risen, and therefore money has sunk. But that rise does not affect the female servants, and it does affect those who feed them like fighting cocks. A droller piece of logic than the rise of fed servants' pocket-money because unfed servants' wages are raised, I never encountered even in Anglo-Saxony. However, the upshot is that any half-starved sempstress who will read this crude letter of mine, and make diligent inquiries, will find that I am right in the main; that domestic servants are trampling too hard upon the people who are called their masters and mistresses; and that three thousand homes are open to a young woman who can prove that she is not a thief, and six thousand hands are offering not only plenty, but repletion, and liberal pocket-money to boot. The pay of a housemaid, in rent, fire, food, washing, beer, and pocket-money, is about £70 a year, and this hungry sempstresses can obtain if they will set about it, and without any loss of dignity; for, as a rule, servants nowadays hold their heads as high or a little higher than their mistresses do.—I am, Sir, your faithful servant,

CHARLES READE.

OUTRAGES ON THE JEWS IN RUSSIA

To the Editor of the "Daily Telegraph"

Sir,—I am one of the many persons who are moved by
your denunciation of the lawless cruelties perpetrated on
the Jews in Russia, and the apparent connivance or apathy
of the varnished savages who misgovern those barbarians.
If the latter persist in that course and so make that a
national crime which might otherwise remain the crime
of numerous individuals, some great calamity will fall on
them, or history is a blind guide; and by the same rule
you give friendly advice when you urge our Government
and people to protest and wash their hands before God
and man of this terrible crime. I fear, however, that a
mere Government protest will be slighted or evaded by
Russian mendacity. Fortunately our nation can speak and
act by other organs besides our Government, and now is
the time to show ourselves men, and men whose hearts are
horrified at the cowardly cruelty of this Tartar tribe to God's
ancient people.

Let us take a wide view of this situation, since it is so
great and so new in our day; for wholesale persecution of
the Jews is not of this epoch, but "a reversion" to the
dark ages. One of the signs that distinguish a true
Christian from a sham one is that the former studies
the Greek and Hebrew Scriptures with care and reverence, and there learns the debt his heart, soul, and understanding owe to historians, poets, philosophers, prophets,
preachers, and teachers, some writing Greek, some Hebrew,
but every one of them Jews; and also learns to pity and
respect the Jewish nation, though under a cloud, and to
hope for the time when they will resume their ancient

territory, which is so evidently kept waiting for them. This, the hope of every Christian, is the burning and longing desire of many, for another reason—because the prophecies we receive, though obscure in matters of detail, are clear as day on two points: That the Jews are to repossess Palestine, and, indeed, to rule from Lebanon to Euphrates; and that this event is to be the first of a great series of changes, leading to a vast improvement in the condition of poor suffering mankind and of creation in general. Now we have here in prospect a glorious event as sure as that the sun will rise to-morrow. The only difference is that the sun will rise at a certain hour, and the Jews will occupy Syria and resume their national glory at an uncertain day.

No doubt it is the foible of mankind to assume that an uncertain date must be a distant one. But that is unreasonable. Surely it is the duty of wise and sober men not to run before the Almighty in this thing; but, on the other hand, to watch precursory signs and lend our humble cooperation, should so great a privilege be accorded to us. This sudden persecution of the Jews in the very nation where they are most numerous—may it not be a precursory sign and a reminder from Providence that their abiding city is not in European Tartary? I almost think some such reminder was needed; for when I was a boy the pious Jews still longed for the Holy Land. They prayed, like Daniel, with their windows open towards Jerusalem. Yet, now that the broken and impoverished Saracen would cede them territory at one-tenth of its agricultural and commerical value, a cold indifference seems to have come over them. I often wonder at this change of sentiment about so great a matter and in so short a period, comparatively speaking, and puzzle myself as to the reason. Two solutions occur to me: 1. Dispersed in various nations, whose average inhabitants are inferior in intelligence and forethought to themselves, they thrive as individual aliens more than they may think so great a multitude of Jews could thrive in a land of their own, where blockheads would be scarce. 2. They have for centuries contracted their abilities to a limited number of peaceful arts and trades; they may distrust their power to diversify their abilities, and be suddenly a complete nation, with soldiers, sailors, merchants, husbandmen, as well as financiers and artists.

If I should happen to be anywhere near the mark in these suggestions, let me offer a word in reply to both objections. In the first place, they both prove too much, for they would keep the Jews dispersed for ever. It is certain, therefore, they will have to be got over some day, and therefore the sooner the better. As to objection one, it is now proved that sojourning among inferior nations has more drawbacks than living at home. True, the Russian yokel has for years been selling to the Jews his summer labour in winter, and at a heavy discount. But the silly, improvident brute has turned like a wild beast upon them, and, outwitted lawfully, has massacred them contrary to law: and truly Solomon had warned them there is no animal more dangerous than a fool and a brute beast without understanding. Besides, they need not evacuate other countries in a hurry and before the resources of their own land are developed. *Dimidium facti qui bene cœpit, habet.* Palestine can be colonised effectually from Russia alone, where there are 3,000,000 Jews trembling for life and property; and the rest would follow. As to the second objection, History is a looking-glass at our backs. Turn round and look into it with your head as well as your eyes, and you shall see the future. Whatever Jews have done Jews may do. They are a people of genius, and genius is not confined by Nature, but by will, by habit, or by accident. To omit to try is not to fail. What have this people tried heartily and failed in? Warriors, writers, builders, merchants, law-givers, husbandmen, and supreme in all !

When they will consent to rise to their destiny I know not, but this I do know, that, whenever they do, not excessive calculations, but some faith, will be expected from them, as it always has been, as a condition of their triumphs, and they will prove equal to the occasion, and be great in the arts of peace and war, and their enemies melt away before them like snow off a dyke. Should they seem to require help, at starting, from any other nation, blessed will be the nation that proffers it ; and the nation that persecutes them will be made an example of in some way or other. Therefore, if by any chance this recent outrage should decide the Jewish leaders to colonise Palestine from Russia, let us freely offer ships, seamen, money—whatever we are asked for. It will be a better national investment than Egyptian, Brazilian, or Peruvian bonds. Meantime, I implore our divines to separate themselves, and all the souls under their charge, in all the churches and chapels of the land, from the crime of those picture-worshipping idolaters and cowardly murderers, by public disavowal and prayerful humiliation, since the monsters call themselves Christians.—Yours faithfully,

CHARLES READE.

3 BLOMFIELD VILLAS, UXBRIDGE ROAD.

PRIVATE BILLS AND PUBLIC WRONGS

To the Editor of the "Daily Telegraph"

Sir,—Not being a Member of Parliament, I must either submit in silence to a bitter wrong, or avert it by publicity. The matter is national. Other grave interests are at stake besides my own, and unless the House of Commons is warned in time it may be ensnared into an act it would look back upon with some dismay. I suppose if anybody were to propose in a private bill to do away with the House of Lords, or repeal the whole common law, people would see that the promoter could not be allowed to enjoy the unfair advantages of a private bill in such discussion. Yet there is a private bill which aims at high game; for it proposes to unsettle the property of the nation, and make it all insecure and liable to surprises and night attacks in Parliament. There is a bill called "Albert Terrace Improvement," which proposes to rob a substantial freeholder of property which I am justified in valuing at £120,000, and several substantial leaseholders who have laid out from £850 to £4600 a-piece, and most of them over £2000, by the odious and oppressive measure of compulsory purchase. For certain reasons, which I will explain should it ever be necessary, the freeholder would never get under that system one-third of the value. The leaseholders' case is come. They could not get their real value, and they live in the houses, and no money could compensate them, because no money could enable them to get houses like these, with gardens running to the wall of Hyde Park. Such properties are relics of the past.

The bill proposes to give these houses, gardens, and sites— not to the public as Northumberland House was given, nor yet by voluntary purchase—but to a single individual, who wants them for a building speculation. The operation commenced thus: We the leaseholders received visits, not from road-makers, nor Peers of the realm, but from architects and builders. These showed us plans of enormous houses with a turret, and sounded us as to our willingness to turn out of our sweet *rus in urbe*—the only one left in the hideous monotony of masonry. We objected, as we have done to similar attempts before now.

Presently out comes the bill, and lo! our architects and builders have melted away before the eye of Parliament, and no projector figures in the bill, but a road-maker and patriot Peer. This public benefactor wants to make a new road into the park and dedicate it to the public. That he distinctly advances as his main object. But he insinuates that he cannot do this act of patriotism without taking seven of his neighbours' houses, and perhaps more. To carry out this object, a gentleman of good descent, who, nevertheless, is in the House of Lords only an obscure Baron, is at this moment in the Commons Emperor Elect of Knightsbridge, for he asks from that House powers so unconstitutional and ill-defined, as he knows from history the Commons would not concede to his Sovereign.

The Queen has a park; he proposes to break into it. The State has its road-makers; he is for kicking them out of their business. The nation values almost beyond everything else upon God's earth the equal security of property in the hands of Lords and Commons. He proposes to trample on the nation's feeling, and on those equal rights by the odious measure of compulsory purchase. To be sure he puts forward what he calls a public object, viz., a new public road into the park. Now, I am not going to argue the whole case, but merely to give Parliament the means of arguing it soundly.

1. His public road is not a public road, but a new private carriage drive, down which the public would not be allowed to run a wheel; and so great a preference is already shown for private carriages in the park and its entrances, that to open a new drive, and not a road, to traverse the park, would offend the public and rouse unpleasant discussions.

2. This "oligarch's alley," miscalled in the bill a public road, is to be 44 feet wide. The property it demands in the bill is 156 feet wide.

3. The undertaker or his associates, or both, are possessed, in some way, of property lying between Sloane Street and Hyde Park; for they are taking down the houses. He solicits in the bill the right to deviate. He can deviate into

rectitude and buy land ; he need not deviate into built houses and misappropriation.

There are many other public objections to his "oligarch's alley," which he calls a public road. But those I leave to the House of Commons ; and I leave to that House with perfect confidence the Albert Terrace Spoliation Bill, divested of its plausible pretext. I will not be so unjust to the Commons and their history as to let your million readers suppose that House needs to be exhorted by me when private cupidity stands nude on one side and the constitutional rights of Englishmen on the other.

But what may not be done in the dark ? When private bills come on there is nobody in the House but the personal friends of the projectors. A job of this kind glides from a bill into an Act in less time than it would take to hatch a serpent, and the House becomes the cat's-paw of a tyranny quite foreign to its own heart and principles.

This is where the shoe really pinches. Only a few members have time or inclination to attend to these cursed little private bills, especially when they are up to the neck in the Hellespont —and who can blame them ?—and so a very little varnish carries them through. John Milton says truly that even wisdom has its blind side. The times are high-minded and the high-minded are unsuspicious ; and so, " At Wisdom's gate Suspicion sleeps, and thinks no ill where no ill seems."

This letter, then, is written partly to warn the nation that its rights are at stake, but still more to warn our historical champions of these rights. I submit that, without a *primâ facie* case, it is not fair that worthy, well-affected citizens, all paying taxes to the State, should be juggled in a private bill out of the unremitting protection of the State. It is even hard, and very hard, we should be put to the suspense, anxiety, and expense of fighting such a bill in committee. At present, however, all I ask for is numbers. Oh ! do, pray, give the nation and us, on Thursday afternoon, not a handful, but a House ; and let the nation know from high-minded Tories and high-minded Liberals whether it has lost the love of both, and lost the greatest protector of its sacred rights it has ever had.

CHARLES READE.

NABOTH'S VINEYARD,
February 5th.

"A TERRIBLE TEMPTATION"

TO THE EDITOR OF THE "DAILY GLOBE," TORONTO

SIR,—Three columns of your journal have been sent me, headed "A Terrible Temptation," yet mainly devoted to reviving stale misrepresentations of my older works. The writer even goes beyond my original detractors—most of them now my converts—for he slanders the character and sincerity of the author; and that in terms so defamatory, and so evidently malicious, that I could sue him, or even indict him, if he was worth it. But I know by experience what would follow : an anonymous slanderer is always a coward; he would run away and hide the moment he saw the dog-whip of the law coming, and I should have to punish some unguarded editor, publisher, or printer, less criminal than the real culprit, but more of a man. I prefer, therefore, to deal with the slanderer as I may; only I expect you, who have published the poison, to publish the antidote.

The anonymous slanderer, in his rifle-pit, has so many unfair advantages over the more manly author, that it is impossible to expose him without first naming and ticketing his habitual blunders and frauds. This necessity compelled me long ago to invent a new science. I call it

LITERARY ZOOLOGY.

Of that science certain terms are indispensable in this discussion : unfortunately they are new to the Canadian public, so I must explain them.

THE CRITICASTER,

first pinned on cork by me in 1859. A very curious little animal, with singular traits; the most distinctive is, that in literary questions easily soluble by direct evidence he flies to cant, conjecture, or "the depths of his inner consciousness," and that means "the shallows of his ignorance." He is a mediæval reasoner, who has lived over into the nineteenth century by some miracle, but no more belongs to it than the Patagonian does, with his implements of stone. This little creature's mind and method are the exact opposite of the lawyer's, the naturalist's, and the critic's.

THE PRURIENT PRUDE.

(First introduced by me to the American public in 1864.)

This is a lewd hypocrite, who passes over all that is sweet, and pure, and innocent in a book, with genuine disrelish, and fixes greedily on whatever a foul mind can misinterpret or exaggerate into indecency. He makes arbitrary additions to the author's meaning, and so ekes out the indelicacy to suit his own true taste, which is for the indelicate; this done, he turns round upon the author, whom he has defiled, and says, "You are unclean." And so the poor author is. But why? A lump of human dirt has been sitting on him, and discolouring him.

THE SHAM-SAMPLE-SWINDLER.

This is a kind of vermin that works thus. He finds an objectionable passage or two in a good book, or a borrowed idea or two in an original book. He quotes these exceptional flaws, and then adds slyly, "*And this is the character of all the rest.*" Here a little bit of truth is made the cover to an enormous lie; but, unfortunately for the public, the bit of truth is compact and visible, the huge lie is in the dark. There is no cure to the sham-sample-swindler except reading the whole book; but the sham sample deters its reader from reading the book. Here, therefore, we have an impregnable circle of fraud. The sham-sample-swindle, as applied to grain, is seldom tried by farmers; their morals are not the morals of scribblers: God forbid they ever should be! It was once tried in Reading market, when I was a boy; but the swindler was flogged out of the market, and never dared show his face there again while he lived. Not so with his literary brethren; they are never flogged, never hung, never nailed on barn-doors. Rarely detected, never effectually exposed, they pursue, without a blush, or a single throb of conscience, the easiest, surest, neatest, and meanest swindle in creation.

The True Anonymuncule.

This little creature must not be confounded with the anonymous writers, who supply narratives of current events, and discuss public measures with freedom, but deal largely in generalities, and very little in personalities. Those are the working bees that gather honey for the public. Reade's anonymuncule is no great producer, he can do little but sting. He is of two kinds—the anonymous letter-writer, pest of families; and the anonymous literary detractor, pest of the fine arts. Both varieties have this essential trait in common, they abuse the shelter and the obscurity of the anonymous. The literary anonymuncule often abuses it doubly : he belies his superior in one organ of criticism, then flies to another, and says the same thing in other words. Then the duped public believes that two disinterested judges have condemned its favourite ; whereas the poor editors are only a couple of unguarded puppets, pulled by one unscrupulous anonymuncule raging with literary envy.

I make no apology for this preface, because it is of general utility ; all, who study it with a little care, can apply it to a thousand cases—past, present, and to come—in which I have no personal interest.

Now to the ephemeral application of these immortal truths. I am a popular author, bearing an indifferent character for temper and moderation, where injustice is done to others, or even to myself, but a high character for sincerity and humanity. As to my literary fame, it has been acquired fairly, as my very enemies admit : the Press has never been favourable to me, nor even just ; the one incorruptible judge of authors has used its own judgment, and gradually accorded me its esteem, I might say its reverence. Now comes an anonymuncule and undertakes to prove that I am an immoral writer, an indecent writer, a writer by the foot and the month, a writer on a false system, the opposite of Scott's and Shakespeare's, and all great masters ; and, above all, a social firebrand, and a *public criminal.* This latter phrase the anonymuncule thinks so appropriate, so decent, and so humane, that he *repeats* it with evident gusto and self-satisfaction. Now you are aware that no man of honour ever brings such charges against a gentleman of high repute, without some slight show of decent regret, and that none but a low-born villain equivocates, exaggerates, or tampers in any way with facts advanced to support a charge of public crime. Bear that indisputable position in mind, while I dissect my anonymuncule.

He opens his libel by saying that I have shocked public morality; and the following are his main proofs:

A.—I have made a brilliant adventuress of the Demimonde the most interesting female character, if not technically the heroine.

B.—I have thrown her vulgarity into the background.

C.—I have thrown her uncleanness into the background, and praised her by faint blame, &c., &c.

Answer to *B.*—It is a direct falsehood. How does this writer know that Rhoda Somerset was vulgar? He knows it only from me. My fearless honesty has put an oath into the woman's mouth, and plenty of Billingsgate beside. Lie 1.

C.—Behold the "prurient prude." This word "uncleanness," applied to vice, is one of his sure signs. Illicit connections are vicious, but they are no more unclean than matrimonial connections. To apply a term which is nasty, without being strictly appropriate, betrays to a philosopher's eye the prurient prude. Whenever in a newspaper you see the word "filth" applied to adultery or other frailty, the writer is a lewd hypocrite, a prurient prude. Remember that: it is well worth remembering. Divested of that false and repulsive expression, what does this charge come to? That I have but coldly stated the illicit connection between Rhoda Somerset and Sir Charles Bassett; I have gratified this prurient prude's real taste with no amorous scenes, no pictures of frailty in action. This is quite true. I have given the virtuous loves of Sir Charles and Bella Bruce in full detail, to gain my reader's sympathy with virtue: and the vicious connection I have coldly stated, like a chronicler. Mine is an art that preaches by pictures. I draw the illicit love with decent reserve; I paint the virtuous love in the purest and sweetest colours I can command. Who but a prurient prude, *with no relish for my scenes of virtuous love,* would distort this to my discredit?

What writer has ever produced scenes purer and sweeter than the innocent loves of Ruperta and Compton Bassett in this book? Yet how have the prurient prudes, one and all, received them? With marked distaste; they call the scenes a bore. Poor shallow hypocrites! These scenes of virgin snow are inconvenient: they do but fidget and obstruct a dirty fellow groping the soil for the thing he denounces and loves.

Is daylight breaking in ?

A.—This is a double falsehood. In the first place, I have made Lady Bassett by far the most interesting character. Were Rhoda Somerset cut out, the deeper interest would still remain, and the story be still rather a strong story. In the next place, Rhoda Somerset is not one character all through the book, as this anonymuncule infers. She is first a frail woman—then a penitent woman. Now it is only in the latter character I admit her to the second place of interest. Even Ruperta Bassett is more interesting than Somerset impenitent. Let any lover of truth study the book, and he will find that no sympathy is conceded to Somerset until her penitence commences, and that the sympathy enlarges as the woman gets better and better. Yet here is an anonymuncule who utterly ignores a woman's penitence in summing up her character. Is there one precedent for this reasoning, that has stood the test of time and reason? No doubt some contemporary females and contemporary criticasters reviled Mary Magdalene to her dying day, and said, "Once a harlot, always a harlot." But what has been the verdict of posterity? And what, in any case, is the verdict of posterity, but the verdict that contemporaries might, and ought to, have arrived at ?

If fifteen years' penitence are to go for nothing in summing up Rhoda Somerset, for how much less than nothing ought ten minutes' penitence to count for in that thief, whom, nevertheless, a venerable Church has summed up a saint ?

John Bunyan was a blaspheming blackguard. He repented, and wrote a novel that has done more good to men's souls than most sermons. Would this anonymuncule sum him up a blaspheming blackguard ?

Kotzebue's Mrs. Haller is an adulteress less excusable than Rhoda Somerset, a low girl with mercenary parents. Do Mrs. Haller's years of penitence go for nothing? Or does Kotzebue being dead, and Reade being alive, make the penitent adulteress a penitent, and the penitent Anonyma an unmitigated Anonyma? Yet, divest the argument of this idiotic blunder, and that part of the libel falls to earth.

D.—He says I have made Sir Charles Bassett the model man of the book. This is untrue. I have not pretended that he was ever much worse than many other young men of fortune ; but I have openly disapproved his early life—have represented him as heartily regretting it, so soon as the virtuous love dawned on him ; and yet I have shown some consequences of

264

his early frailties following him for years. If this is not fiction teaching morality in its own unobtrusive way—what is?

E.—He says that there is a strain of the Somerset through the whole book, and that a nurse giving suck is described more sexually than it ought to be. This is a deliberate falsehood. That great maternal act is described, not sensually, but poetically; and attention is fixed, not on that which the prurient prude was itching for, but on the exquisite expression of the maternal face while nursing—a poetical beauty the sculptors, Chantrey and all, have missed, to their discredit as artists.

F.—He says Lady Bassett was on the brink of adultery. This is another deliberate falsehood. Mr. Angelo may have been in danger; but it takes two to commit adultery; and it is clear the woman was never in danger for a moment.

The anonymuncule then proceeds to say that I have given a true picture; that in England the "kept mistress" has become an institution; that Anonyma did beckon our Countesses and Duchesses across the park, and they followed her, &c.: in short, he delivers a complete defence of the man he has just slandered; for vices are like diseases—to cure them you must ventilate them. Well, I have ventilated the English concubine in my way, and my anonymuncule has slandered me, and imitated me, in the same column of the same newspaper. Having detected himself in this latter act, he catches a faint glimpse of his own conduct, drops the slanderer, and announces that he is going to discourse artistically. Well, when he gets out of slander he is like a fish out of water; I wander through a waste of syllables, hunting, fishing, and diving for an idea; and at last I detect the head of an idea in one paragraph, and the tail in another—these scribblers never can articulate their topics—and I drag its *disjuncta membra* together "with oxen and wainropes," and so get to this—

Whatever a publisher publishes from week to week, the author must have so composed: *ergo*, Mr. Reade writes so many feet per week, and that makes him a crude accumulator of nothings. Now, where did he get his major premiss? From the depths of his inner consciousness. If he knew anything about authors, as distinct from scribblers and anonymuncula, he would be aware that we never write, as they do, from hand to mouth. Between the publication of my last novel and the issue of the first weekly number of the tale, eleven months elapsed. The depths of this man's inner consciousness inform him that I did not write one line of the story in those eleven months. Well, they tell him a lie, for I wrote it all—except a few chapters—in those eleven months; and it was all written, copied, and corrected before the Canadian public saw the first line of it.

He now carries the same system, the criticaster's, into a matter of more general importance. He says that I found my fictions on fact, and so tell lies; and that the chiefs of Fiction did not found fictions on fact and so told only truths.

Now, where does he discover that the chiefs of Fiction did not found their figments upon facts? Where?—why, in that little asylum of idiots, the depths of his inner consciousness! It could be proved in a court of law that Shakespeare founded his fictions on fact, wherever he could get hold of fact. Fact is that writer's idol. It was his misfortune to live in an age when the supplies of fact were miserably meagre. Could he be resuscitated, and a copy of the *Toronto Globe* handed him at the edge of the grave, he would fall on his knees and thank God for that marvel, a newspaper, and for the rich vein of ore, whose value to the theatre he would soon show us, to our utter amazement. Living in that barren age, he did his best. He ransacked Belleforest, Baker, Hollinshed, for facts. He transplanted whole passages from the latter bodily into "Macbeth," and from Plutarch into his "Coriolanus." His historical dramas are crammed with facts, or legends he believed to be fact. Wolsey's speech interwoven with his own—Fact; Henry the Eighth's interjections—Fact; the names of Pistol, Bardolph, and a dozen more—Fact: you may see them on the Court-rolls of Stratford-on-Avon any day you like. His Dogberry and Verges—Fact—from Cricklade in Gloucestershire; his charnel-house in "Romeo and Juliet"—Fact—from Stratford-on-Avon, &c., &c. This anonymuncule can put some limits to his ignorance in twenty-four hours, by reading the "Prolegomena" to Malone's edition, and a few of the notes. Shakespeare habitually interweaves fact with fiction; so this anonymuncule has called him a liar! As for Scott, he is one mass of facts. I know this from various sources—my own mediæval researches, Scott's biography, and Scott's own notes to his own works. He was forty years collecting facts before he wrote a novel. Pure imagination is most ardent in youth; why then did he not pass his youth in writing? He would, if he had held this anonymuncule's theory. He employed that imaginative period in collecting facts: he raked the Vale of Ettrick for facts; he ransacked the Advocates' Library for facts; and so far from disguising his method, he has revealed it fully in his notes. His ability is his own, but his plan, though not his genius, is mine. Now I will substitute the method of the critic for the method of the criticaster, and sift this question in the person of a single artist. Daniel Defoe wrote a narrative on the plan this anonymuncule praises, and says it never leads to lying; it is called "The Apparition of Mrs. Veal." He also wrote a narrative on the method I have adopted, called "Robinson Crusoe." Now, the private history of the latter composition is truly instructive. Daniel Defoe came to his work armed with facts from three main sources: 1. Facts derived in conversation from Selkirk, or Selcraig, who spent some months in London on his way to Largo, and was what we now call a lion. 2. The admirable narrative of Selkirk, by Woodes Rogers. 3. Dampier's Voyages, in which book, and not in his imagination, he found the Mosquito Indian Friday, and certain moral reflections he has put into Robinson Crusoe's mouth. With these good hard facts he wrote a volume beyond praise. His rich storehouse of rare facts exhausted, he still went on—peopled his island, and produced a mediocre volume, such as anybody could write in his age, or ours. The immortal volume dragged its mediocre brother about with it, as men were attached to corpses under the good King Mezentius. The book was so great a success, that its author tried my anonymuncule's theory; he took the field armed with his imagination only, unadulterated by facts. What was the result? The same writer produced another "Robinson Crusoe," which the public read for its title, and promptly damned upon its merits: it has literally disappeared from literature.

"The Apparition of Mrs. Veal" is written on a plan which, according to my anonymuncule, breeds general truths, and no lies. What! The sham certificate of the magistrate, and the sham apparition, minutely related with a single dishonest purpose, to trepan the public into buying the dead stock of "Drelincourt on Death"—these are not lies? I congratulate him on both branches of his theory.

The charge of public criminality my anonymuncule rests on this—"That I went upon a single case of habitual cruelty, and traduced a whole system and all the officials, and did all I could to make a great social experiment miscarry." This is one tissue of falsehoods. That no sanguinary abuses existed, except in one gaol, is a lie. The ordinary Bluebooks, written with rosewater, to please Colonel Jebb the Gaol King, revealed a shocking number of suicides, and a percentage of insanity, which, in a place where the average rate was reduced by stoppage of spirituous liquors, gave me just alarm. I had also personally inspected many gaols, and discovered terrible things : a cap of torture and infection in one northern gaol : in a southern gaol the prisoners were wakened several times at night, and their reason shaken thereby. In another gaol I found an old man sinking visibly to his grave under the system ; nobody doubted it, nobody cared. In another, the chaplain, though a great enthusiast, let out that a woman had been put into the "black hole" by the gaoler, against his advice, and taken out a lunatic, and was still a lunatic, and the visiting justices had treated the case with levity. Then I studied the two extraordinary Bluebooks, viz., the Royal Commissioners' Report on Birmingham Gaol, and also on Leicester Gaol, of which last this impudent, ignorant person has evidently never heard. Then I conversed with one of the Royal Commissioners, and he told me the horrors of Leicester Gaol had so affected one of the Commissioners that it had made him seriously ill for more than a month. Enlightened by all these studies, and being also a man qualified to see deeper into human nature than the Gaol King, or any of his military subordinates, I did what the anonymous Press had done on a vast scale without reproach from any anonymuncule : I struck a blow in defence of outraged law and outraged humanity. But unlike the Press, to whom the prison rules are unknown, I did *not* confound the system with all its abuses; on the contrary, I conducted the case thus : I placed before the reader not one government official, but two—the gaoler and the chaplain : the gaoler eternally breaking *the prison rules,* and the chaplain eternally appealing to the prison rules. At last, after inflicting many miseries by repeated breaches of the prison rules, the gaoler does a poor boy to death ; and then I bring in a *third government official,* who dismisses the gaoler. Now, since the prison rules were the conditions of the national experiment, I clearly supported the national experiment in most particulars. I admit that, in two respects, I did try hard to modify the experiment: I urged on practical men its extreme liability to abuse, and I wrote down the crank, and gave my reasons. This irritated government officials for months ; but at last they saw I was right, and abolished the crank, which was a truly hellish invention to make labour contemptible and unremunerative, and theft eternal. They have since conceded to me other points I had demanded; and, in virtue of these improvements, I am, on a small scale, a public benefactor, and have modified, not disturbed, the national experiment.

Now let any one examine the files of September, 1853, and see what an onslaught a hundred anonymous writers made on the gaols. How is it that not one of these is dubbed a national malefactor? Simply, because my anonymuncule is not jealous of *them*. They, like me, did their duty to the nation; they lashed that Birmingham Hell, which disgraced, not England only, but human nature, and eighteen months afterwards they lashed the English judges for not inflicting a proper punishment on the criminal gaoler. These men, like me, wrote humanity, philosophy, sound law, and good gospel, in a case that cried aloud to God and man for all four. To be sure they wrote on sand, I wrote on brass. But those immortal things are not changed by sand or brass. Whether you print them didactically or dramatically makes no moral difference. I was a national benefactor, one of many. Let me go with the rest, undistinguished. Whoever singles me out, and calls one national benefactor a national criminal, is a liar and a scoundrel. I beg pardon, he would be, if he was a man; but your anonymuncule is not a man, as I understand the word—he is a creature with no genuine convictions whatever. He will write against barbarity in prisons, asylums, hospitals, poorhouses, and all dark places; and, if a man with higher powers writes more effectually against those barbarities, he will eat his own words, and defend Hell. There are several anonymuncula of this sort in England, who would deny their God on the spot, if they caught Mr. Reade singing a hymn. I begin to suspect this is one of them strayed into an honester country, and disgracing it.

His objections to "Put Yourself in His Place" are a tissue of lies. He says I have attacked Trades Unions. A direct falsehood. I have distinctly defended them, and do defend them.

He intimates I draw a vital distinction between my club and an Union. A direct falsehood. I have plainly disowned all such distinctions.

He says I have slurred the faults of the masters. A lie. I have detailed and denounced them again and again.

He intimates I have not read the Bluebooks on Mines and Factories. A mistake. I am deeply versed in them, as he will find, if I live.

He complains that I have not taken into account the diseases and short lives of the Sheffield cutlers. A falsehood. I have gone more minutely into them than any living man but Dr. Hall; have pointed out the remedies, and blamed the masters for not employing their superior intelligence to save the men. "You call your men 'Hands,'" say I: "learn to see they are men."

Understand me, I would not apply harsh terms to my anonymuncule, if these several mistakes were advanced in a literary notice. But the whole article is an *indictment;* and in·an indictment a falsehood is a lie. He has either been to the depths of his inner consciousness to learn the contents of my book, or else he has employed another anonymuncule, or some inaccurate woman, to read it for him, and so between two fools—you know the proverb. "Put Yourself in His Place" is at issue with this writer on one point only. I am not so sloppy-minded as to confound the Manchester district with the town of Manchester. That district numbers two million people, is infected with trade outrage, is losing its sympathy with the law even in face of murder, and is ceasing to be England. Nothing is more shallow than the frivolity with which Mr. Harrison and other one-sided men dismiss this terrible phenomenon as exceptional. He, who has studied human nature, and the Bluebooks, so deeply as I have, and searched the provincial journals, knows that not two but forty trades have committed outrages, and that the exceptional ruffianism of certain Manchester trades is not a genuine exception, but only the uneducated workman's ruffianism carried fairly out. That the Sheffield outrages were stale when I wrote—is a lie. They have never intermitted. Blue-book exposure did not affect them for a moment. The town turned Roebuck out of Parliament for not burking the exposure; and went on with their petards and other deadly practices; see the journals *passim.* Last year they knocked a whole row of non-union houses to pieces, and tried to slaughter the inmates. Were the miscreants at Thorncliffe cutlers? I thought they were this anonymuncule's pets, the miners. The fact is that the Union miners' hands, from John o' Groat's to Lizard Point, are red with the blood of non-union men. In the United States the trades are already steeped in human blood. Is America Sheffield, or Manchester?

The masters are just as egotistical as the men: but, unlike the men, they have never had recourse to violence. How long will that last? Does this dreamer imagine that capital *cannot* buy fighting agents, and ten thousand Colt revolvers, and a million grapeshot; and kill lawless ruffians by the hundred, when they commit felony by the hundred? When we come to this, and when the Unions have upset the British Constitution through the servility of the Commons and the blindness of the Peers, let it be remembered that a thinking novelist, a lover of his kind, encouraged the workmen in lawful combination, but wrote against their beastly ignorance and dirt, and their bloody violence and foul play. In such a case it is either books or bayonets. I have tried a book. Others will try bayonets, and anonymuncula will cry "Bravo!"—unless they catch sight of a popular author in the front ranks.

The author of "Put Yourself in His Place" is, in a very small way, a public benefactor. Whoever calls him a public criminal, is a liar and a scoundrel.

That in "Hard Cash" I painted all asylums as abodes of cruelty—is a lie. One of my asylums is governed by a most humane person, though crotchety. The solitary asylum in "A Terrible Temptation" is also a stronghold of humanity. Even in "Hard Cash" the only cruel asylum is governed, not by a physician, but a pawnbroker. As to the abuses pointed out in "Hard Cash," they really existed, and exist.

Can any man offer a fairer test of a book's veracity than I did? I said, in my preface to "Hard Cash," that the whole thing rested on a mass of *legal evidence*—Bluebooks, pamphlets, newspapers, private letters, diaries of alleged lunatics, reports of tried cases. I offered, in print, to show these, at my own house, to any anonymous writer who might care to profit by my labour—the labour of Hercules. I lived eighty yards from Piccadilly, a great fashionable thoroughfare, down which many of these gentry pass every fine day. How many do you suppose accepted this infallible test of mendacity or veracity in my book?

NOT ONE!

Not one of these hypocrites, who pretend to love truth, would walk eighty yards to reap a whole harvest of truth with next to no trouble.

No, they preferred to lie, unshackled by evidence, and to accuse me of being a liar like themselves..

This anonymuncule has read that printed challenge, and knows it was shirked. Yet he repeats the contemporary lie —which is now a greater lie than ever; for fresh evidence has poured in, both public and private. A gentleman in Dublin has recently been incarcerated, on certificates, in an asylum; has gone to the court with a *habeas corpus,* and been at once pronounced sane. A Manx drunkard has just been cajoled into Scotland, and incarcerated, on a medical certificate, as insane. These are public cases; so is *Hall* v. *Semple,* where a turbulent and drunken wife bought a doctor, and incarcerated her husband. Husband has sued doctor, and got damages. Add private cases. A tradesman in the North had a pretty wife. She went to a magistrate, and said he was mad; "And do, please, lock him up for me." "My pretty dear," says the magistrate, "I can't do that, unless you are sure he is mad." "Mad as a March hare!" replies that fair and tender spouse. Thereupon the magistrate issues his warrant, and the man is locked up. He was no more insane than his neighbours. He got his discharge, and came to me directly. I employed him in several matters.

A respectable tradesman in Cheltenham was incarcerated by his wife, and kept eleven years, while she maintained an illicit connection. He made his escape, and came to me. I lent him a solicitor, and told the parties interested to let him alone. They have never laid a finger on him since. The man is perfectly sane, and always was.

At Hanwell Asylum alone the keepers have murdered three lunatics, by breaking from eight to ten ribs and the breast-bone. The doctor, in every case, has told the coroner that the science he professes does not enable him to say positively that all these ribs were not broken by the man slipping down in a room; and I say that, if medicine was a science, it would possess the statistics of falls; which statistics are at present confined to my notebooks, and these reveal, that in mere tumbles, men break the projecting bones before they break the ribs; and that during the last twenty years only one man has broken so many as four of his own ribs, and *he fell* 120 *feet.*

I told the public, in the *Pall Mall Gazette,* the precise mode in which lunatics are murdered at Hanwell—viz., by the keepers walking up and down the victim on their knees, and pressing on him with their knees. A month later, two keepers were indicted for killing a man in Lancaster Asylum. The doctors puzzled a bit over his broken ribs, and conjectured that nine ribs were broken by pressure on the breast-bone; which is simply idiotic, as will be found by experiment on a skeleton. A witness went into the box, and swore he had seen the man murdered by repeated blows of the keepers' knees. For once, thank God, we nailed these miscreants, and they got seven years' penal servitude.

The author of "Hard Cash" is a public benefactor, in a small way. Whoever, after this, calls him a public criminal, is a liar and a scoundrel.

The last charge is trifling. Here is an ill-natured egotist accusing me of good-natured egotism. The charge, made with moderation, might perhaps have been sustained; but his malice and mendacity have overshot the mark, and given me a right to correct him.

He begins with the Sham-Sample-Swindle. He cites a single passage from my letter to Bushnan. That passage, so taken, is egotistical, but not if you consider the context and its purpose. Bushnan was a humbug, who wrote at me publicly, and said there were no abuses in asyla. You will smile, perhaps, when I tell you that, at that moment, there were abuses in his own asylum so serious, that, very soon after, he was turned out of it. Well, I knocked Bushnan on the head with a lot of examples this anonymuncule has read and shirked, the better to repeat Bushnan's falsehood. From that list of facts I could not afford to exclude my own experience—it was too good evidence to suppress. Yes, at a time when my income was not large, I did, for love of justice, humanity, and law, protect an injured fellow-citizen, in whom I had no other interest. He was a sane man, unjustly incarcerated. I fed him, clothed him, backed him, and, after a bitter and costly struggle, got him an annuity of £100 a year for life from those who incarcerated him. Perhaps, if an anonymuncule were capable of such an action, he might mention it spontaneously and more than once. It was dragged out of *me* by a liar, and I never repeated it in my own person.

For an author to introduce his own character into a novel looks like egotism; but it is not so uncommon as this illiterate person imagines. Eccentric characters are rare, and valuable to the artist; and this eccentric character was intruded not egotistically but artistically. It fitted the occasion and forced itself on me.

"Oh, but," says the anonymuncule, "your sketch is one strain of eulogy on the person and mind of Rolfe." Was ever so impudent a lie as this? It is the exact opposite of the truth. It should be remembered that, in fiction, I am not a satirist; I am one who sees the bright side of a mixed character, and I dare say Rolfe has benefited a little by that, along with a score more characters that I have drawn. But compare Rolfe with his predecessors in his own line of business—with Mr. Eden, Dr. Sampson, Dr. Amboyne. Have I ever handled him with the reverence, the affection, the gusto I have shown *them*? Have I disguised his foibles? Have I not let Dr. Suaby get the better of him in dialogue? Who gets the better of Eden or Amboyne?

"But," says my anonymuncule, "you have said the best judges adore his works." This is an impudent lie; I never said a syllable of the kind.

"Personally he is most striking and interesting," &c. This whole sentence is an impudent lie. I have described the man as personally uninteresting and commonplace: an unwieldy person, a rolling gait, commonplace features, a mild brown eye, not bright. I have told the truth *pro* and *con*, just as I should of any other person I was inspecting with an artist's eye.

But the best possible answer to this falsehood is to republish the comment of an American critic, that has come to me:—
"It is alleged that in this character Reade has intended to represent himself, and a cry of horror is raised by those who have never read 'Copperfield,' 'Pendennis,' or 'Amelia,' and never seen Raphael's portrait of himself. We are inclined to think that Rolfe and Reade are one, because the novels of the latter could scarcely be as perfect as they are, without the patient, unremitting drudgery ascribed to the former, and also because the character is drawn in a pitiless fashion, which Reade never elsewhere employs towards his virtuous personages. The plain exterior of the man, and his self-conceit, all his foibles, are kept persistently before the reader, in a style which seems to indicate conscientious self-analysis, and in gratitude for the picture we fail to blame the artist."—*The Charleston Courier.*

One of these writers is clearly tampering with truth. Let the book itself decide which.

Two virulent critiques on my works, in Canadian papers, end rather suspiciously with the same suggestion. This indicates the same hand, and is an abuse of the anonymous. See my preliminary remark *in voce* anonymuncule. The suggestion of which the anonymuncule is so proud is this, that Mr. Rolfe, previously identified with Mr. Reade, may perhaps end his days in a madhouse.

That shall be as God pleases. He gave me whatever good gifts I have, my hatred of inhumanity and injustice, and my loathing of everything that is dastardly and mean, from a British anonymuncule up to a Carolina skunk; and he can take these gifts away in a moment, by taking   my reason.

I shall be no nearer that calamity for this writer's suggestion, and he will be no farther off it, since such suggestions sometimes offend God, as well as disgust men.

But this is certain: should he ever transplant into any business less base and below the law's lash than anonymous detraction, the morals and practices he has shown in slandering me, he will, soon or late, find his way, not to an asylum, but a gaol.—Your obedient servant, CHARLES READE.

October 1871.

This letter was written in reply to a malicious and defamatory libel by Mr. Goldwin Smith in the *Toronto Globe*. The character of that libel can be divined by the reply. I sent it to the *Globe*, but, as criticasters dare not encounter superior writers, on fair terms, it was suppressed.

C. R.

Aug. 5, 1882.

A SUPPRESSED LETTER

The *Athenæum* has lately published some critiques on dramatic authors, signed " Q.," and written with more confidence than knowledge. The article on Mr. Tom Taylor shocked Mr. Charles Reade's sense of justice and propriety, and he wrote a letter to the editor of the *Athenæum*. That gentleman suppressed the letter. Mr. Reade objects to this as doubly unfair, and requests the editor of the paper to which this is sent to give the letter, and its suppression, due publicity.

To the Editor of the "Athenæum."

2 Albert Terrace, Knightsbridge,
April 25th, 1871. .

Sir,—An article appeared in last week's *Athenæum* entitled "Mr. Tom Taylor," and written by one " Q." The article is unjust and needlessly discourteous to a writer of merit, and I must appeal to your sense of justice to let a disinterested critic correct your " Q.," and undeceive your public.

I will take the two writers in their intellectual order.

Mr. Tom Taylor

first distinguished himself as a scholar ; obtained a fellowship at Trinity College, Cambridge. " Mutatis Studiis " he wrote for the theatre ; and his early pieces were nearly all original, though, at that time, originality was rarer than now. Between the years 1852 and 1856 I had myself the honour of working with him on four original dramas. I found him rich in knowledge, fertile in invention, and rapid in execution. Of late years he has been a very busy man ; he is the head of a public office, and the nation takes the cream of his day : he is a steady contributor to the *Times* and to *Punch*, has published two biographies of great research, and yet has contrived to write many good dramas in prose and verse. The mind is finite, so is the day; and I observe that, writing for the stage in the mere fragments of his time, he now invents less, and imitates more, than he did some years ago. But, taking his whole career, the title of a dramatic inventor cannot be honestly denied him. He may not be a dramatist of the highest class—what living Englishman is?—but he resembles the very highest in this, that he sometimes adapts or imitates, without servility, and sometimes invents. This accomplished writer in so many styles is the only man who of late years has filled a theatre by poetical dramas. His last is "Joan of Arc."

Is not this a remarkable man, as times go, and entitled to decent respect from the mere shrimps and minnows, who write *about* literature, because they cannot write literature?

MR. Q.

is a variety of the literary insect "Criticaster." He has been good enough to reveal his method: he went to the Queen's Theatre to see "Joan of Arc," and weigh the author's lines, and the author himself, in his little balance. He qualified himself as follows: he turned his back on the stage, and fell to talking with another criticaster—the illustrious P. ?—about other plays of Mr. Taylor. They did not talk improvingly, for they merely played off a stale literary fraud which I exposed two years ago under the title of the "Sham Sample Swindle." For all that, this part of Q.'s narrative is interesting to me: I have long been asking myself to what class of society, and to what depths of the human intellect, belong those chattering snobs, who always spoil a play for poor me, whenever I go to the public part of a theatre.

"Revealed the secret stands of Nature's work."

They are criticasters; sent in there, by too confiding editors, to hold their tongues and give their minds to the play.

At the last scene it suddenly occurred to "Q." that he must not go away knowing nothing of the play he was sent there to know all about, and this led to a dialogue I reproduce verbatim, simply remarking that to me, who am a critic, it reads like bad fiction.

"'May I venture to ask,' said I, 'if you have reason to

suppose that the drama we are now witnessing is derived from any foreign original?' My friend was expanding his crush-hat. 'Certainly not,' he replied with emphasis, pointing to the stage, whereon they were roasting Mrs. Rousby: 'I know no other dramatic author who, left to himself, would conceive the notion of presenting before an audience such brutal realism as that.' And my friend left."

Now " P." never uttered those words. Every nation has two languages; the spoken, and the written; so uncouth and involved a sentence never flowed from a bad writer's mouth, it could only wriggle from a bad writer's pen. However, there it is—a monument of impudence, insolence, and ignorance. What these poor gropers in the back slums of the drama stigmatise as unprecedented realism has been enacted before admiring Europe, by the most poetical actress of the century, in the first theatre, and the most squeamish, of the civilised world. " Joan of Arc " was one of Rachel's characters, and, in her hands, was burned to death night after night. The burning was represented with what a critic would call " terrible fidelity," a criticaster " brutal realism." She stood on a small working platform arranged to fall about two feet to a stop. The effect was truthful, but appalling; for, when the fire had burned a little time, the great actress, who did nothing by halves, turned rigid, and seemed to fall like a burnt log from her supports. It conveyed, and was intended to convey, that the lower extremities had been burned away, and the figure dropped into the flames. Of course the curtain fell like lightning then, and, up to the moment preceding that awful incident, the face of the actress shone like an angel's, and was divine with the triumph of the great soul over the very flames that were destroying the mortal body.

Believe me, sir, no author, French or English, can give this actress a nobler opportunity than this of rising to the level of Poetry and History.

As to the notion that death by fire is unfit to be presented *corum populo,* this is the chimera of a few Anglo-Saxon dunces afflicted with the known intellectual foible of their race—the trick of drawing distinctions without a difference; in other words, the inability to generalise. Death by fire is neither more nor less fit to be presented faithfully than death by poison, or cold steel. Only the death of " Joan d'Arc " by fire, with her rapt eyes fixed on the God she is going to, is of a grander and more poetical nature than the death of " Hamlet " or of " Macbeth."

That the performance of this great scene at the Queen's Theatre suggested nothing nobler and more poetic to " P." and " Q." than *an actress roasted,* is not the fault of Mr. Taylor, nor of History, which dictated the situation.

No Frenchman was ever the hog to comment on the same situation in a similar spirit, and I am therefore driven reluctantly to the conclusion, that the brutal nation, which burned the maid of Orleans, is still, in some respects, at the bottom of mankind.

Of course, if the part was vilely acted there would be some excuse for " P." and " Q." But, on the contrary, I hear it is well acted. The fault then lies with the criticasters. It is the old, old story: *Parvis omnia parva.* When little men, with little heads, little hearts, little knowledge, little sensibility, and great vanity, go into a theatre, not to take in knowledge and humanity, but to give out ignorance and malice, not to profit by their mental superior, but to disparage him, they are steeled against ennobling influences, and bonded to beauties however obvious. But the retribution is sure. " Depreciation " is the writer's road to ruin. Men see, in our difficult art, by the divine gift, and the amiable habit, of appreciation : to appreciate our gifted contemporaries, is to gather unconsciously a thousand flowers for our own basket.

The depreciator despises his gifted contemporaries, and so gathers nothing but weeds and self-deception. The appreciator makes a name, a fortune, and a signature. The depreciator tickles his own vanity, but gets to admire nothing, feel nothing, create nothing, and be nothing—but a cypher signed by an Initial.—I am, Sir, your obedient servant,

CHARLES READE.

"FOUL PLAY"

To the Editor of the "Examiner and Times"

Sir,—The *Manchester Examiner*, of June 25, contains some remarks upon the above drama, which amount to this, that it is respectably written, but poorly acted, at the Theatre Royal. This summary is calculated to mislead the public, and to wound artists of merit. Permit me, then, to correct the error.

A dramatist is entirely at the mercy of his actors; let him write like an angel, they can reduce him to the level of Poor Poll. You may, therefore, lay it down as a mathematical certainty that a drama is very well acted if it holds an audience tight for three hours and forty minutes, eliciting laughter, tears, applause, and few or no yawns. To go into detail, which is the surest way, Mr. Coleman plays Robert Penfold with the variations of manner that difficult character requires. Easy and natural in the prologue, he warms with the advancing action. His manner of dealing with the difficult tirade in the fourth act shows a thorough knowledge of his art, and he works the act up to a climax with a fire that is invaluable to me, and rare on any stage. On the whole, his is an earnest, manly performance. Miss Henrietta Simms is an actress—young in years, but old in experience—who has often played leading business at the Adelphi Theatre, London. She has presence and dignity, yet can be sprightly without effort. She lacks neither fire, tenderness, nor variety; and, as one example how far she can carry those three qualities, let me point to four speeches she delivers in the principal island scene. They follow upon Robert Penfold's defence, and might be profitably studied both by actors and critics. But elocution is only a part of the great histrionic art. In fact, what reveals the true artist at once, is his dumb play; by which I mean the play of the countenance while another actor is speaking. The faces of second-rate actors become less expressive when they are silent, but the dumb play of first-rate actors never intermits, and is in as high a key as their play. Now in this branch of her art Miss Simms has hardly a living rival. Let anybody who cares to test this statement, watch the changes of her countenance when Robert Penfold and the others are speaking to her. Let him observe her when Arthur Wardlaw places in her hands the pearl from Godsend Island; gradually her eyes dilate, her lips part, and, long before she speaks the commonplace line I have given her, all the sweet memories of love and Godsend Island seem to flow into her face, and elevate it with a tenderness that has really something divine. Such strokes of genius as this partake of inspiration, and are the glory of that enchanting art, which is so plentifully written about, but, alas! so little comprehended. Now for the smaller parts, which, as your contributor seemed to think, play themselves. I know the London stage by heart, and there is not an actor on it who can look and play Wylie as well as Mr. Horsman does. Mrs. Horsman's performance has, upon the whole, breadth and geniality. Mr. Edwards is a tragedian, who plays a part he dislikes to oblige us. The part contains few of those strong effects which suit him, but he never misses one. The fourth act of this play reveals a sailor lying on a bank, sick, and near his end. He is left alone, and has a soliloquy of eight lines. With these eight lines, and the business that belongs to them, an actor holds a large audience hushed and breathless, and draws many a tear from men and women. And who is this magician? It is Mr. Royce, the low comedian of Mr. Coleman's company. Is it usual in this city for low comedians to draw more tears with eight lines than our tragedians draw with eight plays? If not, why pass over Mr. Royce as if I had written *him* along with the lines he delivers so exquisitely? Mr. Chute, a manager, and a veteran actor, plays the little part of Wardlaw Senior to oblige me, and I begin to fear he plays it too well. The purity, the quiet dignity, and gentlemanly ease with which he invests it are too rare upon the stage to be promptly appreciated. All I can say is, that since Dowton's time I have seen nothing of this class so easy, natural, and perfect.

I fear, sir, I have trespassed on your courtesy; but I am

sure you would not willingly lend yourself to an injustice, and I even think and hope that, should your critic revisit the theatre, he will come round to my opinion—viz., that " Foul Play " owes a large share of its success to the talent and zeal of the performers, and especially of those who play the small characters.—I am, Sir, your obedient servant,

CHARLES READE.

PALATINE HOTEL,
June 26th, 1868.

THE SHAM SAMPLE SWINDLE

"FOUL PLAY"

THE world is so wicked and so old, that it is hard to invent a new knavery. Nevertheless, certain writers are now practising an old fraud with a new face and gulling the public and the Press.

Nothing baffles the literary detective so much as a nameless knavery. I begin, therefore, by depriving the fraud in question of that unfair advantage, and I call it—

THE SHAM SAMPLE SWINDLE.

Examples.—1. A farmer prepares his sample of wheaten grain for market. His duty is to put his two hands fairly into the bulk and so fill his sample-bag. But one day, in my experience, a Berkshire farmer picked his grain for show, that is, he went through the sample, and merely removed the inferior grains. He stood in the market with the sham sample, and readily sold twenty load of grain at more than its value. The fraud was detected, and the farmer driven out of the market.

2. Suppose some malicious rogue had access to a farmer's sample-bag, and were to remove the fine grains, and leave the inferior—that would destroy the farmer's sale and be also a sham sample swindle. Of course nothing so wicked was ever done in agriculture; but there is a baser trade in the world than agriculture, and plied by dirtier hands than those which scatter dung upon our fields.

3. I read one day an article in a *Quarterly Review,* in which these two expressions occurred more than once, "the author of ' Robinson Crusoe,' " and " the author of the ' Lily and the Bee.' " Now, Defoe wrote several stupid stories, and one masterpiece ; Warren wrote several powerful stories and one

foolish rhapsody; yet here, in the name of science (for criticism is science, or it is nothing) is Warren defined by his exceptional failure, and Defoe by his exceptional success; and that is one form of the sham sample swindle. [*N.B.* The dead are apt to get the sunny side of this swindle, and the living the windy side.]

4. A writer produces a great book. With all its beauties it is sure to have flaws, being written by man, who is an imperfect creature. The sham sample swindler picks out the flaw or flaws, quotes them bodily, which gives an air of honesty, and then says, "*We could give a host of other examples, but these will serve to show the general character of the work.*"

The swindle lies in the words italicised. They declare a sham sample to be a true sample; and, observe, this is a falsehood that cannot fail to deceive the reader. For why? The grain of truth that supports the falsehood is shown; the mass of truth that contradicts the falsehood is hidden.

5. A great work of fiction is written; it is rich in invention and novel combination; but, as men of genius have a singularly keen appreciation of all that is good, and can pick out pearls where obscure scribblers could see nothing but rubbish, the author has, perhaps, borrowed one or two things from other written sources, and incorporated them happily with the bulk of his invention. If so, they ought to be pointed out to the public, and are, of course, open to stricture from unlearned critics, who do not know to what an extent Shakespeare, Virgil, Molière, Corneille, Defoe, Le Sage, Scott, Dumas, &c., have pursued this very method, and how much the public gain by it. But the sham sample swindler is not content to point out the borrowed portion, and say honestly, so and so is not original, the rest may be. His plan is to quote the plagiarism, and then add, "*And that part of the work we do not quote is all cut from the same cloth.*"

He tells this lie in cold blood, with his eyes upon the truth; and, as I said before, it is a fraud that can never fail on the spot, because the borrowed part of the work is in sight, the bulk of the work is out of sight.

So much by way of general description.

I come now to a remarkable example : Several journalists not blessed with much power of reasoning on literary subjects are repeating that "Foul Play," a three volume novel, which originally appeared in this magazine, is a servile copy of an obscure French drama, called *Le Portefeuille Rouge.*

Not to waste time on echoes, I have traced this rumour to

its source, a monthly magazine, called the *Mask*. Here, the writer, in a form, the modesty and good taste of which I shall leave to the judge in whose court I may select to try the proprietors of the *Mask* for the libel, conveys to the public a comparison of the two works, and contemptuously comments upon the more brilliant and important of the two.

He conducts the comparison on a two-fold plan. First he deals with the incidents of the two works. Secondly, with the dialogue. But how? In the first branch of comparison he suppresses nine-tenths of the striking incidents in "Foul Play," and at least eight-tenths of the strong incidents in *Le Portefeuille Rouge,* and then, by slightly twisting the few incidents that survive this process, and by arbitrarily wording this double sham sample swindle in similar language (which language is his, not ours), he makes the two works appear much alike in incident, although they are on the whole quite unlike in incident.

Secondly, he comes to the dialogue. And here he is met by a difficulty none of the sham samplers who preceded him had to face. He could not find a line in "Foul Play" that had been suggested by a line in *Le Portefeuille Rouge.* What was to be done? He hit upon the drollest expedient. He selected a dialogue from *Le Portefeuille Rouge* and set it cheek by jowl, not with parallel passages in "Foul Play," which was what his argument demanded, but with a lame and incorrect translation of itself. Here is a specimen of his method :—

LE PORTEFEUILLE ROUGE	THE PLACE WHERE "FOUL PLAY" OUGHT TO BE.
KERVEGUEN.	**KERVEGUEN.**
Pour rien au monde, je n'aurais voulu vous laisser seul ici ; mais, d'un autre côté, quels risques n'auriez-vous pas courus en vous embarquant avec nous ? . . .	For nothing in the world I would not wish to leave you ; but, on the other hand, what risks would you not run in your embarking with us ?
HÉLÈNE.	**HELENE.**
Quoi ! mon père, auriez-vous donc l'idée de parti sans lui ?	What, my father, had you then the idea to go without him ?
KERVEGUEN.	**KERVEGUEN.**
Le bâtiment que je monte appartient à l'Etat, et je ne saurais	The ship which I mount belongs to the State, and I should not

prendre avec moi un homme con-damné par les lois françaises.	know how to take with me a man condemned by the French laws.

HÉLÈNE.	HELENE.
Injustement condamné, mon père; M. Maurice est innocent.	Unjustly condemned, my father.

KERVEGUEN.	KERVEGUEN.
Dieu m'est témoin que je le souhaite de toute mon âme !	Heaven is my witness that I hope it with all my soul.

And so on for *seventy* speeches. By this method it is craftily insinuated to the reader that seventy speeches of " Foul Play " *could* be quoted to prove the plagiarism, though not one speech *is* quoted. Curious, that a manœuvre so transparent should succeed. But it has succeeded—for a time.

Unfortunately for truth and justice, the sham sample swindle, being founded on suppression, has the advantage of brevity; whereas its exposure must always be long and tedious. But, since in this case it has attacked not my ability only, but my probity in business, I hope my readers will be patient, and consider for once how hard it is, after many months of ardent and successful labour and invention, to be not only decried, but slandered and insulted for my pains !

I know no positive antidote to a dishonest comparison, except an honest comparison. A novel is not the same thing as a drama; but no doubt they have three essentials in common. 1. Characters. 2. Incidents. 3. Dialogue. Let us, then, compare the two works on that treble basis.

CHARACTERS IN *LE PORTE-FEUILLE ROUGE.*

1. Duromé, a banker and loose-liver.

2. De Folbert, a daring, middle-aged ruffian, fearing nothing, loving nothing. The trite monster of Melodrama, that never existed in nature.

3. Maurice, a young layman, interesting by his sufferings and adventures, but as to character, utterly commonplace.

CHARACTERS IN "FOUL PLAY."

1. Old Wardlaw, an honourable merchant.

2. Young Wardlaw, a weak youth, led into crime by cowardice; a knave tortured by remorse and rendered human by an earnest love.

3. Michael Penfold, a worthy timid old man, cashier to Wardlaw, Senior.

4. Faustin, Duromé's servant.
5. Bouquin, a sailor.
6. Le Père Lajoie.

4. Robert Penfold, his son, a clergyman, and a man of rare gifts, muscular, learned, inventive, patient, self - denying, delicate- minded : a marked character ; new in fiction.

7. Daniel.
8. Garnier, a surgeon.
9. Vestris.
10. Chasse.
11. Le Comte de Kerveguen, captain of a vessel,—who has got a daughter.

5. General Rolleston, governor of a penal settlement, and a soldier, who, however, has got a daughter.

12. Hélène, daughter of the pre- ceding,—a weak, amiable girl, who parts with her virtue the first fair opportunity. This character is undistinguishable from a thou- sand others in French fiction.

6. Helen (daughter of the pre- ceding), a young lady of marked character, hard to win and hard to lose, virtuous under temptation, and distinguished by a tenacity of purpose which is rarely found in her sex. Upon the whole, a char- acter almost new in fiction.

13. Madame Delaunay, aunt to the preceding.
14. Miss Deborah, Hélène's gouvernante.
15. Jacqueline, Faustin's wife.
16. Mesdemoiselles Dufréne, Duthé, and Fel, young ladies it may be as well not to describe too minutely.
17. Ursule, a lady's-maid.
18. Marcel, a French Cockney, who gets sent to sea, an admirable character ; indeed, the only new character in the drama.
19. An ape.

7. Hiram Hudson, captain of the *Proserpine*, a good seaman, who has been often employed to cast away ships. When drunk, he de- scants on his duty to his employers. This character is based on reality, and is entirely new in fiction.
8. Joseph Wylie, his mate, a man of physical strength, yet cunning ; a rogue, but a manly one, goaded by avarice, but stung by remorse.

9. Cooper, a taciturn sailor, with an antique friendship for talkative Welch.

10. Welch, a talkative sailor, with antique friendship for taciturn Cooper. These two sailors are characters entirely new in fiction. So are their adventures and their deaths.

11. Joshua Fullalove, a character created by myself in "Hard Cash" and reproduced in "Foul Play" with the consent of my collaborateur.

12. Burt, a detective.

13. Undercliff, an expert; a character based on reality, but entirely new in fiction. He reads handwriting wonderfully, but cannot read circumstances.

14. Mrs. Undercliff, mother to the expert, a woman who has no skill at handwriting, but reads faces and circumstances keenly.

15. Tollemache, a barrister.

16. Meredith, a barrister of a different stamp.

17. Sarah Wilson.

18. A squinting barber, who sees a man in trouble, and so demands 10s. for shaving him.

19. Adams, a bill-broker.

20. Somebody, an underwriter.

21. Nancy Rouse, a lodging-house keeper and washerwoman, and a character new in fiction.

Now it is an axiom in literary criticism, that to invent incidents is a lower art than to invent characters; and the writer in the *Mask* fires off this axiom at me. So be it. I find nineteen distinct characters in *Le Portefeuille Rouge,* and out of the nineteen, fifteen bear no shadow of resemblance, in act or word, to any character in " Foul Play : " yet of these fifteen many are the very engines of the play. I find twenty-one distinct characters in " Foul Play," and, out of these, seventeen bear no resemblance, either in deed or word, to any character in *Le Portefeuille Rouge.* Yet these seventeen are busy characters, and take a large share in the plot. As to the small balance of four persons, the two heroines are so opposite in characters that no writer, whose eye was on the French Hélène, could possibly have created the English Helen. The same remark applies to De Folbert and Arthur Wardlaw: they are both rogues; but then they are opposite rogues. Why, they differ as widely as a bold highwayman and an anonymous slanderer.

Setting aside Incident, which awaits its turn in this comparison, I can find no character—except that of General Rolleston—which resembles a character in "Foul Play." Kerveguen is a sailor and the captain of a ship; so far he corresponds, not with General Rolleston, but with the Captain Hudson of "Foul Play." But then this sailor has a resolute character and a daughter, and she is the heroine of the drama. Now the soldier Rolleston has also a resolute character, and a daughter who is the heroine of "Foul Play." The plagiarism of character, if any, is manifestly confined to the heroine's father, one character out of thirty-eight and more, who act, and speak, and think, and feel in the two works. How far does this correspond with the impression the sham sampler has sought to create?

We come now to the incidents of the two works, and these, handled on the above honest method, yield precisely the same result. But to work this out on paper would take a volume. Something however may be done in a shorter compass by the help of figures. "Foul Play," then, is contained in 25 numbers of *Once a Week*. And these numbers average, I believe, 14 columns each, or rather more. The first number is very busy, and deals with crime and love. The prologue of the French drama does not deal with love at all, and with crime of quite another character. In the story the crime is forgery; and that crime remains part of the plot to the end. In the drama the true generative incident is murder. That murder is committed by a villain who had, previously, forged; but the previous forgery could be omitted without affecting the plot. The fundamental incident of the drama is murder. The two fundamental incidents of "Foul Play" are forgery, and the scuttling of a ship to defraud the underwriters.

From No. 1 to No. 4, "Foul Play," though full of incidents, has not an idea in common with the drama. In the 4th number the two works have this in common, that the hero and heroine are on board one ship, and that ship gets lost. But in the drama the father is there, and in the story he is not; the hero and heroine are brought on board by entirely different incidents in the two works, and the French ship is fired by mere accident. Not so the English ship; that is scuttled by order of the heroine's lover; and so the knave is made the means of throwing the woman he loves upon the protection of the friend he has ruined. This is invention and combination of a high order. But calling upon an unforeseen accident to effect a solitary purpose and then dismissing the accident for ever, is just what any fool can do at any moment, and it is all the authors of the French drama have attempted to do in that situation. From the 4th number to the last page but one of the 17th number, "Foul Play" diverges entirely from the drama, and the drama from "Foul Play." The existence of those thirteen numbers (more than one-half of the entire story) is virtually denied by the sham sampler in these words:—

"Construction and incidents are French, and taken from the defendant's drama."

Yet these thirteen numbers are the most admired of the whole. They are the poem of the work. They deal with the strange, the true, the terrible, and the beautiful. Here are to be found the only numbers which I received complete in form as well as in substance from my accomplished collaborateur, and it was this half of the work which drew in one week *forty notices from American journals*. Those journals, commenting on the adventures and contrivances of certain persons wrecked on the Auckland Islands, remarked that *History was imitating fiction*, and so sent their readers to "Foul Play." History will never imitate *Le Portefeuille Rouge*, any more than I have descended to imitate *Le Portefeuille Rouge*. At the end of the 17th number of "Foul Play," General Rolleston lands on the unknown island, and finds his daughter and the innocent convict living alone together. And in the 9th scene of the 2nd act of *Portefeuille Rouge*, Kerveguen comes with other characters, and finds his daughter, the innocent convict, and Marcel. This is a good and generative situation, and looks like plagiarism in the novel. But the moment we come to the treatment, the acts and the words of all the three interlocutors are so remarkably different in the two works, that no honest and discerning man can believe the writer of that scene in "Foul Play" had his eye on the drama. In the story the father and daughter meet alone with wild raptures equal to the occasion; a sacred scene. In the play they meet before witnesses, and the French dramatists with very bad judgment have allowed the low comedian to be present. He opens his mouth, and of course the scene goes to the devil at once.

In the subsequent dialogue and business, I find great variations.

IN THE DRAMA	IN THE NOVEL
Hélène sides at once with Maurice, and argues the case with her father, and Maurice is almost passive. Maurice is never master of the situation. On the contrary, he tries to follow Hélène on board, and is shot like a dog in the attempt. Hélène never undertakes to clear him. All is left to accident.	Helen puts Robert Penfold on his defence, and on his convincing her he is innocent, declares her love. Then Robert Penfold becomes master of the situation, and it is by his own will, and high sense of honour, he remains, and the parting is effected. And Helen and her father undertake to clear him in England; which promise, on Helen's part, with its many consequences, is the very plot of the sequel.

From this to the end of the work, we have seven numbers of " Foul Play," and two acts of *Portefeuille Rouge,* and not an idea in common between the two. So that twenty-three numbers out of twenty-five, " Foul Play," have not an idea in common with the French drama ; two numbers out of twenty-five have each a bare situation which looks like one in the drama, but on closer inspection prove to be handled so differently that the charge of plagiarism is untenable.

" Foul Play " is illustrated by Mr. Du Maurier. The said Du Maurier is a good actor, and has dramatic tendencies. He is sure to have picked out some of the more dramatic situations in " Foul Play " for illustration, and if the incidents of " Foul Play " came from the *Portefeuille Rouge,* Mr. Du Maurier's sketches would serve to illustrate that drama. I have examined his illustrations, twelve in number; I cannot find one that fits any scene or incident in the French drama. If they were all pasted into the *Portefeuille Rouge,* no reader of that drama would be able to apply any one of them to anything in the whole composition. Bring your minds to bear on this fact. It is worth study.

And now I come to the dialogue of the works. Here the comparison is a blank. There is nothing to compare. The writer in the *Mask* dared not put seventy speeches from " Foul Play " by the side of his seventy speeches from *Porte-*

feuille Rouge. He dared not deal thus honestly with even seven speeches. And shall I tell you why? Because there is not one line in " Foul Play " that corresponds with a line in *Portefeuille Rouge.*

Shakespeare, in the " Merry Wives of Windsor," has the following line :

" I'll rather be unmannerly than troublesome."

And Molière, in his *Bourgeois Gentilhomme,* has this line

" *J'aime mieux être incivil qu'importun.*"

I can find no such apparent plagiarism in all the pages of " Foul Play " and *Le Portefeuille Rouge.*

I conclude this subject with the following statements of matters known to me :—

1. I have carefully examined all the MS. contributed to " Foul Play " by Mr. Dion Boucicault. This MS. consists of two or three numbers complete in form as well as in substance ; and also of a great many plans of numbers, sketches, materials, and inventive ideas of singular merit and value. In all this MS. I find only one word that can have come from *Portefeuille Rouge,* and that word is—Helen.

2. I myself never saw *Le Portefeuille Rouge* until after the article in the *Mask* appeared—never saw it nor heard of it.

3. The one valuable situation the two works contain in common may have come to me from Mr. Boucicault, but if so it came *in conversation,* along with many other things quite as good, and the guilt, if any, of selecting the naked idea which is all we have used, lies with me, who never saw the *Porte-feuille Rouge.*

4. I handled, treated, and wrote every line, on which the charge of unprincipled plagiarism has been founded, and I have got my MS. to prove it.

5. Any person connected with literature can compare the *Portefeuille Rouge* and " Foul Play " at my house : and I shall be grateful to any literary brother who may have the honesty and patience to do it.

6. The writer in the *Mask* has done this, and having done it, he must have known that his charge of unprincipled plagiarism was false and disingenuous. Yet, knowing this, he was not content to do me a moderate injury : it was not enough to defraud an honoured writer of his reputation as an inventor ; he must attack my character as a gentleman, and as a

fair dealer with publishers and managers. On this account I am going to make an example of him. I shall sue him for libel, and, when we meet in the Court of Common Pleas, I shall repeat upon my oath as a Christian all the statements, which now I make in these columns upon my honour as a gentleman.

I shall ask leave to return to the sham sample swindle on some other occasion, and in a way that will be less egotistical and more interesting to your readers. It is the most potent swindle in creation, and all honest writers should combine to expose it.

CHARLES READE.

2 ALBERT TERRACE, KNIGHTSBRIDGE,
August 13*th*, 1868.

"IT IS NEVER TOO LATE TO MEND"

FROM THE "READER," *October 28th*, 1865

SIR,—You have published (inadvertently, I hope) two columns of intemperate abuse aimed at my drama, and mendacious personalities levelled at myself.

The author of all this spite is not ashamed to sympathise with the heartless robbers from whom justice and law have rescued my creation and my property.

(*Query*—Was he not set on by those very robbers?)

He even eulogises a ruffian who, on the 4th October, raised a disturbance in the Princess's Theatre, and endeavoured to put down my play by clamour, but was called to order by the respectable portion of the audience.

Have you any sense of justice and fair play where the party assailed is only an author of repute, and the assailant has the advantage of being an obscure scribbler? If so, you will give me a hearing in my defence. I reply in one sentence to two columns of venom and drivel. I just beg to inform honest men and women that your *anonymous contributor*, who sides with piratical thieves against the honest inventor, and disparages Charles Reade, and applauds one Tomlins—is *Tomlins*.—I am, your obedient servant, CHARLES READE.

92 ST. GEORGE'S ROAD, SOUTH BELGRAVIA,
October 21st, 1865.

THE "EDINBURGH REVIEW" AND THE "SATURDAY REVIEW"

A LETTER

SATURDAY REVIEW,—You have brains of your own, and good ones. Do not you echo the bray of such a very small ass as the *Edinburgh Review*. Be more just to yourself and to me. Reflect! I must be six times a greater writer than ever lived, ere I could exaggerate suicide, despair, and the horrors that drove young and old to them; or (to vary your own phrase) write "a libel upon Hell."—Yours sincerely,

CHARLES READE.

GARRICK CLUB,
July 22nd, 1857.

THE PRURIENT PRUDE

SIR,—There is a kind of hypocrite that has never been effectually exposed, for want of an expressive name. I beg to supply that defect in our language, and introduce to mankind the PRURIENT PRUDE. Modesty in man or woman shows itself by a certain slowness to put a foul construction on things, and also by unobtrusively shunning indelicate matters and discussions. The "PRURIENT PRUDE," on the contrary, itches to attract attention by a parade of modesty (which is the mild form of the disease), or even by rashly accusing others of immodesty (and this is the noxious form).

"Doctor Johnson," said a lady, "what I admire in your dictionary is that you have inserted no improper words."

"What! you looked for them, madam?" said the Doctor.

Here was a "PRURIENT PRUDE," that would have taken in an ordinary lexicographer.

The wickeder kind of "PRURIENT PRUDE" has committed great ravages in our English railways, where the carriages, you must know, are small and seldom filled. Respectable men found themselves alone with a shy-looking female, addressed a civil remark to her, were accused at the end of the journey of attempting her virtue, and punished unjustly, or else had to buy her off: till at last, as I learn from an article in the *Saturday Review*, many worthy men refused to sit in a carriage where there was a woman only ; such terror had the " PRURIENT PRUDE " inspired in manly breasts. The last of these heroines, however, came to grief; her victim showed fight; submitted to trial, and set the police on her : she proved to be, as any one versed in human nature could have foretold, a woman of remarkably loose morals ; and she is at this moment expiating her three P's—Prudery, Prurience, and Perjury—in one of her Majesty's gaols.

Some years ago an English baronet was nearly ruined and separated from his wife by one of these ladies. He was from the country, and by force of habit made his toilet nearer the window than a Londoner would.   A "PRURIENT PRUDE" lurked opposite, and watched him repeatedly; which is just what no modest woman would have done once; and, interpreting each unguarded action by the light of her own foul imagination, actually brought a criminal charge against the poor soul.   The charge fell to the ground the moment it was sifted; but in the meantime, what agony had the "PRURIENT PRUDE" inflicted on an innocent family !

Unfortunately the "PRURIENT PRUDE" is not confined to the female sex.   It is not to be found amongst men of masculine pursuits; but it exists amongst writers.   Example: a divorce case, unfit for publication, is reported by all the English journals.   Next day, instead of being allowed to die, it is renewed in a leader.   The writer of this leader begins by complaining of the courts of law for giving publicity to *Filth*.
—(N.B. the ridiculous misuse of this term, where not filth but crime is intended, is an infallible sign of a dirty mind, and marks the "PRURIENT PRUDE.") After this flourish of prudery, Pruriens goes with gusto into the details, which he had just said were unfit for publication.   Take down your file of English journals and you will soon lay your hand on this variety of the "PRURIENT PRUDE."   A harmless little humbug enough.

But, as amongst women, so amongst writers, the "PRURIENT PRUDE" becomes a less transparent and more dangerous impostor, when, strong in the shelter of the Anonymous, which hides from the public his own dissolute life and obscene conversation, he reads his neighbour by the light of his own corrupt imagination, and so his prurient prudery takes the form of slander, and assassinates the fair fame of his moral, intellectual, and social superior.

Now the five or six "Prurient Prudes" who defile the American Press have lately selected me, of all persons, for their victim.   They are trying hard to make the American public believe two monstrous falsehoods: first, that they are pure-minded men; secondly, that I am an impure writer.

Of course, if these five or six "Prurient Prudes" had the courage to do as I do, sign their names to their personalities, their names and their characters would be all the defence I should need.   But, by withholding *their* signatures, they give the same weight to their statements that an honest man gives by appending *his* signature, and compel me, out of respect to the American public, whose esteem I value, to depart from the usual practice of authors in my position, and to honour mere literary vermin with a reply. The case, then, stands thus. I have produced a story called " Griffith Gaunt, or Jealousy." This story has, ever since December 1865, floated *The Argosy*, an English periodical, and has been eagerly read in the pages of *The Atlantic Monthly*. In this tale I have to deal, as an artist and a scholar, with the very period Henry Fielding has described—to the satisfaction of Prurient Prudes; a period in which manners and speech were somewhat blunter than nowadays; and I have to portray a great and terrible passion, Jealousy, and show its manifold consequences, of which even Bigamy (in my story) is one, and that without any violation of probability. Then I proceed to show the misery inflicted on three persons by Bigamy, which I denounce as a crime. In my double character of moralist and artist, I present, not the delusive shadow of Bigamy, but its substance. The consequence is, that instead of shedding a mild lustre over Bigamy, I fill my readers with a horror of Bigamy, and a wholesome indignation against my principal male character, so far as I have shown him. Of course "Griffith Gaunt," like "Hard Cash," is not a child's book, nor a little girl's book : it is an ambitious story, in which I present the great passions that poets have sung with applause in all ages ; it is not a boatful of pap ; but I am not paid the price of pap. By the very nature of my theme I have been compelled now and then to tread on delicate ground ; but I have trodden lightly and passed on swiftly, and so will all the pure-minded men and women who read me. No really modest woman will ever suffer any taint by reading " Griffith Gaunt," unless, indeed, she returns to its perusal, unsexed, and filled with prurient curiosity, by the foul interpretations of the " Prurient Prudes." Then come a handful of scribblers, whose lives are loose and their conversation obscene : they take my text, and read it, not by its own light, but by the light of their own foul imaginations ; and, having so defiled it by mixing their own filthy minds with it, they sit in judgment *on the compound*. To these impostors I say no more. The two words, " Prurient Prude," will soon run round the Union, and render its citizens somewhat less gullible by that class of impostor. One person, however, has slandered me so maliciously and so busily, that I am compelled to notice him individually, the more so as I am about to sue an English weekly for merely quoting him. The editor of a New York weekly called *The Round Table* has printed a mass of scurrility direct and vicarious to this purport :—

1. That " Griffith Gaunt " is an indecent publication ;
2. That it is immoral ;
3. That, like other novelists, the author deals in adultery, bigamy, and nameless social crimes ;
4. But that, unlike the majority of my predecessors, I side with the crimes I depict ;
5. That the modesty and purity of women cannot survive the perusal of " Griffith Gaunt ; "
6. That this story was declined by some of the lowest sensational weekly papers of New York *on the ground that they did not dare to undertake its publication.*
7. Passing from personal to vicarious slander, he prints the letter of an animal calling itself G. S. H., who suggests that some inferior writer wrote " Griffith Gaunt," and that I lent my name to it for a foreign market, and so he and I combined to swindle the Boston publishers.—This, in England, we call felony.

Now, sir, I have often known some obscure dunce, who had the advantage of concealing his nameless name, treat an esteemed author with lofty contempt in the columns of a journal, and call his masterpiece a sorry production. I myself am well accustomed to that sort of injustice and insolence from scribblers, who could not write my smallest chapter, to save their carcasses from the gallows, and their souls from premature damnation. But the spite and vanity of our inferiors in the great, profound, and difficult art of writing, are generally satisfied by calling us dunces, and bunglers, and coxcombs, and that sort of thing.

In all my experience I never knew the Press guilty of such a crime as the editor of *The Round Table* has committed. It is a deliberate attempt to assassinate the moral character of an author and a gentleman, and to stab the ladies of his own family to the heart, under pretence of protecting the women of a nation from the demoralising influence of his pen.

You will see at once that I could not hold any communication with *The Round Table* or its editor, and I must, therefore, trust to American justice and generosity, and ask leave to reply in respectable columns.

In answer to statements 1, 2, 4, and 5, I pledge the honour of a gentleman that they are deliberate and intentional falsehoods, and I undertake to prove this before twelve honest American citizens, sworn to do justice between man and man.

As to No. 3, I really scarce know what my slanderer means. Griffith Gaunt, under a delusion, commits Bigamy: and of course Bigamy may by a slight perversion of terms be called Adultery. But no truthful person, attacking character, would apply both terms to a single act. Is Bigamy more than Polygamy? And is Polygamy called that, and Adultery too, in every district of the United States?

As to "the nameless social crimes," what does the beast mean? Did he find these in his own foul imagination, or did he find them in my text? If it was in the latter, of course he can point to the page. He shall have an opportunity.

Statement 6 is a lie by way of equivocation. The truth is, that before "Griffith Gaunt" was written, an agent of mine proposed to me to sound some newspaper proprietors who had hitherto stolen my works, as to whether they would like to buy a story of me, instead of stealing it. I consented to this preliminary question being put, and I don't know what they replied to my agent. Probably the idea of buying, where they had formed a habit of stealing, was distasteful to them. But this you may rely on, that I never submit a line of manuscript to the judgment of any trader whatever, either in England or in America, and never will. Nothing is ever discussed between a trader and me except the bulk and the price. The price is sometimes a high one; but always a fair one, founded on my sales. If he has not the courage to pay it, all the worse for him. If he has, the bargain is signed, and then and not till then, he sees the copy.

I never intrusted a line of "Griffith Gaunt" to an agent. I never sent a line of it across the Atlantic to any human being, except to the firm of Ticknor & Fields: and even to that respectable firm, one of the partners in which is my valued friend, I did not send a line of it until they had purchased of me the right to publish it in the United States. And this purchase was made on the basis of an old standing agreement.

Compare these facts with the impression a miserable prevaricator has sought to create, to wit, that the proprietor of some low journal was allowed to *read the manuscript, or unpublished sheets,* of "Griffith Gaunt," and declined it *on the score of morality.*

Statement 7, which accuses me of a literary felony, is a deliberate, intentional falsehood. *The Argosy* is sold in New York in great numbers, price sixpence. The editor of *The Round Table* is aware of this, and has seen "Griffith Gaunt" in

it, with my name attached; yet he was so bent on slandering
me by hook or by crook, that he printed the letter of G. S. H.
without contradiction, and so turned the conjecture of a mere
fool into a libel and a lie.

I shall only add that I mean to collar the editor of *The
Round Table,* and drag him and his slanders before a jury
of his countrymen. He thinks there is no law, justice, or
humanity for an Englishman in the great United States. We
shall see.

Pending the legal inquiry, I earnestly request my friends
in the United States to let me know who this editor of *The
Round Table* is, and all about him, that so we may meet on
fair terms before the jury.

All editors of American journals who have any justice, fair
play, or common humanity to spare to an injured stranger,
will print this letter, in which one man defends himself against
many; and will be good enough to accept my thanks for the
same in this writing. CHARLES READE.

3 ALBERT TERRACE,
  HYDE PARK, LONDON.

P.S.—I demand as my right the undivided honour of all the
insults that have been misdirected against Messrs. Ticknor
and Fields, of Boston. Those gentlemen have had no alternative: they could not bow to slander, and discontinue
"Griffith Gaunt" in *The Atlantic Monthly,* without breaking
faith with me, and driving their subscribers to *The Argosy.*
The whole credit, and discredit, of "Griffith Gaunt," my
masterpiece, belongs to me, its sole author, and original
vendor.

SECOND-HAND LIBEL

To the Editor of the "Globe"

Sir,—You have read my letter to the American press, cited one paragraph, and perverted that from its true intention, by suppressing its context. By this means you exaggerate my arrogance, and stir the bile of the publishers. I must request you to be more scrupulous, and to print the whole truth. *The Round Table* had stated that "'Griffith Gaunt' was declined by some of the lowest sensational weekly papers of New York, on the ground that they did not dare to undertake its publication." This was a monstrous piece of insolence; and I had to show a distant public that it *must* be a falsehood. But this I had no means whatever of doing, except by revealing my real way of treating with traders at home and abroad. You are welcome to blarney the publishers by telling them that artists (penny-a-liners excepted) write for money, but publishers publish for glory. I cannot go quite this length with you, not wanting their advertisements; but still I do not wish to affront these gentlemen without provocation, and so I insist on your printing this explanation, which your own disingenuousness has rendered necessary.

On the 17th October "Griffith Gaunt" was published in three volumes; on the 19th a copy was probably in your hands. On that day you revived and circulated a slander that tends to injure its sale very seriously, and to destroy the personal character of its author: you announced in your columns that *"an American critic declares the story to be indecent and immoral; and that, on this point, having vainly attempted to read it, you offer no opinion."*

Now it may be very polite of cold hashed mutton to affect a singular contempt for venison: but in your case it is not reasonable; you are familiar with drudgery; you contrive to read dozens of novels that are the very offal

302

of the human mind; ay, and to praise them too. You know why.

Now, advertisements are a fine thing; but justice is a finer, whatever you may think. And justice required of you either to hold your tongue about "Griffith Gaunt," or else to read it.

But even assuming that you really had not the brains to read "Griffith Gaunt" for pleasure, nor yet the self-respect and prudence to wade through it before lending your columns to its defamation, at least you have read my letter to the American press; and, having read that, you cannot but *suspect* this charge of immorality and indecency to be a libel and a lie. Yet you have circulated the calumny all the same, and suppressed the refutation.

I am afraid the truth is, you have got into your head that the law will allow you to indulge a perverse disposition, by defaming and blackening the moral character of a respected author, provided you use another man's blacking. Pure chimera! The law draws no such distinction. It serves tale-bearers with the same sauce as tale-makers; it protects honest men alike against the originators and the reckless circulators of calumny. Believe me, your only chances to avoid very serious consequences are two: you must either meet me before a jury, and justify the American libel you have Anglicised and circulated; or else you must contradict it at once, and apologise to the man you have wronged. I offer you three days to read "Griffith Gaunt" and decide upon your course. If at the end of that time, you do not distinctly and categorically state that "Griffith Gaunt" is *not* an indecent and immoral book—and apologise to its author—I shall sue the proprietor of the *Globe*, as I am suing the proprietor of the *London Review*, for composing and printing an American libel with English type, and then publishing and selling it in English columns; in other words, for collecting foreign dirt with English hands, and flinging it upon the personal character of an English citizen. CHARLES READE.

5 ALBERT TERRACE,
   October 22nd, 1866.

The editor of the *Globe* having made public comments on this letter, yet kept the letter private, the writer requests less unscrupulous editors to repair this injustice.

"FACTS MUST BE FACED"

To the Editor of the "Times"

Sir,—The *Times* of the 24th of August contains a notice of
"A Terrible Temptation," done upon a new plan. It is a
careful synopsis of all the main incidents in my story, only
my abridger has divested them of every charm. It is rather
hard my name should be attached to a bad story told by
another man when I have told a goodish one with the same
materials; but I console myself by reflecting that the same
ingenious process applied to Homer's *Iliad* would prove it a
contemptible work. There is something more serious, reflecting on me both as a writer and a man, which I cannot
leave uncontradicted in columns so powerful as yours. My
abridger has said that I have written about things which should
not be spoken of, much less written about—alluding to my
sketch of Rhoda Somerset—and that innocent girls ought not
to be informed on such subjects. He even hints that mothers
would do well to forbid my first volume to their unmarried
daughters. You must admit, sir, this is a very serious thing
to say in print, and very cruel to a writer of my age; then do,
please, give me fair play for once, and let me be heard in
reply. The character of Rhoda Somerset was not invented
by me, but copied from a master hand. It was you who
first introduced her, ponies and all, to the public, on the 3rd
day of July 1862, in an admirable letter, headed " Anonyma."
On another occasion you discussed the whole subject, day
after day, in leaders and a vast correspondence, so that for
one lady who knows about the *demi-monde* from my pages,
twenty know a great deal more from yours. Should this
lose you the esteem of my abridger, permit me to offer you,
as a small substitute, the thanks of a better judge. You did
your duty to the public in 1862, as you had often done it
before, and were true to your own invaluable maxim, " Facts

must be faced." For 18 years, at least, the journal you conduct so ably has been my preceptor, and the main source of my works—at all events of the most approved. A noble passage in the *Times* of September 7 or 8, 1853, touched my heart, inflamed my imagination, and was the germ of my first important work, " It is Never Too Late to Mend." That column, a monument of head, heart, and English, stands now dramatised in my pages, and embellishes the work it had inspired. Some years later you put forth an able and eloquent leader on private asylums, and detailed the sufferings there inflicted on persons known to you. This took root in me, and brought forth its fruit in the second volume of " Hard Cash." Later still, your hearty and able, but temperate leaders, upon trades unions and trade outrages incited me to an ample study of that great subject, so fit for fiction of the higher order, though not adapted to the narrow minds of bread-and-butter misses, nor of the criticasters who echo those young ladies' idea of fiction and its limits, and thus " Put Yourself in His Place " was written. Of " A Terrible Temptation," the leading idea came to me from the *Times*—viz., from the report of a certain trial, with the comments of counsel, and the remarkable judgment delivered by Mr. Justice Byles. The character of Rhoda Somerset I culled from your pages, and having observed with what firmness, yet coldness, you treated that character and topic, I have kept your method in view, and, at all events, tried to imitate it. Whatever warmth I have shown is in the scenes of virtuous love; in the Somerset's scenes I am cold and sarcastic. Up to the period of her repentance how do I treat this character? Do I whitewash the hussy, or make her a well-bred, delicate-minded woman, as your refined and immoral writers would? I present her illiterate, coarse, vain, with good impulses, a bad temper, and a Billingsgate tongue. In close contrast to this unattractive photograph I am careful to place my portrait of an English virgin, drawn in the sweetest colours my rude art can command, that every honest reader may see on which side my sympathies lie, and be attracted to virtue by the road of comparison. Believe me, sir, a thousand innocent girls are at this moment being corrupted by writers of their own sex, with novels instinctively adapted to the female reader, to her excessive sexuality, and her sense of propriety. These writers, being women, know how to work on the former without alarming the latter, and so, by fine degrees and with soft insidious pertinacity, they reconcile their female readers to illicit love, and shed a mild lustre over adultery itself. Yet so destitute of the true critical faculty are the criticasters of the day that these canny corrupters of female youth escape censure; it has gone astray after a writer in whose hands vice startles and offends, not captivates. My pen has never corrupted a soul; it never will, it never can, till water shall run uphill.

Should this argument fall into abler hands than an abridger's, I expect to be told, not that it is the duty of all writers to ignore certain vices, and so do their best to perpetuate them, but that many subjects open to the journalist are closed to the novelist. This is true and reasonable. The answer is—journals must, of necessity, report in their small type some crimes and vices quite unfit to be mentioned in a novel; but that a journalist has any right to put into his leaded type and to amplify, discuss, and dwell upon any subject whatever, and that the poet or the novelist has not an equal right to deal with that subject in fiction, this is monstrous and the mere delusion of a rabid egotism.

Since, therefore, I have taken Anonyma from your hands and have presented her in no voluptuous scenes, and have made her a repulsive character until she repents, no mother need forbid my book to her daughter; at all events, until she has forbidden her daughters to enter Hyde Park and the *Times* to enter her drawing-room, and has locked up every Bible on her premises.—I have the honour to be, Sir, your obedient servant and pupil, CHARLES READE.

2 ALBERT TERRACE, KNIGHTSBRIDGE,
August 26th, 1871.

SIR,—Those who read the late controversy between the *Times* and me must, I think, have been surprised and somewhat shocked—if they admire the *Times* as much as I do—at its rude and ungenerous reply to a courteous letter, in which I taught it that great lesson of superior minds—appreciation. A retort so conceited, so silly, and so rude, entitled me to a reply. I sent a short one; it is suppressed. This is foul play: and, as Englishmen in general abhor foul play, I venture to ask you to give publicity to these few lines, which, mild as they are, the editor of the *Times* had not the courage to face.

"FACTS MUST BE FACED."

Sir,—My generous tribute to the *Times* referred to those able men who write in the *Times* on public questions—not to the small fry, who write about literature because they cannot write literature. I touched my hat to the Tritons of the *Times*, not to the minnows : yet one of these latter has coolly adopted the compliment, and actually made it a handle for impertinence that outrages truth and common decency. This is base ; and I wonder you could be betrayed into lending your name to it. Where gentlemen are concerned, appreciation on the one side begets decent civility on the other. I shall not descend to bandy invectives with my inferior, but shall pick his one grain of argument out of his peck of scurrility. I have driven him from his first position, which was, that nobody ought to print anything about Anonyma. Now that he finds who first introduced her to the public, he sings quite another song. "Journals," says he, "deal in such facts as these, but not in fictions." This is a distinction without a difference. It does not matter one straw whether a young lady reads facts about Anonyma, or figments founded on facts, for the effect on her mind is precisely the same in both cases. The distinction is not only muddle-headed, but inapplicable ; for the *Times* has done a little fiction in this thing. Of the letters printed in the *Times* about the *Demi-monde*, a good many were written to order by the staff of the *Times*, though signed " Paterfamilias," " A Belgravian Mother," or what not. Now that is fiction—fiction as pure as anything in " A Terrible Temptation." The late Mr. Joseph Addison did mightily affect this form ; he wrote himself letters from coquettes and other sprightly correspondents, and so enlivened his didactic columns ; for Fiction improves whatever it touches. Your reviewer now hangs to his chimera by one thread. " Ours," says he, " are public duties ; his are private." So much for young gentlemen writing about literature with no knowledge of the business. " Private ! " Why, my English circulation is larger than that of the *Times ;* and in the United States three publishers have already sold three hundred and seventy thousand copies of this novel — which, I take it, is about thirty times the circulation of the *Times* in the United States, and nearly six times its English circulation.

Writing for so vast a variety of human beings, for more than one great nation, and for more than one generation, I cannot afford to adopt novel and narrow views of my great art; I cannot consent to make myself, by artificial contraction, smaller than the journalists. The world is big enough for a few creators as well as for a shoal of commentators. I do not howl because two thousand journalists deal, in their leaded type, with Lunacy, Prisons, Trades Unions, Divorce, Murder, Anonyma, and other great facts; and those who aspire to represent so large a body of sensible men, should bridle their egotism, discourage their pitiable jealousy, and cease to howl because five or six masters of Fiction have the judgment and the skill to weave the recorded facts, and published characters, of this great age, into the forms of Art. —Your obedient servant,   CHARLES READE.

DIALOGUE BETWEEN A JUDGE
AND A GAOLER

To the Editor of the "Daily Telegraph"

Sir,—At Christmas imagination runs rife; Pantomimes threaten, wherein Wisdom will be kept within bounds by Fancy; and even in your columns I have just read a Dream, and found it interesting. May I then profit by your temporary leniency and intrude into the sacred *Telegraph* a dialogue? It is imaginary, but not idle: it may do good, and make Power think instead of thinking it thinks—a common but hurtful habit.

Scene—*The Old Bailey.*

The Judge. Is the gaoler present?

Mr. Holdfast. Here, my lord.

Judge. I sentence this man to four months' imprisonment, with hard labour: you understand?

Holdfast. Perfectly, my lord. You mean unwholesome labour, as much as he can do and a little more. So then when he falls short, we reduce his diet to increase his strength, since it has proved unequal; this to be continued in a circle, and take his bed every now and then and let him lie on a plank.

Judge. What! hard labour, yet short diet, with the addition of cold at night and broken rest! Why, this is not Detention, it is Destruction—either to man or beast. No, sir, I do not condemn this man to imprisonment for life—he is not a murderer—I give him just four months, no more, no less; and in that sentence it is clearly implied that at the end of four months he is to come out, improved in his habits by labour, and in his body by regular meals, of simple, nourishing food, with no alcohol.

Holdfast. Excuse me, my lord; the Act of Parliament authorises a gaoler to reduce a prisoner's diet, and inflict other punishments.

Judge. Ay, at safe intervals; but not in quick repetition, nor in unreasonable conjunction—hard labour on the heels of privation, and cold on the top of both. These things *united* soon exhaust the body. Your Act of Parliament contains no clause, that can be read in a court of law, to repeal the law of England, regarding so great a matter as homicide. That immortal law, which was here before these little trumpery Acts of Parliament, made to-day to be repealed to-morrow, and will be here after Parliament itself has run its course, deals with the case thus : If A., having the legal charge of B., and keeping him in *duresse,* so that he cannot possibly obtain the necessaries of life elsewhere, subjects him to privation of food, rest, &c., and otherwise so shortens his life directly or indirectly by sheer exhaustion of the body, or by any disease which is a natural result of multiplied privations and hardships, A. can be indicted for a felony; and he will be tried, not by any officer of State assuming unconstitutional powers, but constitutionally, by the Queen in the person of her judge, and by the country in the person of its jury.

Holdfast. They would never find a gaoler guilty, not if a dozen of the scum died in their term of imprisonment.

Judge. It is not for me to say. They are getting more intelligent, like the rest of us. Certainly it would be their duty to demand good evidence, and the true facts are hard to get at in a gaol. Acton and Fleetwood destroyed many prisoners, yet were acquitted on trial. But at all events dismiss from your mind that a gaoler can plead the Act of Parliament, or any purely legal defence, to bloodless destruction of a British subject in *duresse.* Keep strictly to my sentence. It is not only the sentence of the Queen and the law, but it is expressly proportioned to the verdict of the country. Four months in a house of detention, not destruction, a house of correction, not a subtle shambles. The sentence has two limits, both equally absolute. If, during the four months, you turn this man into the street, you are indictable for a misdemeanour; if, during the four months, you thrust him cannily into his grave, you are indictable for a felony ; and, should I be the judge to try you, it will be my duty to tell the jury that you took this prisoner, not from the clouds, nor from any Government official, with no power to sentence man, woman, nor child, where I sit, but from me; and that I sentenced him, in your hearing, to four months' imprisonment, and not to imprisonment for life.—I am, Sir, your obedient servant,

CHARLES READE

KNIGHTSBRIDGE, *Christmas Day.*

NOTE TO A SICK FRIEND

My friend, with age come grief and care
   To every son of man,
Sickness or sorrow, hard to bear,
   Though life is but a span.

Since last we met, my heart has bled,
   And will bleed till I die ;
And you, confined to a sick bed,
   In pain and languor lie.

We all should do the best we may
   To cheer a friend in need.
Expect to-morrow, or next day,
   A visit from

CHARLES READE.

19 ALBERT GATE, KNIGHTSBRIDGE.

BIBLE CHARACTERS

BIBLE CHARACTERS

A LITERARY MARVEL

THE characters in Scripture are a literary marvel.

It is very hard to write characters in one country to be popular in every land and age.

Especially hard in narrative. (Drama parades characters by numberless speeches, and autographs them by soliloquy—an expedient false in nature, but convenient in art.)

Hardest of all to create such world-wide and everlasting characters in few words, a bare record of great things said and done.

One test of difficulty is rarity: number, then, the world-wide characters—if any—in Thucydides and Herodotus, and observe whether Josephus, when he leaves watering the Bible and proceeds to supplement it, has added one deathless character to the picture-galleries of Holy Writ. Shall we carry the comparison higher, and include poetic narrative? then go to the top of the tree at once, and examine the two great epics of antiquity.

The " Æneid "—what a stream of narrative! what fire of description! what march and music of words! But the characters?—Æneas mediocre, his staff lay figures. Dido just interesting enough to make one angry with Æneas. Perhaps the strongest colour is in the friendship and fate of Nisus and Euryalus; and there a Jewish pen had shown the way.

The less polished but mightier Homer has achieved the highest feat of genius; he has made puny things grand, and fertilised pebbles. He has bewitched even scholars into thinking his Greeks wiser and braver than the Trojans; whereas, if you can shut your ears to his music, his Greeks were barbarians besieging a civilised city for a motive and in a manner incompatible with one ray of civilisation. The motive: from the first dawn of civilisation no country with independent states ever got those states to unite in leaving home and besieging a distant city to recover the person of a solitary adulteress. The manner: the first dawn of civilisation showed men that cities placed like Troy can always be taken by one of two methods, blockade or assault. But Homer Zulus had neither the sense to blockade that civilised city and starve it out, nor the invention to make ladders, covered ways, and battering-rams, nor the courage to scale walls, nor even to burn or break through a miserable gate. The civilised Trojans had a silver currency, the Tyrian shekel, called by scholars with Homer on the brain "the Homeric shekels." Homer never mentions it, never saw it. The uncivilised Greeks had no currency but bullocks; no trade but exchange of commodities. The attack and defence of Troy were of a piece with the two currencies: the civilised Orientals, with a silver currency, barred out the Zulus, with a bullock currency and calves' brains, like a pack of schoolboys, and showed their contempt of them by coming out and attacking them in the open with their inferior numbers. Yet the genius of Homer could dazzle men's eyes, and bewitch their ears, and confound their judgments, and sing black white. So behold the barbarians gilt for ever, and the civilised people smirched. *Carent quia vate sacro.*

But turn from the glories of the wondrous tale this magician has built on a sorry subject—fitter for satire than epic—to his characters, and he is no longer supreme.

To be sure, he does not dose us with monotonies, abstractions, lay figures; *fortemque Gyan, fortemque Cloanthum*: he discriminates the brute courage of Ajax and the airy valour of Tydides, the wisdom of Nestor and the astuteness of Ulysses. But his gods and goddesses?—mere human animals; blue blood for red, and there ends his puerile invention in things divine. His leading heroes are characters, but not on a par with his descriptions, his narrative, and his music. They are the one ephemeral element in an immortal song. Achilles with his unsoldierlike egotism, his impenetrable armour, his Zulu cruelty to his helpless foe, and his antique tender friendship, is a brave Greek of the day, but he is not for all time; two-thirds of him no modern soldier would deign to copy.

The twenty-four books devoted by so great a poet to Ulysses have not engraved "the much enduring man" on the Western heart. In short, the leading heroes of Homer's epics are immortal in our libraries, but dead in our lives.

Now take the two little books called Samuel. The writer is not a great master like Homer and Virgil; he is artless, and careless to boot; forgets what he had said a few pages before, and spoils more than one good incident by putting the cart before the horse—I mean by false transposition, by presenting events out of their true and interesting sequence: a sad fault in composition. But the characters that rise from the historical strokes of that rude pen are immortal: so solid, and full of colour, too, that they stand amidst the waves of time like rocks, carved into statues by Phidias, and coloured by Apelles.

Yet this writer has no monopoly of the art in ancient Palestine; he shares it with about sixteen other historians, all Hebrews, though some of them write Hebrew and some Greek.

In our day character-painting is much attempted by certain writers of fictitious narrative; but their method excludes them from a serious comparison with Homer, Virgil, and the sacred historians. They do not evolve characters by simple narration. They clog the story with a hundred little essays on the character of each character. They keep putting their heads from behind the show, and openly analysing their pale creations, and dissecting them, and eking them out with comments, and microscoping their poodles into lions. These are the easy expedients of feeble art. They succeed with contemporaries, and, indeed, are sure to be popular for a time, because most readers have slow or lazy minds, and love a writer who will save them the trouble of studying and penetrating character by doing it for them in the very text of the story. But it would be paying this false method—which microscopes real mediocrity into false importance—too great a compliment to compare its fruits with the characters that are self-evolved in the sacred writers, and, indeed, in Homer and Virgil, for their *method* was, at all events, the true one, though its results in the single particular of character were inferior.

In further support of my present position let me submit a few truths to be taken in conjunction.

First. Moderate excellence in writing is geographical; loses fifty per cent. in human esteem by crossing a channel or a frontier.

Second. Translation lowers it ten per cent.

Third. But when you carry into the West a translation of a work the East admires ever so much, ten to one it will miss the Western mind. Eastern music is a dreamy noise to a

Western ear, but one degree beyond the sweet illogical wail of an Æolian harp. Eastern poetry is to the Western a glue of honeyed words, a tinkling cymbal, or a drowsy chime. The sacred Koran, the Bible of a hundred million Orientals, is to your Anglo-Saxon the weakest twaddle that ever drivelled from a human skull. It does not shock an Occidental Christian, or rouse his theological ire. It is a mild emetic to his understanding, and there's an end of it.

Fourth. The world is a very large place : Palestine is a small province *in the East.*

Fifth. What the whole world outside Palestine could very seldom do at all, this petty province did on a very large scale. About seventeen writers, all Israelites, some of them with what would now-a-days be called a little learning, some without, some writing in Hebrew, some in Greek, all achieved one wonder. They sat down to record great deeds done, and great words spoken in Egypt, Syria, Mesopotamia, and Palestine, which districts united are but a slice of the East, and they told them wondrous briefly, yet so that immortal and world-wide characters rise like exhalations from the record.

Written in the East, these characters live for ever in the West; written in one province, they pervade the world; penned in rude times, they are prized more and more as civilisation advances; product of antiquity, they come home to the business and bosoms of men, women, and children in modern days.

Then, is it any exaggeration to say that " THE CHARACTERS OF SCRIPTURE ARE A MARVEL OF THE MIND ? "

II

AIDS TO FAITH

OF a remarkable phenomenon the cause or causes must be remarkable. Any humdrum explanation of a marvel denounces itself; in the matter of solution " inadequate " means " unscientific."

Perhaps the wisest plan will be not to hurry to an explanation, but examine the phenomenon in detail, and that may give us glimpses of a real and sufficient solution.

THE CHARACTERS OF SCRIPTURE ARE A PART OF ITS TRUTH,

AIDS TO FAITH

AND AIDS TO REASONABLE FAITH IN A MATTER WHERE FAITH IS A
BOON AND DISBELIEF A CALAMITY.

The Bible contains many things that were hard to believe
at the time, and many things that are very hard to believe
now. It was the prophecies, I think, that encountered the
most reasonable incredulity at the date of their delivery ; but
now it is the histories, or portions of them ; for in our day so
many of the prophecies, minute and improbable at the time,
have been fulfilled to the letter, that old prophecy tends to
convert the reason to faith. Well, in a minor degree the
close study of character in Scripture commends to our reason
the truth of many strange incidents with which these true
characters are indissolubly united.

This is mere preliminary discourse, so an example or two
must serve. Many more will follow, if God should enable a
broken old man to complete the work he has had the hardi-
hood to begin.

Well, then, we are told in Judges, chapter xiii., that an
angel, in the likeness of a man, foretold to Manoah, and also
to his wife, that they should have a son, who should deliver
Israel. The hospitable pair desired to feast this friendly
prophet with a kid. But he declined, and advised them to
offer it to God. So they offered the kid as a burnt-offering.
Lo ! as the fire rose high, their visitor went up in the flame,
and then melted into the air. They fell trembling on their
faces, quivering with terror.

This is a miracle ; we never see miracles now-a-days ; and as
it is natural, though fallacious, to think our narrow experience
is the experience of all time and place, we find it very hard
to believe them.

But please follow this narrative into character.

"And Manoah said unto his wife, We shall surely die,
because we have seen God. But his wife said unto him, If
the Lord were pleased to kill us, He would not have received
a burnt-offering and a meat offering at our hands, neither
would He have showed us all these things, nor would, as at
this time, have told us such things as these."

A great emergency always reveals people's characters, and
here are two characters suddenly developed in a pair that
looked alike till then ; but now one is all blind superstitious
terror, the other all clear logic and good sense. Was this
invented, and blind superstition assigned to the male, clear
logic to the female ? And that in the East, where women were
deemed inferior, and by sure consequence made inferior.

Youth has its difficulties; but so has scepticism. Learned reason cannot readily believe that an Oriental writer invented this un-Oriental dialogue.

Reason suggests that this character-dialogue was really spoken by some superstitious man and logical woman.

Well, but if so, à *propos* of what were both speeches spoken?

Clearly it was à *propos* of something strange and thrilling that had *stirred* these two characters to their depths, and elicited the hitherto unsuspected superiority of the wife, though Oriental.

It is hard to find a fact that could fit this character-dialogue so thoroughly as the recorded miracle does with all its details; yet the character-dialogue bears Truth engraved on its face, and so it becomes one of the aids to Faith—a humble one, of course.

John relates that Mary Magdalene told Peter and the other disciple Christ's sepulchre was open, and His body risen again, and immediately both those disciples ran to the sepulchre; the other disciple outran Peter, and got there first, but hesitated at the entrance; then Peter came up and rushed in at once, and the other followed him.

Now, John did not trouble himself to account for this apparent inconsistency in the rapidity of those two disciples; he merely recorded the facts. But we, who study his lines far more than he ever studied them, come to this passage with the knowledge (1) that Peter was not a youth, and (2) that he was the most ardent and impetuous of all the Apostles. We therefore see what John does not indicate, the true significance of the two seemingly incongruous facts he records so simply; it was just this—the younger *legs* got first to the outside of the tomb; the more ardent and impetuous *character* rushed first into the awe-inspiring place where his Lord had lain. This stroke of character, unconsciously revealed by simple statement of fact, lays hold of our reason, and aids it—so far as it goes—to believe a thing that would be utterly incredible but for the weight and variety of the evidence, cotemporary, continuous, and monumental.

Mary and Martha of Bethany are presented to us in three fragments of narrative—one by Luke, two by John, and no apparent concert between the writers—indeed, a clear absence of it.

In the first passage, which is by Luke, they appear, one as

a bustling housewife, the other a pious student; very distinct characters, though both thoroughly feminine; and there Luke leaves them (Luke x. 38–42).

In the second passage, which is by John, bereavement effaces their superficial distinction for a time, and they are both tender women (John xi. 21–25).

In the third passage the keynote, struck by Luke, is returned to by John, and the women seem to differ entirely in his page as they had done in Luke's (John xii. 2, 3).

BEFORE THE SICKNESS OF LAZARUS.

"And a certain woman named Martha received Him into her house. And she had a sister called Mary, which also sat at Jesus' feet, and heard His word. But Martha was cumbered about much serving, and came to Him, and said, Lord, dost Thou not care that my sister hath left me to serve alone? bid her therefore that she help me" (Luke x. 38–40).

Mary, not a word.

WHEN LAZARUS WAS LYING DEAD.

Martha, who was the greater gossip, and heard news soonest, ran to meet Jesus outside the village, and at sight of Him, the first cry of her true woman's heart was, "Lord, if Thou hadst been here, my brother would not have died."

An hour later Mary heard He was in the village, and she ran, the gentle Mary, and clung passionately to His knees; and what was the first cry of her woman's heart? "Lord, if Thou hadst been here, my brother would not have died."

The very words Martha had spoken; and if you ask me why such opposite characters said the same thing, I must reply out of Molière: "*Ne voyez-vous pas que c'est la Nature pure qui vous parle?*"

Calamity effaces even broad distinctions, if they lie above the hearts. Behold the bustling housewife and the gentle student equally merged in loving, trusting woman! (John xi. 21–32).

AFTER LAZARUS WAS RESTORED TO LIFE.

Jesus came to Bethany, and supped with that family He had made the happiest in Judæa. Lazarus was amongst those who sat at meat.

Martha *served*.

Mary took a pound of ointment of spikenard—very precious —and anointed the feet of Jesus (John xii. 2, 3).

Now, did physician Luke sit down in one place and coin these two names, and invent their characters, so opposite in household matters?

Did fisherman John sit down in another place, and adopt Luke's names, yet out of his own invention present Luke's bustling housewife and his absorbed student as one woman in the depths of the heart?

Did this same John afterwards go back in his invention, Heaven knows how, to Luke's keynote, and present his one-hearted mourners as women differing greatly in every-day life, and especially in their way of honouring a beloved guest?

This solution is incredible, and no man sees its absurdity more clearly than a veteran writer of fiction; such a man knows the artifices of art and the limits of art. Now, here the artifices are absent, and the limits surpassed.

No; the sisters of Bethany were real creatures, written about piecemeal by two independent writers, who each recorded what little he knew about them.

Thus handled, they differ from each other in domestic character, but agree in the deeper affections, and they never differ so much from each other as they both do from the male of our species.

But in truth nobody doubts that these were real characters that differed, and real hearts that agreed.

What has not been universally observed is that the reality of the characters is inseparable from the truth of the narrative, and stands or falls with it.

The whole record occupies only five verses in Luke and fourteen in John, and the characters are not created on the modern plan; they exist only by the facts. Try to believe the characters, yet doubt the facts; you will find you cannot really do it. If you are as honest and resolute as the thing deserves, you will come to this: either both the characters are a daring fiction concocted *miraculously* by a fisherman and a doctor, writing in different places and at different times, or else the facts, which exhale the characters like a rose its perfume, are as true as those characters are.

If the Old and New Testament, looked into, should be found to teem with examples of this sort, was I wrong to say that "The characters of Scripture are a part of its truth, and aids to reasonable faith in a matter where faith is a boon and disbelief a calamity?"

But if the characters of Scripture are both a marvel of the mind and also aids to faith, surely we ought to give up skimming them, and study them. Put them at their lowest, and they are a gold-mine; and in that mine surface-washing has been productive; but to dig is better.

I begin purposely with one of the smaller characters. A place is not vouchsafed him in the old collections of Bible characters, and even of late he has been disposed of in a page or two as one of "the lesser lights." But who knows? we may rate him higher if we study, not skim, him.

III

NEHEMIAH

ONCE in the history of mankind a mortal man told a nation its history in detail, predicting the near and the distant future so distinctly that both seemed to lie equally close to his eye on one map of events. (Deuteronomy xxviii., xxix., xxx.)

In our little (so-called) predictions we go by two guides— experience of the past, and shrewd calculation of the future founded on that experience. But this diviner had no help from either of those guides to the future; on the contrary, the things he foretold were unprecedented, inconsistent with each other, incredible, and to human reason absurd.

(1.) You shall drive out all the nations that now inhabit Canaan; shall take that land and hold it.

(2.) If you keep the divine law I have just promulgated, you shall enjoy that country, and its soil shall teem with fruitfulness.

(3.) If you do not keep this divine law, that land and you shall wither under every curse that can strike man, beast, and soil, and at last you shall be driven out of it.

(4.) If after that you shall repent, and turn again to God and His commandments, He will pity you, and turn your captivity, and restore you, and punish your enemies, who have afflicted you with His consent, but with no good motive on their part.

Now, here was a string of inconsistent improbabilities.

(1.) The land of Canaan was held by warlike tribes, with cavalry, chariots of war, and walled cities.

The Hebrews were a half-armed infantry, encumbered with

a mob of women and children. They had no strongholds, but must advance on the Canaanites from tents, and retreat to tents whenever worsted, either in skirmish or drawn battle.

(2.) To conquer Canaan and its cities from tents, they must by degrees master the art of war so thoroughly that, with their proved superiority as soldiers, and the fortresses acquired by that conquest, no nation could dispossess them, still less transplant them to a distance.

(3.) Suppose, as a wild hypothesis, the improbable conquest and incredible transplantation of such a people accomplished ; that expatriated mass would then, as a matter of course, blend with the greater nation that received them.

(4.) In two more generations the absorbed and absorbing people would be so compact, that it could not possibly be decomposed, and the Hebrew multitude return spontaneously by miracle as they had been exported by miracle.

Yet every tittle of the incredible and contradictory romance Moses foretold came true.

That half-armed infantry drove out the warriors of Canaan, and took their land, and obeyed God's law there, and reaped the promised blessings *till Joshua and the elders who knew him and survived him were all dead:* a remarkable fact, which merits profound study, and has been skimmed accordingly. But they left a few idolaters, and these leavened them, so that in time idolatry and the true worship flourished side by side. Sometimes one had the upper hand, sometimes the other. Neither was ever extinct. Now, nations are not like individuals ; they cannot be judged at all in the next world, and even in this world they must be judged by their majorities. This people, then, were judged in this world by their fluctuating majorities, and alternately cursed and blessed for about nine hundred years. Yet, though the double prediction of Moses was all this time recorded, and read out at times to the people, and though alternate blessings and curses were its running comment and illustration, they could never make up their minds unanimously whether to worship the God of Israel and be blessed, or false gods and be cursed.

At last, when they were proved incurable in Canaan, the long-predicted chastisement fell on them. Israel, being the greater idolater, was carried away captive first. Judah soon followed, and her desecrated Temple was despoiled and destroyed. Part of the nation was slaughtered in battle or famished on the road; a few thousands of the lower sort remained at home, but without their Temple, their rites, their national existence. The cream of Judah and Israel were really transported to Babylon and its neighbourhood, by a monarchy which had long practised that prodigious kind of transplantation. (See Herodotus, *passim.*)

Even now, according to Moses, this people might repent; and if so, they would return to their own land, and their captors suffer in turn.

But humanly speaking, what chance was there that Israelites or Jews would unlearn idolatry at Babylon? Why, what had all their idolatry come of?—Imitation. Under the early Judges they could not as a nation withstand the example of a few conquered idolaters, who worshipped false gods in groves for want of temples. In the height of their glory their wisest king was decoyed into idolatry by the example of his intellectual inferiors, his wives and concubines. Imitation and example set them bowing at one time to a contemptible fish-god; at another to a fiend whose worship entailed the burning of their children. Now, at Babylon idolatry was example and authority into the bargain. At Babylon idolatry was glorious, sublime; had every charm and seduction to win the sensual understanding and divert it from the unseen God.

If you and I and an archangel had been endowed with absolute power, but left to our own wisdom, human and angelic, I am persuaded that neither that archangel nor you nor I should have sent the Hebrews to Babylon to unlearn idolatry; so wide and impassable is the gulf between the sagacity of created beings and the genuine prescience that marks their Creator—for constant prescience implies omniscience.

Babylon, bright centre of captivating idolatry, commenced an everlasting cure of Jewish idolatry, which punishments, blessings, miracles, could never effect in the land of Canaan. I keep in reserve a comment or two on this historical curiosity.

Meantime, "sweet were the uses of adversity." The captivity roused great examples of faith, revived the necessity for miracles—and so miracles came—reawakened the lyre of Judah, which had slept since the days of David, and stirred up the noblest army of prophets that ever preached in any period of Hebrew story.

The Book of Daniel, the most sustained and grandest of all the prophetical and historical books, was written in Babylon itself, and partly in the Chaldaic tongue.

Ere long that impregnable city, Babylon, falsified its past history, defied all human probability, and bowed to Hebrew prophecy. Behind its enormous walls, it had laughed invaders to scorn for centuries; yet it was taken a few years after it had torn that suffering people from their land.

Cyrus, descendant of the conqueror, had no sooner succeeded to the throne of Persia, to which Babylon and Palestine were now equally subject, than he issued a most remarkable edict; he alleged Divine inspiration, and by order of the Most High—as he declared—invited the Jews to go up to Jerusalem and build the Temple to Him whom he, Cyrus, proclaimed to be the true God. He restored to the Jews their sacred vessels, and assisted them with his vast resources.

The leader of this return was Zerubbabel. When the returned captives laid the foundation of the new Temple, there came a touch of nature which never, whilst books endure, shall pass from the memory of mankind. The young and the middle-aged praised God with shouts of joy; but many of the priests and Levites, who were ancient men, and had seen the first Temple in its glory, wept with a loud voice; so that such as stood apart could not discern the noise of the shouts of joy from the noise of the wailing of those aged men.

Yet the leaders of the heathen nations that were settled in Judea baffled this good work by their intrigues for twenty-one years, and then at last the Temple was built and dedicated. But none of those poor old men lived to weep again, comparing the finished Temple with Solomon's in all its glory.

Besides the new Temple and its services, the restored Jews had prophets, especially Haggai and Zachariah, and no doubt there was a great revival. But it is clear that in the course of years there was a decline; and fifty-seven years after the rebuilding of the Temple, Ezra went up from Babylon to purify the degenerating descendants of those pious patriots.

The support Ezra had from Artaxerxes, King of Persia, and consequently of Babylon, his touching gratitude to that monarch and to Him who "is enthroned in the heart of kings," the abuses he found rampant, his tears and ardent prayers to God, his temporary success, and the great revival of the law he inaugurated, *Dei gratiâ*, are written in the last four chapters of the book that bears his name.

About fourteen years after this revival, and ninety-two years after the edict of Cyrus, Singleheart stepped upon the scene. He was a Jew, born probably in Persia, and rose, in spite of his origin, by rare ability, to a high place in the service of Artaxerxes. His title was cup-bearer; but all such titles are misleading. He was a statesman and a courtier, and it was only one of his duties to taste the wine before he poured out for the king, and so secure him at his own risk against poison. This royal favourite, bred in soft Persia and lodged in those earthly paradises, the summer palace and winter palace of his monarch, had yet "Jerusalem written on his heart."

It was what they call winter in Persia, but what we should call balmy spring. Singleheart, better known as Nehemiah, was leading a life of delights with the king at Shushan, when Hanani, a pious Jew, who had gone with a company to visit Jerusalem, returned from that journey. Nehemiah questioned him eagerly about their city and countrymen.

Then Hanani and his fellows hung their heads, and told Nehemiah that the remnant of the captivity in that land were in great affliction and reproach; the wall of Jerusalem, also, was broken down, and the gates burned with fire.

See now how Jerusalem was beloved by her exiled sons! Born, bred, and thriving in soft, seductive Persia, the true-hearted Jew Nehemiah was struck down directly by these words. He who had a right to stand on the steps of the greatest throne in the world, sat down upon the ground, and fasted and wept, and prayed before the God of heaven; and this was his confession and his prayer: "O Lord God of heaven . . . we have dealt very corruptly against Thee, and have not kept the commandments, nor the statutes, nor the judgments, which Thou commandedst Thy servant Moses. Remember, I beseech Thee, the word that Thou commandedst Thy servant Moses, saying, If ye transgress, I will scatter you abroad among the nations: but if ye turn unto Me, and keep My commandments, and do them; though there were of you cast out unto the uttermost part of the heaven, yet will I gather them from thence, and will bring them unto the place that I have chosen to set My name there. . . . O Lord, I beseech Thee, let now Thine ear be attentive to the prayer of Thy servant and to the prayer of Thy servants, who desire to fear Thy name: and prosper, I pray Thee, Thy servant this day, and grant him mercy in the sight of this man."

Public men are slaves as well as masters, their conscience seldom their own, their time never. Neither their pleasures nor their griefs can be long indulged. The bereaved states-man is not allowed to be quiet and to mourn; he must leave

the new grave and the desolate home for his arena, sometimes must even take part in a public festivity with a bleeding heart. This very thing befell Nehemiah. Like the poor
actor who must go from a home with a coffin to play his part
in comedy, and laugh and fool with the rest, sad Singleheart
had soon to rise from his knees, and don his gay raiment and
mingle in a brilliant and jocund scene.

Great Artaxerxes gave a superb banquet to his nobility :
the queen was there—no every-day event. You may let
loose your imagination without fear ; it will not go beyond the
splendours of the Persian court on that occasion. Gold plate
by the ton, gorgeous silk dresses of every hue, marble pillars,
fountains, music, lights to turn night into day, slaves, sultanas,
courtiers resplendent as stars, and all worshipping their sun
Artaxerxes; smiling when he smiled, laughing when he
laughed, applauding him to the echo, and thinking it little
to say of this king of monarchs what Eastern adulation could
say later on of a little trumpery prince, " It is the voice of
a god."

It was Singleheart's duty to present the cup to this earthly
divinity. So he took up the golden goblet, filled it cere-
moniously, and offered it with a deep obeisance, as he had often
done before ; but now for the first time with a sorrowful face.

This was so strange a thing in him, or indeed in any
courtier, that the king noticed it at once ; even as he took
the cup his eye dwelt on this sad face, and he said directly,
" Why is your countenance sad ? "

Nehemiah was too much taken aback to reply. The king
questioned him again. " You are not sick ? "

Still no reply.

" This is sorrow, and nothing else. "

Then Nehemiah was sore afraid, and I will tell you why.
His life was in danger. Even a modern autocrat like Louis
XIV. expected everybody's face to shine if he did but appear,
and how much more an Artaxerxes ! What, wear a sorrowful
face when he was presiding over joy and gaiety, and gilding
them by his presence ! If he had ordered this melancholy
visage away to prison or death, it would have been justified
by precedent, and loudly applauded on the spot by all the
guests.

But though Nehemiah felt his danger, yet the king's actual
words were not menacing, and the courtier found courage to
tell the simple truth. He salaamed down to the ground.
" Let the king live for ever ! " After this propitiatory

formula he replied, " Why should not my countenance be sad, when the city, the place of my fathers' sepulchres, lieth waste, and its gates are burned with fire ? "

These are brave words, and can be read aggressively ; only that is not how Nehemiah spoke them. It was his to propitiate, not to offend, and his tones were broken-hearted and appealing, not contumacious.

You must read the words so, if you would be one in a thousand, and really understand them.

The king answered him accordingly. " What do you ask me ? " said he.

Then Nehemiah set us all an example. He did not answer the king out of his own head, and pray for wisdom six hours afterwards, because it was bed-time. He prayed standing on the spot, and, like a skilful gunner, shot the occasion flying. Strengthened by ejaculatory prayer, the soul's best weapon, he said, " If it please the king, and if thy servant has found favour in thy sight, pray send me to Judah, unto the city of my fathers' sepulchres, that I may build it."

The king's answer was rather favourable. He was unwilling to lose a good servant for ever, and asked him how long he wished to be away ; but this was as much as to say he should go upon conditions.

When that one point was settled, and leave of absence conceded, Nehemiah got bolder and bolder. He asked for passports where needed, and an order on Asaph for timber, &c. The liberal monarch granted all, and even volunteered a cavalry escort to see him safe to the end of that long and perilous journey. In recording the first of these petitions the autobiographer, Nehemiah, suddenly informs us that the queen was sitting by the king's side. This looks as if he connected her somehow in his own mind with his petition and the king's bounty, and rather favours the notion that she was the famous Esther, and sympathised then and there with her sad countryman by look or gesture.

So Singleheart left the lap of luxury and rode with his escort from Shushan to Jerusalem. This ride passes for nothing in the Biblical account ; whether it is so we can best ascertain by doing it ourselves.

He reached Jerusalem, and showed rare wisdom the first day. Instead of proclaiming himself and his credentials, and going boldly to work, he lay quiet three days, doing nothing and learning everything, especially who would be likely to support him, who to oppose him.

On the third day, in the middle of the night, he rose and took with him, not his Persian escort to make a clatter of hoofs and a parade, but a few trusty men on foot, and even to them he did not reveal what "God had put into his heart to do at Jerusalem." So, with his secret locked at present in his breast, he passed out by the gate of the valley and round the city, and under the silver light of the moon and stars viewed the clean gaps, the burned fragments of the gates, and the jagged breaches in the walls of the holy city. It was the right time to gaze on a great and fallen city: such a ruin is sad but beautiful in that tender light.

The same stars that shone above it and upon it had glittered upon Solomon's Temple, his impregnable walls, his imperial power.

As Nehemiah looked on this contrast, piteous yet lovely beneath those unchanging stars, he wept, he prayed, he drank in the scene; and methinks it never left his mind in the good fight he fought thereafter by night as well as day.

Nehemiah was a layman, and had a layman's good sense in religion; walls were necessary to the safety and glory of the city. They were also necessary to true religion. Idolaters must be kept out of the city, or idolatry could never be kept out of the Jewish mind. The whole history of the nation showed this.

Fresh from that starlight picture Nehemiah went to the Jewish nobles, priests, and princes, showed the powers he held under the hand of Artaxerxes, and urged them to rebuild the walls and revive the national glory. He has not told us what he said; but it is clear he found words of rare eloquence; for they all caught fire directly, and cried out, "Let us rise and build."

IV

NEHEMIAH'S WORK

Singleheart, Builder.

Then this wise man strengthened zeal with method. Under his advice each powerful man took his own piece of the dilapidated wall, and repaired it with his people.

This may seem a small thing to hasty readers, but it was a master-stroke of genius. Not only was it a grand division of labour, but it animated the work with a noble emulation and a personal pride. "See how fast my work goes on!" "See how well my piece is done!" "Now, my sons, gird up your tunics, or Rephaiah the son of Hur will get ahead of us."

There were forty-six building parties, and leading women amongst them, the daughters of Shallum, a powerful man. I apprehend the individual builders were not less than three thousand; so the walls began to rise like an exhalation.

The good cannot monopolise foresight. Evil men soon see when their interests are threatened. The heathen leaders showed their teeth at once; but at first they underrated the power of zeal under a wise and earnest leader. Their weapon was scorn. Sanballat, Tobiah, and Geshem inquired ironically whether Nehemiah meant to take the place of Artaxerxes. Nehemiah replied, "I am God's servant, and mind your own business; you have no portion, nor right, nor memorial in Jerusalem."

When the walls began to rise as if by magic, Sanballat got frightened, but still brazened out his anxiety with ridicule. "What are these feeble Jews up to? Will they fortify themselves? Will they set up their sacrifices again? Will they turn the rubbish back into stones to build with?"

"A stone wall," says Tobiah, "ay, the sort of wall a fox couldn't clamber over without knocking it down."

We writers get used to this sort of criticism after some great exhausting labour; and I should not have thought Nehemiah would have much minded such sneers.

But ridicule is wonderfully stinging to those who are not hardened to it by use, and he felt it bitterly; he appealed to God to judge these scorners, and went on building.

Then the heathen leaders dropped their sorry jests, and prepared to attack the builders with armed men, and so crush the work with violence and blood. So sure of the result were they that they let out their tactics. They said: "These builders shall not see us, nor know at what part to expect us; in a moment we will be in the midst of them, and slay them, and cause the work to cease."

SINGLEHEART, CAPTAIN.

Forewarned, forearmed. Nehemiah instantly withdrew a number of men from the works, and armed them to the teeth, and disposed them in stations as for the defence of a city. He also girt a sword on every builder, and put a javelin into one of his hands. Then he took a lofty station, with a band of warriors round him, and a trumpeter by his side. He circulated an order that wherever the trumpet should sound, thither all his men should run, with their weapons, from every side.

So wrought they, trowel in one hand, javelin in another, swords by their side, and a great leader's eye over all; and one-half their force paraded with shield and spear "from the rising of the morn till the stars appeared at eve." At night they all watched under arms, and no man put off his clothes except to wash them. Night and day were one to these gallant men till the mighty work was done: so can the spirit of a great leader animate a host, and make each pawn a knight, each mason a hero.

The heathen leaders swallowed their boast, and never made a single attack. By that means they saved their skins, for if they had attacked a weak part of the walls, Nehemiah would have seen them from his elevation, and run to meet them with his picked men, sounding the trumpet as he ran. Then his soldiers and armed builders would have run in upon the foe from every side, and cut them to pieces in a moment. So the heathen leaders did not fight, but tried assassination.

SINGLEHEART, POLITICIAN.

Sanballat and Geshem sent a friendly message to decoy Nehemiah to his death. "Come," said they, "why should we quarrel over the matter? No doubt we can come to some friendly arrangement. Meet us in the plains of Ono; there are several villages there; choose which you like for this amicable meeting."

Sorry schemers! Fancy these shallow traitors sending this to an Oriental statesman!—a bare hook without a bait. He did not condescend to be angry, or show them he saw through them. He parried the proposal with cool contempt. "I am doing a great work; why should I leave it and interrupt it to come to *you* ?"

They sent a similar message four times. Then Nehemiah did a first-rate thing. Instead of varying his reply in the least, he sent the same formula four times, and I am all admiration at this; for, after all, when you have given a good answer, why admit even a shadow of imperfection in that answer by altering a word or two? And then, how like a rock it makes a man seem, to give the waves but one answer : immovability, whether they surge up or ripple up, come at him smiling or foaming.

Irritated by this granite contempt, Sanballat deviated from the Oriental into the ruffian ; he did what corresponds in our day to sending an abusive post-card. He actually sent a letter, wide open, for everybody to read before it reached Nehemiah, and thus ran this ill-bred pagan's lines :

"It is reported among the heathen, and Gashmu confirms it, that you and the Jews mean to rebel against Artaxerxes, and that you have built the wall with this object, and to be king yourself; and that you have bribed prophets to say there is a king in Jerusalem. We shall report all this to Artaxerxes unless you meet us as invited, and come to terms with us."

This open letter was well calculated to alarm. Lies of the sort sent from Jerusalem had ere now poisoned the monarch's mind in Persia, and arrested a good work in Judea for many a long day.

Nehemiah sent him back an open letter in return. "There are no such things done as you pretend; you are feigning them all out of your own heart."

From that hour the enemy resigned all direct attacks on him, but still endeavoured to detach a few friends from him ; and here they had some success, having inter-married with Jewish families.

His chivalrous Spirit.

The worst trap of all was now laid for him : a singularly wicked one, to catch him by means of his piety, and his desire to know God's will in all things. The prophet Shemaiah and the prophetess Noadiah foretold a great danger, and that he could escape it only by shutting him-self up in the Temple and closing the doors. This time, with all his sagacity, he did not divine treachery. Not his wisdom, but his high spirit, saved Singleheart from this trap.

"What!" said he ; "shall such a man as I am flee? And what man, intrusted with God's work, would skulk into the Temple merely to *save his life* ?

"I will not go in."

Talk of lines like the sound of a trumpet : why, this was

to speak thunder-bolts and act lightning. Here we see in action what the heathen poet taught in noblest song :

> " Summum crede nefas animam præferre pudori
> Et propter vitam vivendi perdere causas."

After Singleheart had escaped this trap by his courage and his fidelity to a single purpose, he found that these prophecies came from lying prophets suborned by Tobiah and Sanballat.

Then in the spirit of his dispensation he invoked on their heads the curse of that God they had blasphemed.

After a feeble attempt to work upon the Jews they had intermarried with, Tobiah and Sanballat disappear from the narrative.

The walls of Jerusalem were rebuilt in fifty-two days, and Singleheart gave the glory to God. Taking the work and the time together, is there a parallel to this achievement? The Chinese Wall and the great Pacific Railway are far greater works, and much of the latter was built with the pick in one hand and the revolver in the other. But then, these vast works took years to complete.

Looking at the size of the city, the great height and breadth of the walls, it was an enormous work ; much greater than the London Law-Courts, that have taken a dozen years to build—greater than the cathedral of Cologne, which has been centuries in hand. And when you consider that these walls were built in the teeth of an armed and implacable foe, built with the trowel in one hand, the javelin in the other, and that the sleep of the workmen was broken with watching, and their clothes never taken off except to wash them, and flung on again half dry, it was an unrivalled feat of labour, zeal, judgment, courage, and piety, and will so remain to the end of time.

Nehemiah, Reformer.

Ezra came to Jerusalem fourteen years before Nehemiah ; he left the holy seed of Judah pure at Babylon, but found it at Jerusalem mingled with that of idolaters.

When he discovered this he rent his garment and mantle, and plucked off the hair of his head and beard, and sat down astonied until the evening sacrifice.

But during that solemnity he rose and threw himself down at the gate of the Temple, and prayed and wept and confessed the sins of his people.

His sorrow and his eloquence touched many hearts, and led to a public confession and to solemn pledges of reformation, especially from such of the offenders as belonged to Levi, Ezra's own tribe.

But it is clear from Nehemiah's own account that intermarriage with heathen, and other abuses, proved too strong for Ezra in the long-run. Nehemiah found this malpractice and many others at Jerusalem. Indeed, his great enemy, the heathen Tobiah, owed much of his power to having married a Jewess of good family. Nehemiah set himself to reform this, but not this alone. He was not a better, but a greater, man than Ezra, and made wiser reforms, and kept them alive, which Ezra failed to do.

One thing that shocked him much was the usurious practices of the wealthier Jews, and their cruelty in selling their poor debtors into bondage. "What!" said he; "we have redeemed our brethren that were sold unto the heathen, and will ye sell your brethren?" and they found nothing to answer.

Then he reminded them he had power to levy large exactions upon *them,* and besought them to imitate his moderation.

Such was the power of his example and his remonstrances that he actually induced the creditors to restore to the ruined debtors their houses, vineyards, and olive-yards, and a little of the forfeited produce to keep them alive through the famine.

When the relenting creditors had bound themselves to this by oath, he took his tunic in both hands, and shook it, and said, " May God so shake out every man from his house and from his labour who performeth not this promise."

This was a master-stroke, and shows the man of genius. Such appeals to the senses as well as to the conscience take the whole mind by assault, and fix the matter for ever in the memory. His hearers cried " Amen !" and praised the Lord, and—kept their promise.

All preceding governors of Jerusalem had acted on their powers and bled the people themselves, and even let their servants oppress and pillage them. Not so Nehemiah ; with him it was more blessed to give than to receive. He kept a noble table, and entertained one hundred and fifty Jews every day from the city, besides hungry souls from the villages; but all this at his own expense; the governor's allowance he never touched, because, as he said, the people were burdened enough without that. His mind runs forward, and he relates this a little out of place—chapter v. 13-19. I have but placed it in its true sequence. It is a noble trait, and every generous heart goes with him, when with honest simplicity he burst out, "Think on me, my God, for good, according to all I have done for this people."

Though he was nominal governor of Jerusalem for twelve years from the date of his first visit, it would seem, on a careful comparison of all his statements, that Hanani and Hananiah acted for him by his own appointment during a portion of that time as well as after it had expired. But as Ezra, both before and after Nehemiah's arrival, was unable to cope persistently with the abuses of the day, so Nehemiah's own lieutenants failed to withstand them.

Probably Nehemiah himself felt there was no one in whom he could place a blind confidence; for, twelve years after his first visit, he came back to Jerusalem with enlarged powers, and this time he showed priests as well as laymen he was not a man to be trifled with.

Eliashib the priest had given his kinsman Tobiah the heathen an apartment in the Temple, and Tobiah had furnished it.

Nehemiah bundled out all his furniture and effects, and had the rooms purified after him.

He found a priest, grandson of this very Eliashib, married to a heathen. He chased him out of the Temple.

On the other hand, he found that certain lay rulers, whose business it was to see the tithes paid to the priests and Levites, had so neglected them that many of that sacred tribe were working in the fields for a bare subsistence.

Nehemiah rebuked these negligent officials, and established storehouses for the tithes of corn, new wine, and oil; and to secure the Levites against any future neglect in the distribution of these stores, he selected Shelemiah, a priest, Zadok, a scribe, and Pedaiah, a Levite, as almoners or distributors of these stores, and associated with them one Hanan, a man of approved fidelity.

Both priests and laymen had become loose in observing the Sabbath day. He found Jews treading the wine-presses, gathering in the harvests and trading on the Sabbath day, and men of Tyre bringing fish and other wares into the markets of the city.

He treated natives and aliens alike, stopped the home trade, and closed the gates of the city against the Tyrians.

But the Tyrians were hard to deal with; they lodged outside the wall, and offered their wares outside. "Do that again," said Nehemiah, "and I will lay hands on you." This frightened them away for good.

Then came his worst trouble, the persistent intermarriage with heathen.

Ezra had withstood this for years in vain. Nehemiah had combated it with partial success; yet now Nehemiah found Jews who had married wives of Ashdod, Ammon, and Moab, and their children could not speak Hebrew, but naturally spoke their mother-tongue.

Then he came out in a new character. He contended with them, and cursed them, and smote certain of them, and plucked off their hair, and made them swear by God not to give their daughters to heathen husbands nor their sons to heathen wives again.

After this outburst of impassioned zeal, which at first takes the student of his mind a little by surprise, he returned to his grave character, and reasoned the matter with those he had terrified into submission.

"What Jew," said he, "was ever so wise, so great, so beloved of God, as King Solomon? Yet outlandish women could make even him sin against God, and commit idolatry."

Nehemiah prevailed, and there is reason to believe that idolatry received its deathblow under his rule.

He ends his brief but noble record with his favourite prayer, "Remember me, O my God, for good." That prayer has long been granted. But the children of God on earth have not seen all his value. Do but enumerate the various parts he played, the distinct virtues he showed, the strokes of genius he extemporised—and all to serve, not himself, but his country and his God. Faithful courtier, yet true patriot; child of luxury, yet patient of hardship; inventive builder, impromptu general, astute politician, high-spirited gentleman, inspired orator, resolute reformer—born leader of men, yet humble before God.

He rebuilt the walls of Jerusalem; he restored the law of Moses. Tradition says he lived fifty years after the events he records; he probably returned to Persia; but if he did, he was not the man to stay there half a century and leave the city and the law to take care of themselves.

Character is a key to facts; and it was not in Nehemiah's character to live and desert the two great works of his life for fifty years or so.

When, after two centuries of small events, small men, and no history, big events and the big men they generate came again to Judea and raised history from the dead, we find the stamp of Nehemiah and his pupils marked on the Jewish mind so plainly that the story of the Maccabees seems but a natural sequence of Nehemiah's chronicle.

Nehemiah fought tooth and nail for all the law of Moses, and especially the Sabbath day. Nehemiah tore the holy seed out of the embraces of the heathen, and ended the moral influences of idolatry.

This was sure to drive the idolater, sooner or later, from the bloodless weapons that alone can conquer the mind, to persecution and brute force; and accordingly, in the next Hebrew record, behold those weapons levelled against constant souls, and the sword of heroic Judas.

Nehemiah, then, is not what hasty judges have called him, "one of the lesser lights." He is a gigantic figure that stalked across the page of history luminous, then glided into the dark abyss of time, but scattered sparks of historic light, and left, not one, but two immortal works behind him.

As to the character of his piety, he relies on God, seeks His glory, and is unceasing in good works for his nation. But then, he despised lucre, and sought not the praise of men for those works.

It is no small matter to look to God alone, with much light or little. He lived under a covenant of works, and thought accordingly; yet methinks he needed but a word or two from Christ's own lips to be a Christian saint.

V

JONAH

JONAH, the son of Amittai, figures amongst the prophetical writers, but he was not one; he was only a seer, like Nathan, Elijah, Elisha, the prophet that came out of Judah, and many others. Like them, his inspiration was occasional, but taught him something of the mind of God (Jonah iv. 1).

His other predictions are lost for want of a chronicler, but a master-hand has recorded his great prophecy and the strange events that preceded and followed it. This little Hebrew seer suddenly received a grand and startling commission— to go to the banks of the Tigris and threaten the oldest, largest, and wickedest city in the world with speedy destruction for its sins. That still, small voice, which no mortal had ever defied, thrilled Jonah's ear. "Arise, go to Nineveh, that great city, and cry against it; for their wickedness is come up before Me."

Here was an honour for a petty seer. His betters would have received it with pious exultation. Samuel, or Nathan, Elijah, Elisha, John the Baptist, or Paul, would have risen like lions, and gone forth with strong faith and pious pride to thunder against great Nineveh. But this strange man received the order silently, and silently evaded it. He did not hang his head and object like poor crushed Moses, when the hot patriotism of his youth had been cooled into apathy by exile, family ties, and forty years' intercourse with Midianitish bullocks. Jonah received the Divine command, quietly turned his back upon it and on Nineveh, fled to the seaport Joppa, and sailed in a ship for distant Tarshish.

So imperfect was his inspiration at this time that he thought the hand of the God that he served could not reach him on a foreign sea.

They got into blue water, and such was his confidence that he told the ship's company he was flying from the tutelary God of Palestine. His hearers, no more enlightened than himself, received his communication with no misgivings.

But presently a mighty tempest from the Lord fell upon the sea, and the ship was in mortal danger. The mariners were terrified, and cried every man to his God, and, not trusting too much to that, threw the cargo overboard. But there was one man who did not share their apprehensions. He went quietly to sleep, and neither the roaring sea, the whistling wind, nor the poor, creaking, labouring ship disturbed him. And of all the people whose lives were in such peril, who was this one calm sleeper?

It was Jonah.

But the shipmaster came to him, and shook him, and insisted on his calling on his God. But lo! the peril increased, and from the suddenness and violence of the storm, they began to suspect the anger of the gods against some person in that doomed vessel. So they cast lots to learn who was the culprit, and the lot fell on Jonah. Then they questioned him as to his country and occupation, hoping, somehow or other, to gather how he had offended heaven.

Then Jonah, who now realised his folly and the narrow views he had taken of Him who is omnipresent and almighty, replied, "I am an Hebrew; and I fear the Lord, the God of heaven, *who hath made the sea and the dry land.*"

Then the quaking mariners remembered he had told them he was flying from his God: and now behold that God, by his own confession, was not a local divinity, but the creator of sea and land.

Connecting this new revelation with the sudden tempest and their increasing peril, the men were in mortal fear, and put a terrible question to Jonah: "What shall we do to you to save our own lives?"

Then Jonah, faulty as his character was, shone out like the sun. No shirking; no craven subterfuges. He looked them in the face and said:

"What you must do is, lay hold on me, and cast me into the sea, so shall the sea be calm to you; for I know that for my sake this great tempest is upon you."

Thus did Jonah show himself a prophet and a man. Though terror-stricken, murderous eyes glared on him, and the fearful sea yawned and raged for him, he was so true and so just that he delivered his own doom unflinchingly.

Nobility begets nobility; and the partners of his peril could not bear to sacrifice a man in whom they saw no evil, but, on the contrary, justice, heroism, and self-sacrifice. The poor, honest fellows said, "Anything but that," and chose rather to be wrecked on shore. Their ship, after all, was but a galley lightened of its cargo, so they got out their long oars and made a gallant effort to row their trireme ashore, and there leave her bones, but save their own lives and that self-sacrificing hero. This was not to be. Sixty hands labouring at those oars could not prevail against the one hand that hurled the raging sea at that labouring galley and drove her from the land.

Then these doomed men resigned themselves to the will of Jonah's God. They cried to Him most pathetically, "We beseech Thee, O Lord, we beseech Thee, let us not perish for this man's life." And on the other hand, they begged that if Jonah was innocent his blood might not be laid on them, since they had done all they could to learn the Divine will. And when they had so prayed, they took up Jonah and cast him into the sea.

No doubt, as that pale but unflinching face went down without a cry or murmur, they looked on awhile with horror and misgiving; but not for long; the sea subsided as if by magic. The waves were calmed, the wind abated, the vessel was saved. The rescued mariners worshipped the God of Jonah.

To his late companions Jonah was lost for ever. But God chastises His rebellious servants—not destroys them. Some monster of the deep was sent to that ship's side, and swallowed up Jonah as he sank.

It was a terrible punishment. Think of it! For all these things are skimmed so superficially that they never really come home to the mind, least of all to the mind that is bent on preaching doctrines and not on comprehending facts. The man found himself in a place cold as death and dark as pitch; no room to move hand or foot. After the first shock of utter amazement, the sliminess, the smell, the water rushing through the fish's gills, must have told him where he was. Oh, then conceive his horror! So he was not to die in the sea and there an end; but to lie in the belly of a great fish till he rotted away; or to be brought up within range of the creature's teeth and gnawed away piecemeal and digested in fragments.

Take my word for it, the poor wretch passed many hours of agony, expecting a slow death of torment, and would have given the world to be vomited into the raging sea and perish by drowning—a mild and common death.

But as the hours rolled on and death came no nearer, he began to hope a little, and to repent more and more. The man was soon crushed into that state of self-abasement and penitence, out of which a forgiving God often raises His faulty servants to great honour and happiness. He prayed to God out of the fish's belly, and said:

"I cried by reason of mine affliction unto the Lord, and He heard me: out of the belly of hell cried I, and Thou heardest my voice. For Thou hadst cast me into the deep, in the midst of the seas; and the floods compassed me about: all Thy billows and Thy waves passed over me. Then I said, I am cast out of Thy sight; yet I will look again toward Thy holy temple. The waters compassed me about, even to the soul: the depth closed me round about, the weeds were wrapped about my head. I went down to the bottoms of the mountains; the earth with her bars was about me for ever: yet hast Thou brought up my life from corruption, O Lord my God. When my soul fainted within me I remembered the Lord : and my prayer came in unto Thee, into Thine holy temple. I will sacrifice unto Thee with the voice of thanksgiving : I will pay that that I have vowed. Salvation is of the Lord. And the Lord spake unto the fish, and it vomited out Jonah upon the dry land."

Who was now the happiest man in all the world? Why, this forgiven sinner; this punished, humbled, rewarded rebel.

To him life was ten times sweeter ; the sunshine, the shelly beach, the purple sea, with its myriad dimples and prismatic hues, ten times more lovely than to other men.

Lazarus was happy, returning from the grave to his beloved Master, and his darling sisters that wept on his neck for joy.

Happy was the widow's only son, whom the Master, mighty yet tender, delivered with His own hand from his coffin to his bereaved mother, wild with amazement and maternal love. But both these men came back from the neutral state of mere unconsciousness to daylight and the joys of life.

Not so Jonah. He had been buried alive, and came back from the sickening horror of a living tomb, from a darkness and a death that he felt, to the warm bright sunshine, the glittering sand painted with radiant shells, the purple sea smiling myriad dimples and rainbowed with prismatic hues.

Whilst he gazed at these things with a rapture they had never yet created in him, and poured out his soul in gratitude, there came to him once more the still, small voice of his Master, clear, silvery, dispassionate, and divinely beautiful.

" Arise, go to Nineveh, that great city, and preach unto it the preaching that I bid thee."

Jonah now obeyed with alacrity and went to Nineveh, strong in his Divine commission.

Nineveh having perished about two centuries before Herodotus visited the Tigris, we have no better authority as to its size and population than the words of the Book of Jonah. We may, however, rely on the universal tradition that it was a city of vast size and magnificence, and three days' journey in circuit by Jewish computation, or 480 Greek stadia, which two measurements agree, being sixty English miles.

It was a brilliant and luxurious city, at the head of the world in general magnificence and in the fine arts.

A rude Hebrew seer came from a country inferior in every mental quality but knowledge of God, and threatened this magnificent city with destruction in forty days, if the people did not repent their sins and turn to the true God.

The thing to be expected was that the townspeople would laugh at him for a day or two, and then drag him through their gutters, or whip him through the streets with his prophecy pinned to his back in cuneiform letters.

But Jonah, inspired by God, and being, so to speak, a prophet raised from the dead to do a great work, preached with supernatural power, and bowed these Assyrian hearts, from the throne to the cabin. The King of Nineveh, the greatest monarch of the day, rose up from his throne at the preaching of Jonah, laid his royal robe in the dust and sat on the ground in sackcloth and ashes, a picture of lowly penitence and an example which all his people followed. They fasted, not by halves, but to the confines of torture. They tasted neither food nor drink, and they kept food and drink from their herds, their flocks, and their beasts of burden. They covered themselves and their cattle with sackcloth ; they abstained from the sins that Jonah had denounced, and cried for mercy to the God of this Boanerges. Then God saw, pardoned, and spared.

Here was a triumph for Jonah—alone, and with no human help, he had terrified and converted the greatest city in the world. Even egotism, if humanised by benevolence, could have found gratification in this. But poor Jonah was all egotism. A witty Frenchman has defined an egotist as a character who will burn down another man's house to cook himself two eggs. Jonah was quite up to the mark of this definition. He would have burned down a populous and penitent city to enjoy his one egg, the *amour propre* of a seer.

He was sore displeased, and complained to the Lord. He even said—though I cannot say I *quite* believe him—that this was the only reason why he had fled to Tarshish. He knew his prophecy would prove an empty menace, for, said he, " I know that Thou art a gracious God, and merciful, slow to anger, and of great kindness, and repentest Thee of the evil. *I wish I were dead.*"

Now, if any one of us had been allowed to speak for God, we should have come down on this egotist like a sledge-hammer.

What! do you cast in God's teeth that quality by which alone you have yourself escaped destruction? Return, then, to the belly of that shark, and there, in the darkness of your eyes, let light visit your soul blinded by egotism.

Come, now—shall penitent Jonah and penitent Nineveh be destroyed for their repented sins? or shall both be saved, and God be consistent, though man, Jonah included, is not?

But God never talks like that. He is better than man at man's best. Man forgives, but remembers, and sometimes even alludes. God, when He forgives, obliterates. It is so throughout the sacred books, and although neither the Hebrew writers nor any other writers can comprehend or describe the infinite God, yet they all reveal this fragment of His infinite nature with a consistency that bears the stamp of truth and excludes the idea of invention.

When Jonah stood by the seaside saved from death, God did not say to him, "See what comes of resisting My will!" He obliterated what He had forgiven, and merely repeated His command about Nineveh without an unkind word. And now that His wayward servant reproached Him with His weakness in forgiving penitent Chaldeans, He only said to him with more than maternal sweetness, "Doest thou well to be angry?"

This did not melt the angry Jonah. He turned his back on the city, which he hated for not fulfilling his prediction punctually. He went out into the fields and sat down to see whether God would really be so cruel as to mortify Jonah and save 600,000 people, not one of whom was Jonah.

God pitied His servant exposed to the midday heat, and prepared a gourd to comfort his aching head, and afterwards instruct his heart.

Then Jonah enjoyed great happiness. All the day he looked upon a wonder of nature. A lovely gourd came up from the ground, growing slowly but perceptibly, and reared and expanded its huge succulent leaves till they formed a thick canopy over the head of the favoured prophet.

Then Jonah rejoiced in the impenetrable shade of this lovely plant, and began to be half reconciled to the prolonged existence of Nineveh.

Then the gourd entered on its second office. The Almighty had planted a worm in the gourd, and the worm was enabled to destroy it as rapidly as it had grown.

Then did the sun and the hot wind beat on Jonah's head,

and he cried once more, as our foolish women do when things go wrong, " I wish I were dead."

Then God said to Jonah tenderly, " Doest thou well to be angry ? "

Ungracious Jonah replied roughly, " I do well to be angry, even unto death."

Then came the still, small voice, sweet yet clear, gentle yet mighty and penetrating, which no patriarch but Jonah ever resisted so long ; and even he must yield to it at last. "Thou hast had pity on the gourd, for the which thou hast not laboured, neither madest it grow ; which came up in a night, and perished in a night : and should not I spare Nineveh, that great city, wherein are more than six score thousand persons that cannot discern between their right hand and their left ; and also much cattle ? "

Now, if the reader of Jonah is curious to know whether he left Nineveh as great an egotist as he entered it, I can only give him one man's opinion, but it is not a hasty one. In the first place, the Omniscient is not to be defeated ; why should Jonah's egotism resist Him to the end, any more than Jonah's flight baffled Him for more than a day or two?

Primâ facie, the Almighty must conquer the heart of Jonah, since He knows the way to every heart.

Starting from this safe position, I ask myself why so faulty a man as Jonah was so honoured ? Clearly it was not because of his rebellious spirit, nor his egotism ; but in spite of them.

Probably he was a man of pure life and morals ; certainly he was the soul of truth. Why should not the God of truth select as a vehicle of prophecy the brave, truthful man, who, facing desperate men with the sea raging on him at his back, could say, "The truth is, you must take me up and fling me into the sea ; for with my just execution the storm will abate."

Jonah did not write the book, but he must have communicated the facts and the main particulars of the dialogue.

Now, no *unconverted* egotist tells a tale so fairly throughout, and the concluding dialogue so thoroughly against himself, as it is done in this book. You read this dialogue between God and a man ; and the writer is a man. A man yourself, you are shocked at the man, and you bless God.

Moreover, he has given God the last word and the best. Now, no unconverted egotist ever did that, nor ever will. The unconverted egotist is to be found in a thousand autobiographies ; catch him giving an opponent the last word, or the best !

I have little doubt, therefore, that Jonah went home a converted egotist, and that when he came to think quietly over it all, he yielded to Divine instruction, and that his character kept improving to the last day of his life.

Of course I reject the conventional theory that Jonah, being a prophet, had no personal weakness under his skin, and wished penitent Nineveh to be destroyed only because he feared for his own nation if it was left standing. If he foresaw the captivity at all, he must have known that the danger was to be from Babylon, after Nineveh had been centuries extinct. Long after Jonah, Nahum threatened Nineveh, but did not fear it.

These skimmers forget that, if Jonah was faultless, God must have been imperfect, since God and he were in direct opposition; and that not once, but twice. The Book of Jonah is generally underrated; one reason is, it is judged by commentators, who have never tried to tell an immortal story, so they underrate a man immeasurably their superior, since the able narrator is above the able commentator, and high as heaven above the conventional commentator, who is mad after types, and who follows his predecessors, who follows theirs, "ut anser trahit anserem."

The truth is, that "Jonah" is the most beautiful story ever written in so small a compass.

Now, in writing it is condensation that declares the master; verbosity and garrulity have their day, but only hot-pressed narratives live for ever. The Book of Jonah is in forty-eight verses, or one thousand three hundred and twenty-eight English words.

Now, take one thousand three hundred and twenty-eight words in our current narratives: how far do they carry you? Why, ten to one, you get to nothing at all but chatter, chatter, chatter. Even in those close models "Robinson Crusoe," the "Vicar of Wakefield," "Candide," "Rasselas," one thousand three hundred and twenty-eight words do not carry the reader far; yet in the one thousand three hundred and twenty-eight words of Jonah you have a wealth of incident, and all the dialogue needed to carry on the grand and varied action. You have also character, not stationary, but growing just as Jonah's grew, and a plot that would bear volumes, yet worked out without haste or crudity in one thousand three hundred and twenty-eight words.

Then there is another thing. Only the great artists of the pen hit upon the perfect proportions of dialogue and narrative. With nineteen story-tellers out of twenty there is a weary excess of dialogue. Nor are all the sacred narratives so nicely proportioned as Jonah. In Job the narrative is so short as to be crude and uninteresting compared with the events handled, and the dialogue is excessive, and in some places false, since similar sentiments and even similar words are given to different speakers. In the Apocrypha, "Judith" and "Tobit" are literally massacred by verbosity and bungling; not so, however, in "Susannah and the Elders" —that is a masterpiece as far as it goes.

To my mind, speaking merely as an artist, the Acts of the Apostles eclipses all human narratives,

"Stellas exortus uti Ætherius sol ; "

and in the Old Testament, Genesis, Samuel, Jonah, and Ruth stand pre-eminent, and Jonah above sweet Ruth by the greater weight of the facts and the introduction of the Deity. And oh, the blindness of conventional critics, groping Hebrew records not for pearls of facts, but pebbles of dogma ! They have failed to observe that the God of Jonah is the God of the New Testament. Yet it is so, and this great book connects the two Bibles, instead of contrasting them and sore perplexing every honest mind with a changeable Deity.

No doubt the God of the New Testament can be found, or heavenly glimpses of Him, in the Hebrew prophets. But how about the historians? The truculent writers of Joshua, Judges, and Samuel have surely now and then coloured the unchangeable God from their own minds and their own state of civilisation.

The Book of Jonah is not a book of prophecy, but just as much a history as Samuel ; yet in the history of Jonah, written long before Isaiah, God is the God of the New Testament ; the God we all hope to find in this world and the next.

Were there no other reason, every Christian may well cling to the Book of Jonah. As to the leading miracle which staggers some people who receive other miracles, these men are surely inconsistent. There can be no scale of the miraculous. To infinite power it is no easier to pick up a pin than to stop all the planets in their courses for a time and then send them on again.

Say there never was a miracle and never will be, and I differ with, but cannot confute, you. Deny the creation and the possibility of a re-creation or resurrection ; call David a fool for saying, " It is he that hath made us and not we ourselves," and . . . . a wise man for suggesting that, on the contrary, molecules created themselves without a miracle, and we made ourselves out of molecules without a miracle; and although your theory contradicts experience as much as, and staggers credulity more than, any miracle that has ever been ascribed by Christians or Jews to infinite power, I admit it is consistent, though droll.

But once grant the creation of a hundred thousand suns and a million planets, though we never in our short span saw one created; grant the creation of men, lions, fleas, and sea anemones, though all such creations are contrary to our experience; and it is a little too childish to draw back and say that our Creator and re-Creator is only the Lord of flesh, and that fish are beyond His control.

Clearly, infinite power can create a new fish in Jewish waters, or despatch an old fish in the millionth of a second from the Pacific to the shores of Palestine.

Now to go from power to wisdom, is this miracle a childish one? does it smack of human invention?

What were the objects to be gained by it? A rebellious servant was to be crushed into submission, yet not destroyed. He was to feel the brief agony of death by drowning, then to be laid in a horrible dark prison till he repented, then to be restored to the world in a fit state of mind and body to take a long journey and threaten the greatest city in the world.

Tackle all those difficulties, effect all those just and wise objects, invent your own miracle, and perhaps when you compare it with Jonah's, you will think very highly of the latter, and not so highly of the whole army of skimmers, who have discredited and sneered at a record they have never tried hard to comprehend:

"Facile judicat qui pauca considerat."

VI

DAVID

THIS is the widest character on record. Of course there are other famous men who fill more pages. But, remember, three lives of David, written in his own time, are lost; and the books that survive give only the man's cream. Had his chroniclers pursued the modern method, our shelves would have groaned under their tomes. But in their age, if pure discourse was sometimes diffuse, narrative was always severely concise : they sank a thousand minor details that would be sure to interest us now, and kept strictly to those great deeds and words which seemed peculiar to David, and indeed remain so to this hour.

History thus compressed is a crucible of character : in it mediocrity evaporates, and even celebrity shrivels. In Holy Writ, Moses, Elijah, and Paul : in profane history, Solon, Alexander, Cæsar, Charlemagne, Napoleon, and others, excelled David greatly in one quality or another. David presents a greater number of distinct and striking features than any one of those great men ; and that is why I style him the widest character on record—a shepherd, a soldier, a courtier, a famous friend, a fugitive, an actor, a marauder, a general, a king, a statesman, an exile, a priest, a prophet, a saint, a criminal, a penitent : and nothing by halves.

This boy killed a lion hand to hand, and knocked down a mail-clad giant like a sparrow. This man was hunted for his life like a wolf, and spared his pursuer like a lamb. This warrior conquered armies, and even his own passions, yet one day unruly desire laid him low. He became the heartless assassin of a husband he had abused.

This hero invented chivalry two thousand years before the knights who have gained the credit for it. This bard versified the sorrows of his soul, and sang them to boot, long before we were told of poets that

"They learn in suffering what they teach in song."

This magnanimous minstrel lauded and bewailed his dead foe in deathless lines ; this tuneful preacher, in an Eastern province and a bygone age, has comforted bleeding hearts throughout the globe, and will while earth shall last. Merciful in an age of blood ; yet sometimes extremely hard and cruel. Brave, generous, meek, irritable, forgiving, vindictive, pious, sensual, criminal, contrite—greatest of all in penitence, man's most redeeming quality ; for his repentance had no limit but his light. He never saw a sin in himself that he did not mourn and weep for it heart, soul, and body.

And, to conclude the chapter of his anomalies, he foretold the Saviour of the world, and lived, upon the whole, as if he knew Him. Yet when he came to die, far from forgiving his enemies, he drew back his pardon from those he had forgiven, and left his own son a legacy of blood—a sad heathen act for a dying saint, to whom the Great Forgiver had pardoned worse crimes than Shimei's; yet as profitable to the upright reader as anything in all his strange, eventful history, since here he left mankind an exemplary proof how much Christ's personal teaching was needed, and how great a boon it was, and is, to mortal man.

VII

PAUL'S PERSEVERANCE

"And with these sayings scarce restrained they the people, that they had not done sacrifice unto them. And there came thither certain Jews from Antioch and Iconium, who persuaded the people, and having stoned Paul, drew him out of the city, supposing he had been dead. Howbeit, as the disciples stood round about him, he rose up, and came into the city; and the next day he departed with Barnabas to Derbe. And when they had preached the gospel to that city, and had taught many, they returned again to Lystra, and to Iconium, and Antioch, confirming the souls of the disciples, and exhorting them to continue in the faith, and that we must through great tribulation enter into the kingdom of God."—ACTS xiv. 18–22.

SCRIPTURE is so full of heavenly food, that often a single text furnishes more than one sermon. In these cases the text is generally a precept. In the narrative portion matters are of necessity not so condensed as all that, and a whole passage, containing several verses, takes the place of a *text*.

For example, here are four verses it would be unwise to separate for the purposes of discourse, and wise to read them all four with care, and consider what they reveal: what a picture of human nature, and of God's grace !

These marvellous passages of Divine story are so briefly and so simply told, compared with other narratives, that people too often read them and hear them read, without discovering all that lies in them for our edification. They require intelligent and prayerful study, and they repay it, as a mine repays the spade.

Now and then these gems of narrative are lost in part, through a mistaken notion in the mind that they record prodigies—acts we are to admire at a distance, but not try nor hope to imitate them, even at a distance.

Many people look on the Apostles and Saints as super-human creatures, or as so upheld by the ever-present arm of God that they did their great work, and suffered their great trials, with none of that difficulty and pain we should have encountered in their place, and are bound to encounter if necessary.

Now, it is wise to revere Apostles and Saints; but it is most unwise to take them for prodigies. For no man imitates a prodigy—he feels it would be useless. But it is our duty to imitate, to follow the steps of Apostles and Saints, and, more than that, it is our duty to follow them exactly, though it be at ever so humble a distance.

And in this Scripture encourages us. It *tells* us that our Lord Himself was tempted in all things as we are, though without sin, and it *shows* us that He actually suffered much innocent sorrow, grief, mortification, and one dark hour of despairing agony.

We are not invited to believe that, when He wept over Lazarus and the sorrows of his bereaved sisters, He did not feel as brave men feel when they weep for others; we are not to assume—without a word to justify it—that when He was scourged, buffeted, and spat upon, His poor cheek did not burn with shame; that when beaten, and fastened with cruel nails to a cross, His whole human frame did not quiver with pain; nor that when the disciples, whose faith He had so carefully armed for the trial with His earnest, loving words and the commemorative supper, all forsook Him and fled, a sword did not pierce His human heart.

How much more His Apostles, who were entirely human, must have felt their trials just as we should, though grace gave them the victory!

Now, first realise this simple truth, and then put yourself in the place of Paul at Lystra.

His good work among the heathen began hopefully at Iconium; but by-and-by it was baffled by the unbelieving Jews. Men who worshipped one God, actually sided with idolatry through mere hatred of Christ, and, though they never troubled their heads to correct the worship of devils, stirred up the heathen against the ministration of the Gospel, and nearly succeeded in putting those two Apostles to death by stoning, which was the punishment of blasphemy.

They prevailed in part. Paul and Barnabas, the two greatest benefactors that ever entered Iconium, were com-pelled to slink out of the place like criminals, or die the death of the blasphemer. Here was mortification and disappointment, all the more bitter that their hopes had been raised at first.

Well, they retired, and did not lose heart, as most of us would have done. They carried their great, rejected boon to Lystra.

Paul was an extempore preacher, and therefore his eye was never on the wrong place, a book or manuscript, but always on the right place, his hearers. He preached to the heathen at Lystra, and observed his hearers keenly—habit of all real orators. Presently he noticed two eyes fixed on him with faith. The great orator saw that those eyes were drinking in the Gospel in earnest. He also observed that this man, who heard so eagerly, and *believed,* was a cripple. Paul stopped in his discourse, and said, with a loud voice : " Stand upright on thy feet."

To the amazement of the audience, the man stood up, leaped, and walked.

Lystra was not a large place ; doubtless this man, a cripple from his birth, was known ; the miracle was evident ; the heathen were not—like the Jews—fortified by prejudice against the evidence of their senses. They took the Apostles for gods, the imaginary gods they had been accustomed to worship, and they proceeded to offer sacrifices to them ; the very priest of Jupiter claimed his part in the ceremony.

Now, this was a temptation of the evil one. We ought not to underrate it merely because it failed. There is no other recorded instance of its failing. Alexander the Great accepted flattery in this impious form. So did Augustus Cæsar and his successors. So did Herod, to his cost.

But Paul and Barnabas were struck with pious horror ; they ran in among the people and rent their clothes, and declared their common humanity, and diverted the blind piety and gratitude of these poor heathen to the true God.

So much for grace.

Now for human nature.

This same fickle mob were presently talked over by the Jews, and made to believe the Apostles were impostors.

Impostors !—and they had cured the lame.

Impostors !—and they had refused divine honours !

This fickle heathen mob acted in concert with these stiff-necked Jews, and amongst them they actually stoned the man they had proposed to worship, and dragged his breathless body outside the city. Lystra was not to be defiled by dead Paul.

A monstrous act, yet perfectly natural. The unwise always run from one extreme to the other, and probably the vanity of these unstable men was wounded at the very thought that they had been on the point of worshipping a couple of Jews, whom their own countrymen now came and denounced as impostors.

Now, stoning a man did not mean flinging small stones at him from a distance. Their way was to drag the victim to his knees, and raise heavy stones with both hands, and hurl them down on his back, his loins, his neck, his head, till the life was battered out of him.

So was that holy man crushed and pounded to death. He was breathless—he was insensible. So far as the pain of dying was concerned, his poor body suffered all and more than it did a few years later at Rome, when one swift blow of a sword—the most merciful of all his foes, and indeed his kindest friend—released him at once from the burden of the flesh and the battle with sin.

This battered body—the body of the greatest benefactor that ever visited their paltry city—the men of Lystra dragged outside the gates with ignominy, and then returned in contemptuous triumph.

Now realise the scene that followed, ye skimmers of Bible facts, and divers into Bible guesses, and quibblers of dogmas. The murderers are gone. There lies the body of Paul, crushed, bloody, ghastly pale, dirty, deserted by all but a few disciples who stood sadly round, and being new converts, their faith is oozing fast out of them as they look on that pale and battered saint, who could heal the lame, but could not defend his own life.

But stay—what is this? The body stirs—the crushed one sighs—he moves—he rises feebly, with a little aid. He utters no word of complaint; blames neither his foes for their cruelty, nor his friends for their cowardice. He is unable to travel—he is assisted back into that murderous city: and there he lies racked in every joint.

How long? Six months? Well, then, three?

One afternoon. The next day he limped to Derbe. What for? For medical advice probably; for repose, if he could not afford a physician; for a soft couch to lie on and ease his aching frame?

No—to preach the Gospel.

We read his fortitude and his zeal. What it cost him we

must learn from our own common-sense. No man is nearly killed by many violent blows and not much hurt. After such cruel usage pain may intermit, but it does not leave a man in a day, nor yet in a week. Let the saints of this our day, who do God's work in spite of pain, and disease, and weakness, take comfort by example, and be assured that many a throe wrung Paul's stout heart, long after he was stoned and left for dead at Lystra, yet neither pain nor threat could quell him; with aching body, but undaunted heart, he preached God's word at Derbe.

After some bitter trial God often rewards His soldier, even in this world. The Apostles preached at Derbe with great success, and made many converts.

This done, they marched into a neighbouring town. Its name was Lystra.

What Lystra? No doubt there are two Lystras. That was no uncommon thing. This was doubtless some Lystra a hundred miles distant from the Lystra that stoned Paul and dragged his body outside the walls.

No; it was the Lystra that stoned him. He returned to it, not from a tour of towns, but direct from Derbe, with the pain still in his body, but the Gospel in his indomitable heart.

Iconium had tried to stone him, so he will go there soon, we may be sure; but Lystra had already stoned him, so he will go there first; and, if not killed there, he will go to Iconium and Antioch, the very centres which sent forth those very Jews who all but destroyed him at Lystra. He will beard those very men in their own dens, with the sword of the Gospel and the shield of Faith.

Was this premature return to Lystra bravado or desperation?

It was neither. It was courage and wisdom. Religion, like philosophy, can teach by examples. Paul had a great lesson to teach in those three cities. He had, as the sacred narrative informs us, to confirm the souls of the disciples in those cities, and exhort them to continue in the faith, and teach them that we must through much tribulation enter the Kingdom of Heaven. Now, Paul could do more than *preach* this lesson at Lystra; he could *show* it as powerfully in his own person, as he had shown the power of God in healing their lame citizen.

Just imagine, for one moment, how the men of Lystra stared with amazement when these two Apostles walked back into their market-place and resumed their preaching, as if no serious interruption had ever occurred.

No details are given of this second visit; but the result speaks for itself. Reaction reigned ; their lame fellow-citizen had been walking those streets, showing his limbs, and speaking his mind, we may be sure. No Jews ventured a second experiment upon heathen credulity. Faith, Patience, Fortitude, were more than conquerors even at vile Lystra.

In that terrible conflict of spiritual powers, of which this world is the arena, Satan often wins the skirmish and God the battle.

Now, this great heroic story, told in four verses, reveals nothing absolutely new in Scripture history, and nothing that will ever become obsolete, least of all the great lesson that we must enter Heaven by the Gate of Tribulation.

EVIDENCES OF REVELATION [*]

In the summer of 1880, some fanatics having revived the notion that the pseudo-Tichborne impostor is an illegitimate son of Roger Tichborne's father, I wrote some letters in my nephew's weekly publication *Fact*, entitled "The Doctrine of Coincidences." The leading position in them is that the force of unforeseen coincidences is great, and increases in a prodigious ratio when they are multiplied and point to one conclusion; and I also there showed that fifteen independent and unforeseen coincidences all point from different points of the compass to one central fact, that this impostor is Arthur Orton, of Wapping.

I mentioned this in outline to my dear friend the Rev. Charles Graham, and he said that unforeseen coincidences were among the evidences of the truth of Scripture. I then remembered that Paley uses them in the "Horæ Paulinæ." I was not aware they had been applied to the Old Testament also. Mr. Graham, however, lent me a volume entitled "Undesigned Coincidences in the Old and New Testament," by the Rev. J. J. Blunt. The writer in his Preface refers to Paley as the writer who had worked this vein the most remarkably; and to Doddridge on 1st Thessalonians, and Biscoe's "History of the Acts of the Apostles," as predecessors who—to use my own phrase—had fingered the idea before him.

Dr. Blunt extends Paley's method to the Old Testament, and observes many unstudied coincidences of statement in the books of Moses.

These he calls generally coincidences; I myself am not quite clear that they are all coincidences. Many seem to be rather subtle consistences, or statements accidentally corroborative of each other.

A coincidence I should define as two indisputable facts

[*] Apparently the notes for a further statement of the subject.

356

pointing to one conclusion. If so, there are three parts in a coincidence, but only two in a corroborative statement.

If I am right in this distinction, Dr. Blunt discovers (pages 9-21) many coincidences which, taken in conjunction, point clearly to a Patriarchal Church long before Moses, with (1) places of worship; (2) forms of consecrating such places; (3) priests, tithes, and a Sabbath, circumcision, moral enactments against murder, robbery, fornication, adultery (in the limited sense Moses himself understood it), false swearing, disobedience to parents, marriage with idolaters. Also ceremonies: purification, clean and unclean animals (Noah), sacrifices, circumcision.—(Pages 1-23).

Incidental proofs of the promised Christ he finds in the early sacrifices,—and here I would venture to throw in that Cain's sacrifice, which could not typify Christ, was rejected;—in the wild eagerness of the women for offspring—a desire that overcame jealousy, defied nature.

And all this with no design on the part of Moses to elevate those who lived before the law it was his mission to promulgate. This, says the author, is my master-key, explaining and justifying details that are trivial and even offensive without it. Witness the conduct of Sarah, Jacob's wives, Onan, Tamar, &c.

Pages 24-93 are occupied with what I should not call coincidences, but undesigned consistency—one statement unobtrusively confirming another :—

Abraham's intercession for Sodom, and his leaving off at ten.

Lot and his family at Sodom, and Abraham's hope that there would be righteous in that home.

Isaac marrying into a generation below him.

Great age at which Sarah had borne Isaac.

Jochebed, daughter of Levi, marrying a grandson of Levi. Jochebed turns out to have been born in Egypt—child of Levi's old age.

Identity of Jacob's character in so many incidents.

The freight of the camels that carried Joseph into Egypt.

The sepulture of the Egyptians.

The many off-hand indications that Egypt was a great corn-grower.

The historical fact that it was so.

The proportion of oxen and waggons assigned to the descendants of Levi.

The apparent fate of Korah, Dathan, and Abiram, and their families. The subsequent statement that Korah's children died not.

The original account, more closely examined, admitting this solution.

Miraculous water at Horeb.

Altars of Amalekites.

Death of Zimri.

Diminution of the Tribe of Simeon.

The fondness of Joseph for his father, and the way his brothers appeal to it unconsciously.—(Pages 24-93.)

The character of Jacob, a cowed man. Its consistency.

To these I beg to add :

(1.) That the ark is built, or begun, more than one hundred years before the deluge ; and the deluge does not come till Methuselah, the son of righteous Enoch, is just dead. Yet the writer does not observe this, and the reader only discovers it by arithmetical computation.

(2.) That Rebekah's trait, parental partiality, is found in her favourite son, yet not noticed by the author. And that Jacob, the younger son, blesses the younger son of Joseph before the elder. Yet the writer seems only to notice the bare fact.

(3.) That the typical offering of Abel was accepted, but the non-typical offering of Cain rejected. Yet the writer has no theory on the matter.

Balaam slain among the Midianites. Compare with the invitation just given to him.

MONUMENTAL EVIDENCE AND DOCUMENTAL

MONUMENTAL, by physical destruction after its existence has been recorded in words, may pass into mixed evidence ; or documental evidence of a quondam monumental.

Example : The writer of Genesis points his readers to the pillar of Rachel's grave, on the way from Bethel to Ephrath, but he does not refer to the pillar of salt that once was Lot's wife, as still existing (Joshua iv. 21).

The period of time, a week, and its universal existence, is a monumental proof of the truth of Moses. Years, months, and days are derivable from the sun and moon ; but the week is an unnatural division. Yet there never was an age when it did not prevail in India, China, Assyria, Egypt, and it migrated to Greece and Rome.

The world is large, and full of conflicting opinions. How many solutions exist of this arbitrary division—seven days ! There is only one known to creation, and that is adequate, for it says the parents of all mankind were taught it by their Creator.

Now try any other solution and it will be found inadequate, and evidently to accept an inadequate solution of an undeniable fact is credulity in one of its weakest forms.

THE END

Printed by BALLANTYNE, HANSON & CO.
Edinburgh and London

AN ALPHABETICAL CATALOGUE
OF BOOKS IN FICTION AND
GENERAL LITERATURE
PUBLISHED BY
CHATTO & WINDUS
III ST. MARTIN'S LANE
CHARING CROSS
LONDON, W.C.

[MAR., 1902.]

Adams (W. Davenport), Works by.
A Dictionary of the Drama: being a comprehensive Guide to the Plays, Playwrights, Players, and Playhouses of the United Kingdom and America, from the Earliest Times to the Present Day. Crown 8vo. half-bound, 12s. 6d. *[Preparing.*
Quips and Quiddities. Selected by W. DAVENPORT ADAMS. Post 8vo, cloth limp, 2s. 6d.

Agony Column (The) of 'The Times,' from 1800 to 1870. Edited with an Introduction, by ALICE CLAY. Post 8vo, cloth limp, 2s. 6d.

Alexander (Mrs.), Novels by. Post 8vo, illustrated boards, 2s. each.
Maid, Wife, or Widow? | **Blind Fate.**
Crown 8vo, cloth, 3s. 6d. each; post 8vo, picture boards, 2s. each.
Valerie's Fate. | **A Life Interest.** | **Mona's Choice.** | **By Woman's Wit.**
Crown 8vo, cloth 3s. 6d. each.
The Cost of her Pride. | **Barbara, Lady's Maid and Peeress.** | **A Fight with Fate.**
A Golden Autumn. | **Mrs. Crichton's Creditor.** | **The Step-mother.**
A Missing Hero.

Allen (F. M.).—Green as Grass. Crown 8vo, cloth, 3s. 6d.

Allen (Grant), Works by. Crown 8vo, cloth, 6s. each.
The Evolutionist at Large. | **Moorland Idylls.**
Post-Prandial Philosophy. Crown 8vo, art linen, 3s. 6d.

Crown 8vo, cloth extra, 3s. 6d. each; post 8vo, illustrated boards, 2s. each.
Babylon. 12 Illustrations. | **The Devil's Die.** | **The Duchess of Powysland.**
Strange Stories. | **This Mortal Coil.** | **Blood Royal.**
The Beckoning Hand. | **The Tents of Shem.** | **Ivan Greet's Masterpiece.**
For Maimie's Sake. | **The Great Taboo.** | **The Scallywag.** 24 Illusts.
Philistia. | **Dumaresq's Daughter.** | **At Market Value.**
In all Shades. | **Under Sealed Orders.**
Dr. Palliser's Patient. Fcap. 8vo, cloth boards, 1s. 6d.

Anderson (Mary).—Othello's Occupation. Crown 8vo, cloth, 3s. 6d.

Antrobus (C. L.), Novels by. Crown 8vo, cloth, gilt top, 6s. each.
Quality Corner: A Study of Remorse. | **Wildersmoor.**

Appleton (G. Webb).—Rash Conclusions. Crown 8vo, cloth, 3s. 6d.

Arnold (Edwin Lester), Stories by.
The Wonderful Adventures of Phra the Phœnician. Crown 8vo, cloth extra, with 12 Illustrations by H. M. PAGET, 3s. 6d.; post 8vo, illustrated boards, 2s.
The Constable of St. Nicholas. With Frontispiece by S. L. WOOD. Crown 8vo, cloth, 3s. 6d.; picture cloth, flat back, 2s.

Artemus Ward's Works. With Portrait and Facsimile. Crown 8vo, cloth extra, 3s. 6d.—Also a POPULAR EDITION post 8vo, picture boards, 2s.

Ashton (John), Works by. Crown 8vo, cloth extra, 7s. 6d. each.
Humour, Wit, and Satire of the Seventeenth Century. With 82 Illustrations.
English Caricature and Satire on Napoleon the First. With 115 Illustrations.
Social Life in the Reign of Queen Anne. With 85 Illustrations. Crown 8vo, cloth, 3s. 6d.
Crown 8vo, cloth, gilt top, 6s. each.
Social Life under the Regency. With 90 Illustrations.
Florizel's Folly: The Story of GEORGE IV. With Photogravure Frontispiece and 12 Illustrations.

Bacteria, Yeast Fungi, and Allied Species, A Synopsis of. By W. B. GROVE, B.A. With 87 Illustrations. Crown 8vo, cloth extra, 3s. 6d.

Baildon (H. B.).—Robert Louis Stevenson: A Life Study in Criticism. With 2 Portraits. Crown 8vo, buckram, 6s.

Bardsley (Rev. C. Wareing, M.A.), Works by.
English Surnames : Their Sources and Significations. Crown 8vo, cloth, 7s. 6d.
Curiosities of Puritan Nomenclature. Crown 8vo, cloth, 3s. 6d.

Barr (Robert : Luke Sharp), Stories by. Cr. 8vo, cl., 3s. 6d. each.
In a Steamer Chair. With Frontispiece and Vignette by DEMAIN HAMMOND.
From Whose Bourne, &c, With 47 Illustrations by HAL HURST and others.
Revenge ! With 12 Illustrations by LANCELOT SPEED and others.
A Woman Intervenes. With 8 Illustrations by HAL HURST.
The Unchanging East : Notes on a Visit to the Farther Edge of the Mediterranean. With a Frontispiece. Crown 8vo, cloth, gilt top, 6s.
A Royal Tramp. With 12 Illustrations by E. J. SULLIVAN. Crown 8vo, cloth, gilt top, 6s.

Barrett (Frank), Novels by.
Post 8vo, illustrated boards, 2s. each; cloth, 2s. 6d. each.

The Sin of Olga Zassoulich.	**John Ford ;** and **His Helpmate.**
Between Life and Death.	**A Recoiling Vengeance.**
Folly Morrison. | **Little Lady Linton.**	**Lieut. Barnabas.** | **Found Guilty.**
A Prodigal's Progress. | **Honest Davie.**	**For Love and Honour.**

Crown 8vo, cloth, 3s. 6d. each ; post 8vo, picture boards, 2s. each ; cloth limp, 2s. 6d. each.
Fettered for Life. | **The Woman of the Iron Bracelets.** | **The Harding Scandal**
A Missing Witness. With 8 Illustrations by W. H. MARGETSON.

Crown 8vo, cloth, 3s. 6d. each.
Under a Strange Mask. With 19 Illusts. by E. F. BREWTNALL. | **Was She Justified ?**

Barrett (Joan).—Monte Carlo Stories. Fcap. 8vo, cloth, 1s. 6d.

Besant (Sir Walter) and James Rice, Novels by.
Crown 8vo, cloth extra, 3s. 6d. each ; post 8vo, illustrated boards, 2s. each ; cloth limp, 2s. 6d. each.

Ready-Money Mortiboy.	**This Son of Vulcan.**	**The Seamy Side.**
The Golden Butterfly.	**The Monks of Thelema.**	**The Case of Mr. Lucraft.**
My Little Girl.	**By Celia's Arbour.**	**'Twas in Trafalgar's Bay.**
With Harp and Crown.	**The Chaplain of the Fleet.**	**The Ten Years' Tenant.**

*** There are also LIBRARY EDITIONS of all the above, excepting the first two. Large crown 8vo cloth extra, 6s. each.

Besant (Sir Walter), Novels by.
Crown 8vo, cloth extra, 3s. 6d. each ; post 8vo, illustrated boards, 2s. each ; cloth limp, 2s. 6d. each.
All Sorts and Conditions of Men. With 12 Illustrations by FRED. BARNARD.
The Captains' Room, &c. With Frontispiece by E. J. WHEELER.
All in a Garden Fair. With 6 Illustrations by HARRY FURNISS.
Dorothy Forster. With Frontispiece by CHARLES GREEN.
Uncle Jack, and other Stories. | **Children of Gibeon.**
The World Went Very Well Then. With 12 Illustrations by A. FORESTIER.
Herr Paulus : His Rise, his Greatness, and his Fall. | **The Bell of St. Paul's.**
For Faith and Freedom. With Illustrations by A. FORESTIER and F. WADDY.
To Call Her Mine, &c. With 9 Illustrations by A. FORESTIER.
The Holy Rose, &c. With Frontispiece by F. BARNARD.
Armorel of Lyonesse : A Romance of To-day. With 12 Illustrations by F. BARNARD.
St. Katherine's by the Tower. With 12 Illustrations by C. GREEN.—Also in picture cloth, flat back, 2s.
Verbena Camellia Stephanotis, &c. With a Frontispiece by GORDON BROWNE.
The Ivory Gate. | **The Rebel Queen.**
Beyond the Dreams of Avarice. With 12 Illustrations by W. H. HYDE.
In Deacon's Orders, &c. With Frontispiece by A. FORESTIER. | **The Revolt of Man.**
The Master Craftsman. | **The City of Refuge.**

Crown 8vo, cloth, 3s. 6d. each.
A Fountain Sealed. | **The Changeling.** | **The Fourth Generation.**

Crown 8vo, cloth, gilt top, 6s. each.
The Orange Girl. With 8 Illustrations by F. PEGRAM.
The Lady of Lynn. With 12 Illustrations by G. DEMAIN-HAMMOND.
No Other Way. With Illustrations. *[Preparing.*

POPULAR EDITIONS, Medium 8vo, 6d. each.
The Golden Butterfly. | **The Chaplain of the Fleet.**
Ready-Money Mortiboy. | **The Orange Girl.**

The Charm, and other Drawing-room Plays. By Sir WALTER BESANT and WALTER H. POLLOCK. With 50 Illustrations by CHRIS HAMMOND and JULE GOODMAN. Crown 8vo, cloth, 3s. 6d.
Fifty Years Ago. With 144 Illustrations. Crown 8vo, cloth, 3s. 6d.
The Eulogy of Richard Jefferies. With Portrait. Crown 8vo, cloth, 6s.
London. With 125 Illustrations. Demy 8vo, cloth, 7s. 6d.
Westminster. With an Etched Frontispiece by F. S. WALKER, R.E., and 130 Illustrations by WILLIAM PATTEN and others. LIBRARY EDITION, demy 8vo, cloth gilt and gilt top, 18s.; POPULAR EDITION, demy 8vo, cloth, 7s. 6d.
South London. With an Etched Frontispiece by F. S. WALKER, R.E., and 118 Illustrations. Demy 8vo, cloth gilt and gilt top, 18s. ; POPULAR EDITION, demy 8vo, cloth, 7s. 6d.
East London. With an Etched Frontispiece by F. S. WALKER, and 55 Illustrations by PHIL MAY, L. RAVEN HILL, and JOSEPH PENNELL. Demy 8vo, cloth, 18s.
Jerusalem : The City of Herod and Saladin. By WALTER BESANT and E. H. PALMER. Fourth Edition. With a new Chapter, a Map, and 11 Illustrations. Small demy 8vo, cloth, 7s. 6d.
Sir Richard Whittington. With Frontispiece. Crown 8vo, art linen, 3s. 6d.
Gaspard de Coligny. With a Portrait. Crown 8vo, art linen, 3s. 6d.
The Art of Fiction. Fcap. 8vo, cloth, red top, 1s. net.
As We Are, and As We May Be. Crown 8vo, buckram, gilt top, 6s. *[Shortly.*
Essays and Historiettes. Crown 8vo, buckram, gilt top, 6s. *[Shortly.*

Baring Gould (Sabine, Author of 'John Herring,' &c.**), Novels by.**
Crown 8vo, cloth extra, 3s. 6d. each ; post 8vo, illustrated boards, 2s. each.
Red Spider. | **Eve.**

Beaconsfield, Lord. By T. P. O'CONNOR, M.P. Cr. 8vo, cloth, 5s.

Bechstein (Ludwig).—As Pretty as Seven, and other German
Stories. With Additional Tales by the Brothers GRIMM, and 98 Illustrations by RICHTER. Square 8vo, cloth extra, 6s. 6d. ; gilt edges, 7s. 6d.

Bellew (Frank).—The Art of Amusing: A Collection of Graceful
Arts, Games, Tricks, Puzzles, and Charades. With 300 Illustrations. Crown 8vo, cloth extra, 4s. 6d.

Bennett (Arnold).—The Grand Babylon Hotel. Crown 8vo, cloth,
gilt top, 6s.

Bennett (W. C., LL.D.).—Songs for Sailors. Post 8vo, cl. limp, 2s.

Bewick (Thomas) and his Pupils. By AUSTIN DOBSON. With 95
Illustrations. Square 8vo, cloth extra, 3s. 6d.

Bierce (Ambrose).—In the Midst of Life: Tales of Soldiers and
Civilians. Crown 8vo, cloth extra, 3s. 6d. ; post 8vo, illustrated boards, 2s.

Bill Nye's Comic History of the United States. With 146 Illustrations by F. OPPER. Crown 8vo, cloth extra, 3s. 6d.

Bindloss (Harold), Novels by.
Ainslie's Ju-Ju: A Romance of the Hinterland. Crown 8vo, cloth, 3s. 6d.
A Sower of Wheat. Crown 8vo, cloth, gilt top, 6s.

Bodkin (M. McD., K.C.), Books by.
Dora Myrl, the Lady Detective. Crown 8vo, cloth, 3s. 6d. ; picture cloth, flat back, 2s.
Shillelagh and Shamrock. Crown 8vo, cloth, 3s. 6d.

Bourget (Paul).—A Living Lie. Translated by JOHN DE VILLIERS.
With special Preface for the English Edition. Crown 8vo, cloth, 3s. 6d.

Bourne (H. R. Fox), Books by.
English Merchants: Memoirs in Illustration of the Progress of British Commerce. With 32 Illus-
trations. Crown 8vo, cloth, 3s. 6d.
English Newspapers: Chapters in the History of Journalism. Two Vols., demy 8vo, cloth, 25s.
The Other Side of the Emin Pasha Relief Expedition. Crown 8vo, cloth, 6s.

Boyd.—A Versailles Christmas-tide. By MARY STUART BOYD. With
53 Illustrations by A. S. BOYD. Fcap. 4to, cloth gilt and gilt top, 6s.

Boyle (Frederick), Works by. Post 8vo, illustrated bds., 2s. each.
Chronicles of No-Man's Land. | **Camp Notes.** | **Savage Life.**

Brand (John).— Observations on Popular Antiquities; chiefly
illustrating the Origin of our Vulgar Customs, Ceremonies, and Superstitions With the Additions of Sir
HENRY ELLIS. Crown 8vo, cloth, 3s. 6d.

Brayshaw (J. Dodsworth).—Slum Silhouettes: Stories of London
Life. Crown 8vo, cloth, 3s. 6d.

Brewer (Rev. Dr.), Works by.
**The Reader's Handbook of Famous Names in Fiction, Allusions, References,
Proverbs, Plots, Stories, and Poems.** Together with an ENGLISH AND AMERICAN
BIBLIOGRAPHY, and a LIST OF THE AUTHORS AND DATES OF DRAMAS AND OPERAS. A
New Edition, Revised and Enlarged. Crown 8vo, cloth. 7s. 6d.
A Dictionary of Miracles: Imitative, Realistic, and Dogmatic. Crown 8vo, cloth, 3s. 6d.

Brewster (Sir David), Works by. Post 8vo, cloth, 4s. 6d. each.
More Worlds than One: Creed of the Philosopher and Hope of the Christian. With Plates.
The Martyrs of Science: GALILEO, TYCHO BRAHE, and KEPLER. With Portraits.
Letters on Natural Magic. With numerous Illustrations.

Brillat-Savarin.—Gastronomy as a Fine Art. Translated by
R. E. ANDERSON, M.A. Post 8vo, half-bound, 2s.

Bryden (H. A.).—An Exiled Scot: A Romance. With a Frontispiece, by J. S. CROMPTON, R.I. Crown 8vo, cloth, 6s.

Brydges (Harold).—Uncle Sam at Home. With 91 Illustrations.
Post 8vo illustrated boards, 2s. ; cloth limp, 2s. 6d.

Buchanan (Robert), Poems and Novels by.

The Complete Poetical Works of Robert Buchanan. 2 vols., rown 8vo, buckram, with Portrait Frontispiece to each volume, 12s.

Crown 8vo, cloth, 6s. each.
The Devil's Case: a Bank Holiday Interlude. With 6 Illustrations.
The Earthquake; or, Six Days and a Sabbath.
The Wandering Jew: a Christmas Carol.

Crown 8vo, cloth, 3s. 6d. each.
The Outcast: a Rhyme for the Time.
The Ballad of Mary the Mother: a Christmas Carol.
St. Abe and his Seven Wives. Crown 8vo, cloth, 2s. 6d.

Crown 8vo, cloth, 3s. 6d. each ; post 8vo, illustrated boards, 2s. each.

The Shadow of the Sword.	**Love Me for Ever.** With Frontispiece.
A Child of Nature. With Frontispiece.	**Annan Water.** | **Foxglove Manor.**
God and the Man. With 11 Illustrations by	**The New Abelard.** | **Rachel Dene.**
Lady Kilpatrick. [FRED. BARNARD.	**Matt:** A Story of a Caravan. With Frontispiece.
The Martyrdom of Madeline. With	**The Master of the Mine.** With Frontispiece.
Frontispiece by A. W. COOPER.	**The Heir of Linne.** | **Woman and the Man.**

Crown 8vo, cloth, 3s. 6d. each.
Red and White Heather. | **Andromeda:** An Idyll of the Great River.

The Charlatan. By ROBERT BUCHANAN and HENRY MURRAY. Crown 8vo, cloth, with a Frontispiece by T. H. ROBINSON, 3s. 6d. ; post 8vo, picture boards, 2s.

Burton (Robert).—The Anatomy of Melancholy. With Transla-
tions of the Quotations. Demy 8vo, cloth extra, 7s. 6d.
Melancholy Anatomised: An Abridgment of BURTON'S ANATOMY. Post 8vo, half-cl., 2s. 6d.

Caine (Hall), Novels by. Crown 8vo, cloth extra, 3s. 6d. each. ; post
8vo, illustrated boards, 2s. each ; cloth limp, 2s. 6d. each.
The Shadow of a Crime. | **A Son of Hagar.** | **The Deemster.**
Also LIBRARY EDITIONS of **The Deemster** and **The Shadow of a Crime,** set in new type, crown 8vo, and bound uniform with **The Christian,** 6s. each; and CHEAP POPULAR EDITIONS of **The Deemster, The Shadow of a Crime,** and **A Son of Hagar,** medium 8vo, portrait-cover, 6d. each.—Also the FINE-PAPER EDITION of **The Deemster,** pott 8vo, cloth, gilt top, 2s. net ; leather, gilt edges, 3s. net.

Cameron (Commander V. Lovett).—The Cruise of the 'Black
Prince' Privateer. Post 8vo, picture boards, 2s.

Canada (Greater) : The Past, Present, and Future of the Canadian
North-West. By E. B. OSBORN, B.A. With a Map. Crown 8vo, cloth, 3s. 6d.

Captain Coignet, Soldier of the Empire: An Autobiography.
Edited by LOREDAN LARCHEY. Translated by Mrs. CAREY. With 100 Illustrations. Crown 8vo, cloth, 3s. 6d.

Carlyle (Thomas).—On the Choice of Books. Post 8vo, cl., 1s. 6d.
Correspondence of Thomas Carlyle and R. W. Emerson, 1834-1872. Edited by C. E. NORTON. With Portraits. Two Vols., crown 8vo, cloth, 24s.

Carruth (Hayden).—The Adventures of Jones. With 17 Illustra-
tions. Fcap. 8vo, cloth, 2s.

Chambers (Robert W.), Stories of Paris Life by.
The King in Yellow. Crown 8vo, cloth, 3s. 6d.; fcap. 8vo, cloth limp, 2s. 6d.
In the Quarter. Fcap. 8vo, cloth, 2s. 6d.

Chapman's (George), Works. Vol. I., Plays Complete, including the
Doubtful Ones.—Vol. II., Poems and Minor Translations, with Essay by A. C. SWINBURNE.—Vol. III., Translations of the Iliad and Odyssey. Three Vols., crown 8vo, cloth, 3s. 6d. each.

Chapple (J. Mitchell).—The Minor Chord: The Story of a Prima
Donna. Crown 8vo, cloth, 3s. 6d.

Chaucer for Children: A Golden Key. By Mrs. H. R. HAWEIS. With
8 Coloured Plates and 30 Woodcuts. Crown 4to, cloth extra, 3s. 6d.
Chaucer for Schools. With the Story of his Times and his Work. By Mrs. H. R. HAWEIS. A New Edition, revised. With a Frontispiece. Demy 8vo, cloth, 2s. 6d.

Chess, The Laws and Practice of. With an Analysis of the Open-
ings. By HOWARD STAUNTON. Edited by R. B. WORMALD. Crown 8vo, cloth, 5s.
The Minor Tactics of Chess: A Treatise on the Deployment of the Forces in obedience to Strategic Principle. By F. K. YOUNG and E. C. HOWELL. Long fcap. 8vo, cloth, 2s. 6d.
The Hastings Chess Tournament. Containing the Authorised Account of the 230 Games played Aug.-Sept., 1895. With Annotations by PILLSBURY, LASKER, TARRASCH, STEINITZ, SCHIFFERS, TEICHMANN, BARDELEBEN, BLACKBURNE, GUNSBERG, TINSLEY, MASON, and ALBIN ; Biographical Sketches of the Chess Masters, and 22 Portraits. Edited by H. F. CHESHIRE. Cheaper Edition. Crown 8vo, cloth, 5s.

Clare (Austin), Stories by.
For the Love of a Lass. Post 8vo, illustrated boards, 2s.; cloth, 2s. 6d.
By the Rise of the River: Tales and Sketches in South Tynedale. Crown 8vo cloth, 3s. 6d.

Clive (Mrs. Archer), Novels by.
Post 8vo, cloth, 3s. 6d. each; picture boards, 2s. each.
Paul Ferroll. | Why Paul Ferroll Killed his Wife.

Clodd (Edward, F.R.A.S.).—Myths and Dreams. Cr. 8vo, 3s. 6d.

Coates (Anne).—Rie's Diary. Crown 8vo, cloth, 3s. 6d.

Cobban (J. Maclaren), Novels by.
The Cure of Souls. Post 8vo, Illustrated boards, 2s.
The Red Sultan. Crown 8vo, cloth extra, 3s. 6d.; post 8vo, illustrated boards, 2s.
The Burden of Isabel. Crown 8vo, cloth extra, 3s. 6d.

Coleridge (M. E.).—The Seven Sleepers of Ephesus. Fcap. 8vo,
leatherette, 1s.; cloth, 1s. 6d.

Collins (C. Allston).—The Bar Sinister. Post 8vo, boards, 2s.

Collins (John Churton, M.A.), Books by.
Illustrations of Tennyson. Crown 8vo, cloth extra, 6s.
Jonathan Swift. A Biographical and Critical Study. Crown 8vo, cloth extra, 8s.

Collins (Mortimer and Frances), Novels by.
Crown 8vo, cloth extra, 3s. 6d. each; post 8vo, illustrated boards, 2s. each.
From Midnight to Midnight. | Blacksmith and Scholar.
You Play me False. | The Village Comedy.

Post 8vo, illustrated boards, 2s. each.
Transmigration. | Sweet Anne Page. | Frances.
A Fight with Fortune. | Sweet and Twenty.

Collins (Wilkie), Novels by.
Crown 8vo, cloth extra, many Illustrated, 3s. 6d. each; post 8vo, picture boards, 2s. each;
cloth limp, 2s. 6d. each.

*Antonina.	My Miscellanies.	Jezebel's Daughter.
*Basil.	Armadale.	The Black Robe.
*Hide and Seek.	Poor Miss Finch.	Heart and Science.
*The Woman in White.	Miss or Mrs.?	'I Say No.'
*The Moonstone.	The New Magdalen.	A Rogue's Life.
*Man and Wife.	The Frozen Deep.	The Evil Genius.
*The Dead Secret.	The Law and the Lady.	Little Novels.
After Dark.	The Two Destinies.	The Legacy of Cain.
The Queen of Hearts.	The Haunted Hotel.	Blind Love.
No Name.	The Fallen Leaves.	

, Marked * have been reset in new type, in uniform style.

POPULAR EDITIONS. Medium 8vo, 6d. each; cloth, 1s. each.
The Moonstone. | Antonina. | The Dead Secret.

Medium 8vo, 6d. each.
The Woman in White. | The New Magdalen. | Man and Wife.

Colman's (George) Humorous Works: 'Broad Grins,' 'My Night-
gown and Slippers,' &c. With Life and Frontispiece. Crown 8vo, cloth extra, 3s. 6d.

Colquhoun (M. J.).—Every Inch a Soldier. Crown 8vo, cloth,
3s. 6d.; post 8vo, illustrated boards, 2s.

Colt-breaking, Hints on. By W. M. HUTCHISON. Cr. 8vo, cl., 3s. 6d.

Compton (Herbert).—The Inimitable Mrs. Massingham: a
Romance of Botany Bay. Crown 8vo, cloth, 3s. 6d.

Convalescent Cookery. By CATHERINE RYAN. Cr. 8vo, 1s.; cl., 1s. 6d.

Cooper (Edward H.).—Geoffory Hamilton. Cr. 8vo, cloth, 3s. 6d.

Cornish (J. F.).—Sour Grapes: A Novel. Cr. 8vo, cloth, gilt top, 6s.

Cornwall.—Popular Romances of the West of England; or, The
Drolls, Traditions, and Superstitions of Old Cornwall. Collected by ROBERT HUNT, F.R.S. With
two Steel Plates by GEORGE CRUIKSHANK. Crown 8vo, cloth, 7s. 6d.

Cotes (V. Cecil).—Two Girls on a Barge. With 44 Illustrations by
F. H. TOWNSEND. Crown 8vo, cloth extra, 3s. 6d.; post 8vo, cloth, 2s. 6d.

Craddock (C. Egbert), Stories by.
The Prophet of the Great Smoky Mountains. Crown 8vo, cloth, 3s. 6d.; post 8vo
illustrated boards, 2s.
His Vanished Star. Crown 8vo, cloth, 3s. 6d.

Cram (Ralph Adams).—Black Spirits and White. Fcap. 8vo, cloth, 1s. 6d.

Crellin (H. N.), Books by.
Romances of the Old Seraglio. With 28 Illustrations by S. L. WOOD. Crown 8vo, cloth, 3s. 6d.
Tales of the Caliph. Crown 8vo, cloth, 2s.
The Nazarenes: A Drama. Crown 8vo, 1s.

Crim (Matt.).—Adventures of a Fair Rebel. Crown 8vo, cloth extra, with a Frontispiece by DAN. BEARD, 3s. 6d.; post 8vo, illustrated boards, 2s.

Crockett (S. R.) and others. — Tales of Our Coast. By S. R. CROCKETT, GILBERT PARKER, HAROLD FREDERIC, 'Q.,' and W. CLARK RUSSELL. With 2 Illustrations by FRANK BRANGWYN. Crown 8vo, cloth, 3s. 6d.

Croker (Mrs. B. M.), Novels by. Crown 8vo, cloth extra, 3s. 6d. each; post 8vo, illustrated boards, 2s. each; cloth limp, 2s. 6d. each.
Pretty Miss Neville. | Interference. | Village Tales & Jungle
Proper Pride. | A Family Likeness. | Tragedies.
A Bird of Passage. | A Third Person. | The Real Lady Hilda.
Diana Barrington. | Mr. Jervis. | Married or Single?
Two Masters.

Crown 8vo, cloth extra, 3s. 6d. each.
Some One Else. | Miss Balmaine's Past. | Beyond the Pale.
In the Kingdom of Kerry. | Jason, &c. | Infatuation.
Terence. With 6 Illustrations by SIDNEY PAGET.

'To Let,' &c. Post 8vo, picture boards, 2s.; cloth limp, 2s. 6d.
The Cat's-paw. With 12 Illustrations by FRED. PEGRAM. Crown 8vo, cloth, gilt top, 6s.

Cruikshank's Comic Almanack. Complete in Two SERIES: The FIRST, from 1835 to 1843; the SECOND, from 1844 to 1853. A Gathering of the Best Humour of THACKERAY, HOOD, MAYHEW, ALBERT SMITH, A'BECKETT, ROBERT BROUGH, &c. With numerous Steel Engravings and Woodcuts by GEORGE CRUIKSHANK, HINE, LANDELLS, &c. Two Vols., crown 8vo, cloth gilt, 7s. 6d. each.
The Life of George Cruikshank. By BLANCHARD JERROLD. With 84 Illustrations and a Bibliography. Crown 8vo, cloth extra, 3s. 6d.

Cumming (C. F. Gordon), Works by. Large cr. 8vo, cloth, 6s. each.
In the Hebrides. With an Autotype Frontispiece and 23 Illustrations.
In the Himalayas and on the Indian Plains. With 42 Illustrations.
Two Happy Years in Ceylon. With 28 Illustrations.
Via Cornwall to Egypt. With a Photogravure Frontispiece.

Cussans (John E.).—A Handbook of Heraldry; with Instructions for Tracing Pedigrees and Deciphering Ancient MSS., &c. Fourth Edition, revised, with 408 Woodcuts and 2 Coloured Plates. Crown 8vo, cloth extra, 6s.

Daudet (Alphonse).—The Evangelist; or, Port Salvation. Crown 8vo, cloth extra, 3s. 6d.; post 8vo, illustrated boards, 2s.

Davenant (Francis, M.A.).—Hints for Parents on the Choice of a Profession for their Sons when Starting in Life. Crown 8vo, cloth, 1s. 6d.

Davidson (Hugh Coleman).—Mr. Sadler's Daughters. With a Frontispiece by STANLEY WOOD. Crown 8vo, cloth extra, 3s. 6d.

Davies (Dr. N. E. Yorke-), Works by. Cr. 8vo, 1s. ea.; cl., 1s. 6d. ea.
One Thousand Medical Maxims and Surgical Hints.
Nursery Hints: A Mother's Guide in Health and Disease.
Foods for the Fat: The Dietetic Cure of Corpulency and of Gout.
Aids to Long Life. Crown 8vo, 2s.; cloth limp, 2s. 6d.

Davies' (Sir John) Complete Poetical Works. Collected and Edited, with Introduction and Notes, by Rev. A. B. GROSART, D.D. Two Vols., crown 8vo, cloth, 3s. 6d. each.

De Guerin (Maurice), The Journal of. Edited by G. S. TREBUTIEN. With a Memoir by SAINTE-BEUVE. Translated from the 20th French Edition by JESSIE P. FROTH-INGHAM. Fcap. 8vo, half-bound, 2s. 6d.

De Maistre (Xavier).—A Journey Round my Room. Translated by HENRY ATTWELL. Post 8vo, cloth limp, 2s. 6d.

Derby (The): The Blue Ribbon of the Turf. With Brief Accounts of THE OAKS. By LOUIS HENRY CURZON. Crown 8vo, cloth limp, 2s. 6d.

Dewar (T. R.).—A Ramble Round the Globe. With 220 Illustrations. Crown 8vo, cloth extra, 7s. 6d.

De Windt (Harry), Books by.
Through the Gold-Fields of Alaska to Bering Straits. With Map and 33 full-page Illustrations. Cheaper Issue. Demy 8vo, cloth, 6s.
True Tales of Travel and Adventure. Crown 8vo, cloth, 3s. 6d.

Dickens (Charles), About England with. By ALFRED RIMMER. With 57 Illustrations by C. A. VANDERHOOF and the AUTHOR. Square 8vo, cloth, 3s. 6d.

Dictionaries.

The Reader's Handbook of Famous Names in Fiction, Allusions, References, Proverbs, Plots, Stories, and Poems. Together with an ENGLISH AND AMERICAN BIBLIOGRAPHY. and a LIST OF THE AUTHORS AND DATES OF DRAMAS AND OPERAS, By Rev. E. C. BREWER, LL.D A New Edition, Revised and Enlarged. Crown 8vo, cloth, 7s. 6d.

A Dictionary of Miracles: Imitative, Realistic, and Dogmatic. By the Rev. E. C. BREWER, LL.D. Crown 8vo, cloth, 3s. 6d.

Familiar Short Sayings of Great Men. With Historical and Explanatory Notes by SAMUEL A. BENT, A.M. Crown 8vo, cloth extra, 7s. 6d.

The Slang Dictionary: Etymological, Historical, and Anecdotal. Crown 8vo, cloth, 6s. 6d.

Words, Facts, and Phrases: A Dictionary of Curious, Quaint, and Out-of-the-Way Matters. By ELIEZER EDWARDS. Crown 8vo, cloth extra, 3s. 6d.

Dilke (Rt. Hon. Sir Charles, Bart., M.P.).—The British Empire.
Crown 8vo, buckram, 3s. 6d.

Dobson (Austin), Works by.
Thomas Bewick and his Pupils. With 95 Illustrations. Square 8vo, cloth, 3s. 6d.
Four Frenchwomen. With Four Portraits. Crown 8vo, buckram, gilt top, 6s.
Eighteenth Century Vignettes. IN THREE SERIES. Crown 8vo, buckram, 6s. each.
A Paladin of Philanthropy, and other Papers. With 2 Illusts. Cr. 8vo, buckram, 6s.

Dobson (W. T.).—Poetical Ingenuities and Eccentricities. Post
8vo, cloth limp, 2s. 6d.

Donovan (Dick), Detective Stories by.
Post 8vo, illustrated boards, 2s. each ; cloth limp, 2s. 6d. each.

The Man-Hunter.	Wanted!	Suspicion Aroused.	Riddles Read.
Caught at Last.	Tracked to Doom.	A Detective's Triumphs.
Tracked and Taken.	Link by Link.	In the Grip of the Law.
Who Poisoned Hetty Duncan?		From Information Received.

Crown 8vo, cloth extra, 3s. 6d. each ; post 8vo, illustrated boards, 2s. each ; cloth, 2s. 6d. each.
The Man from Manchester. With 23 Illustrations.
The Mystery of Jamaica Terrace. | **The Chronicles of Michael Danevitch.**

Crown 8vo, cloth, 3s. 6d. each.
The Records of Vincent Trill, of the Detective Service.—Also picture cloth, flat back, 2s.
The Adventures of Tyler Tatlock, Private Detective.
Deacon Brodie ; or, Behind the Mask. | **Tales of Terror.**
Dark Deeds. Crown 8vo, picture cloth, flat back, 2s.

Dowling (Richard).—Old Corcoran's Money. Crown 8vo, cl., 3s. 6d.

Doyle (A. Conan).—The Firm of Girdlestone. Cr. 8vo, cl., 3s. 6d.

Dramatists, The Old. Cr. 8vo, cl. ex., with Portraits, 3s. 6d. per Vol.
Ben Jonson's Works. With Notes, Critical and Explanatory, and a Biographical Memoir by WILLIAM GIFFORD. Edited by Colonel CUNNINGHAM. Three Vols.
Chapman's Works. Three Vols. Vol. I. contains the Plays complete ; Vol. II., Poems and Minor Translations, with an Essay by A. C. SWINBURNE ; Vol. III., Translations of the Iliad and Odyssey.
Marlowe's Works. Edited, with Notes, by Colonel CUNNINGHAM. One Vol.
Massinger's Plays. From GIFFORD'S Text. Edited by Colonel CUNNINGHAM. One Vol.

Dublin Castle and Dublin Society, Recollections of. By A
NATIVE. Crown 8vo, cloth, gilt top. 6s.

Duncan (Sara Jeannette: Mrs. EVERARD COTES), Books by.
Crown 8vo, cloth extra, 7s. 6d. each.
A Social Departure. With 111 Illustrations by F. H. TOWNSEND.
An American Girl in London. With 80 Illustrations by F. H. TOWNSEND.
The Simple Adventures of a Memsahib. With 37 Illustrations by F. H. TOWNSEND.

Crown 8vo, cloth extra, 3s. 6d. each.
A Daughter of To-Day. | **Vernon's Aunt.** With 47 Illustrations by HAL HURST.

Dutt (Romesh C.).—England and India: A Record of Progress
during One Hundred Years. Crown 8vo, cloth, 2s.

Early English Poets. Edited, with Introductions and Annotations,
by Rev. A. B. GROSART, D.D. Crown 8vo, cloth boards, 3s. 6d. per Volume.
Fletcher's (Giles) Complete Poems. One Vol.
Davies' (Sir John) Complete Poetical Works. Two Vols.
Herrick's (Robert) Complete Collected Poems. Three Vols.
Sidney's (Sir Philip) Complete Poetical Works. Three Vols.

Edgcumbe (Sir E. R. Pearce).—Zephyrus: A Holiday in Brazil
and on the River Plate. With 41 Illustrations. Crown 8vo, cloth extra, 5s.

Edwardes (Mrs. Annie), Novels by.
A Point of Honour. Post 8vo, illustrated boards, 2s. | **A Plaster Saint.** Cr. 8vo, cl., 3s. 6d.
Archie Lovell. Crown 8vo, cloth, 3s. 6d. ; illustrated boards, 2s.

Edwards (Eliezer).—Words, Facts, and Phrases: A Dictionary
of Curious, Quaint, and Out-of-the-Way Matters. Cheaper Edition. Crown 8vo, cloth, 3s. 6d.

Egerton (Rev. J. C., M.A.).— Sussex Folk and Sussex Ways.
With Introduction by Rev. Dr. H. WACE, and Four Illustrations. Crown 8vo, cloth extra, 5s.

Eggleston (Edward).--Roxy: A Novel. Post 8vo, illust. boards, 2s.

Englishman (An) in Paris. Notes and Recollections during the Reign of Louis Philippe and the Empire. Crown 8vo, cloth, 3s. 6d.

Englishman's House, The: A Practical Guide for Selecting or Building a House. By C. J. RICHARDSON. Coloured Frontispiece and 534 Illusts. Cr. 8vo, cloth, 3s. 6d.

Ewald (Alex. Charles, F.S.A.).—The Life and Times of Prince Charlie Stuart, Count of Albany (THE YOUNG PRETENDER). With a Portrait. Crown 8vo, cloth extra, 7s. 6d.

Eyes, Our: How to Preserve Them. By JOHN BROWNING. Cr. 8vo, 1s.

Familiar Short Sayings of Great Men. By SAMUEL ARTHUR BENT, A.M. Fifth Edition, Revised and Enlarged. Crown 8vo, cloth extra, 7s. 6d.

Faraday (Michael), Works by. Post 8vo, cloth extra, 4s. 6d. each.
The Chemical History of a Candle: Lectures delivered before a Juvenile Audience. Edited by WILLIAM CROOKES, F.C.S. With numerous Illustrations.
On the Various Forces of Nature, and their Relations to each other. Edited by WILLIAM CROOKES, F.C.S. With Illustrations.

Farrer (J. Anson).—War: Three Essays. Crown 8vo, cloth, 1s. 6d.

Fenn (G. Manville), Novels by.
Crown 8vo, cloth extra, 3s. 6d. each; post 8vo, illustrated boards, 2s. each.
The New Mistress. | **Witness to the Deed.** | **The Tiger Lily.** | **The White Virgin.**

Crown 8vo, cloth 3s. 6d. each.

A Woman Worth Winning.	**Double Cunning.**	**The Story of Antony Grace**
Cursed by a Fortune.	**A Fluttered Dovecote.**	**The Man with a Shadow.**
The Case of Ailsa Gray.	**King of the Castle.**	**One Maid's Mischief.**
Commodore Junk.	**The Master of the Cere-**	**This Man's Wife.**
Black Blood.	**monies.**	**In Jeopardy.**

Crown 8vo, cloth, gilt top, 6s. each.
The Bag of Diamonds, and Three Bits of Paste.
Running Amok: a Story of Adventure.
The Cankerworm: being Episodes of a Woman's Life.
A Crimson Crime. Crown 8vo, cloth, gilt top, 6s.; picture cloth, flat back, 2s.

Feuerheerd (H. L.).—The Gentleman's Cellar; or, The Butler and Cellarman's Guide. SECOND EDITION. Fcap. 8vo, cloth, 1s.

Fiction, A Catalogue of, with Descriptive Notices and Reviews of over NINE HUNDRED NOVELS, will be sent free by Messrs. CHATTO & WINDUS upon application.

Fin-Bec.—The Cupboard Papers: Observations on the Art of Living and Dining. Post 8vo, cloth limp, 2s. 6d.

Firework-Making, The Complete Art of; or, The Pyrotechnist's Treasury. By THOMAS KENTISH. With 267 Illustrations. Crown 8vo, cloth, 3s. 6d.

First Book, My. By WALTER BESANT, JAMES PAYN, W. CLARK RUSSELL, GRANT ALLEN, HALL CAINE, GEORGE R. SIMS, RUDYARD KIPLING, A. CONAN DOYLE, M. E. BRADDON, F. W. ROBINSON, H. RIDER HAGGARD, R. M. BALLANTYNE, I. ZANGWILL, MORLEY ROBERTS, D. CHRISTIE MURRAY, MARY CORELLI, J. K. JEROME, JOHN STRANGE WINTER, BRET HARTE, 'Q.,' ROBERT BUCHANAN, and R. L. STEVENSON. With a Prefatory Story by JEROME K. JEROME, and 185 Illustrations. A New Edition. Small demy 8vo, art linen, 3s. 6d.

Fitzgerald (Percy), Works by.
Little Essays: Passages from the Letters of CHARLES LAMB. Post 8vo, cloth, 2s. 6d.
Fatal Zero. Crown 8vo, cloth extra, 3s. 6d.; post 8vo, illustrated boards, 2s.

Post 8vo, illustrated boards, 2s. each.

Bella Donna.	**The Lady of Brantome.**	**The Second Mrs. Tillotson.**
Polly.	**Never Forgotten.**	**Seventy-five Brooke Street.**

Sir Henry Irving: Twenty Years at the Lyceum. With Portrait. Crown 8vo, cloth, 1s. 6d.

Flammarion (Camille), Works by.
Popular Astronomy: A General Description of the Heavens. Translated by J. ELLARD GORE, F.R.A.S. With Three Plates and 288 Illustrations. Medium 8vo, cloth, 10s. 6d.
Urania: A Romance. With 87 Illustrations. Crown 8vo, cloth extra, 5s.

Fletcher's (Giles, B.D.) Complete Poems: Christ's Victorie in Heaven, Christ's Victorie on Earth, Christ's Triumph over Death, and Minor Poems. With Notes by Rev. A. B. GROSART, D.D. Crown 8vo, cloth boards, 3s. 6d.

Forbes (Archibald).—The Life of Napoleon III. With Photogravure Frontispiece and Thirty-six full-page Illustrations. Cheaper Issue. Demy 8vo, cloth, 6s.

Forbes (Hon. Mrs. Walter R. D.).—Dumb. Cr. 8vo, cl., gilt top, 6s.

Francillon (R. E.), Novels by.
Crown 8vo, cloth extra, 3s. 6d. each; post 8vo, illustrated boards, 2s. each.
One by One. | **A Real Queen.** | **A Dog and his Shadow.** | **Ropes of Sand.** Illust

Post 8vo, illustrated boards, 2s. each.
Queen Cophetua. | **Olympia.** | **Romances of the Law.** | **King or Knave?**
Jack Doyle's Daughter. Crown 8vo, cloth, 3s. 6d.

Frederic (Harold), Novels by. Post 8vo, cloth extra, 3s. 6d. each;
Illustrated boards. 2s. each.

| Seth's Brother's Wife. | The Lawton Girl. |

French Literature, A History of. By HENRY VAN LAUN. Three
Vols., demy 8vo, cloth boards, 22s. 6d.

Fry's (Herbert) Royal Guide to the London Charities, 1901-2.
Edited by JOHN LANE. Published Annually. Crown 8vo, cloth, 1s. 6d.

Gardening Books. Post 8vo, 1s. each; cloth limp. 1s. 6d. each.
A Year's Work in Garden and Greenhouse. By GEORGE GLENNY.
Household Horticulture. By TOM and JANE JERROLD. Illustrated.
The Garden that Paid the Rent. By TOM JERROLD.

Gardner (Mrs. Alan).—Rifle and Spear with the Rajpoots: Being
the Narrative of a Winter's Travel and Sport in Northern India. With numerous Illustrations by the
Author and F. H. TOWNSEND. Demy 4to, half-bound, 21s.

Gaulot (Paul).—The Red Shirts: A Tale of 'The Terror.' Trans-
lated by JOHN DE VILLIERS. With a Frontispiece by STANLEY WOOD. Crown 8vo, cloth, 3s. 6d. ;
picture cloth, flat back, 2s.

Gentleman's Magazine, The. 1s. Monthly. Contains Stories,
Articles upon Literature, Science, Biography, and Art, and 'Table Talk' by SYLVANUS URBAN.
** Bound Volumes for recent years kept in stock, 8s. 6d. each. Cases for binding, 2s. each.

Gentleman's Annual, The. Published Annually in November. 1s.

German Popular Stories. Collected by the Brothers GRIMM and
Translated by EDGAR TAYLOR. With Introduction by JOHN RUSKIN, and 22 Steel Plates after
GEORGE CRUIKSHANK. Square 8vo, cloth, 6s. 6d. ; gilt edges, 7s. 6d.

Gibbon (Chas.), Novels by. Cr. 8vo, cl., 3s. 6d. ea.; post 8vo, bds., 2s. ea.

| Robin Gray. With Frontispiece. | Loving a Dream. | The Braes of Yarrow. |
| The Golden Shaft. With Frontispiece. | Of High Degree. | |

Post 8vo, illustrated boards, 2s. each.

The Flower of the Forest.	A Hard Knot.	By Mead and Stream.
The Dead Heart.	Queen of the Meadow.	Fancy Free.
For Lack of Gold.	In Pastures Green.	In Honour Bound.
What Will the World Say?	In Love and War.	Heart's Delight.
For the King.	A Heart's Problem.	Blood-Money.

Gibney (Somerville).—Sentenced ! Crown 8vo, cloth, 1s. 6d.

Gilbert (W. S.), Original Plays by. In Three Series, 2s. 6d. each.
The FIRST SERIES contains: The Wicked World—Pygmalion and Galatea—Charity—The Princess—
The Palace of Truth—Trial by Jury.
The SECOND SERIES: Broken Hearts—Engaged—Sweethearts—Gretchen—Dan'l Druce—Tom Cobb
—H.M.S. 'Pinafore'—The Sorcerer—The Pirates of Penzance.
The THIRD SERIES: Comedy and Tragedy—Foggerty's Fairy—Rosencrantz and Guildenstern—
Patience—Princess Ida—The Mikado—Ruddigore—The Yeomen of the Guard—The Gondoliers—
The Mountebanks—Utopia.

Eight Original Comic Operas written by W. S. GILBERT. In Two Series. Demy 8vo, cloth,
2s. 6d. each. The FIRST containing: The Sorcerer—H.M.S. 'Pinafore'—The Pirates of Penzance—
Iolanthe—Patience—Princess Ida—The Mikado—Trial by Jury.
The SECOND SERIES containing: TheGondoliers—The Grand Duke—The Yeomen of the Guard—
His Excellency—Utopia, Limited—Ruddigore—The Mountebanks—Haste to the Wedding.
The Gilbert and Sullivan Birthday Book: Quotations for Every Day in the Year, selected
from Plays by W. S. GILBERT set to Music by Sir A. SULLIVAN. Compiled by ALEX. WATSON.
Royal 16mo, Japanese leather, 2s. 6d.

Gilbert (William). — James Duke, Costermonger. Post 8vo,
Illustrated boards, 2s.

Gissing (Algernon), Novels by. Crown 8vo, cloth, gilt top, 6s. each.

| A Secret of the North Sea. | The Wealth of Mallerstang. |

Glanville (Ernest), Novels by.
Crown 8vo, cloth extra, 3s. 6d. each ; post 8vo, illustrated boards, 2s. each.
The Lost Heiress: A Tale of Love, Battle, and Adventure. With Two Illustrations by H. NISBET.
The Fossicker: A Romance of Mashonaland. With Two Illustrations by HUME NISBET.
A Fair Colonist. With a Frontispiece by STANLEY WOOD.

The Golden Rock. With a Frontispiece by STANLEY WOOD. Crown 8vo, cloth extra, 3s. 6d.
Kloof Yarns. Crown 8vo, cloth, 1s. 6d.
Tales from the Veld. With Twelve Illustrations by M. NISBET. Crown 8vo, cloth, 3s. 6d.
Max Thornton. With 8 Illustrations by J. S. CROMPTON, R.I. Large crown 8vo, cloth, gilt
edges, 5s. ; cloth, gilt top, 6s.

Glenny (George).—A Year's Work in Garden and Greenhouse:
Practical Advice as to the Management of the Flower, Fruit, and Frame Garden. Post 8vo, 1s. ; cloth, 1s. 6d

Godwin (William).—Lives of the Necromancers. Post 8vo, cl., 2s.

Golden Treasury of Thought, The: A Dictionary of Quotations from the Best Authors. By THEODORE TAYLOR. Crown 8vo, cloth, 3s. 6d.

Goodman (E. J.).—The Fate of Herbert Wayne. Cr. 8vo, 3s. 6d.

Grace (Alfred A.).—Tales of a Dying Race. Cr. 8vo, cloth, 3s. 6d.

Greeks and Romans, The Life of the, described from Antique Monuments. By ERNST GUHL and W. KONER. Edited by Dr. F. HUEFFER. With 545 Illustrations. Large crown 8vo, cloth extra, 7s. 6d.

Grey (Sir George).—The Romance of a Proconsul: Being the Personal Life and Memoirs of Sir GEORGE GREY, K.C.B. By JAMES MILNE. With Portrait. SECOND EDITION. Crown 8vo, buckram, 6s.

Griffith (Cecil).—Corinthia Marazion: A Novel. Crown 8vo, cloth extra, 3s. 6d.

Gunter (A. Clavering, Author of 'Mr. Barnes of New York').— **A Florida Enchantment.** Crown 8vo, cloth, 3s. 6d.

Hair, The: Its Treatment in Health, Weakness, and Disease. Translated from the German of Dr. J. PINCUS. Crown 8vo, 1s.; cloth. 1s. 6d.

Hake (Dr. Thomas Gordon), Poems by. Cr. 8vo, cl. ex., 6s. each.
New Symbols. | **Legends of the Morrow.** | **The Serpent Play.**

Maiden Ecstasy. Small 4to. cloth extra, 8s.

Halifax (C.).—Dr. Rumsey's Patient. By Mrs. L. T. MEADE and CLIFFORD HALIFAX, M.D. Crown 8vo, cloth, 3s. 6d.

Hall (Mrs. S. C.).—Sketches of Irish Character. With numerous Illustrations on Steel and Wood by MACLISE, GILBERT, HARVEY, and GEORGE CRUIKSHANK. Small demy 8vo, cloth extra, 7s. 6d.

Hall (Owen), Novels by.
The Track of a Storm. Crown 8vo, cloth, 3s. 6d.; picture cloth, flat back, 2s.
Jetsam. Crown 8vo, cloth, 3s. 6d.
Eureka. Crown 8vo, cloth, gilt top, 6s.

Halliday (Andrew).—Every-day Papers. Post 8vo, boards, 2s.

Hamilton (Cosmo), Stories by. Crown 8vo, cloth gilt, 3s. 6d. each.
The Glamour of the Impossible. | **Through a Keyhole.**

Handwriting, The Philosophy of. With over 100 Facsimiles and Explanatory Text. By DON FELIX DE SALAMANCA. Post 8vo, half-cloth, 2s. 6d.

Hanky-Panky: Easy and Difficult Tricks, White Magic, Sleight of Hand, &c. Edited by W. H. CREMER. With 200 Illustrations. Crown 8vo, cloth extra, 4s. 6d.

Hardy (Rev. E. J., Author of ' How to be Happy though Married ').— **Love, Courtship, and Marriage.** Crown 8vo, cloth, 3s. 6d.

Hardy (Iza Duffus), Novels by. Crown 8vo, cloth, gilt top, 6s. each.
The Lesser Evil. | **Man, Woman, and Fate.**

Hardy (Thomas).—Under the Greenwood Tree. Post 8vo, cloth extra, 3s. 6d.; illustrated boards, 2s.; cloth limp, 2s. 6d.—Also the FINE PAPER EDITION, pott 8vo, cloth, gilt top, 2s. net; leather, gilt edges, 3s. net.

Haweis (Mrs. H. R.), Books by.
The Art of Beauty. With Coloured Frontispiece and 91 Illustrations. Square 8vo, cloth bds., 6s.
The Art of Decoration. With Coloured Frontispiece and 74 Illustrations. Sq. 8vo, cloth bds., 6s.
The Art of Dress. With 32 Illustrations. Post 8vo, 1s.; cloth, 1s. 6d.
Chaucer for Schools. With the Story of his Times and his Work. A New Edition, revised. With a Frontispiece. Demy 8vo, cloth, 2s. 6d.
Chaucer for Children. With 38 Illustrations (8 Coloured). Crown 4to, cloth extra, 3s. 6d.

Haweis (Rev. H. R., M.A.).—American Humorists: WASHINGTON IRVING, OLIVER WENDELL HOLMES, JAMES RUSSELL LOWELL, ARTEMUS WARD, MARK TWAIN, and BRET HARTE. Crown 8vo, cloth, 6s.

Hawthorne (Julian), Novels by.
Crown 8vo, cloth extra, 3s. 6d. each; post 8vo, illustrated boards, 2s. each.
Garth. | **Ellice Quentin.** | **Beatrix Randolph.** With Four Illusts.
Sebastian Strome. | | **David Poindexter's Disappearance.**
Fortune's Fool. | **Dust.** Four Illusts. | **The Spectre of the Camera.**

Post 8vo, illustrated boards, 2s. each.
Miss Cadogna. | **Love—or a Name.**

Harte's (Bret) Collected Works. Revised by the Author. LIBRARY
EDITION, in Ten Volumes, crown 8vo, cloth extra, 6s. each.

Vol.   I. COMPLETE POETICAL AND DRAMATIC WORKS. With Steel-plate Portrait.
  ,,   II. THE LUCK OF ROARING CAMP—BOHEMIAN PAPERS—AMERICAN LEGEND.
  ,, III. TALES OF THE ARGONAUTS—EASTERN SKETCHES.
  ,, IV. GABRIEL CONROY. | Vol. V. STORIES—CONDENSED NOVELS, &c.
  , VI. TALES OF THE PACIFIC SLOPE.
  ,, VII. TALES OF THE PACIFIC SLOPE—II. With Portrait by JOHN PETTIE, R.A.
  ,, VIII. TALES OF THE PINE AND THE CYPRESS. ·
  ,, IX. BUCKEYE AND CHAPPAREL.
  ,, X. TALES OF TRAIL AND TOWN, &c.

Bret Harte's Choice Works. In Prose and Verse. With Portrait of the Author and 40 Illustrations. Crown 8vo, cloth, 3s. 6d.
Bret Harte's Poetical Works. Printed on hand-made paper. Crown 8vo, buckram, 4s. 6d.
Some Later Verses. Crown 8vo, linen gilt, 5s.
In a Hollow of the Hills. Crown 8vo, picture cloth, flat back, 2s.

Crown 8vo, cloth extra, 3s. 6d. each ; post 8vo, picture boards, 2s. each.
Gabriel Conroy.
A Waif of the Plains. With 60 Illustrations by STANLEY L. WOOD.
A Ward of the Golden Gate. With 59 Illustrations by STANLEY L. WOOD.

Crown 8vo, cloth extra, 3s. 6d. each.
A Sappho of Green Springs, &c. With Two Illustrations by HUME NISBET.—Also in picture cloth, flat back, 2s.
Colonel Starbottle's Client, and Some Other People. With a Frontispiece.
Susy: A Novel. With Frontispiece and Vignette by J. A. CHRISTIE.
Sally Dows, &c. With 47 Illustrations by W. D. ALMOND and others.
A Protegee of Jack Hamlin's, &c. With 26 Illustrations by W. SMALL and others.
The Bell-Ringer of Angel's, &c. With 39 Illustrations by DUDLEY HARDY and others.
Clarence: A Story of the American War. With Eight Illustrations by A. JULE GOODMAN.
Barker's Luck, &c. With 39 Illustrations by A. FORESTIER, PAUL HARDY, &c.
Devil's Ford, &c. With a Frontispiece by W. H. OVEREND.
The Crusade of the "Excelsior." With a Frontispiece by J. BERNARD PARTRIDGE.
Three Partners ; or, The Big Strike on Heavy Tree Hill. With 8 Illustrations by J. GULICH.
Tales of Trail and Town. With Frontispiece by G. P. JACOMB-HOOD.

Post 8vo, illustrated boards, 2s. each.
An Heiress of Red Dog. | **The Luck of Roaring Camp.** | **Californian Stories.**

Post 8vo, illustrated boards, 2s. each ; cloth, 2s. 6d. each.
Flip. | **Maruja.** | **A Phyllis of the Sierras.**

Heckethorn (C. W.), Books by.
London Souvenirs. | **London Memories: Social, Historical, and Topographical.**

Helps (Sir Arthur), Books by. Post 8vo, cloth limp, 2s. 6d. each.
Animals and their Masters. | **Social Pressure.**

Ivan de Biron: A Novel. Crown 8vo, cloth extra, 3s. 6d. ; post 8vo, illustrated boards, 2s.

Henderson (Isaac).—Agatha Page: A Novel. Cr. 8vo, cl., 3s. 6d.

Henty (G. A.), Novels by.
Rujub, the Juggler. With Eight Illustrations by STANLEY L. WOOD. Small demy 8vo, cloth, gilt edges, 5s. ; post 8vo, illustrated boards, 2s.
Colonel Thorndyke's Secret. With a Frontispiece by STANLEY L. WOOD. Small demy 8vo, cloth, gilt edges, 5s.

Crown 8vo, cloth, 3s. 6d. each.
The Queen's Cup. | **Dorothy's Double.**

Herman (Henry).—A Leading Lady. Post 8vo, cloth, 2s. 6d.

Herrick's (Robert) Hesperides, Noble Numbers, and Complete
Collected Poems. With Memorial-Introduction and Notes by the Rev. A. B. GROSART, D.D., Steel Portrait, &c. Three Vols., crown 8vo, cloth boards, 3s. 6d. each.

Hertzka (Dr. Theodor).—Freeland: A Social Anticipation. Translated by ARTHUR RANSOM. Crown 8vo, cloth extra, 6s.

Hesse-Wartegg (Chevalier Ernst von).—Tunis: The Land and
the People. With 22 Illustrations. Crown 8vo, cloth extra, 3s. 6d.

Hill (Headon).—Zambra the Detective. Crown 8vo, cloth, 3s. 6d.;
post 8vo, picture boards, 2s.

Hill (John), Works by.
Treason-Felony. Post 8vo, boards, 2s. | **The Common Ancestor.** Cr. 8vo, cloth, 3s. 6d.

Hinkson (H. A.).—Fan Fitzgerald. Crown 8vo, cloth, gilt top, 6s.

Hoey (Mrs. Cashel).—The Lover's Creed. Post 8vo, boards, 2s.

Holliday, Where to go for a. By E. P. SHOLL, Sir H. MAXWELL,
Bart., M.P., JOHN WATSON, JANE BARLOW, MARY LOVETT CAMERON, JUSTIN H. McCARTHY, PAUL LANGE, J. W. GRAHAM, J. H. SALTER, PHŒBE ALLEN, S. J. BECKETT, L. RIVERS VINE and C. F. GORDON CUMMING. Crown 8vo, cloth, 1s. 6d.

Hollingshead (John).—According to My Lights. With a Portrait.
Crown 8vo, cloth, gilt top, 6s.

Holmes (Oliver Wendell), Works by.
The Autocrat of the Breakfast-Table. Illustrated by J. GORDON THOMSON. Post 8vo, cloth limp, 2s. 6d. Another Edition, post 8vo, cloth, 2s.
The Autocrat of the Breakfast-Table and **The Professor at the Breakfast-Table.** In One Vol. Post 8vo, half-bound, 2s.

Hood's (Thomas) Choice Works in Prose and Verse. With Life of the Author, Portrait, and 200 Illustrations. Crown 8vo, cloth, 3s. 6d.
Hood's Whims and Oddities. With 85 Illustrations. Post 8vo, half-bound, 2s.

Hook's (Theodore) Choice Humorous Works; including his Ludicrous Adventures, Bons Mots, Puns, and Hoaxes. With a Life. A New Edition, with a Frontispiece. Crown 8vo, cloth, 3s. 6d.

Hooper (Mrs. Geo.).—The House of Raby. Post 8vo, boards, 2s.

Hopkins (Tighe), Novels by.
For Freedom. Crown 8vo, cloth, 6s.
Crown 8vo, cloth, 3s. 6d. each.
'Twixt Love and Duty. With a Frontispiece. | **The Incomplete Adventurer.**
The Nugents of Carriconna. | **Nell Haffenden.** With 8 Illustrations by C. GREGORY.

Horne (R. Hengist). — Orion: An Epic Poem. With Photograph Portrait by SUMMERS. Tenth Edition. Crown 8vo, cloth extra, 7s.

Hornung (E. W.).—The Shadow of the Rope. Crown 8vo, cloth, gilt top, 6s.

Hugo (Victor).—The Outlaw of Iceland (Han d'Islande). Translated by Sir GILBERT CAMPBELL. Crown 8vo, cloth, 3s. 6d.

Hume (Fergus), Novels by.
The Lady from Nowhere. Crown 8vo, cloth, 3s. 6d. ; picture cloth, flat back, 2s.
The Millionaire Mystery. Crown 8vo, cloth, gilt top, 6s.

Hungerford (Mrs., Author of ' Molly Bawn '), Novels by.
Post 8vo, illustrated boards, 2s. each : cloth limp, 2s. 6d. each.
In Durance Vile. | **An Unsatisfactory Lover.**
Crown 8vo, cloth extra, 3s. 6d. each ; post 8vo, illustrated boards, 2s. each : cloth limp, 2s. 6d. each.
A Maiden All Forlorn. | **Peter's Wife.** | **The Professor's Experiment.**
Marvel. | **Lady Patty.** | **The Three Graces.**
A Modern Circe. | **Lady Verner's Flight.** | **Nora Creina.**
April's Lady. | **The Red-House Mystery.** | **A Mental Struggle.**
Crown 8vo, cloth extra, 3s. 6d. each.
An Anxious Moment. | **The Coming of Chloe.** | **A Point of Conscience.** | **Lovice.**

Hunt's (Leigh) Essays: A Tale for a Chimney Corner, &c. Edited by EDMUND OLLIER. Post 8vo, half-bound, 2s.

Hunt (Mrs. Alfred), Novels by.
Crown 8vo, cloth extra, 3s. 6d. each ; post 8vo, illustrated boards, 2s. each.
The Leaden Casket. | **Self-Condemned.** | **That Other Person.**
Mrs. Juliet. Crown 8vo, cloth extra, 3s. 6d.

Hutchison (W. M.).—Hints on Colt-breaking. With 25 Illustrations. Crown 8vo, cloth extra, 3s. 6d.

Hydrophobia: An Account of M. PASTEUR's System ; The Technique of his Method, and Statistics. By RENAUD SUZOR, M.B. Crown 8vo, cloth extra, 6s.

Impressions (The) of Aureole. Post 8vo, cloth, 2s. 6d.

Indoor Paupers. By ONE OF THEM. Crown 8vo, 1s. ; cloth, 1s. 6d.

Inman (Herbert) and Hartley Aspden.—The Tear of Kalee. Crown 8vo, cloth, gilt top, 6s.

In Memoriam: Verses for every Day in the Year. Selected and arranged by LUCY RIDLEY. Small square 8vo. cloth, 2s. 6d. net : leather, 3s. 6d net.

Innkeeper's Handbook (The) and Licensed Victualler's Manual. By J. TREVOR-DAVIES. A New Edition. Crown 8vo, cloth, 2s.

Irish Wit and Humour, Songs of. Collected and Edited by A. PERCEVAL GRAVES. Post 8vo, cloth limp, 2s. 6d.

Irving (Sir Henry): A Record of over Twenty Years at the Lyceum. By PERCY FITZGERALD. With Portrait. Crown 8vo, cloth, 1s. 6d.

James (C. T. C.). — A Romance of the Queen's Hounds. Post 8vo, cloth limp, 1s. 6d.

Jameson (William).—My Dead Self. Post 8vo, cloth, 2s. 6d.

Japp (Alex. H., LL.D.).—Dramatic Pictures, &c. Cr. 8vo, cloth, 5s.

Jefferies (Richard), Books by. Post 8vo, cloth limp, 2s. 6d. each.
Nature near London. | The Life of the Fields. | The Open Air.
*** Also the HAND-MADE PAPER EDITION, crown 8vo, buckram, gilt top, 6s. each ; and the FINE
PAPER EDITION of **The Life of the Fields.** pott 8vo, cloth, gilt top, 2s. net ; leather, gilt edges, 3s. net.
The Eulogy of Richard Jefferies. By Sir WALTER BESANT. With a Photograph Portrait.
Crown 8vo, cloth extra, 6s.

Jennings (Henry J.), Works by.
Curiosities of Criticism. Post 8vo, cloth limp, 2s. 6d.
Lord Tennyson : A Biographical Sketch. With Portrait. Post 8vo, cloth, 1s. 6d.

Jerome (Jerome K.), Books by.
Stageland. With 64 Illustrations by J. BERNARD PARTRIDGE. Fcap. 4to, picture cover, 1s.
John Ingerfield, &c. With 9 Illusts. by A. S. BOYD and JOHN GULICH. Fcap. 8vo, pic. cov. 1s. 6d.

Jerrold (Douglas).—The Barber's Chair; and The Hedgehog
Letters. Post 8vo, printed on laid paper and half-bound. 2s.

Jerrold (Tom), Works by. Post 8vo, 1s. ea. ; cloth limp, 1s. 6d. each.
The Garden that Paid the Rent.
Household Horticulture : A Gossip about Flowers. Illustrated.

Jesse (Edward).—Scenes and Occupations of a Country Life.
Post 8vo, cloth limp, 2s.

Jones (William, F.S.A.), Works by. Cr. 8vo, cl. extra, 3s. 6d. each.
Finger-Ring Lore : Historical, Legendary, and Anecdotal. With Hundreds of Illustrations.
Crowns and Coronations : A History of Regalia. With 91 Illustrations.

Jonson's (Ben) Works. With Notes Critical and Explanatory, and
a Biographical Memoir by WILLIAM GIFFORD. Edited by Colonel CUNNINGHAM. Three Vols.
crown 8vo, cloth extra, 3s. 6d. each.

Josephus, The Complete Works of. Translated by WHISTON. Con-
taining 'The Antiquities of the Jews' and 'The Wars of the Jews.' With 52 Illustrations and Maps.
Two Vols., demy 8vo, half-cloth, 12s. 6d.

Kempt (Robert).—Pencil and Palette : Chapters on Art and Artists.
Post 8vo, cloth limp, 2s. 6d.

Kershaw (Mark). — Colonial Facts and Fictions : Humorous
Sketches. Post 8vo, illustrated boards, 2s. ; cloth, 2s. 6d.

King (R. Ashe), Novels by. Post 8vo, illustrated boards, 2s. each.
'The Wearing of the Green.' | Passion's Slave. | Bell Barry.
A Drawn Game. Crown 8vo, cloth, 3s. 6d. ; post 8vo, illustrated boards, 2s.

Kipling Primer (A). Including Biographical and Critical Chapters,
an Index to Mr. Kipling's principal Writings, and Bibliographies. By F. L. KNOWLES, Editor of
'The Golden Treasury of American Lyrics.' With Two Portraits. Crown 8vo, cloth, 3s. 6d.

Knight (William, M.R.C.S., and Edward, L.R.C.P.). — The
Patient's Vade Mecum : How to Get Most Benefit from Medical Advice. Cr. 8vo, cloth, 1s. 6d.

Knights (The) of the Lion : A Romance of the Thirteenth Century.
Edited, with an Introduction, by the MARQUESS OF LORNE, K.T. Crown 8vo, cloth extra, 6s.

Lambert (George).—The President of Boravia. Crown 8vo, cl., 3s. 6d.

Lamb's (Charles) Complete Works in Prose and Verse, including
'Poetry for Children' and 'Prince Dorus.' Edited, with Notes and Introduction, by R. H. SHEP-
HERD. With Two Portraits and Facsimile of the 'Essay on Roast Pig.' Crown 8vo, cloth, 3s. 6d.
The Essays of Elia. Post 8vo, printed on laid paper and half-bound, 2s.
Little Essays : Sketches and Characters by CHARLES LAMB, selected from his Letters by PERCY
FITZGERALD. Post 8vo, cloth limp, 2s. 6d.
The Dramatic Essays of Charles Lamb. With Introduction and Notes by BRANDER MAT-
THEWS, and Steel-plate Portrait. Fcap. 8vo, half-bound, 2s. 6d.

Landor (Walter Savage).—Citation and Examination of William
Shakspeare, &c. before Sir Thomas Lucy, touching Deer-stealing, 19th September, 1582. To which
is added, A Conference of Master Edmund Spenser with the Earl of Essex, touching the
State of Ireland, 1595. Fcap. 8vo, half-Roxburghe, 2s. 6d.

Lane (Edward William).—The Thousand and One Nights, com-
monly called in England The Arabian Nights' Entertainments. Translated from the Arabic,
with Notes. Illustrated with many hundred Engravings from Designs by HARVEY. Edited by EDWARD
STANLEY POOLE. With Preface by STANLEY LANE-POOLE. Three Vols., demy 8vo, cloth, 7s. 6d. ea.

Larwood (Jacob), Works by.
Anecdotes of the Clergy. Post 8vo, laid paper, half-bound, 2s.
Post 8vo, cloth limp, 2s. 6d. each.
Forensic Anecdotes. | Theatrical Anecdotes.

Lehmann (R. C.), Works by. Post 8vo, cloth, 1s. 6d. each.
Harry Fludyer at Cambridge.
Conversational Hints for Young Shooters: A Guide to Polite Talk.

Leigh (Henry S.).—Carols of Cockayne. Printed on hand-made paper, bound in buckram, 5s.

Leland (C. Godfrey). — A Manual of Mending and Repairing. With Diagrams. Crown 8vo, cloth, 5s.

Lepelletier (Edmond). — Madame Sans-Gène. Translated from the French by JOHN DE VILLIERS. Post 8vo, cloth, 3s. 6d. ; picture boards, 2s.

Leys (John K.), Novels by.
The Lindsays. Post 8vo, picture bds., 2s. | A Sore Temptation. Cr. 8vo, cloth, gilt top, 6s.

Lilburn (Adam).—A Tragedy in Marble. Crown 8vo, cloth, 3s. 6d.

Lindsay (Harry, Author of 'Methodist Idylls'), Novels by.
Crown 8vo, cloth, 3s. 6d. each.
Rhoda Roberts. | The Jacobite: A Romance of the Conspiracy of 'The Forty.'
Judah Pyecroft, Puritan. Crown 8vo, cloth, gilt top, 6s.

Linton (E. Lynn), Works by.
An Octave of Friends. Crown 8vo, cloth, 3s. 6d.
Crown 8vo, cloth extra, 3s. 6d. each ; post 8vo, illustrated boards, 2s. each.
Patricia Kemball. | Ione.   Under which Lord? With 12 Illustrations.
The Atonement of Leam Dundas.   'My Love!' | Sowing the Wind.
The World Well Lost. With 12 Illusts.   Paston Carew, Millionaire and Miser.
The One Too Many.   Dulcie Everton. | With a Silken Thread.
                    The Rebel of the Family.
                    Post 8vo, cloth limp, 2s. 6d. each.
Witch Stories. | Ourselves: Essays on Women.
Freeshooting: Extracts from the Works of Mrs. LYNN LINTON.

Lowe (Charles, M.A.).—Our Greatest Living Soldiers. With 8 Portraits. Crown 8vo, cloth, 3s. 6d.

Lucy (Henry W.).—Gideon Fleyce: A Novel. Crown 8vo, cloth extra, 3s. 6d. ; post 8vo, illustrated boards, 2s.

Macalpine (Avery), Novels by.
Teresa Itasca. Crown 8vo, cloth extra, 1s.
Broken Wings. With Six Illustrations by W. J. HENNESSY. Crown 8vo, cloth extra, 6s.

MacColl (Hugh), Novels by.
Mr. Stranger's Sealed Packet. Post 8vo, illustrated boards, 2s.
Ednor Whitlock. Crown 8vo, cloth extra, 6s.

Macdonell (Agnes).—Quaker Cousins. Post 8vo, boards, 2s.

MacGregor (Robert).—Pastimes and Players: Notes on Popular Games. Post 8vo, cloth limp, 2s. 6d.

Mackay (Charles, LL.D.). — Interludes and Undertones; or, Music at Twilight. Crown 8vo, cloth extra 6s.

Mackenna (Stephen J.) and J. Augustus O'Shea.—Brave Men in Action: Thrilling Stories of the British Flag. With 8 Illustrations by STANLEY L. WOOD. Small demy 8vo, cloth, gilt edges, 5s.

McCarthy (Justin), Works by.
A History of Our Own Times, from the Accession of Queen Victoria to the General Election of 1880. LIBRARY EDITION. Four Vols., demy 8vo, cloth extra, 12s. each.– Also a POPULAR EDITION, in Four Vols., crown 8vo, cloth extra, 6s. each.–And the JUBILEE EDITION, with an Appendix of Events to the end of 1886, in Two Vols., large crown 8vo, cloth extra, 7s. 6d. each.
A History of Our Own Times, from 1880 to the Diamond Jubilee. Demy 8vo, cloth extra, 12s. ; or crown 8vo, cloth, 6s.
A Short History of Our Own Times. One Vol., crown 8vo, cloth extra, 6s.–Also a CHEAP POPULAR EDITION, post 8vo, cloth limp, 2s. 6d.
A History of the Four Georges and of William the Fourth. By JUSTIN MCCARTHY and JUSTIN HUNTLY MCCARTHY. Four Vols., demy 8vo, cloth extra, 12s. each.
The Reign of Queen Anne. 2 vols., demy 8vo, cloth, 12s each.   [Preparing.
Reminiscences. With a Portrait. Two Vols., demy 8vo, cloth, 24s.   [Vols. III. & IV. shortly.
Crown 8vo, cloth extra, 3s. 6d. each ; post 8vo, illustrated boards, 2s. each ; cloth limp, 2s. 6d. each.
The Waterdale Neighbours.   Donna Quixote. With 12 Illustrations.
My Enemy's Daughter.   The Comet of a Season.
A Fair Saxon. | Linley Rochford.   Maid of Athens. With 12 Illustrations.
Dear Lady Disdain. | The Dictator.   Camiola: A Girl with a Fortune.
Miss Misanthrope. With 12 Illustrations. Red Diamonds. | The Riddle Ring.
The Three Disgraces, and other Stories. Crown 8vo, cloth, 3s. 6d.
Mononia: A Love Story of "Forty-eight." Crown 8vo, cloth, gilt top, 6s.
'The Right Honourable.' By JUSTIN MCCARTHY and Mrs. CAMPBELL PRAED. Crown 8vo, cloth extra, 6s.

McCarthy (Justin Huntly), Works by.
The French Revolution. (Constituent Assembly, 1789-91). Four Vols., demy 8vo, cloth, 12s. each.
An Outline of the History of Ireland. Crown 8vo, 1s.; cloth, 1s. 6d.
Ireland Since the Union: Sketches of Irish History, 1798-1886. Crown 8vo, cloth, 6s.
Hafiz in London: Poems. Small 8vo, gold cloth, 3s. 6d.
Our Sensation Novel. Crown 8vo, picture cover, 1s.; cloth limp, 1s. 6d.
Doom: An Atlantic Episode. Crown 8vo, picture cover, 1s.
Dolly: A Sketch. Crown 8vo, picture cover, 1s.; cloth limp, 1s. 6d.
Lily Lass: A Romance. Crown 8vo, picture cover, 1s.; cloth limp, 1s. 6d.
A London Legend. Crown 8vo, cloth, 3s. 6d.
The Royal Christopher. Crown 8vo, cloth, 3s. 6d.

MacDonald (George, LL.D.), Books by.
Works of Fancy and Imagination. Ten Vols., 16mo, cloth, gilt edges, in cloth case, 21s.; or the Volumes may be had separately, in Grolier cloth, at 2s. 6d. each.
Vol. I. WITHIN AND WITHOUT.—THE HIDDEN LIFE.
" II. THE DISCIPLE.—THE GOSPEL WOMEN.—BOOK OF SONNETS.—ORGAN SONGS.
" III. VIOLIN SONGS.—SONGS OF THE DAYS AND NIGHTS.—A BOOK OF DREAMS.—ROADSIDE POEMS.—POEMS FOR CHILDREN.
" IV. PARABLES.—BALLADS.—SCOTCH SONGS.
" V. & VI. PHANTASTES: A Faerie Romance. | Vol. VII. THE PORTENT.
" VIII. THE LIGHT PRINCESS.—THE GIANT'S HEART.—SHADOWS.
" IX. CROSS PURPOSES.—THE GOLDEN KEY.—THE CARASOYN.—LITTLE DAYLIGHT.
" X. THE CRUEL PAINTER.—THE WOW O' RIVVEN.—THE CASTLE.—THE BROKEN SWORDS.—THE GRAY WOLF.—UNCLE CORNELIUS.
Poetical Works of George MacDonald. Collected and Arranged by the Author. Two Vols. crown 8vo, buckram, 12s.
A Threefold Cord. Edited by GEORGE MACDONALD. Post 8vo, cloth, 5s.
Phantastes: A Faerie Romance. With 25 Illustrations by J. BELL. Crown 8vo, cloth extra, 3s. 6d.
Heather and Snow: A Novel. Crown 8vo, cloth extra, 3s. 6d.; post 8vo, illustrated boards, 2s.
Lilith: A Romance. SECOND EDITION. Crown 8vo, cloth extra, 6s.

Machray (Robert).—A Blow over the Heart. Crown 8vo, cloth,
gilt top, 6s.

Maclise Portrait Gallery (The) of Illustrious Literary Charac-
ters: 85 Portraits by DANIEL MACLISE; with Memoirs—Biographical, Critical, Bibliographical, and Anecdotal—illustrative of the Literature of the former half of the Present Century, by WILLIAM BATES, B.A. Crown 8vo, cloth extra, 3s. 6d.

Macquoid (Mrs.), Works by. Square 8vo, cloth extra, 6s. each.
In the Ardennes. With 50 Illustrations by THOMAS R. MACQUOID.
Pictures and Legends from Normandy and Brittany. 34 Illusts. by T. R. MACQUOID.
Through Normandy. With 92 Illustrations by T. R. MACQUOID, and a Map.
About Yorkshire. With 67 Illustrations by T. R. MACQUOID.

Magician's Own Book, The: Performances with Eggs, Hats, &c.
Edited by W. H. CREMER. With 200 Illustrations. Crown 8vo, cloth extra, 4s. 6d.

Magic Lantern, The, and its Management: Including full Practical
Directions. By T. C. HEPWORTH. With 10 Illustrations. Crown 8vo, 1s.; cloth, 1s. 6d.

Magna Charta: An Exact Facsimile of the Original in the British
Museum, 3 feet by 2 feet, with Arms and Seals emblazoned in Gold and Colours, 5s.

Mallory (Sir Thomas). — Mort d'Arthur: The Stories of King
Arthur and of the Knights of the Round Table. (A Selection.) Edited by B. MONTGOMERIE RANKING. Post 8vo, cloth limp, 2s.

Mallock (W. H.), Works by.
The New Republic. Post 8vo, cloth, 3s. 6d.; picture boards, 2s.
The New Paul and Virginia: Positivism on an Island. Post 8vo, cloth, 2s. 6d.
Poems. Small 4to, parchment, 8s. | **Is Life Worth Living?** Crown 8vo, cloth extra, 6s.

Margueritte (Paul and Victor).—The Disaster. Translated by
FREDERIC LEES. Crown 8vo, cloth, 3s. 6d.

Marlowe's Works. Including his Translations. Edited, with Notes
and Introductions, by Colonel CUNNINGHAM. Crown 8vo, cloth extra, 3s. 6d.

Massinger's Plays. From the Text of WILLIAM GIFFORD. Edited
by Col. CUNNINGHAM. Crown 8vo, cloth extra, 3s. 6d.

Matthews (Brander).—A Secret of the Sea, &c. Post 8vo, illus-
trated boards, 2s.; cloth limp, 2s. 6d.

Max O'Rell, Books by. Crown 8vo, cloth, 3s. 6d. each.
Her Royal Highness Woman. | **Studies in Cheerfulness.**

Merivale (Herman).—Bar, Stage, and Platform: Autobiographic
Memories. Crown 8vo, cloth, 6s.

Merrick (Leonard), Novels by.
The Man who was Good. Post 8vo, picture boards, 2s.
Crown 8vo, cloth, 3s. 6d. each.
This Stage of Fools. | **Cynthia:** A Daughter of the Philistines.

Meade (L. T.), Novels by.
A Soldier of Fortune. Crown 8vo, cloth, 3s. 6d.; post 8vo, illustrated boards, 2s.

Crown 8vo, cloth, 3s. 6d. each.

The Voice of the Charmer. With 8 Illustrations. | A Son of Ishmael.
In an Iron Grip. | On the Brink of a Chasm. | An Adventuress.
The Siren. | The Way of a Woman. | The Blue Diamond.
Dr. Rumsey's Patient. By L. T. MEADE and CLIFFORD HALIFAX, M.D.

Crown 8vo, cloth. gilt top, 6s. each.

This Troublesome World. SECOND EDITION. | A Stumble by the Way.

Mexican Mustang (On a), through Texas to the Rio Grande. By
A. E. SWEET and J. ARMOY KNOX. With 265 Illustrations. Crown 8vo, cloth extra, 7s. 6d.

Miller (Mrs. F. Fenwick).—Physiology for the Young; or, The
House of Life. With numerous Illustrations. Post 8vo, cloth limp, 2s. 6d.

Milton (J. L.), Works by. Post 8vo, 1s. each ; cloth, 1s. 6d. each.
The Hygiene of the Skin. With Directions for Diet, Soaps, Baths, Wines, &c.
The Bath in Diseases of the Skin.
The Laws of Life, and their Relation to Diseases of the Skin.

Minto (Wm.).—Was She Good or Bad? Crown 8vo, cloth, 1s. 6d.

Mitchell (Edmund), Novels by. Crown 8vo, cloth, gilt top, 6s. each.
The Lone Star Rush. With 8 Illustrations by NORMAN H. HARDY.
Only a Nigger.

Crown 8vo, picture cloth, flat backs, 2s. each.

Plotters of Paris. | The Temple of Death. | Towards the Eternal Snows.

Mitford (Bertram), Novels by. Crown 8vo, cloth extra, 3s. 6d. each.
The Gun-Runner: A Romance of Zululand. With a Frontispiece by STANLEY L. WOOD.
The King's Assegai. With Six full-page Illustrations by STANLEY L. WOOD.
Renshaw Fanning's Quest. With a Frontispiece by STANLEY L. WOOD.
The Luck of Gerard Ridgeley. Crown 8vo, picture cloth, flat back, 2s.
The Triumph of Hilary Blachland. Crown 8vo, cloth, gilt top, 6s.

Molesworth (Mrs.).—Hathercourt Rectory. Crown 8vo, cloth,
3s. 6d.; post 8vo, illustrated boards, 2s.

Moncrieff (W. D. Scott-).—The Abdication: An Historical Drama.
With Seven Etchings by JOHN PETTIE, W. Q. ORCHARDSON, J. MACWHIRTER, COLIN HUNTER,
R. MACBETH and TOM GRAHAM. Imperial 4to, buckram, 21s.

Montagu (Irving).—Things I Have Seen in War. With 16 full-
page Illustrations. Crown 8vo, cloth, 6s.

Moore (Thomas), Works by.
The Epicurean; and Alciphron. Post 8vo, half-bound, 2s.
Prose and Verse; including Suppressed Passages from the MEMOIRS OF LORD BYRON. Edited
by R. H. SHEPHERD. With Portrait. Crown 8vo, cloth extra, 7s. 6d.

Morrow (W. C.).—Bohemian Paris of To-Day. With 106 Illustra-
tions by EDOUARD CUCUEL. Small demy 8vo, cloth, gilt top, 6s.

Muddock (J. E.), Stories by.
Crown 8vo, cloth extra, 3s. 6d. each.

Maid Marian and Robin Hood. With 12 Illustrations by STANLEY WOOD.
Basile the Jester. With Frontispiece by STANLEY WOOD.
Young Lochinvar. | The Golden Idol.

Post 8vo, illustrated boards, 2s. each.

The Dead Man's Secret. | From the Bosom of the Deep.
Stories Weird and Wonderful. Post 8vo, illustrated boards, 2s.; cloth, 2s. 6d.

Murray (D. Christie), Novels by.
Crown 8vo, cloth extra, 3s. 6d. each ; post 8vo, illustrated boards, 2s. each.

A Life's Atonement. | A Model Father. | Bob Martin's Little Girl.
Joseph's Coat. 12 Illusts. | Old Blazer's Hero. | Time's Revenges.
Coals of Fire. 3 Illusts. | Cynic Fortune. Frontisp. | A Wasted Crime.
Val Strange. | By the Gate of the Sea. | In Direst Peril.
Hearts. | A Bit of Human Nature. | Mount Despair.
The Way of the World. | First Person Singular. | A Capful o' Nails.
The Making of a Novelist: An Experiment in Autobiography. With a Collotype Portrait. Cr.
8vo, buckram, 3s. 6d.
My Contemporaries in Fiction. Crown 8vo, buckram, 3s. 6d.
His Own Ghost. Crown 8vo, cloth, 3s. 6d.; picture cloth, flat back, 2s.

Crown 8vo, cloth, 3s. 6d. each.

This Little World. | A Race for Millions.
Tales in Prose and Verse. With Frontispiece by ARTHUR HOPKINS.

Crown 8vo, cloth, gilt top, 6s. each.

The Church of Humanity. | Despair's Last Journey.

Murray (D. Christie) and Henry Herman, Novels by.
Crown 8vo, cloth extra, 3s. 6d. each ; post 8vo, illustrated boards, 2s. each.

One Traveller Returns. | The Bishops' Bible.
Paul Jones's Alias, &c. With Illustrations by A. FORESTIER and G. NICOLET.

Murray (Henry), Novels by.
Post 8vo, cloth, 2s. 6d. each.

A Game of Bluff. | A Song of Sixpence.

Newbolt (H.).—Taken from the Enemy. Post 8vo, leatherette, 1s.

Nisbet (Hume), Books by.
'Bail Up.' Crown 8vo, cloth extra, 3s. 6d. ; post 8vo, illustrated boards, 2s.
Dr. Bernard St. Vincent. Post 8vo, illustrated boards, 2s.

Lessons in Art. With 21 Illustrations. Crown 8vo, cloth extra, 2s. 6d.

Norris (W. E.), Novels by. Crown 8vo, cloth, 3s. 6d. each ; post 8vo,
picture boards, 2s. each.
Saint Ann's. | Billy Bellew. With a Frontispiece by F. H. TOWNSEND.

Miss Wentworth's Idea. Crown 8vo, cloth, 3s. 6d.

Oakley (John).—A Gentleman in Khaki: A Story of the South
African War. Demy 8vo, picture cover, 1s.

Ohnet (Georges), Novels by. Post 8vo, illustrated boards, 2s. each.
Doctor Rameau. | A Last Love.

A Weird Gift. Crown 8v cloth, 3s. 6d. ; post 8vo, picture boards, 2s.
Love's Depths. Translated by F. ROTHWELL. Crown 8vo, cloth, 3s. 6d.

Oliphant (Mrs.), Novels by. Post 8vo, illustrated boards, 2s. each.
The Primrose Path. | Whiteladies.
The Greatest Heiress in England.

The Sorceress. Crown 8vo, cloth, 3s. 6d.

O'Shaughnessy (Arthur), Poems by :
Fcap. 8vo, cloth extra, 7s. 6d. each.
Music and Moonlight. | Songs of a Worker.

Lays of France. Crown 8vo, cloth extra, 10s. 6d.

Ouida, Novels by. Cr. 8vo, cl., 3s. 6d. ea.; post 8vo, illust. bds., 2s. ea.
Held in Bondage. | A Dog of Flanders. | In Maremma. | Wanda.
Tricotrin. | Pascarel. | Signa. | Bimbi. | Syrlin.
Strathmore. | Chandos. | Two Wooden Shoes. | Frescoes. | Othmar.
Cecil Castlemaine's Gage | In a Winter City. | Princess Napraxine.
Under Two Flags. | Ariadne. | Friendship. | Guilderoy. | Ruffino.
Puck. | Idalia. | A Village Commune. | Two Offenders.
Folle-Farine. | Moths. | Pipistrello. | Santa Barbara.

POPULAR EDITIONS. Medium 8vo, 6d. each ; cloth, 1s. each.
Under Two Flags. | Moths.

Medium 8vo, 6d. each.
Held in Bondage. | Puck.

The Waters of Edera. Crown 8vo, cloth, 3s. 6d. ; picture cloth, flat back, 2s.
Wisdom, Wit, and Pathos, selected from the Works of OUIDA by F. SYDNEY MORRIS. Post
8vo, cloth extra, 5s.—CHEAP EDITION, illustrated boards, 2s.

Pandurang Hari; or, Memoirs of a Hindoo. With Preface by Sir
BARTLE FRERE. Post 8vo, illustrated boards, 2s.

Paris Salon, The Illustrated Catalogue of the, for 1902. (Twenty-
fourth Year.) With over 300 Illustrations. Demy 8vo, 3s. [May.

Payn (James), Novels by.
Crown 8vo, cloth extra, 3s. 6d. each ; post 8vo, illustrated boards, 2s. each.

Lost Sir Massingberd. | The Family Scapegrace.
A County Family. | Holiday Tasks.
Less Black than We're Painted. | The Talk of the Town. With 12 Illusts.
By Proxy. | For Cash Only. | The Mystery of Mirbridge.
High Spirits. | The Word and the Will.
A Confidential Agent. With 12 Illusts. | The Burnt Million.
A Grape from a Thorn. With 12 Illusts. | Sunny Stories. | A Trying Patient.

Post 8vo illustrated boards, 2s. each.

Humorous Stories. | From Exile. | Found Dead. Gwendoline's Harvest.
The Foster Brothers. | Mirk Abbey. A Marine Residence.
Married Beneath Him. | The Canon's Ward.
Bentinck's Tutor. | Walter's Word. | Not Wooed, But Won.
A Perfect Treasure. | Two Hundred Pounds Reward.
Like Father, Like Son. | The Best of Husbands.
A Woman's Vengeance. | Halves. | What He Cost Her.
Carlyon's Year. | Cecil's Tryst. | Fallen Fortunes. Kit: A Memory.
Murphy's Master. | At Her Mercy. | Under One Roof. Glow-worm Tales.
The Clyffards of Clyffe. | A Prince of the Blood.
Some Private Views.

A Modern Dick Whittington ; or, A Patron of Letters. With a Portrait of the Author. Crown
8vo, cloth, 3s. 6d. ; picture cloth, flat back, 2s.
In Peril and Privation. With 17 Illustrations. Crown 8vo, cloth, 3s. 6d.
Notes from the 'News.' Crown 8vo, cloth, 1s. 6d.

Pascal's Provincial Letters. A New Translation, with Historical Introduction and Notes by T. M'CRIE, D.D. Post 8vo, half-cloth, 2s.

Paul (Margaret A.).—Gentle and Simple. Crown 8vo, cloth, with Frontispiece by HELEN PATERSON, 3s. 6d.; post 8vo, illustrated boards, 2s.

Payne (Will).—Jerry the Dreamer. Crown 8vo, cloth, 3s. 6d.

Pennell (H. Cholmondeley), Works by. Post 8vo, cloth, 2s. 6d. ea.
Puck on Pegasus. With Illustrations.
Pegasus Re-Saddled. With Ten full-page Illustrations by G. DU MAURIER.
The Muses of Mayfair: Vers de Société. Selected by H. C. PENNELL.

Phelps (E. Stuart), Works by. Post 8vo, cloth, 1s. 6d. each.
An Old Maid's Paradise. | **Burglars in Paradise.**
Beyond the Gates. Post 8vo, picture cover, 1s.; cloth, 1s. 6d.
Jack the Fisherman. Illustrated by C. W. REED. Crown 8vo, cloth, 1s. 6d.

Phil May's Sketch-Book. Containing 54 Humorous Cartoons. Crown folio, cloth, 2s. 6d.

Phipson (Dr. T. L.), Books by. Crown 8vo, art canvas, gilt top, 5s. ea.
Famous Violinists and Fine Violins.
Voice and Violin: Sketches, Anecdotes, and Reminiscences.

Planche (J. R.), Works by.
The Pursuivant of Arms. With Six Plates and 209 Illustrations. Crown 8vo, cloth, 7s. 6d.
Songs and Poems, 1819-1879. With Introduction by Mrs. MACKARNESS. Crown 8vo, cloth, 6s.

Plutarch's Lives of Illustrious Men. With Notes and a Life of Plutarch by JOHN and WM. LANGHORNE, and Portraits. Two Vols., demy 8vo, half-cloth 10s. 6d.

Poe's (Edgar Allan) Choice Works: Poems, Stories, Essays. With an Introduction by CHARLES BAUDELAIRE. Crown 8vo, cloth, 3s. 6d.

Pollock (W. H.).—The Charm, and other Drawing-room Plays. By Sir WALTER BESANT and WALTER H. POLLOCK. With 50 Illustrations. Crown 8vo, cloth gilt, 6s.

Pond (Major J. B.).—Eccentricities of Genius: Memories of Famous Men and Women of the Platform and the Stage. With 91 Portraits. Demy 8vo, cloth, 12s.

Pope's Poetical Works. Post 8vo, cloth limp, 2s.

Porter (John).—Kingsclere. Edited by BYRON WEBBER. With 19 full-page and many smaller Illustrations. Cheaper Edition. Demy 8vo, cloth, 7s. 6d.

Praed (Mrs. Campbell), Novels by. Post 8vo, illust. bds., 2s. each.
The Romance of a Station. | **The Soul of Countess Adrian.**
Crown 8vo, cloth, 3s. 6d. each; post 8vo, boards, 2s. each.
Outlaw and Lawmaker. | **Christina Chard.** With Frontispiece by W PAGET.
Mrs. Tregaskiss. With 8 Illustrations by ROBERT SAUBER.
Crown 8vo, cloth, 3s. 6d. each.
Nulma. | **Madame Izan.** | **'As a Watch in the Night.'**

Price (E. C.).—Valentina. Crown 8vo, cloth, 3s. 6d.

Princess Olga.—Radna: A Novel. Crown 8vo, cloth extra, 6s.

Pryce (Richard).—Miss Maxwell's Affections. Crown 8vo, cloth, with Frontispiece by HAL LUDLOW, 3s. 6d.; post 8vo, illustrated boards, 2s.

Proctor (Richard A.), Works by.
Flowers of the Sky. With 55 Illustrations. Small crown 8vo, cloth extra, 3s. 6d.
Easy Star Lessons. With Star Maps for every Night in the Year. Crown 8vo, cloth, 6s.
Familiar Science Studies. Crown 8vo, cloth extra, 6s.
Saturn and its System. With 13 Steel Plates. Demy 8vo, cloth extra, 10s. 6d.
Mysteries of Time and Space. With numerous Illustrations. Crown 8vo, cloth extra, 6s.
The Universe of Suns, &c. With numerous Illustrations. Crown 8vo, cloth extra, 6s.
Wages and Wants of Science Workers. Crown 8vo, 1s. 6d.

Rambosson (J.).—Popular Astronomy. Translated by C. B. PITMAN. With 10 Coloured Plates and 63 Woodcut Illustrations. Crown 8vo, cloth, 3s. 6d.

Randolph (Col. G.).—Aunt Abigail Dykes. Crown 8vo, cloth, 7s. 6d.

Read (General Meredith).—Historic Studies in Vaud, Berne, and Savoy. With 31 full-page Illustrations. Two Vols., demy 8vo, cloth, 28s.

Richardson (Frank).—The King's Counsel. Cr. 8vo, cl., gilt top, 6s.

Riddell (Mrs. J. H.), Novels by.
A Rich Man's Daughter. Crown 8vo, cloth, 3s. 6d.
Weird Stories. Crown 8vo, cloth extra, 3s. 6d.; post 8vo, illustrated boards, 2s.
Post 8vo, illustrated boards, 2s. each.
The Uninhabited House. | **Fairy Water.**
The Prince of Wales's Garden Party. | **Her Mother's Darling.**
The Mystery in Palace Gardens. | **The Nun's Curse.** | **Idle Tales.**

Reade's (Charles) Novels.

The New Collected LIBRARY EDITION, complete in Seventeen Volumes, set in new long primer type, printed on laid paper, and elegantly bound in cloth, price 3s. 6d. each.

1. Peg Woffington; and Christie Johnstone.
2. Hard Cash.
3. The Cloister and the Hearth. With a Preface by Sir WALTER BESANT.
4. 'It is Never Too Late to Mend.'
5. The Course of True Love Never Did Run Smooth; and Singleheart and Doubleface.
6. The Autobiography of a Thief; Jack of all Trades; A Hero and a Martyr; and The Wandering Heir.
7. Love Me Little, Love me Long.
8. The Double Marriage.
9. Griffith Gaunt.
10. Foul Play.
11. Put Yourself in His Place.
12. A Terrible Temptation.
13. A Simpleton.
14. A Woman-Hater.
15. The Jilt, and other Stories: and Good Stories of Man and other Animals.
16. A Perilous Secret.
17. Readiana; and Bible Characters.

In Twenty-one Volumes, post 8vo, illustrated boards, 2s. each.

Peg Woffington. | Christie Johnstone.
'It is Never Too Late to Mend.'
The Course of True Love Never Did Run Smooth.
The Autobiography of a Thief; Jack of all Trades; and James Lambert.
Love Me Little, Love Me Long.
The Double Marriage.
The Cloister and the Hearth.
Hard Cash. | Griffith Gaunt.
Foul Play. | Put Yourself in His Place.
A Terrible Temptation.
A Simpleton. | The Wandering Heir.
A Woman-Hater.
Singleheart and Doubleface.
Good Stories of Man and other Animals.
The Jilt, and other Stories.
A Perilous Secret. | Readiana.

LARGE TYPE, FINE PAPER EDITIONS. Pott 8vo, cl., gilt top, 2s. net ea.; leather, gilt edges, 3s. net ea.
The Cloister and the Hearth. | 'It is Never Too Late to Mend.'

POPULAR EDITIONS. Medium 8vo, 6d. each; cloth, 1s. each.
Peg Woffington; and Christie Johnstone. | Hard Cash.

Medium 8vo, 6d. each.
'It is Never Too Late to Mend.' | The Cloister and the Hearth. | Foul Play.

Christie Johnstone. With Frontispiece. Choicely printed in Elzevir style. Fcap. 8vo, half-Roxb. 2s. 6d.
Peg Woffington. Choicely printed in Elzevir style. Fcap. 8vo, half-Roxburghe, 2s. 6d.
The Cloister and the Hearth. In Four Vols., post 8vo, with an Introduction by Sir WALTER BESANT, and a Frontispiece to each Vol., buckram, gilt top, 6s. the set.
The Cloister and the Hearth. NEW ILLUSTRATED EDITION, with 16 Photogravure and 84 half-tone Illustrations by MATT B. HEWERDINE. Small 4to, cloth gilt and gilt top, 10s. 6d. net.
Bible Characters. Fcap. 8vo, leatherette, 1s.
Selections from the Works of Charles Reade. With an Introduction by Mrs. ALEX. IRELAND. Post 8vo, cloth limp, 2s. 6d.

Rimmer (Alfred), Works by. Large crown 8vo, cloth, 3s. 6d. each.

Rambles Round Eton and Harrow. With 52 Illustrations by the Author.
About England with Dickens. With 58 Illustrations by C. A. VANDERHOOP and A. RIMMER.

Rives (Amelie, Author of 'The Quick or the Dead?'), Stories by.

Crown 8vo, cloth, 3s. 6d. each.
Barbara Dering. | Meriel: A Love Story.

Robinson Crusoe. By DANIEL DEFOE. With 37 Illustrations by

GEORGE CRUIKSHANK. Post 8vo, half-cloth, 2s.

Robinson (F. W.), Novels by.

Women are Strange. Post 8vo, illustrated boards, 2s.
The Hands of Justice. Crown 8vo, cloth extra, 3s. 6d.; post 8vo illustrated boards, 2s.
The Woman in the Dark. Crown 8vo, cloth, 3s. 6d.; post 8vo, illustrated boards, 2s.

Robinson (Phil), Works by. Crown 8vo, cloth extra, 6s. each.

The Poets' Birds. | The Poets' Beasts.
The Poets and Nature: Reptiles, Fishes, and Insects.

Roll of Battle Abbey, The: A List of the Principal Warriors who

came from Normandy with William the Conqueror, 1066. Printed in Gold and Colours, 5s.

Rosengarten (A.).—A Handbook of Architectural Styles. Trans-

lated by W. COLLETT-SANDARS. With 639 Illustrations. Crown 8vo, cloth extra, 6d.

Ross (Albert).—A Sugar Princess. Crown 8vo, cloth, 3s. 6d.

Rowley (Hon. Hugh), Works by. Post 8vo, cloth, 2s. 6d. each.

Puniana: Riddles and Jokes. With numerous Illustrations.
More Puniana. Profusely Illustrated.

Runciman (James), Stories by.

Schools and Scholars. Post 8vo, cloth, 2s. 6d.
Skippers and Shellbacks. Crown 8vo, cloth, 3s. 6d.

Russell (Dora), Novels by.

A Country Sweetheart. Post 8vo, picture boards, 2s.
The Drift of Fate. Crown 8vo, cloth, 3s. 6d.; picture cloth, flat back 2s.

Russell (Herbert).—True Blue; or, 'The Lass that Loved a Sailor.'

Crown 8vo, cloth, 3s. 6d.

Russell (W. Clark), Novels, &c., by.

Crown 8vo, cloth extra, 3s. 6d. each; post 8vo, illustrated boards, 2s. each; cloth limp, 2s. 6d. each.

Round the Galley-Fire.	An Ocean Tragedy.
In the Middle Watch.	My Shipmate Louise.
On the Fo'k'sle Head.	Alone on a Wide Wide Sea.
A Voyage to the Cape.	The Good Ship 'Mohock.'
A Book for the Hammock.	The Phantom Death.
The Mystery of the 'Ocean Star.'	Is He the Man?	The Convict Ship.
The Romance of Jenny Harlowe.	Heart of Oak.	The Last Entry.

The Tale of the Ten.

Crown 8vo, cloth, 3s. 6d. each.

A Tale of Two Tunnels. | The Death Ship.

The Ship: Her Story. With 50 Illustrations by H. C. SEPPINGS WRIGHT. Small 4to, cloth, 6s.
The 'Pretty Polly': A Voyage of Incident. With 12 lustrations by G. E. ROBERTSON. Large crown 8vo, cloth, gilt edges, 5s.

Saint Aubyn (Alan), Novels by.

Crown 8vo, cloth extra, 3s. 6d. each; post 8vo, illustrated boards, 2s. each.

A Fellow of Trinity. With a Note by OLIVER WENDELL HOLMES and a Frontispiece.

The Junior Dean.	The Master of St. Benedict's.	To His Own Master.
Orchard Damerel.	In the Face of the World.	The Tremlett Diamonds

Fcap. 8vo, cloth boards, 1s. 6d. each.

The Old Maid's Sweetheart. | Modest Little Sara.

Crown 8vo, cloth, 3s. 6d. each.

The Wooing of May.	A Tragic Honeymoon.	A Proctor's Wooing.
Fortune's Gate.	Gallantry Bower.	Bonnie Maggie Lauder.
Mary Unwin. With 8 Illustrations by PERCY TARRANT.		Mrs. Dunbar's Secret.

Saint John (Bayle).—A Levantine Family. A New Edition.
Crown 8vo, cloth, 3s. 6d.

Sala (George A.).—Gaslight and Daylight. Post 8vo, boards, 2s.

Scotland Yard, Past and Present: Experiences of Thirty-seven Years.
By Ex-Chief-Inspector CAVANAGH. Post 8vo, illustrated boards, 2s.; cloth, 2s. 6d.

Secret Out, The: One Thousand Tricks with Cards; with Entertaining Experiments in Drawing-room or 'White' Magic. By W. H. CREMER. With 300 Illustrations. Crown 8vo, cloth extra, 4s. 6d.

Seguin (L. G.), Works by.
The Country of the Passion Play (Oberammergau) and the Highlands of Bavaria. With Map and 37 Illustrations. Crown 8vo, cloth extra, 3s. 6d.
Walks in Algiers. With Two Maps and 16 Illustrations. Crown 8vo, cloth extra, 6s.

Senior (Wm.).—By Stream and Sea. Post 8vo, cloth, 2s. 6d.

Sergeant (Adeline), Novels by. Crown 8vo, cloth, 3s. 6d. each.
Under False Pretences. | Dr. Endicott's Experiment.

Shakespeare for Children: Lamb's Tales from Shakespeare.
With Illustrations, coloured and plain, by J. MOYR SMITH. Crown 4to, cloth gilt, 3s. 6d.

Shakespeare the Boy. With Sketches of the Home and School Life,
the Games and Sports, the Manners, Customs, and Folk-lore of the Time. By WILLIAM J. ROLFE, Litt.D. A New Edition, with 42 Illustrations, and an INDEX OF PLAYS AND PASSAGES REFERRED TO. Crown 8vo, cloth gilt, 3s. 6d.

Sharp (William).—Children of To-morrow. Crown 8vo, cloth, 6s.

Shelley's (Percy Bysshe) Complete Works in Verse and Prose.
Edited, Prefaced, and Annotated by R. HERNE SHEPHERD. Five Vols., crown 8vo, cloth, 3s. 6d. each.
Poetical Works, in Three Vols.:
Vol. I. Introduction by the Editor; Posthumous Fragments of Margaret Nicholson; Shelley's Correspondence with Stockdale; The Wandering Jew; Queen Mab, with the Notes; Alastor, and other Poems; Rosalind and Helen; Prometheus Unbound; Adonais, &c.
,, II. Laon and Cythna: The Cenci; Julian and Maddalo; Swellfoot the Tyrant; The Witch of Atlas; Epipsychidion; Hellas.
,, III. Posthumous Poems; The Masque of Anarchy; and other Pieces.
Prose Works, in Two Vols.:
Vol. I. The Two Romances of Zastrozzi and St. Irvyne; the Dublin and Marlow Pamphlets; A Refutation of Deism; Letters to Leigh Hunt, and some Minor Writings and Fragments.
,, II. The Essays; Letters from Abroad; Translations and Fragments, edited by Mrs. SHELLEY. With a Biography of Shelley, and an Index of the Prose Works.

Sherard (R. H.).—Rogues: A Novel. Crown 8vo, cloth, 1s. 6d.

Sheridan's (Richard Brinsley) Complete Works, with Life and
Anecdotes. Including his Dramatic Writings, his Works in Prose and Poetry, Translations, Speeches, and Jokes. Crown 8vo, cloth, 3s. 6d.
The Rivals, The School for Scandal, and other Plays. Post 8vo, half-bound, 2s.
Sheridan's Comedies: The Rivals and The School for Scandal. Edited, with an Introduction and Notes to each Play, and a Biographical Sketch, by BRANDER MATTHEWS. With Illustrations. Demy 8vo, half-parchment, 12s. 6d.

Shiel (M. P.).—The Purple Cloud. Crown 8vo, cloth, gilt top, 6s.

Sidney's (Sir Philip) Complete Poetical Works, including all those in 'Arcadia.' With Portrait, Memorial-Introduction, Notes, &c., by the Rev. A. B. GROSART, D.D. Three Vols., crown 8vo, cloth boards, 3s. 6d. each.

Signboards: Their History, including Anecdotes of Famous Taverns and Remarkable Characters. By JACOB LARWOOD and JOHN CAMDEN HOTTEN. With Coloured Frontispiece and 94 Illustrations. Crown 8vo, cloth extra, 3s. 6d.

Sims (George R.), Works by.
Post 8vo, illustrated boards, 2s. each; cloth limp, 2s. 6d. each.

The Ring o' Bells. | My Two Wives. | Memoirs of a Landlady.
Tinkletop's Crime. | Tales of To-day. | Scenes from the Show.
Zeph: A Circus Story, &c. | The Ten Commandments: Stories.
Dramas of Life. With 60 Illustrations.

Crown 8vo, picture cover, 1s. each; cloth, 1s. 6d. each.
The Dagonet Reciter and Reader: Being Readings and Recitations in Prose and Verse selected from his own Works by GEORGE R. SIMS.
The Case of George Candlemas. | Dagonet Ditties. (From *The Referee*.)
How the Poor Live; and Horrible London. With a Frontispiece by F. BARNARD. Crown 8vo, leatherette, 1s.
Dagonet Dramas of the Day. Crown 8vo, 1s.

Crown 8vo, cloth, 3s. 6d. each; post 8vo, picture boards, 2s. each; cloth limp, 2s. 6d. each.
Mary Jane's Memoirs. | Mary Jane Married. | Rogues and Vagabonds.
Dagonet Abroad.

Crown 8vo, cloth, 3s. 6d. each.
Once upon a Christmas Time. With 8 Illustrations by CHARLES GREEN, R.I.
In London's Heart: A Story of To-day.—Also in picture cloth, flat back, 2s. | A Blind Marriage.
Without the Limelight: Theatrical Life as it is. | The Small-part Lady, &c.

Sister Dora: A Biography. By MARGARET LONSDALE. With Four Illustrations. Demy 8vo, picture cover, 4d.; cloth, 6d.

Sketchley (Arthur).—A Match in the Dark. Post 8vo, boards, 2s.

Slang Dictionary (The): Etymological, Historical, and Anecdotal. Crown 8vo, cloth extra, 6s. 6d.

Smart (Hawley), Novels by.
Crown 8vo, cloth 3s. 6d. each; post 8vo, picture boards, 2s. each.
Beatrice and Benedick. | Long Odds.
Without Love or Licence. | The Master of Rathkelly.

Crown 8vo, cloth, 3s. 6d. each.
The Outsider | A Racing Rubber.
The Plunger. Post 8vo, picture boards, 2s.

Smith (J. Moyr), Works by.
The Prince of Argolis. With 130 Illustrations. Post 8vo, cloth extra, 3s. 6d.
The Wooing of the Water Witch. With numerous Illustrations. Post 8vo, cloth, 6s.

Snazelleparilla. Decanted by G. S. EDWARDS. With Portrait of G. H. SNAZELLE, and 65 Illustrations by C. LYALL. Crown 8vo, cloth, 3s. 6d.

Society in London. Crown 8vo, 1s.; cloth, 1s. 6d.

Somerset (Lord Henry).—Songs of Adieu. Small 4to Jap. vel., 6s.

Spalding (T. A., LL.B.).—Elizabethan Demonology: An Essay on the Belief in the Existence of Devils. Crown 8vo, cloth extra, 5s.

Speight (T. W.), Novels by.
Post 8vo, illustrated boards, 2s. each.

The Mysteries of Heron Dyke. | The Loudwater Tragedy.
By Devious Ways, &c. | Burgo's Romance.
Hoodwinked; & Sandycroft Mystery. | Quittance in Full.
The Golden Hoop. | Back to Life. | A Husband from the Sea.

Post 8vo, cloth limp, 1s. 6d. each.
A Barren Title. | Wife or No Wife?

Crown 8vo, cloth extra, 3s. 6d. each.
A Secret of the Sea. | The Grey Monk. | The Master of Trenance.
A Minion of the Moon: A Romance of the King's Highway.
The Secret of Wyvern Towers. | The Doom of Siva. | The Web of Fate.
The Strange Experiences of Mr. Verschoyle.

Spenser for Children. By M. H. TOWRY. With Coloured Illustrations by WALTER J. MORGAN. Crown 4to, cloth extra, 3s. 6d.

Sprigge (S. Squire).—An Industrious Chevalier. Crown 8vo, cloth, gilt top, 6s.

Spettigue (H. H.).—The Heritage of Eve. Crown 8vo, cloth, 6s.

Stafford (John), Novels by.
Doris and I. Crown 8vo, cloth, 3s. 6d. | Carlton Priors. Crown 8vo, cloth, gilt top, 6s.

Starry Heavens (The); A POETICAL BIRTHDAY BOOK. Royal 16mo, cloth extra, 2s. 6d.

Stag-Hunting with the 'Devon and Somerset.' An Account of
the Chase of the Wild Red Deer on Exmoor, 1887-1901. By PHILIP EVERED. With 70 Illustrations by H. M. LOMAS. Crown 4to, cloth gilt, 16s. net.

Stedman (E. C.).—Victorian Poets. Crown 8vo, cloth extra, 9s.

Stephens (Riccardo, M.B.).—The Cruciform Mark: The Strange
Story of RICHARD TREGENNA, Bachelor of Medicine (Univ. Edinb.) Crown 8vo, cloth, 2s. 6d.

Stephens (Robert Neilson).—Philip Winwood: A Sketch of the
Domestic History of an American Captain in the War of Independence. Crown 8vo, cloth, 3s. 6d.

Sterndale (R. Armitage).—The Afghan Knife: A Novel. Post
8vo, cloth, 3s. 6d.; illustrated boards, 2s.

Stevenson (R. Louis), Works by.
Crown 8vo, buckram, gilt top, 6s. each.
Travels with a Donkey. With a Frontispiece by WALTER CRANE.
An Inland Voyage. With a Frontispiece by WALTER CRANE.
Familiar Studies of Men and Books.
The Silverado Squatters. With Frontispiece by J. D. STRONG.
The Merry Men. | **Underwoods:** Poems.
Memories and Portraits.
Virginibus Puerisque, and other Papers. | **Ballads.** | **Prince Otto.**
Across the Plains, with other Memories and Essays.
Weir of Hermiston. | **In the South Seas.**
Familiar Studies of Men and Books. LARGE TYPE, FINE PAPER EDITION. Pott 8vo, cloth, gilt top, 2s. net; leather, gilt edges, 3s. net.
A Lowden Sabbath Morn. With 27 Illustrations by A. S. BOYD. Fcap. 8vo, cloth, 6s.
Songs of Travel. Crown 8vo, buckram, 5s.
New Arabian Nights. Crown 8vo, buckram, gilt top, 6s.; post 8vo, illustrated boards, 2s.
—POPULAR EDITION, medium 8vo, 6d.
The Suicide Club; and The Rajah's Diamond. (From NEW ARABIAN NIGHTS.) With Eight Illustrations by W. J. HENNESSY. Crown 8vo, cloth, 3s. 6d.
The Stevenson Reader: Selections from the Writings of ROBERT LOUIS STEVENSON. Edited by LLOYD OSBOURNE. Post 8vo, cloth, 2s. 6d.; buckram, gilt top, 3s. 6d.
The Pocket R.L.S. Favourite Passages from his Works. Small 16mo, cloth, 2s. net; leather, 3s. 6d. net.
LARGE TYPE, FINE PAPER EDITION. Pott 8vo, cl., gilt top, 2s. net each; leather, gilt edges, 3s. net each.
Familiar Studies of Men and Books. | **New Arabian Nights.**
Robert Louis Stevenson: A Life Study in Criticism. By H. BELLYSE BAILDON. With 2 Portraits. SECOND EDITION, REVISED. Crown 8vo, buckram, gilt top, 6s.

Stockton (Frank R.).—The Young Master of Hyson Hall. With
numerous Illustrations by VIRGINIA H. DAVISSON and C. H. STEPHENS. Crown 8vo, cloth, 3s. 6d.

Storey (G. A., A.R.A.).—Sketches from Memory. With 93
Illustrations by the Author. Demy 8vo, cloth, gilt top, 12s. 6d.

Stories from Foreign Novelists. With Notices by HELEN and
ALICE ZIMMERN. Crown 8vo, cloth extra, 3s. 6d.

Strange Manuscript (A) Found in a Copper Cylinder. Crown
8vo, cloth extra, with 19 Illustrations by GILBERT GAUL, 3s. 6d.; post 8vo, illustrated boards, 2s.

Strange Secrets. Told by PERCY FITZGERALD, CONAN DOYLE, FLOR-
ENCE MARRYAT, &c. Post 8vo, illustrated boards, 2s.

Strutt (Joseph). — The Sports and Pastimes of the People of
England; including the Rural and Domestic Recreations, May Games, Mummeries, Shows, &c., from the Earliest Period. Edited by WILLIAM HONE. With 140 Illustrations. Cr. 8vo, cloth extra, 3s. 6d.

Sundowner, Stories by.
Told by the Taffrail. Crown 8vo, cloth, 3s. 6d.
The Tale of the Serpent. Crown 8vo, cloth, flat back, 2s.

Surtees (Robert).—Handley Cross; or, Mr. Jorrocks's Hunt.
With 79 Illustrations by JOHN LEECH. A New Edition. Post 8vo, cloth, 2s.

Swinburne's (Algernon C.) Works.
Selections from the Poetical Works of A. C. Swinburne. Fcap. 8vo 6s.
Atalanta in Calydon. Crown 8vo, 6s.
Chastelard: A Tragedy. Crown 8vo, 7s.
Poems and Ballads. FIRST SERIES. Crown 8vo, or fcap. 8vo, 9s.
Poems and Ballads. SECOND SER. Cr. 8vo, 9s.
Poems & Ballads. THIRD SERIES. Cr. 8vo, 7s.
Songs before Sunrise. Crown 8vo, 10s. 6d.
Bothwell: A Tragedy. Crown 8vo, 12s. 6d.
Songs of Two Nations. Crown 8vo, 6s.
George Chapman. (See Vol. II. of G. CHAPMAN'S Works.) Crown 8vo, 3s. 6d.
Essays and Studies. Crown 8vo, 12s.
Erechtheus: A Tragedy. Crown 8vo, 6s.
A Note on Charlotte Bronte. Cr. 8vo, 6s.
A Study of Shakespeare. Crown 8vo, 8s.

Songs of the Springtides. Crown 8vo, 6s.
Studies in Song. Crown 8vo, 7s.
Mary Stuart: A Tragedy. Crown 8vo, 8s.
Tristram of Lyonesse. Crown 8vo, 9s.
A Century of Roundels. Small 4to, 8s.
A Midsummer Holiday. Crown 8vo, 7s.
Marino Faliero: A Tragedy. Crown 8vo, 6s.
A Study of Victor Hugo. Crown 8vo, 6s.
Miscellanies. Crown 8vo, 12s.
Locrine: A Tragedy. Crown 8vo, 6s.
A Study of Ben Jonson. Crown 8vo, 7s.
The Sisters: A Tragedy. Crown 8vo, 6s.
Astrophel, &c. Crown 8vo, 7s.
Studies in Prose and Poetry. Cr. 8vo, 9s.
The Tale of Balen. Crown 8vo, 7s.
Rosamund, Queen of the Lombards: A Tragedy. Crown 8vo, 6s.

Swift's (Dean) Choice Works, in Prose and Verse. With Memoir,
Portrait, and Facsimiles of the Maps in 'Gulliver's Travels.' Crown 8vo, cloth, 3s. 6d.
Gulliver's Travels, and **A Tale of a Tub.** Post 8vo, half-bound, 2s.
Jonathan Swift: A Study. By J. CHURTON COLLINS. Crown 8ve, cloth extra, 8s.

Syntax's (Dr.) Three Tours: In Search of the Picturesque, in Search
of Consolation, and in Search of a Wife. With ROWLANDSON'S Coloured Illustrations, and Life of the
Author by J. C. HOTTEN. Crown 8vo, cloth extra, 7s. 6d.

Taine's History of English Literature. Translated by HENRY VAN
LAUN. Four Vols., small demy 8vo, cloth boards, 30s.—POPULAR EDITION, Two Vols., large crown
8vo, cloth extra, 15s.

Taylor (Bayard). — Diversions of the Echo Club: Burlesques of
Modern Writers. Post 8vo, cloth limp, 2s.

Taylor (Tom).—Historical Dramas: 'JEANNE DARC,' ''TWIXT AXE
AND CROWN,' 'THE FOOL'S REVENGE,' 'ARKWRIGHT'S WIFE,' 'ANNE BOLEYNE,' 'PLOT AND
PASSION.' Crown 8vo, 1s. each.

Temple (Sir Richard, G.C.S.I.).—A Bird's-eye View of Pictur-
esque India. With 32 Illustrations by the Author. Crown 8vo, cloth, g lt top, 6s.

Thackerayana: Notes and Anecdotes. With Coloured Frontispiece and
Hundreds of Sketches by WILLIAM MAKEPEACE THACKERAY. Crown 8vo, cloth extra, 3s. 6d.

Thames, A New Pictorial History of the. By A. S. KRAUSSE.
With 340 Illustrations. Post 8vo, cloth, 1s. 6d.

Thomas (Annie), Novels by.
The Siren's Web: A Romance of London Society. Crown 8vo, cloth, 3s. 6d.
Comrades True. Crown 8vo, cloth, gilt top, 6s.

Thomas (Bertha), Novels by.
The Violin-Player. Crown 8vo, cloth, 3s. 6d.
Crown 8vo, cloth, gilt top, 6s. each.
In a Cathedral City. | **The Son of the House.**
The House on the Scar: a Tale of South Devon. SECOND EDITION.

Thomson's Seasons, and The Castle of Indolence. With Introduction by ALLAN CUNNINGHAM, and 48 Illustrations. Post 8vo, half-bound, 2s.

Thoreau: His Life and Aims. By H. A. PAGE. With a Portrait
and View. Post 8vo buckram, 3s. 6d.

Thornbury (Walter), Books by.
The Life and Correspondence of J. M. W. Turner. With Eight Illustrations in Colours and
Two Woodcuts. New and Revised Edition. Crown 8vo, cloth, 3s. 6d.
Tales for the Marines. Post 8vo, illustrated boards, 2s.

Timbs (John), Works by. Crown 8vo, cloth, 3s. 6d. each.
Clubs and Club Life in London: Anecdotes of its Famous Coffee-houses, Hostelries, and
Taverns. With 41 Illustrations.
English Eccentrics and Eccentricities: Stories of Delusions, Impostures, Sporting Scenes,
Eccentric Artists, Theatrical Folk, &c. With 48 Illustrations.

Twain's (Mark) Books.
The Author's Edition de Luxe of the Works of Mark Twain, in 22 Volumes (limited
to 600 Numbered Copies for sale in Great Britain and its Dependencies), price £13 15s. net the
Set ; or, 12s. 6d. net per Volume, is now complete, and a detailed Prospectus may be had. The
First Volume of the Set is SIGNED BY THE AUTHOR. (Sold only in Sets.)
UNIFORM LIBRARY EDITION OF MARK TWAIN'S WORKS.
Crown 8vo, cloth extra, 3s. 6d. each.
Mark Twain's Library of Humour. With 197 Illustrations by E. W. KEMBLE.
Roughing It ; and The Innocents at Home. With 200 Illustrations by F. A. FRASER.
The American Claimant. With 81 Illustrations by HAL HURST and others.
*The Adventures of Tom Sawyer.** With 111 Illustrations.
Tom Sawyer Abroad. With 26 Illustrations by DAN BEARD.
Tom Sawyer, Detective, &c. With Photogravure Portrait of the Author.
Pudd'nhead Wilson. With Portrait and Six Illustrations by LOUIS LOEB.
*A Tramp Abroad.** With 314 Illustrations.
*The Innocents Abroad ; or, The New Pilgrim's Progress. With 234 Illustrations. (The Two Shil-
ling Edition is entitled **Mark Twain's Pleasure Trip.**)
*The Gilded Age.** By MARK TWAIN and C. D. WARNER. With 212 Illustrations.
*The Prince and the Pauper.** With 190 Illustrations.
*Life on the Mississippi. With 300 Illustrations.
*The Adventures of Huckleberry Finn.** With 174 Illustrations by E. W. KEMBLE.
*A Yankee at the Court of King Arthur.** With 220 Illustrations by DAN BEARD.
*The Stolen White Elephant. | *The £1,000,000 Bank-Note.
The Choice Works of Mark Twain. Revised and Corrected throughout by the Author. With
Life, Portrait, and numerous Illustrations.
*** The books marked * may be had also in post 8vo, picture boards, at 2s. each.
Crown 8vo, cloth, gilt top, 6s. each.
Personal Recollections of Joan of Arc. With Twelve Illustrations by F. V. DU MOND.
More Tramps Abroad.
The Man that Corrupted Hadleyburg, and other Stories and Sketches. With a Frontispiece.
Mark Twain's Sketches. Post 8vo, illustrated boards, 2s.

Trollope (Anthony), Novels by.
Crown 8vo, cloth extra, 3s. 6d. each; post 8vo, illustrated boards, 2s. each.
The Way We Live Now. | Mr. Scarborough's Family.
Frau Frohmann. | Marion Fay. | The Land-Leaguers.
Post 8vo, illustrated boards, 2s. each.
Kept in the Dark. | The American Senator. | The Golden Lion of Granpere.

Trollope (Frances E.), Novels by.
Crown 8vo, cloth extra, 3s. 6d. each: post 8vo, illustrated boards, 2s. each.
Like Ships upon the Sea. | Mabel's Progress. | Anne Furness.

Trollope (T. A.).—Diamond Cut Diamond. Post 8vo, illust. bds., 2s.

Tytler (C. C. Fraser-).—Mistress Judith: A Novel. Crown 8vo, cloth extra, 3s. 6d.; post 8vo, illustrated boards, 2s.

Tytler (Sarah), Novels by.
Crown 8vo, cloth extra, 3s. 6d. each; post 8vo, illustrated boards, 2s. each.
Buried Diamonds. | The Blackhall Ghosts. | What She Came Through.
Post 8vo, illustrated boards, 2s. each.
The Bride's Pass. | The Huguenot Family. | Noblesse Oblige. | Disappeared.
Saint Mungo's City. | Lady Bell. | Beauty and the Beast.
Crown 8vo, cloth, 3s. 6d. each.
The Macdonald Lass. With Frontispiece. | Mrs. Carmichael's Goddesses.
The Witch-Wife. | Rachel Langton. | Sapphira. | A Honeymoon's Eclipse.
A Young Dragon.
Citoyenne Jacqueline. Crown 8vo, picture cloth, flat back, 2s.
Three Men of Mark. Crown 8vo, cloth, gilt top, 6s.

Upward (Allen), Novels by.—A Crown of Straw. Cr. 8vo, cl. 6s.
The Queen Against Owen. Crown 8vo, cloth, 3s. 6d.; post 8vo, picture boards, 2s.
The Prince of Balkistan. Post 8vo, picture boards, 2s.

Vandam (Albert D.).—A Court Tragedy. With 6 Illustrations by J. BARNARD DAVIS. Crown 8vo, cloth, 3s. 6d.

Vashti and Esther. By 'Belle' of The World. Cr. 8vo, cloth, 3s. 6d.

Vizetelly (Ernest A.), Books by. Crown 8vo, cloth, 3s. 6d. each.
The Scorpion: A Romance of Spain. With a Frontispiece.
With Zola in England: A Story of Exile. With 4 Portraits.
Crown 8vo, cloth, gilt top, 6s. each.
A Path of Thorns. | The Lover's Progress.
Bluebeard: An Account of Comorre the Cursed and Gilles de Rais; with Summaries of various Tales and Traditions. With 9 Illustrations. Demy 8vo, cloth, 9s. net.

Wagner (Leopold).—How to Get on the Stage, and how to Succeed there. Crown 8vo, cloth, 2s. 6d.

Walford's County Families of the United Kingdom (1902). Containing Notices of the Descent, Birth, Marriage, Education, &c., of more than 12,000 Distinguished Heads of Families, their Heirs Apparent or Presumptive, the Offices they hold or have held, their Town and Country Addresses, Clubs, &c. Royal 8vo, cloth gilt, 50s.

Waller (S. E.).—Sebastiani's Secret. With 9 Illusts. Cr. 8vo, cl., 6s.

Walton and Cotton's Complete Angler. With Memoirs and Notes by Sir HARRIS NICOLAS, and 61 Illustrations. Crown 8vo, cloth antique, 7s. 6d.

Walt Whitman, Poems by. Edited, with Introduction, by WILLIAM M. ROSSETTI. With Portrait. Crown 8vo, hand-made paper and buckram, 6s.

Warden (Florence), Novels by.
Joan, the Curate. Crown 8vo, cloth, 3s. 6d.; picture cloth, flat back, 2s.
A Fight to a Finish. Crown 8vo, cloth, gilt top, 6s.

Warman (Cy).—The Express Messenger. Crown 8vo, cloth, 3s. 6d.

Warner (Chas. Dudley).—A Roundabout Journey. Cr. 8vo, cl. 6s.

Warrant to Execute Charles I. A Facsimile, with the 59 Signatures and Seals. Printed on paper 22 in. by 14 in. 2s.
Warrant to Execute Mary Queen of Scots. A Facsimile, including Queen Elizabeth's Signature and the Great Seal. 2s.

Wassermann (Lillias).—The Daffodils. Crown 8vo, cloth, 1s. 6d.

Weather, How to Foretell the, with the Pocket Spectroscope. By F. W. CORY. With Ten Illustrations. Crown 8vo, 1s.; cloth, 1s. 6d.

Webber (Byron).—Sport and Spangles. Crown 8vo, cloth, 2s.

Werner (A.).—Chapenga's White Man. Crown 8vo, cloth, 3s. 6d.

Westbury (Atha).—The Shadow of Hilton Fernbrook: A Romance of Maoriland. Crown 8vo, cloth, 3s. 6d.

Westall (William), Novels by.
Trust Money. Crown 8vo, cloth, 3s. 6d. ; post 8vo, illustrated boards, 2s.

Crown 8vo, cloth, 6s. each.

As a Man Sows. | **A Red Bridal.** | **The Old Bank.**
Her Ladyship's Secret. | **As Luck would have it.** |

Crown 8vo, cloth, 3s. 6d. each.

A Woman Tempted Him.   **Nigel Fortescue.**   **The Phantom City.**
For Honour and Life.   **Ben Clough.** | **Birch Dene.**   **Ralph Norbreck's Trust.**
Her Two Millions.   **The Old Factory** (also at 6d.)   **A Queer Race.**
Two Pinches of Snuff.   **Sons of Belial.**   **Red Ryvington.**
With the Red Eagle.   **Strange Crimes.**   **Roy of Roy's Court.**

Wheelwright (E. Gray).—A Slow Awakening. Crown 8vo, 6s.

Whishaw (Fred.), Novels by. Crown 8vo, cloth, gilt top, 6s. each.
A Forbidden Name: A Story of the Court of Catherine the Great. | **Mazeppa.**

White (Gilbert).—Natural History of Selborne. Post 8vo, 2s.

Wilde (Lady). — The Ancient Legends, Mystic Charms, and
Superstitions of Ireland ; with Sketches of the Irish Past. Crown 8vo, cloth, 3s. 6d.

Williams (W. Mattieu, F.R.A.S.), Works by.
Science in Short Chapters. Crown 8vo, cloth extra, 7s. 6d.
A Simple Treatise on Heat. With Illustrations. Crown 8vo, cloth, 2s. 6d.
The Chemistry of Cookery. Crown 8vo, cloth extra, 6s.
A Vindication of Phrenology. With Portrait and 43 Illusts. Demy 8vo, cloth extra, 12s. 6d.

Williamson (Mrs. F. H.).—A Child Widow. Post 8vo, bds., 2s.

Wills (C. J.), Novels by.
An Easy-going Fellow. Crown 8vo, cloth, 3s. 6d. | **His Dead Past.** Crown 8vo, cloth, 6s.

Wilson (Dr. Andrew, F.R.S.E.), Works by.
Chapters on Evolution. With 259 Illustrations. Crown 8vo, cloth extra, 7s. 6d.
Leisure-Time Studies. With Illustrations. Crown 8vo, cloth extra, 6s.
Studies in Life and Sense. With 36 Illustrations. Crown 8vo, cloth 3s. 6d.
Common Accidents: How to Treat Them. With Illustrations. Crown 8vo, 1s. ; cloth, 1s. 6d.
Glimpses of Nature. With 35 Illustrations. Crown 8vo, cloth extra, 3s. 6d.

Winter (John Strange), Stories by. Post 8vo, illustrated boards,
2s. each ; cloth limp, 2s. 6d. each.
Cavalry Life. | **Regimental Legends.**
Cavalry Life and Regimental Legends. LIBRARY EDITION. Crown 8vo, cloth, 3s. 6d.
A Soldier's Children. With 34 Illustrations. Crown 8vo, cloth, 3s. 6d.

Wissmann (Hermann von). — My Second Journey through
Equatorial Africa. With 92 Illustrations. Demy 8vo, cloth, 16s.

Wood (H. F.), Detective Stories by. Post 8vo, boards, 2s. each.
The Passenger from Scotland Yard. | **The Englishman of the Rue Cain.**

Woolley (Celia Parker).—Rachel Armstrong; or, Love and The-
ology. Post 8vo, cloth, 2s. 6d.

Wright (Thomas, F.S.A.), Works by.
Caricature History of the Georges; or, Annals of the House of Hanover. Compiled from
Squibs, Broadsides, Window Pictures, Lampoons, and Pictorial Caricatures of the Time. With
over 300 Illustrations. Crown 8vo, cloth, 3s. 6d.
**History of Caricature and of the Grotesque in Art, Literature, Sculpture, and
Painting.** Illustrated by F. W. FAIRHOLT, F.S.A. Crown 8vo, cloth, 7s. 6d.

Wynman (Margaret).—My Flirtations. With 13 Illustrations by
J. BERNARD PARTRIDGE. Post 8vo, cloth limp, 2s.

Zola (Emile), Novels by. Crown 8vo, cloth extra, 3s. 6d. each.
The Joy of Life. Edited by ERNEST A. VIZETELLY.
The Fortune of the Rougons. Edited by ERNEST A. VIZETELLY.
Abbe Mouret's Transgression. Edited by ERNEST A. VIZETELLY.
The Conquest of Plassans. Edited by ERNEST A. VIZETELLY.
Germinal; or, Master and Man. Edited by ERNEST A. VIZETELLY.
The Honour of the Army. and other Stories. Edited by ERNEST A. VIZETELLY.
His Excellency (Eugene Rougon). With an Introduction by ERNEST A. VIZETELLY.
The Dram-Shop (L'Assommoir). With Introduction by E. A. VIZETELLY.
The Fat and the Thin. Translated by ERNEST A. VIZETELLY.
Money. Translated by ERNEST A. VIZETELLY. | **Work.** Translated by ERNEST A. VIZETELLY.
His Masterpiece. Edited by ERNEST A. VIZETELLY.
The Downfall. Translated by E. A. VIZETELLY.—Also a POPULAR EDITION, medium 8vo, 6d.
The Dream. Translated by ELIZA CHASE. With Eight Illustrations by JEANNIOT.
Doctor Pascal. Translated by E. A. VIZETELLY. With Portrait of the Author.
Lourdes. Translated by ERNEST A. VIZETELLY.
Rome. Translated by ERNEST A. VIZETELLY. | **Paris.** Translated by ERNEST A. VIZETELLY.
Fruitfulness (Fécondité). Translated and Edited, with an Introduction, by E. A. VIZETELLY.
With Zola in England. By ERNEST A. VIZETELLY. With Four Portraits. Crown 8vo, cloth, 3s. 6d.

'ZZ' (L. Zangwill).—A Nineteenth Century Miracle. Cr. 8vo, 3s. 6d.

THE PICCADILLY (3/6) NOVELS—*continued.*

By Sir WALTER BESANT.

All Sorts & Conditions.	Armorel of Lyoness.
The Captains' Room.	S.Katherine's by Tower
All in a Garden Fair.	Verbena Camellia, &c.
Dorothy Forster.	The Ivory Gate.
Uncle Jack.	Holy Rose	The Rebel Queen.
World Went Well Then.	Dreams of Avarice.
Children of Gibeon.	In Deacon's Orders.
Herr Paulus.	The Master Craftsman.
For Faith and Freedom.	The City of Refuge.
To Call Her Mine.	A Fountain Sealed.
The Revolt of Man.	The Changeling.
The Bell of St. Paul's.	The Fourth Generation
The Charm.	

By AMBROSE BIERCE—In Midst of Life.

By HAROLD BINDLOSS. Ainslie's Ju-Ju.

By M. McD. BODKIN.

Dora Myrl.	Shillelagh and Shamrock.

By PAUL BOURGET.—A Living Lie.

By J. D. BRAYSHAW.—Slum Silhouettes.

By ROBERT BUCHANAN.

Shadow of the Sword.	The New Abelard.
A Child of Nature.	Matt.	Rachel Dene
God and the Man.	Master of the Mine.
Martyrdom of Madeline	The Heir of Linne.
Love Me for Ever.	Woman and the Man.
Annan Water.	Red and White Heather.
Foxglove Manor.	Lady Kilpatrick.
The Charlatan.	Andromeda.

R. W. CHAMBERS.—The King in Yellow.
By J. M. CHAPPLE.—The Minor Chord.

By HALL CAINE.

Shadow of a Crime.	Deemster.	Son of Hagar.

By AUSTIN CLARE.—By Rise of River.

By Mrs. ARCHER CLIVE.

Paul Ferroll. | Why Paul Ferroll Killed his Wife.

By ANNE COATES.--Rie's Diary.

By MACLAREN COBBAN.

The Red Sultan.	The Burden of Isabel.

By WILKIE COLLINS.

Armadale.	After Dark.	The New Magdalen.
No Name.	Antonina	The Frozen Deep.
Basil.	Hide and Seek.	The Two Destinies.
The Dead Secret.	'I Say No.'
Queen of Hearts.	Little Novels.
My Miscellanies.	The Fallen Leaves.
The Woman in White.	Jezebel's Daughter.
The Law and the Lady.	The Black Robe.
The Haunted Hotel.	Heart and Science.
The Moonstone.	The Evil Genius.
Man and Wife.	The Legacy of Cain.
Poor Miss Finch.	A Rogue's Life.
Miss or Mrs.?	Blind Love.

By MORT. & FRANCES COLLINS.

Blacksmith & Scholar.	You Play me False.
The Village Comedy.	Midnight to Midnight.

M. J. COLQUHOUN.—Every Inch Soldier.

By HERBERT COMPTON.

The Inimitable Mrs. Massingham.

By E. H. COOPER.—Geoffory Hamilton.

By V. C. COTES.—Two Girls on a Barge.

By C. E. CRADDOCK.

The Prophet of the Great Smoky Mountains.
His Vanished Star.

By H. N. CRELLIN.

Romances of the Old Seraglio.

By MATT CRIM.

The Adventures of a Fair Rebel.

By S. R. CROCKETT and others.

Tales of Our Coast.

By B. M. CROKER.

Diana Barrington.	The Real Lady Hilda.
Proper Pride.	Married or Single?
A Family Likeness.	Two Masters.
Pretty Miss Neville.	In the Kingdom of Kerry
A Bird of Passage.	Interference.
Mr. Jervis.	A Third Person,
Village Tales.	Beyond the Pale.
Some One Else.	Jason.	Miss Balmaine's Past.
Infatuation.	Terence.

By ALPHONSE DAUDET.

The Evangelist ; or, Port Salvation.

H. C. DAVIDSON.—Mr. Sadler's Daughters.

By HARRY DE WINDT.

True Tales of Travel and Adventure.

By DICK DONOVAN.

Man from Manchester.	Tales of Terror.
Records of Vincent Trill	Chronicles of Michael
The Mystery of	Danevitch.	Detective.
Jamaica Terrace.	Tyler Tatlock, Private
Deacon Brodie.	

By RICHARD DOWLING.

Old Corcoran's Money.

By A. CONAN DOYLE.

The Firm of Girdlestone.

By S. JEANNETTE DUNCAN.

A Daughter of To-day. | Vernon's Aunt.

By ANNIE EDWARDES.

Archie Lovell. | A Plaster Saint.

By G. S. EDWARDS.—Snazelleparilla.

By G. MANVILLE FENN.

Cursed by a Fortune.	A Fluttered Dovecote.
The Case of Ailsa Gray.	King of the Castle.
Commodore Junk.	Master of Ceremonies.
The New Mistress.	The Man with a Shadow
Witness to the Deed.	One Maid's Mischief.
The Tiger Lily.	Story of Antony Grace.
The White Virgin.	This Man's Wife.
Black Blood.	In Jeopardy. [n'ng.
Double Cunning.	A Woman Worth Win-

By PERCY FITZGERALD.—Fatal Zero

By R. E. FRANCILLON.

One by One.	Ropes of Sand.
A Dog and his Shadow.	Jack Doyle's Daughter.
A Real Queen.	

By HAROLD FREDERIC.

Seth's Brother's Wife. | The Lawton Girl.

By GILBERT GAUL.

A Strange Manuscript Found in a Copper Cylinder.

By PAUL GAULOT.—The Red Shirts.

By CHARLES GIBBON.

Robin Gray.	The Golden Shaft.
Loving a Dream.	The Braes of Yarrow
Of High Degree	

By E. GLANVILLE.

The Lost Heiress.	The Golden Rock.
Fair Colonist	Fossicker	Tales from the Veld.

By E. J. GOODMAN.

The Fate of Herbert Wayne.

By Rev. S. BARING GOULD.

Red Spider. | Eve.

By ALFRED A. GRACE.

Tales of a Dying Race.

CECIL GRIFFITH.—Corinthia Marazion.

By A. CLAVERING GUNTER.

A Florida Enchantment.

By OWEN HALL.

The Track of a Storm. | Jotsam.

By COSMO HAMILTON.

Glamour of Impossible. | Through a Keyhole.

By THOMAS HARDY.

Under the Greenwood Tree.

By BRET HARTE.

A Waif of the Plains.	A Protegée of Jack
A Ward of the Golden	Hamlin's.
Gate.	Springs.	Clarence.
A Sappho of Green	Barker's Luck.
Col. Starbottle's Client.	Devil's Ford. [celsior.
Susy.	Sally Dows.	The Crusade of the Ex-
Bell-Ringer of Angel's.	Three Partners.
Tales of Trail and Town	Gabriel Conroy.

By JULIAN HAWTHORNE.

Garth.	Dust.	Beatrix Randolph.
Ellice Quentin.	David Poindexter's Dis
Sebastian Strome.	appearance.
Fortune's Fool.	Spectre of Camera.

By Sir A. HELPS.—Ivan de Biron.

By I. HENDERSON.—Agatha Page.

By G. A. HENTY.

Dorothy's Double. | The Queen's Cup.

HEADON HILL.—Zambra the Detective

THE PICCADILLY (3/6) NOVELS—*continued.*

By JOHN HILL.—The Common Ancestor.

By TIGHE HOPKINS.
'Twixt Love and Duty. | Nugents of Carriconna.
The Incomplete Adventurer. | Nell Haffenden.

VICTOR HUGO.—The Outlaw of Iceland.

FERGUS HUME.—Lady from Nowhere.

By Mrs. HUNGERFORD.

Marvel.	A Point of Conscience.
A Modern Circe.	A Maiden all Forlorn.
Lady Patty.	The Coming of Chloe.
A Mental Struggle.	Nora Creina.
Lady Verner's Flight.	An Anxious Moment.
The Red-House Mystery	April's Lady.
The Three Graces.	Peter's Wife.
Professor's Experiment.	Lovice.

By Mrs. ALFRED HUNT.
The Leaden Casket. | Self-Condemned.
That Other Person. | Mrs. Juliet.

By R. ASHE KING.—A Drawn Game.

By GEORGE LAMBERT.
The President of Boravia.

By EDMOND LEPELLETIER.
Madame Sans-Gêne.

By ADAM LILBURN. A Tragedy in Marble

By HARRY LINDSAY.
Rhoda Roberts. | The Jacobite.

By HENRY W. LUCY.—Gideon Fleyce.

By E. LYNN LINTON.

Patricia Kemball.	The Atonement of Leam
Under which Lord?	Dundas.
'My Love!'	Ione.	The One Too Many.
Paston Carew.	Dulcie Everton.
Sowing the Wind.	Rebel of the Family.
With a Silken Thread.	An Octave of Friends.
The World Well Lost.	

By JUSTIN McCARTHY.

A Fair Saxon.	Donna Quixote.
Linley Rochford.	Maid of Athens.
Dear Lady Disdain.	The Comet of a Season.
Camiola.	The Dictator.
Waterdale Neighbours.	Red Diamonds.
My Enemy's Daughter.	The Riddle Ring.
Miss Misanthrope.	The Three Disgraces.

By JUSTIN H. McCARTHY.
A London Legend. | The Royal Christopher

By GEORGE MACDONALD.
Heather and Snow. | Phantastes.

W. H. MALLOCK.—The New Republic.

P. & V. MARGUERITTE.—The Disaster.

By L. T. MEADE.

A Soldier of Fortune.	On Brink of a Chasm.
In an Iron Grip.	The Siren.
Dr. Rumsey's Patient.	The Way of a Woman.
The Voice of the Charmer	A Son of Ishmael.
An Adventuress.	The Blue Diamond.

By LEONARD MERRICK.
This Stage of Fools. | Cynthia.

By BERTRAM MITFORD.
The Gun-Runner. | The King's Assegai.
Luck of Gerard Ridgeley. | Renah. Fanning's Quest.

By Mrs. MOLESWORTH.
Hathercourt Rectory.

By J. E. MUDDOCK.
Maid Marian and Robin Hood. | Golden Idol.
Basile the Jester. | Young Lochinvar.

By D. CHRISTIE MURRAY.

A Life's Atonement.	The Way of the World.
Joseph's Coat.	BobMartin's Little Girl
Coals of Fire.	Time's Revenges.
Old Blazer's Hero.	A Wasted Crime.
Val Strange.	Hearts.	In Direst Peril.
A Model Father.	Mount Despair.
By the Gate of the Sea.	A Capful o' Nails.
A Bit of Human Nature.	Tales in Prose & Verse
First Person Singular.	A Race for Millions.
Cynic Fortune.	This Little World.
	His Own Ghost.

By MURRAY and HERMAN.
The Bishops' Bible. | Paul Jones's Alias.
One Traveller Returns.

By HUME NISBET.—'Bail Up!'

By W. E. NORRIS.
Saint Ann's. | Billy Bellew.
Miss Wentworth's Idea.

By G. OHNET.
A Weird Gift. | Love's Depths.

By Mrs. OLIPHANT.—The Sorceress.

By OUIDA.

Held in Bondage.	In a Winter City.
Strathmore.	Chandos.	Friendship.
Under Two Flags.	Moths.	Ruffino.
Idalia.	(Gage.	Pipistrello.	Ariadne.
Cecil Castlemaine's	A Village Commune.
Tricotrin.	Puck.	Bimbi.	Wanda.
Folle Farine.	Frescoes.	Othmar.
A Dog of Flanders.	In Maremma.
Pascarel.	Signa.	Syrlin.	Guilderoy.
Princess Napraxine.	Santa Barbara.
Two Wooden Shoes.	Two Offenders.
	The Waters of Edera.

By MARGARET A. PAUL.
Gentle and Simple.

By JAMES PAYN.

Lost Sir Massingberd.	The Talk of the Town.
The Family Scapegrace	Holiday Tasks.
A County Family.	For Cash Only.
Less Black than We're	The Burnt Million.
Painted.	The Word and the Will
A Confidential Agent.	Sunny Stories.
A Grape from a Thorn.	A Trying Patient.
In Peril and Privation.	A Modern Dick Whit-
Mystery of Mirbridge.	tington.
High Spirits.	By Proxy.	

By WILL PAYNE.—Jerry the Dreamer

By Mrs. CAMPBELL PRAED.
Outlaw and Lawmaker. | Mrs. Tregaskiss.
Christina Chard. | Nulma. | Madame Izan.
'As a Watch in the Night.'

By E. C. PRICE.—Valentina.

By RICHARD PRYCE.
Miss Maxwell's Affections.

By Mrs. J. H. RIDDELL.
Weird Stories. | A Rich Man's Daughter.

By AMELIE RIVES.
Barbara Dering. | Meriel.

By F. W. ROBINSON.
The Hands of Justice. | Woman in the Dark.

By ALBERT ROSS.—A Sugar Princess.

By HERBERT RUSSELL. True Blue.

By CHARLES READE.

Peg Woffington; and	Griffith Gaunt.
Christie Johnstone.	Love Little, Love Long.
Hard Cash.	The Double Marriage.
Cloister & the Hearth.	Foul Play.
Never Too Late to Mend	Put Y'rself in His Place
The Course of True	A Terrible Temptation.
Love; and Single-	A Simpleton.
heart & Doubleface.	A Woman-Hater.
Autobiography of a	The Jilt, & otherStories;
Thief; Jack of all	& Good Stories of Man.
Trades; A Hero and	A Perilous Secret.
a Martyr; and The	Readiana; and Bible
Wandering Heir.	Characters.

J. RUNCIMAN.—Skippers and Shellbacks.

By W. CLARK RUSSELL.

Round the Galley-Fire.	My Shipmate Louise.
In the Middle Watch.	Alone on Wide Wide Sea.
On the Fo'k'sle Head	The Phantom Death.
A Voyage to the Cape.	Is He the Man?
Book for the Hammock.	Good Ship 'Mohock.'
Mystery of 'Ocean Star'	The Convict Ship.
Jenny Harlowe.	Heart of Oak.
An Ocean Tragedy.	The Tale of the Ten.
A Tale of Two Tunnels.	The Last Entry.
	The Death Ship.

By DORA RUSSELL.—Drift of Fate.

Two-Shilling Novels—*continued.*

By Sir ARTHUR HELPS.
Ivan de Biron.

By G. A. HENTY.
Rujub the Juggler.

By HEADON HILL.
Zambra the Detective.

By JOHN HILL.
Treason Felony.

By Mrs. CASHEL HOEY.
The Lover's Creed.

By Mrs. GEORGE HOOPER.
The House of Raby.

By Mrs. HUNGERFORD.
A Maiden all Forlorn.	Lady Verner's Flight.
In Durance Vile.	The Red-House Mystery
Marvel.	The Three Graces.
A Mental Struggle.	Unsatisfactory Lover.
A Modern Circe.	Lady Patty.
April's Lady.	Nora Creina.
Peter's Wife.	Professor's Experiment.

By Mrs. ALFRED HUNT.
That Other Person.	The Leaden Casket.
Self-Condemned.	

By MARK KERSHAW.
Colonial Facts and Fictions.

By R. ASHE KING.
A Drawn Game.	Passion's Slave.
'The Wearing of the	Bell Barry.
Green.'	

By EDMOND LEPELLETIER
Madame Sans-Gene.

By JOHN LEYS.
The Lindsays.

By E. LYNN LINTON.
Patricia Kemball.	The Atonement of Leam
The World Well Lost.	Dundas.
Under which Lord ?	Rebel of the Family.
Paston Carew.	Sowing the Wind.
'My Love!'	The One Too Many.
Ione.	Dulcie Everton.
With a Silken Thread.	

By HENRY W. LUCY.
Gideon Fleyce.

By JUSTIN McCARTHY.
Dear Lady Disdain.	Donna Quixote.
Waterdale Neighbours.	Maid of Athens.
My Enemy's Daughter	The Comet of a Season.
A Fair Saxon.	The Dictator.
Linley Rochford.	Red Diamonds.
Miss Misanthrope.	The Riddle Ring.
Camiola	

By HUGH MACCOLL.
Mr. Stranger's Sealed Packet.

By GEORGE MACDONALD.
Heather and Snow.

By AGNES MACDONELL.
Quaker Cousins.

By W. H. MALLOCK.
The New Republic.

By BRANDER MATTHEWS.
A Secret of the Sea.

By L. T. MEADE.
A Soldier of Fortune.

By LEONARD MERRICK.
The Man who was Good.

By Mrs. MOLESWORTH.
Hathercourt Rectory.

By J. E. MUDDOCK.
Stories Weird and Won-	From the Bosom of the
derful.	Deep.
The Dead Man's Secret.	

By D. CHRISTIE MURRAY.
A Model Father.	A Bit of Human Nature.
Joseph's Coat.	First Person Singular.
Coals of Fire.	Bob Martin's Little Girl.
Val Strange.	Hearts.	Time's Revenges.
Old Blazer's Hero.	A Wasted Crime.
The Way of the World	In Direst Peril.
Cynic Fortune.	Mount Despair.
A Life's Atonement.	A Capful o' Nails
By the Gate of the Sea.	

By MURRAY and HERMAN.
One Traveller Returns.	The Bishops' Bible.
Paul Jones's Alias.	

By HUME NISBET.
'Bail Up!'	Dr. Bernard St. Vincent.

By W. E. NORRIS.
Saint Ann's.	Billy Bellew.

By GEORGES OHNET.
Dr. Rameau.	A Weird Gift.
A Last Love.	

By Mrs. OLIPHANT.
Whiteladies.	The Greatest Heiress in
The Primrose Path.	England.

By OUIDA.
Held in Bondage.	Two Lit. Wooden Shoes.
Strathmore.	Moths.
Chandos.	Bimbi.
Idalia.	Pipistrello.
Under Two Flags.	A Village Commune.
Cecil Castlemaine's Gage	Wanda.
Tricotrin.	Othmar.
Puck.	Frescoes.
Folle Farine.	In Maremma.
A Dog of Flanders.	Guilderoy.
Pascarel.	Ruffino.
Signa.	Syrlin.
Princess Napraxine.	Santa Barbara.
In a Winter City.	Two Offenders.
Ariadne.	Ouida's Wisdom, Wit,
Friendship.	and Pathos.

By MARGARET AGNES PAUL.
Gentle and Simple.

By Mrs. CAMPBELL PRAED.
The Romance of a Station.	
The Soul of Countess Adrian.	
Outlaw and Lawmaker.	Mrs. Tregaskiss
Christina Chard.	

By RICHARD PRYCE.
Miss Maxwell's Affections.

By JAMES PAYN.
Bentinck's Tutor.	The Talk of the Town.
Murphy's Master.	Holiday Tasks.
A County Family.	A Perfect Treasure.
At Her Mercy.	What He Cost Her.
Cecil's Tryst.	A Confidential Agent.
The Clyffards of Clyffe.	Glow-worm Tales.
The Foster Brothers.	The Burnt Million.
Found Dead.	Sunny Stories.
The Best of Husbands.	Lost Sir Massingberd.
Walter's Word.	A Woman's Vengeance.
Halves.	The Family Scapegrace.
Fallen Fortunes.	Gwendoline's Harvest.
Humorous Stories.	Like Father, Like Son.
£200 Reward.	Married Beneath Him.
A Marine Residence.	Not Wooed, but Won.
Mirk Abbey	Less Black than We're
By Proxy.	Painted.
Under One Roof.	Some Private Views.
High Spirits.	A Grape from a Thorn.
Carlyon's Year.	The Mystery of Mir-
From Exile.	bridge.
For Cash Only.	The Word and the Will.
Kit.	A Prince of the Blood.
The Canon's Ward.	A Trying Patient.

By Mrs. J. H. RIDDELL.
Weird Stories.	The Uninhabited House.
Fairy Water.	The Mystery in Palace
Her Mother's Darling.	Gardens.
The Prince of Wales's	The Nun's Curse.
Garden Party.	Idle Tales.

www.ingramcontent.com/pod-product-compliance
Lightning Source LLC
Chambersburg PA
CBHW051525100726
47898CB00005B/1572